Dear Karen!

Thank you for supporting my first book & I look forward to taking your fermentation class soon! Cheers! ♡ Kathe[...]

What Are the Chances?

The Unconventional First Edition

A young woman's adventures while searching for the truth of life in the profound landscapes, cultures and experiences across America.

A Truth-Based Story Experienced and Written by

K. A. Trainer

Disclaimers

1. This entire book was published **unconventionally**. *This book was lived unconventionally. It was written unconventionally. It was edited unconventionally. Therefore, I felt that the first print was best published unconventionally. Please enjoy the rawness.*

2. **I tried to write a true story**. *This is honestly as true as I could make it be due to certain guidelines. It is based upon a true story.*

3. **I'm not claiming that what I have done is amazing**. *In fact, compared to many others, this is rather common.*

4. Also, **don't take anything I say in this to be the truth.** *However, this is 100% my truth and this is the way that I went about fulfilling my biggest dreams at the time. I feel in my heart that the greatest gift I could give this world now is to share these first-hand encounters in the truest way I can. My true intention for this book is to encourage readers to remain optimistic about their dreams and to inspire others to live with a limitless mindset.*

5. **NOTHING** mentioned or described in this book was in any way licensed, sponsored, endorsed, or otherwise affiliated with any business or prior publication for this first publication of *What Are the Chances?* All references are just experiential moments documented to help inspire and educate the readers to understand the essence of the context in this book. All other quotes not crafted by me are available in the public domain.

6. Most of the names of characters and specific details **have been altered** to protect identities.

7. * marks certain changes and alterations

Editors' Notes

What does 'Unconventional First Edition' mean?

It means that this book is perfectly imperfect.

Some tenses are charming, but off. Some phrases are goofy, yet full of character. Some grammatical details may be imperfect, but they were written in passionate emphasis upon a certain situation or time fluctuations. So, in its entirety, it is written perfectly from an experiential basis.

This edition is the compilation of over 40 editor's works.

After returning from traveling to finish writing this book, I found myself short on funds. So, just like short funds didn't stop my traveling in the first place, I decided to find literary enthusiasts and scholar friends to help me in the final stages of editing. For this first edition, I compiled all of these edits together. *(Note: it would have been a world easier to just hire an editor),* but I only understood this after I was nearly done with my compilation.

So needless to say, after 6 years of editing and re-editing, I decided to suck it up and get it all ready for publishing.

Also, you will notice on the cover that it states 'Soon to be a #1 Best Selling Author'. I put it on here as a joke at the beginning, but realized that this whole book is about getting into alignment with that which you are wanting. So, even though that caption is amusing to read, it is also intentional, hopeful and appropriate in regards to the storyline.

Preface

Here's a little history on how this book manifested.

We are all on the search to fulfill our dreams; to conquer our deepest desires and live out our happiest lives. No matter what the final goal is, everyone has a dream that they think of frequently and wish for someday. I wrote this line in a song in 2006, but I didn't understand it until about seven years later when I finally began living my dream of travel.

"But a dream is just a dream until it becomes a truth."

From the moment of my very first childhood thoughts, I determined that I did not want a typical house with a typical life. When I was growing up, I would say, "I'm going to live in an RV so I can live everywhere." I was told that it wasn't possible. As I have grown, I have switched these dreams to bounce from one concept to the next in a beautifully chaotic fashion. Now I have identified that my absolute truest dreams trickle into every stream of possible life existence on Earth. My biggest desire in life has no boundaries and no restrictions. *My biggest dream is to simply experience life and to share life's truth.* As a 29-year-old woman from the hometown of Lebanon, Pennsylvania *(I began this preface originally written at age 22)*, I have watched hundreds of people leave this small city and move away to follow their hearts or to live out the expectancies of a college education. Many others have stayed behind always longing for more. Learning is a great way to open doors to the future, but the one thing I began to notice was the broken promises to our society's children. The 'recipe to a good life' just didn't work for everyone like our schools assured. After the 2008 recession, many jobs were unavailable or were low paying and hard to find because competition was intense. Many friends of this generation were returning unhappy with a lot of debt. Over and over, I saw many who began waking up to the idea that this 'promised life formula' just wasn't a reality for everyone all the time. But the thing that shocked me most was that even some of those who landed the job right out of college weren't genuinely happy. In fact, many were more stressed than ever. This didn't make sense.

That's when I realized that true happiness was never a factor of the life formula. *Click- Perspective changed.* I saw people blaming unhappiness on their cities. 'This town sucks" And most people seemed to dislike their hometowns from absolutely everywhere. But the thing that amazes me is that everyone is from somewhere. Everyone has a hometown that someone else has moved to because they have fallen in love with it. Here is where we enter into the goldmine of perspective. It is the view of the seer, the perspective of the experiencer that changes everything. Just because I was born in Lebanon, PA and it's a small-minded, judgmental, post-industrial town, doesn't mean that it completely sucks. It's cheap to live and it is a half hour drive to three decent cities, one of them being our state capital. It's a twenty-minute drive to the Appalachian Mountains and has beautiful Dutch landscapes perfect for watching sunrises and sunsets.

Yet, even in my growing appreciation of my hometown, I longed for so much more. I was aware of the lack of happiness, yet didn't know how to find it. Years went by where I talked about going in my car alone, with nowhere to be and nowhere to have to go, except everywhere to be and everywhere to go! And I wanted it so badly, I longed for it so deeply, that even when my life was stable and headed in another direction, I still got what I wanted. Life happens.

So here is my warning.

Be careful what you wish for because your deepest dreams, if desired strongly enough, will happen. The longing inside of you, if continuously thought of, will create the opportunity for it and it might destroy everything you have right now if it doesn't fit the vibration of your desires. Following your dreams could break your heart, make you leave your job and give all your stuff away so you can be fully, truly free to live that life which you deeply long for. At least those are all things that happened to me.

Just remember, if you ask, you shall receive. You simply cannot ask life for answers continuously, but when it offers them to you, back up and wave your hands in front of you exclaiming, *"Uh... Thanks, but Nah. That isn't really what I want. I am not ready yet."*

Ask and Receive. Every religion says it. Every self-empowerment book speaks of it. My advice is to allow the flow of life to happen because the river of life flows whether you row with or against the current. We can either fight the current or we can sit back, steer a little bit, but mostly enjoy the ride and go with the flow. *Welcome to the sweet life of living in alignment.*

This book is written in a way to help readers understand the potential power of overcoming limiting thoughts. I shared struggles, internally and externally, to really embrace this idea of overcoming fear and negative emotions. I paddled against the current almost the entirety of this book. It would have been a lot simpler to just document the travel adventures and exciting stories, but that is not the true purpose of my writing this book. The real purpose unraveled itself over time. *The purpose is to share the truth- the good, the bad and the awkward.* My truth is to share how I fulfilled my deepest dreams in hopes of inspiring a simpler, easier way for others to properly fulfill their deepest dreams.

My truth is to share genuine, straightforward inspiration.

So alas, after six years in the making, over 75 different edits that I had originally assumed to be complete, here she is presented to you for the first time. This is thousands upon thousands of hours of writing, researching, exploring, reconsidering, crying from frustration, hiking intensely overwhelmed by potential clarity leading me laughing like a fool into the sky, editing until my nervous eyes could burst, re-editing until I went crazy and caught another few rides cross-country to rediscover my passions, all the while having this book in the back of my mind like a boulder, grounding me to a burden of thousands of hours of remaining focus; 'twas a lost reminder to share the wealth of experience, a mirage of my greatest imagination hanging a carrot before my eyes, provoking me ceaselessly, trailed by seemingly endless rewriting to ensure that this version captures the purest form of truth that I was able to accurately share by myself. No matter where I went, I couldn't distract myself from the self-induced destiny of producing this precise book in this precise way. Even my dreams woke me time and time again with phrases and subtle changes that resulted in a spring to a pen and rigorous 3 am writings.

Well, let me tell you, I have discovered a thousand ways not to write a book by now... But here she is with all the integrity I could muster. Thus, I created a few pen names, but ultimately decided to use my own name because that is my only justified way to share the raw truth of my experiences.

So my friends, dream on and live life to its juiciest potential.

Sincerely,

K. A. Trainer

In loving memory of my Great-Gramma, Catherine Claire Barry.

August 13, 1917 – April 28, 2012

Also, in dedication to Dad, Momma Minx, Kris, Gator, Nick, Ashley, Mary-Ann, Savannah, Victoria, Elisa, Owen, Baby Belle, Beckett, Emmie, Matt, Julie, Denise, John, Gina, All Family, All Friends, Bogey, Zola, Marshmallow, Honey, Reno and my cat-daughter whom dealt with my frequent disappearances her whole life, Lucy Gaga. This book is also completely in dedication to all who ever were a part of my life. I am entirely thankful for every person who consciously or unconsciously has assisted of this life's journey.

Part One

The Awakening

Noun

1. *an act of waking from sleep.*

2. *an act or moment of becoming suddenly aware of something.*

Adjective

1. *coming into existence or awareness.*

Chapter One

Day One- Lancaster/ Erie, Pennsylvania

"The greatest barrier you will ever cross is the one within your own mind. Everything else is relatively easy."

Idreamt of this moment years ago, this moment of simple peace just being where I am with thousands of miles of beautifully bizarre memories to reflect upon. And she, Callie, a random girl I had run into after a series of synchronized events following my falling out of a tree, sat at that counter smiling wildly, phone in hand as she skimmed through my online photo album. She had so many questions for me. *It felt good. Yeah, this felt really good...* One at a time my vivid recollections were awakened by the simple glance at her bewilderment to the images that she was slipping into. *Yeah, I have seen this before.* This girl had the bug; she absolutely had the travel bug and as she was scrolling through my pictures of places that I'd been, she spoke in sweet excitement with that all too familiar glow in her eye that I've only ever seen in the passionate explorer telling me about their dreams. She stared at me, eyes gleaming with a whole world of possibility reflecting inspired inquiries of my experiences, "Ok... Wow. I am so glad I get to ask you all of this. I have wanted to travel for years, but I don't know how. I just don't know what to do or how to go about it." She looked at me, unsure of what to say next, but her brown eyes peering from beneath her short, blond curls were begging for answers.

I smiled, very familiar with that feeling of craving unknown worldly experience, "Yeah, I am happy to help a soul-seeking explorer. Ask me anything." She looked down and stared at one picture for a while, a particular picture I had forgotten about. I was surprised by what I saw because she wasn't staring at a vast landscape or a crazy occurrence. She was staring at a picture of me the very first day I left. It caught me off guard as I gazed into those forgotten tears in my eyes, those raindrops sprinkling the windows and an uncertainty of survival in that pathetic attempt at an optimistic smile. I felt those dark, unsettled emotions emerge back from whatever suppressed realm I had stored them in all this time. That broken smile, that eager longing blended with absolute desperation in that picture, in that face, in my face… *Oh god…* that picture snapped this ego-driven master-travel certainty right out of my head. I startlingly glanced out the window, catching a reflection of myself and my current eyes and in them I saw something very different. I gasped silently as she asked her question, unaware of all the disturbed uneasiness that had swamped my vision in what felt like an extremely extended instant.

"Out of everything that happened and all of the places that you have been, what was the best day? Like, what is the best day of your life?" Her eyes lit up eagerly. I stared at her, faded, as a vortex of travel history swarmed my eyes. *The best day of my life?* I suddenly was thousands of miles, thousands of lives away in just a moment and just as fast, I returned again with full confidence that I knew exactly what to say.

"This might sound crazy, Callie, but the best day of my life is also the worst day of my life." I laugh as I say this and she brushes those blond curls back over her head as she asks me to explain it further. A few locks of her gold fall elegantly over her forehead. *Gosh, she's possibly the most beautiful woman I have ever seen...* I glanced at that picture again, that picture that she for some odd reason decided to leave on that screen, pleading me to dive into those ancient emotions. I saw the now distant, but well acquainted fear in those innocent eyes. It was a fear of the unknown. In that picture I saw a fear of failing, but as I stared into it I saw something else. I also saw a fear of really living. I blinked it away as I looked out the window again, but my vision shifted from seeing through the window's transparency to seeing it as a faded mirror and here I was greeted by my own current stunned reflection. These eyes were so different. These eyes knew so much more than the eyes in that picture. These eyes have faced death and these eyes have seen the likes of heaven. I sigh and tell her it's going to take a while to explain in detail. She tells me she's got plenty of time. School just ended and she moves back home in a few days for the summer. She wants to hear it all.

I laugh nervously as I look at the picture, those details, those emotions- *Whoa. It all comes back again...*

....

The steering wheel, sweaty and trembling, seemed to be the only thing real in this moment. My eyes were committed to the road and the sides of my cheeks were wrapped in liquid. All types of liquid actually, not just tears, but a blend of stale coffee, saliva, snot, rain and whatever else was streaming out of my inconsistent face. I just couldn't comprehend the fact that there really was no other option at this point other than to just drive away. This forced surrender made me cry even harder, blending my tears into the raindrops on the windshield.

Wow, there really was no going back. I have reached the point of no return- *actual, true, no return,* and it was absolutely terrifying. This was

2

ultimately my fate, not by my choice in the moment, but rather a forced present. To give up and retreat would mean only to stare into the eyes of broken-hearted anger and that was certainly not an option. She said it herself in what seemed to be the worst way possible - silence. That image tattooed itself into my mind. *"Before I get back…"* I read it over and over as if that little, stupid scrap of thoughtless paper, that determined note to destroy my life was just gleaming, holding its middle finger up at me in the reflective surface of the road. *"Be gone before I get back…"* I looked into my rear view mirror as if by some chance she was following me, waving her arms with a wide smile on her face, wanting me to turn around and come back. This would be a repetitive vision for weeks. I just couldn't believe that this is the way that it all ended. This! - This seemingly unrealistic betrayal of love - This is not how it was supposed to happen.

But that is exactly what happened. I remind myself. *This is exactly what happened.*

My eyes drive hard and my ears begin to ring with sounds of her past voices. I think of how she used to climb on top of me, rubbing my back and squeezing my muscles after I was finished landscaping. *"Oh baby, you worked so hard today." She'd whisper softly in my ear, sliding her hands down my chest as we'd kiss. "You just do such a good job at work" Our cat-daughters would hop up on the sofa and roll around and we'd laugh together. After they bounced away, she'd reach for my belt and our kisses would unite our souls into a world of…* And suddenly I'm bawling even harder as I'm driving. Somehow, in a strange sort of separation of self, I find a crooked view of myself from a distance and laugh at how absurd I must look. For some reason within my mental imprisonment, I am still able to step back and wonder what the people driving next to me must be thinking. It's as if I am in this constant duality of how I see myself and how others see me; I laugh at the crying and I cry at the laughing. How foolish I must be to direct my energy to strangers on the road.

I blubber on down the highway.

The rain slows and I quickly remind myself out loud, *"I am headed toward the greatest journey of my life, toward fulfilling my greatest dreams! This is everything I have ever wanted! The freedom of the open road, the bed in the back of the station wagon, the wide view of the universe around me…"* and I laugh at how silly I am for bawling despite such upcoming magnificence, such insistent transformation. *But her eyes hold a strong grasp on my heart. We are not together, yet somehow even though my ship is sailing, I just can't seem to depart.* Many times I turn around in my mind. I turn around at 15, 20, 30, 35, 40 minutes, 45 minutes, 1 hour and so on. I consider it many, many

3

times and I wonder what the response would be if I arrived back again with open arms. But actually, I know what the response would be. And it is not in my favor.

So onward I drive, south on 79 toward- *umm... what? Where am I going?* I think momentarily about how much I can't stand cold weather. I guess I will make finding heat and warmth my destination. So the thought of sun defrosts my eyes and fills my spirit with hope as my mind fills with visions of Florida. But for a realistic now, I guess I will say its Pittsburgh-ish area.

I had been preparing for a journey for a few weeks now and I found a good priced tablet online, but I didn't have time to figure out how to use the maps on it before she 'made' me go. The whole reason I bought it was because I needed to use it for the map since I didn't have nor want a smart phone. Not having a smart phone would prove countless times to be the primary reason for so many unnecessary hours of toil, agony and stress as I traveled. There really is no pride in making life both dangerous and harder. This is a lesson I would have to learn much later though.

So I drive onward and realize that I need to figure out some sort of plan. *My options... wait, what are my options?* My mind has become so misted from my confused tears that I completely forgot to figure out where I am going and it is now an hour into the trip. I remember that I spoke with my cousin, Bri, last week who lives in a small college town in California, Pennsylvania, about an hour and a half south of Pittsburgh. She said I could stay the night tomorrow, but that still leaves me with the problem of tonight. And it is so cold outside right now that I couldn't imagine sleeping in my car, trying to stay bundled up all night long in some odd, distant parking lot scattered with homeless zombies or lot racing outlaws during this harsh Pennsylvania winter. One solution remained: I needed to find free Wi-Fi. I needed to get online so I could send out SofaCruisin requests. But first, I must figure out what the hell I am doing or where I am going.

I see a sign for Pittsburgh. *Ok good. That is the plan for sure. I will do Pittsburgh tonight.* It was nice to have something to look forward to. Or maybe not something, but at least some place just so my first baby travel steps won't lead me falsely down a staircase. Unfortunately, even though I make a good mental attempt to figure out where to go to find free internet, I continue driving in circles, hopelessly lost in the Pittsburgh suburbs. I see all types of races scattering about like multi-colored ants behind glass. They have babies they push around and stroll here and there. They drive and honk and scream. I watch several cars nearly crash into each other on almost every street and I cannot help but to allow this insanity to feed into my own inner personal discomfort. This tension is building a boulder within my eyebrows and my chest and I cannot help but to engage personally with every wrong turn. I just want to find Wi-Fi so that I can find a place to stay!

I need something to be real tonight. I need something to be safe and certain. Several times I consider returning to Alana in Erie, Pennsylvania. *The home that never was. Maybe I can make it my home now!* Yet as quickly as these thoughts flowed in, they flowed right out because I knew these thoughts were insanity. *I cannot return there…*

At least not yet. I've been gone, what… I check the clock… *about three hours…*

"Three hours! Is that all that I have been gone…" It already felt as if weeks of suffering and misery had gone by. *"I haven't even allowed myself the opportunity to experience life yet!"* I make a mental checklist to reconfigure my road exploration.

1. Find a parking space somewhere not too ghetto.
2. Find Wi-Fi as soon as possible.
3. A hot coffee would be pleasant.
4. A bathroom would be agreeable too.
5. Send out and check my sofa requests

A sofa request is in reference to the website *SofaCruisin.com. Anyone can use this site to find places to sleep anywhere in the entire world! You select where you desire to go and send out requests to local people near your destination that have available spare rooms or sofas. It's a simple and safe concept considering that anyone can be a member. There are certified members who have people vouch for them and there are others that have friends and linked accounts. Everyone can rate their time with people and judge if it was a positive experience or a negative one. So, if one uses basic judgment skills and doesn't just click on any available name without any references and hope for the best, it is a very safe site to use.

This is my first time using the site and I was very afraid of who might respond. A friend from high school named Denny uses this site too and we had exchanged reference info so I at least had a valid person on my *page*, making my chances of finding a place to sleep tonight much, much higher and much, much safer.

A million outcomes flashed into my head as I sent out my simple statement to locals asking if anyone had anything available for me to sleep on for the night. It was a bit later than I had expected by the time I got into the parking

5

lot to purchase a coffee, but I had high hopes that something would happen soon. And in fact, it did.

Within five minutes of my posting on a random local event about needing a place to stay, I had a message. Doing this simple action was a huge step toward making a massive change in my life. There was so much fear, so much hesitation and uncertainty inside of me in this moment that my fear of trying almost eclipsed my first pivotal opportunity of finding not just a place to sleep, but a sexy distraction from my broken heart.

Chapter Two

Pittsburgh, PA

"It is true that if you never try, you never fail. But it is also true that you will never know what you have missed out on in life."

I nearly fly out of my seat. *My first Sofa response! Oh boy!* I click on it excited to see that it is a girl, which is a big relief. Then I realize that she is also about my age. *Hey, that's pretty cool! I could probably trust her to maybe listen to my stresses and maybe she'd understand and be able to help me through this a little bit.* I click on her profile and observe that she does not have any prior references. I then look at her picture and instantly realize that she is not just a like-aged girl, but she is definitely a like-aged lesbian. My eyebrows rise slightly as I read her message, filled with so much excitement at how quick I had gotten a response... *Wow! This is my first encounter on this site.* This speed would prove to be a rare thing on the site in later days, but as of now this is exactly what I needed.

She said that she just happened to log into the site, but hadn't used it yet and just saw my post. She lived on the south side of town up a big hill overlooking the city, but if I wanted to meet her at a show tonight, I could. She was working the soundboard for a traveling production at the Rex theatre. Options weighed out. I realize that I shouldn't trust her because she has no prior references, but she is asking me to meet her at not only a public place, but a place that she is either volunteering or employed so there is a great deal of validation there. *And she is a lesbian, so that's pretty awesome.*

Just three hours from show time, I decide that this is a great first night opportunity. We exchange numbers and she explains that it is like a spoken word poetry thing that locals sign up to be a part of. She said she'd put me on the guest list. Eventually I find myself circling around for a much longer time than I expected, a confused vortex now battling time looking for a parking space. I drove down the main street passing the theatre about four times while trying different maneuvers and roads to find a space, but there really was just nothing available. I remember that she had told me that she wouldn't be using her phone at all because of her duty on sound control so I couldn't ask for suggestions on parking. I just knew to go to the front door. Eventually a miraculous parking space does open up and I slide on in like the champion parallel parking official, waving at the cheering crowd within my mind. I check the time and have five minutes until the show begins! *Sweet!*

I start power walking, feeling my booty tighten and the calf pain rush in. I hadn't realized how long I was sitting down for today until this moment of fast paced walking. I finally get to the door and open it only to be surprised to see a disappointed couple walking out. I wonder what that was all about as I happily gallop to the little rope and stand waiting for someone to pay attention to me. The doors were closed and I heard a large laughter erupt from within the darkness. The crowd sounds huge. *Wow, this thing is a pretty big deal, I guess.* A woman comes over and looks me up and down and says, "Sorry, but we are sold out."

Startled, I begin stuttering, "Well, hi. Uh, sorry. I'm late. My name is Katie and I think my name is on a list somewhere or something."

"We are at max capacity and I think I have everyone that was on the list marked off already." She stares at me firmly in the eyes as I feel my last fiber of confidence melt. *Oh no!* This is exactly the opposite of what my fragile broken hearted ego needs right now!

"Are you sure? It's really important. I am friends with Madison, the girl doing sound tonight." I didn't know how to explain meeting a random girl that I don't know off of a website so that I could sleep at her place. That just sounded too strange for this older woman to understand. Friend seemed way more acceptable in this moment.

She flips a page back and I see Madison plus one, but the one is crossed out. "Sorry she already had her plus one sign in here. She just came in right before it started. She signed her name right here next to the plus one. See?" My heart sank and tears began to fill the corners of my eyes. This is a lesson in faith. Accurately timing out the SofaCruisin message without actually planning out the timing was lesson one. Lesson two is trust that my life guided me here for a reason and I must be confident that the world will reveal its inner justification.

She can see that I'm upset. "Hey. Sorry, Hun." But in fact, I am absolutely devastated. Words spill out of my mouth. I haven't even any control over them and I just mumble everything that happened and explain that Madison is a SofaCruisin host and I am so incredibly heart broken and I don't know what to do and I'm not sure where to go and that homeless guy out there stared at me really scary and…

She lifted up the rope, "Five bucks. Go on in. We are above max capacity. Don't tell anyone." She smiled at me. No more questions asked. Disbelief blinked across my face while I eagerly reach into my pocket to pull out my shaking money. I express my absolute gratitude way more sincerely than I should have and walk inside to see the entire room full from sit down space to standing. There is nowhere for me to go so I find a tiny corner in the back where I can stand by the bar on the foot rest about three inches higher than the ground and wedge myself in the cubby area so that I am not in the way of the bartender's space. I think of that previous encounter at the door and consider it to be a lesson in determination and persistence. Yes, my mind was focused on fear of the outdoors and missing my chance to find a place to sleep, but I knew what I wanted the outcome to be, even if it was an unconscious desire, even if it wasn't the least bit graceful! I knew what it was that I was wanting. And despite all odds, and several harsh declines, I got it! *Victory!*

At the halftime intermission, I follow the cute, thin, short haired girl (that spent her time at the corner of the stage) into the lobby. I could only assume her to be Madison so I approach her to say hi. She is wearing a black button up and has a genuine smile that emphasizes her sweet voice. *Mmm… Definitely standard lesbian babe.* I mention how I like the way her hair falls to the side of her face to which she replies "Thanks" and I realize that I may have just hit on her without realizing it. Quick, nervous conversation rises and we say our swift greetings. She returns to the auditorium with the rest of the crowd. I rush to the bathroom and realize that I am surprisingly happy while I am washing my hands. I catch a glimpse of a smile on my face, a rare pleasure as of late and I see in my reflection, a moment of hope. *The lessons of random public restrooms will always hold true in reconnecting me to my divine self.* I laugh at the thought of that and realize that it is actually very true. Great moments of insight have, many times, taken residence in the bathroom. It's a moment where you can be alone with your thoughts, where you can stretch your back and shoulders and recollect your own mind. The bathroom is a sanctuary in and of itself, even if the mindfulness becomes that of analyzing how drunk you actually are. In my case this time, it was realizing where I am in this world. There is no reason for me to be here, now, smiling about meeting a cute lesbian at a show in Pittsburgh, yet here I am.

From behind me, a recognizable face emerges from the stall. "So where have you SofaCruised so far?" the lady originally from the front door comes up and asks me while washing her hands. This completely catches me off guard because she used the term *SofaCruised* as if she knew what it was. I explain that this is my first time and that is why I was so scared. "I SofaCruised all over Europe last year. It was just such a wonderful experience. You are going to love it."

This blew my mind. For the second time tonight, she has blown my mind. I was completely unaware that older, professional people used this site too. Until now, I thought it was just hippies and soul seekers. I really had no idea that sophisticated, established people, especially women also liked it and used it. She explained how she dislikes using hotels because they are so impersonal. She began telling stories of the different types of places that she had stayed in her journey. A family brought her in with their three children and they all ate dinner together every night accepting her as a member of the family. She had taught the children a few English words over the couple days she stayed there before moving onto the next couch in the next city. I hadn't really understood how big this SofaCruisin site really was until this moment. This was one of the first lessons of life's offerings. I wanted the opportunity to better understand SofaCruisin so I could trust it more and was given the chance to speak with the perfect traveler at this point in time in my place of comfort, as strange as it may be, in my bathroom chapel.

After the show, I was following Madison up the treacherous hill, a 45-degree angle that I didn't think any car could drive up, but I trusted that she knew what she was doing and I ushered my little Volkswagen station wagon up that hill. "Come on, Felix. You can do it baby." We dropped off my car and stuff in her charming apartment, a house overlooking the entire city equipped with wooden floors and a fire stove in a newly remodeled kitchen. She offered to drive me around town to show me some of the local areas. We go through what she tells me is the gay district, but I don't know for sure because nothing about it seemed very gay to me. She mentions a bar that she sometimes goes to and we walk into a very darkly lit dive bar and the walls are decorated in naked women art, which both surprises me and excites me. Not in that way, but in the small-eager-mind-introduced-to-big-city-life kind of way. It does seem strange that no one around appears startled by this except for me. This is one of the first realizations that I don't know much about city culture at all.

Madison buys me a beer and then another and we talk about our lives and she is so engaged in our conversation that I just spill everything about Alana and my break up. I think I start crying at one point and the beer goes down way faster than expected so she buys me another and tells me stories about her exes and it just feels so good to really connect with someone like this. I will forever be grateful for the outcome of this night. Talking with someone who really understands is exactly what I needed more than anything else in the whole world and somehow, someway a same-aged sweet-hearted lesbian came to my rescue in Pittsburgh, Pennsylvania on March 12th, 2013. What are the chances?

Back at her house we watch an artistically expressive movie called *Midnight Red Cabin French. I have never seen it before and I am pleasantly surprised by the way that they filmed this movie. It's so fun to watch, so much energy and bizarre color. Then something strange happens. I start to see the movie on a deeper level. I see the genuine love and the terrifying heartbreak, the lust for love, but the lack of the ability to have it. I notice Madison has fallen asleep sitting next to me and my eyes widen as I become fully entranced by this movie like a mentalist's pendulum.

I become part of it. I see how the main character feels; I know what he knows. I have been where he is, hopelessly in love with a beautiful woman and unable to be with her. I see the sickness growing in her on screen and I think of all those miserable hospital visits to Hershey Medical Center with my girlfriend, *uh… I mean my ex-girlfriend…*- Alana. I feel the dread of what we thought would be a horrible health ending for my love. I feel the agony he portrays and I feel the love he displays. I am this movie and I start to cry gently as the curtain closes. While he sits alone in the top of the building, writing and typing his heart's pain, I feel the stab of each word.

"The supreme thing one is to ever experience or learn is just simply to love and allow thyself to be truly loved in return."

And he sits alone, typing in that building with nothing left but her memory as the camera pans out across the lonely city rooftops. It holds strong and true, ringing in the ears of millions now. It's a timeless love that goes beyond just walls, beyond people, beyond anything.

And I bawl. I silently bawl, my eyes, soaking wet and when I close them I see her face. I see her smile and her body. I feel her warmth against me and I kiss her face. And the memory is enough to last me, for now, but I expect to return to her again. *After this journey, I know all will be well with us again.* A fire is ignited within, which is surprising considering this amount of tears should typically put out any type of flame, but the fire is growing stronger. I am growing stronger. *Something about that movie, just… It just…*

It just made me understand why I am here. I wake Madison and tell her I'm going to bed. She retires downstairs and I go into the side room and crawl into the crisp bed, full of determination to succeed in whatever it is I am doing with my life. I am not sure what it is, but I feel great about where it's going. And something about seeing healing through writing guides my mind toward ease. I slip into an exhausted slumber within seconds.

Chapter Three

California, PA

"May soul move as fondly as yoga guides body."

A surprising sentence from Callie halts my story. "So you are a, umm, a, well... a lesbian?" I nod yes. "OH... ok. Hmm... I have some more questions for you then, but I totally thought you were going somewhere else with that story." Callie laughs while touching her wrist watch, an action I identify as nervousness. "So, what did you say earlier, you fell out of a tree?"

"Well, let's not hop ahead too quickly yet." I reply with a bit of confident anticipation at her reaction. *She really is gorgeous...* "Now, where was I? Oh yeah, do you know anything about yoga?"

....

I wake up in an old country style room. I habitually roll out of bed and begin doing sun salutations on the wooden floor. A sun salutation is a series of awakening yoga moves that stretches out the core of the body and elongates the spine through many deep breaths. As I flow through the poses, I notice that with every subtle movement, I create what seems like a loud crack through the floorboards. This produces tension in my temples, a rude guest making a series of annoying noises. This tiny repetitive creak puts a disturbance on my meditative state. I let out a deep breath and decide to walk out to get some water then try yoga in the living room.

I trip over the carpet, a very ungraceful start to the day so far. This makes me laugh; laughter, like yoga, is a good way to start the day too. *Actually, laughter is a great way to start almost anything.* I laugh at that thought, *perpetual motion.* I walk to the window to see a beautiful sunrise over the city. The sky is breathtaking and the air is cold and clear. Since she lives up in this hilltop home, I can see for miles over bridges, trees and city. The sky has glowing sun beams reflecting off the thousands of buildings. Millions of sparkles transfer through my eyes and down to greet my open heart. I feel so fortunate to be where I am right now. *Day one- Success.*

I hear the door behind me open and it startles me slightly. I turn to see Madison walking into the kitchen, arms outstretched above trying to release the night's kinks. "Well, good morning." I say while I smile at her. "This view is just phenomenal. I just can't believe how gorgeous it is from up here."

"Yeah, it is pretty nice." She mentions while walking over to empty out something that looked like a bong. I had never seen one of these glass vases before so I wasn't sure what it was at first.

"No, but I seriously feel as if I can take on another world up here. Like waking up to this, this magnificent masterpiece every single day..." I spread my arms high into the air and outwards as I speak, staring into the powerful landscape. I catch my reflection and see my shape, my form represented over top of this lovely creation of life before me. Suddenly I feel one with all I see. "I just can't imagine how inspired you get every day when you see this."

"Yeah, it is nice, isn't it? Sometimes I forget since I see it every day." I make note to never take advantage of my surroundings and write in my hungry journal, *'No matter where one is in life there is always something beautiful to be observed; something is always worth the gratitude of being in the now. The world will always present you with what you are able to appreciate and if you are unable to appreciate what you currently have, then you will get no more. Always remember gratitude for life.'*

She fresh grinds some coffee beans, filling the air with an intensely warm aroma. She debunks my bong mystery while explaining that it was a French press coffee pot. I watch her move around in her morning eyes and find myself rather attracted to her awkward jerky movements indicating that she's a little nervous. Gosh, *she really is very cute. Am I allowed to think that?* After coffee is made, she pours the thick, black liquid into a cup. I have never seen such a rich cup of coffee before, heavy and genuine. I am actually kind of intimidated by it for some reason. *But the smell, the aroma, ahh yes.* This is the nectar of the gods for sure. This is the way that coffee was intended to be enjoyed. We sit at her large counter and talk about life. These are always my favorite conversations because I love stepping on the sunrise dancefloor of fresh daybreak topics, to flow into a verbal tango with another person, each stepping properly to display the seamless arrangement of conceptual movements. Our laughter erupts from our stimulating language trickling around us, effortlessly gliding us step by step into each other's comfort levels. We began to understand each other very deeply in just minutes.

Our morning coffee verbal dance was followed up by her hopping on her computer. She didn't want to go to the office since I was around today, so she decided to work from home. While she took care of business, I ended up reading some more of Leopold Mountain's, *Contemplate and Welcome Prosperity.* His book is a daily vitamin to me right now, filling me with hope

13

and wisdom to relate to every event I encounter. I feel like I need it every day for strength and proper function, but I can only take so much at a time, otherwise I become oversaturated in determination and burn out my mental fuse. It is just so juicy, so full of material, that if I try to take in too much immediately, it just plugs my head and confuses me. Actually, if I am to be honest, the entire reason I am on this trip is because of this book.

....

Callie devilishly repeats 'verbal tango' before asking me some questions about this, as she put it, 'magical book'. I was intending to graze the surface of this controversial topic, *the law of attraction*, but the more I spoke of it, the more fascinated she became. So, I really began to explain how it related to my journey's development. She then asks me how I first found out about it.

I laugh nervously while rubbing the back of my neck as I reflect on those wild moments of synchronicity. *"Well, Leopold Mountain's main concept is, 'Anything that the mind can perceive and entirely believe the mind can and will always achieve.' He explains that the Law of Attraction energetically attracts that which you think and feel and suggests that there is a 'hidden power' that all the most influential people throughout history have not only understood, but have practiced. * In the mid 1900's, Leopold Mountain was initiated into the highest order of the masonic fraternities, beyond that of just a 32nd degree mason. His initiation and influence during his time as Master of the Royal Secret gained him notoriety and trust, linking him to serve equally as Knight Commander-Court of Honor. But he didn't whole heartedly believe in the secret's need to be kept secret. This highest of praises, just two positions below the Honorary 33 degree and the Active 33 degree, made him a controversial figure being that deep down, he felt that the initiation process needs not be so strict for the fundamental and spiritual laws of society to govern the masses of the people."

Callie looks tangled in my words so I try to break it down a little easier. "He wanted the truth to be set free from only the control of the privileged; those whom were born lucky enough to have their parents teach them that they have power over their own minds. Over several years, a secret initiative was formed between Leopold and a former president of the United States, an undisclosed philanthropist and Sovereign Grand Commander of the Ancient Accepted Scottish Rite, Northern Masonic Junction. This moral question was sparked in this man's later years as he questioned the integrity of his life's choices, the disintegration of mankind for his own wealth. This turned-philanthropist offered to pay Leopold's travel and expenses for the next 25 years if Leopold spent every moment dedicated to acquiring the details of these powerful abundance mindset secrets by interviewing millionaires and the richest people all over the world."

Callie asks, "So, what did he do about it? He wrote a book?"

I respond, "Well, in this book he exclaims that this practice introduced him to the wealthiest, most influential people of this time. He met billionaires and city developers and even assisted in another president's decisions as his right hand man. All of this was ignited by the initial power of his mind since he originally came from nothing. Leopold's family didn't come from wealth, but Leopold had a deep drive for more in his life. Fortunately during his childhood, a local businessman saw this attribute as a rare brilliance and brought Leopold in as his own son, introducing him to the first stages of masonic initiation. He instantly became obsessed with these philosophies and ancient practices of masonic virtue. His first book, titled,* *From Rags to Riches*, explores his personal endeavor to advance his own life based upon hard work and dedication to practicing these universal laws he preaches. His book, *Successes by Universal Laws*, was first published in 1920 and was extremely controversial because of some key phrases dealing with the word *vibration*. The mass distributed 1929 edition is what most are familiar with now, but it does not contain much scientific vibrational theory."

"Hmm... weird. So, how does this whole thing work?" Callie asks.

"Well, the Law of Attraction is essentially a simple, psychological model of life living strategy. 1. Think of anything you desire. 2. Believe it fully and whole-heartedly 3. Feel what it feels like to attain it. 4. Repeat daily. 5. It will manifest itself into the physical world. The Law of Attraction suggests that anything that ever has existed in life has been the product of a thought. So, if you can actively engage your thoughts to be that which you want most, whether it is money, love, a house, a situation, an opportunity, anything- you can have it if you first believe it is possible. He includes many explanations and true stories of those who have applied the Law of Attraction to increase their wealth, happiness or power in society."

"So it's like 'create your own reality' type of thing? Wow. That's crazy. How did you ever hear about this?" She asks. Her arms move from crossed to by her sides, indicating a physical openness for listening to me.

"It's funny actually. In 2008, this whole concept of mind power was explored by another book that was turned into a documentary called 'The Secret' by Rhonda Byrne. '*The Secret*' is relatable to our generation because it focuses on current celebrities and people of great wealth in our lives now. It was endorsed by Oprah Winfrey and features people like Jack Canfield, author of the Chicken Soup series and a host of wellness practitioners, philosophers and motivational speakers. But truthfully, this will sound a little crazy. The first time I ever discovered *The Law of Attraction* was honestly from hiking solo on the Appalachian Trail. I used to go on day long hikes alone several times a week and would meditate after writing at scenic views. It was as if no mysteries were left, as if the whole existence of the universe became unified with my spirit. I could look out over those valleys and understand life as so beautifully simple, yet so simply complex. I could see the patterns of my life reflected in the landscapes before me and it really felt like the universe was talking to me and telling me secrets."

"Ha-ha. What are you talking about? The mountain would speak to you? I hope it spoke better to you than that tree you were hanging with before meeting me this morning." Callie's arms cross again as she laughs. "Are you high?"

"Ha. No, I actually don't smoke and yes, it really felt like the universe was talking to me. I would 'come down' off those mountain 'high' cliffs and later read those written ramblings in my notebooks. It really felt like I was going crazy! But I also felt like there just had to be truth in it somehow. It's as if I was either channeling the mountain's wisdom or going insane, but I didn't know which was true. I did, however, know that I felt more alive than I ever have as I wrote it. I never had met anyone who spoke of such things, especially me being from a small-minded, left for dead steel industry town. But the mountain introduced me to the power of my own thoughts and I felt absolutely insane until I watched *'The Secret'* with Alana. I instantly became obsessed with it; I needed to know more. It felt like I had discovered this secret truth, a treasure of internal wealth, yet never had any proof that it existed beyond my own accidental discovery of it. That is, I felt crazy until my first meeting with that documentary. I unconsciously used the Law of Attraction to attract more information about the Law of Attraction without ever having been aware of it! It's just like electricity. Whether you know how it works or not, you can still plug in a lamp and enjoy the benefits of electrical current. I still wasn't sure if I was crazy though. I needed to figure out what this was all about. After I watched that movie and became aware of how the mind can attract anything, I started to educate myself constantly because I began manifesting everything around me- free coffee, free gas, free food, getting small job offers here and there and suddenly I realized that almost everything I said I was wanting, was happening. Yes, it was all little stuff, like saying "I wish I had a couple extra bucks" and then I would buy a pair of jeans from a thrift store and there would be a $20 bill in the pocket. Or like heading down to my college class wishing I had eaten something before I left and wishing I hadn't forgotten my wallet. I then arrived at school to see it was free pizza and soda day. I don't drink soda anymore, but the point is that I was attracting circumstances and it became increasingly frequent until it seemed that nearly everything I said came true. On many occasions a friend would say, "How did you know that?" or they would often reply, "Whoa! What are the chances?"

"Ok. So, you are telling me that if I say I want a million dollars, it'll just pop up?" Callie seems like she is interested in this, but very uncertain about anything I've said so far. I may not have been explaining myself clearly enough too.

"No, that is not exactly what I am talking about. Action plus intention produces circumstance when mixed with visualization and feeling. Ah, they are such powerful tools in life's toolbox and most people aren't taught to know it exists! I can't emphasize the importance of using imagination. We were taught to color within the lines of society, but by using our thoughts, we can draw our own lines to color in ourselves! We can create our own realities for the most part! And I'm saying that if you believe you'll have a million dollars every day and if you feel worthy of it while you take action, then your life will most likely align with the reality of your thoughts."

Callie bends down and picks up a penny. She holds it up to me. "Hmm... Small step to a million, but I guess it's a step. I guess…"

"See, Callie. In the first few months of my applying the Law of Attraction to my life, everything became magical. In fact, I started to actually feel crazy because everything I was saying became true and I needed to know more. No one I knew ever spoke of any of this, but I proved to myself that the mountain top told me no lies. Callie, I wanted the real truth. I craved it. I longed for a deeper education on it. That's what they say about the Law of Attraction though; whatever you focus on when added to a burning desire, will happen. And it is not exactly about only what you want."

"Well, what is it then?"

It's about what you feel plus what you are focusing on with vibrational intention. It's all about emotion."

"So, I have to feel like a millionaire?"

"Yes! Well, kind of. I am certainly no master on all of this, but I do believe that if you say, *"I want a lot of money.",* but you feel poor, you will not receive a lot of money because the words that are spoken are empty. You are attracting the feeling of 'poor' to you even though you speak of 'rich'. It's all about the emotional vibration blended with the thought vibration, a divine

17

entanglement between the frequencies of the head and the heart. And when those come together with a direct focal point, anything is possible."

Callie makes direct eye contact with me. "Ok, I think I am starting to understand what you are saying now. It's not just like a magic spell or something. That's what I was thinking you were talking about at first. You can attract good or bad depending on what you think about and how you feel. Wow, I have never heard of this before, but I love it."

"In my case, the reason I was on this road trip was because I was knowing what I was wanting, but remaining in a state of *'This is good enough. This is all I need in life.'* And yes, love is what I wanted, I still do, but my sincerest desire at the time was to explore this country, to see new life and to just learn how to think much more positively. I longed to live in limitless possibility and divine freedom within my mind. I felt as if I had lived in a mental cage of a slow, oncoming spiritual death my whole life and I subconsciously knew what I needed to do to create change, yet ignored it. There is no wish more powerful than the subconscious desire. Underneath the folds of my progressive heartbreak existed the unraveling of my deepest desires and I didn't even realize it as my relationship fell apart.

That's what they say, though.

Be careful what you wish for.

Right?"

Chapter Four

"There is never a limitation to the ability to set a new goal."

Callie mentions something about generally being a skeptical person most of the time. She likes the way I speak with enthusiasm and exhilaration. She hesitantly says, "What exactly do you mean by '*Be careful what you wish for?*' I mean, yeah, I have heard that phrase like a thousand times, but what does that mean for you with all of this?"

I laugh as I remark that she really is doing a great job asking me questions that only have lengthy answers. "I mean, I can't really make up a short explanation. This is deep. It's powerful and complex." She replies that she only likes complex things and laughs as she nudges my shoulder. *You want complex? No problem, honey.*

"The unraveling of truths arrived in a surprising way for me. Some of the greatest gifts in life arrive in the package of immense pain. In January 2013, Alana and I packed up our entire apartment in Lebanon, Pennsylvania into a 17 ft. U-Haul and drove some ridiculously windy, snowy six hours to Erie to restart our lives. Living close to family was one of Alana's big dreams and I was dedicated to fulfilling her dreams, especially, well, especially after what happened." Callie notices that I slightly shudder.

"What happened?"

I look out the window and spot an uncomfortable middle-aged woman walking slowly with a cane. She cautiously watches each step, clutching her lower back with her other hand. *Pain…* "I don't want to talk about it now, Callie. I am just not in the mood. After we talk a little bit, if you still want to hear then, I will tell you. But for now, just know that some incredibly extreme circumstances caused me to stumble right upon the only book I was seeking at the time, *Contemplate and Welcome Prosperity.* I was unconsciously attracting the training guide for attracting life circumstances to myself in the frozen season of Erie, PA."

Callie asks me again how it all came to be. I remind her that I just wasn't in the mood to relive that tragic time about Alana verbally right now. "I still want to hear what happened to you before we met today! You said it was an amazing revelation or something, but I can hardly imagine falling from a tree as amazing."

"Yes, I did fall from a tree earlier and it was actually amazing. Ha-ha." I rub my bruised elbows noticing they are entirely brush burned. "The tree story is seriously insignificant now without the rest of the background story. There really isn't a short cut to the experience, but I will definably tell you later on if you still want to hear it."

"Well, I've got time and you've absolutely got my attention. I want to hear all of it."

"Ok, then. Let's start back at day two on the road, day two toward living life limitless. Ya, Ready?"

Chapter Five

*"Deep within our own reservoir of truth, we must find our personal power
and really live in that truth."*

Callie jots down a few words. "Live life limitless? That sounds so
extreme." I watch her write triple L. "So, you really do believe in all of
this, well, this stuff?" I give her a confused look.

"This Law of Attraction stuff. I mean, it's fascinating, but is it real? Or is
it like confirmation bias? You know what I mean, right? You look for answers
because you are aware of it, like if someone buys a red car and now they see
that same red car everywhere. It's just that they are looking for it now, but it's
been there all along. Could all of this stuff just actually be confirmation bias?
Are you just seeing it because you are looking for it?"

I smile at her, unsure of how to respond. I appreciate her debate. The
perspective shift from having no control over one's life to having some
influence over one's life is monumental. I know I could aggravate this
conversation some more, but I decide to play it safe. "You'll have to listen to
my story more and decide for yourself. I won't tell you what to believe, but
I'll tell you what happened to make me believe. 'Live Life Limitless'. She
circles it and smiles. *Challenge accepted.*

....

At Madison's house, I put down that book and take in my surroundings. *I
am not in Erie anymore. Day 2. Pittsburgh...* I return mentally to see
Madison in the kitchen.

Madison wants to take me out to see the city in the daylight. We drive
around and she explains history about the buildings and countless bridges. It
feels so good to just have someone guide my misplaced soul today. It's
exactly what I need. She then suggests going to the Andy Warhol museum
which is a bit pricy, but it is a must do in Pittsburgh for anyone with an
appreciation for art. There are some things about the strangeness in some of
his experimental art pieces that I will never forget. In the video series, he had
people sit in front of the camera for a minute and stare at it. The camera
would record the subtle movements of a person's face as they slowly become
more comfortable. It's like subtle art documentation or experimental

relaxation based upon muscle structure and tension. Some looked so stressed and as the moments went on they would relax. Some would begin it with determination and as they stared, the angles of their face and eyes would reflect doubt or apprehension. Around the next wall, there was a machine which would allow you to partake in the experience. It records visitors in the same manner and emails it to you. It made me nervous as I sat staring at the camera. It made me wonder where that discomfort was based from inside of me. *Where did this nervous tension stem from? Hmm… perplexing and odd.* But something deep inside was unsettled at my inability to just be in front of a camera without moving. We eventually have lunch and our day together ends before sunset and we say our farewells. Our hug is so genuine and feels so very true. I explain, in the best way I can, how important it was for me to meet her. I will always be grateful for her arrival in my life now.

I arrive at my cousin's apartment after an hour of anxiety from being alone with my own thoughts while driving. An actual destination feels so pleasant. Her porch is scattered with huge art pieces in the rain. As I knock on the door, I hear the warm giggle of lots of female laughter fill my ears. *Ahhh… estrogen therapy.* Tension drains from my body.

She greets me with a massive hug and we laugh as she asks me how everything has been. I tell her that I am going to Florida and she tells me about her school plans, introducing me to her friends who are giggling in the basement and putting on makeup. A few empty champagne bottles are on the table as they confess they've each finished one so far. My cousin was already on her second when she offered to do a shot of vodka with me. The house and she were both were very different than I expected. The reason for my uncertainty is vital. (*Don't get me wrong in this description because I do love all my family with absolute compassion.*) My uncle and aunt were very nice to me, but back in the day they were very close-minded: gay hating, black loathing, corporate loving, gun toting, Christian preaching, etc... And when I came out to them when I was in high school, they treated me, well, different. Different is a gentle way to describe their judgement and my disappointment. I had been so excited to share my big secret, the fact that I was in love with my very first girlfriend. I wanted to share this joy with my blood relatives and I was greeted by an invisible wall that they set up between us. For years, they tripped over their words as we spoke. They always watched me with a cautioned eye to ensure that they wouldn't catch "the gay". In fact, this judgmental misunderstood hate was so extreme that after Obama was president, a distant family member produced a series of original art pieces depicting gays, guns and bibles on fire around his angry black presidential body. But off my cousin went to an arts school and when I saw her next, she was an entirely different person. She hugged me deeply with genuine love and it shocked me because I could feel that she meant it. She laughed and drank and was just so filled with life, so filled with joy. I couldn't believe the transformation that took place after three years of college. She told me that she had a boyfriend, but to not tell her parents. When I asked her why, she explained it was because he was black. I was floored that this kind of hesitation still existed in our world. She begged to not ever let her dad know. She confessed that she only finds black men attractive and if her dad knew that, he might disown her or kill her or something. She didn't care about me being gay anymore. I was confused about all of it at the time, until she explained that her best friend, the head of the sorority, was a beautiful lesbian. It was in this moment that I understood the importance of kids leaving their parents influence to go off into the world to figure life out for themselves under their own terms. *Prejudice, intolerance and misguided hate drown in the river of life when there is nothing to keep them afloat.*

They were all getting ready to go out on the town and I smile at how much I appreciate having a group of lovely, wild women to be my friends tonight. They just couldn't wait to go out clubbing and I was really excited to see what it was all about. The first bar was a tiny dive bar and I was certainly surprised that the college students prized bar that 'everyone' went to was such a dump.

The really sexy lesbian head of sorority had a girlfriend, which was good because she stood between my legs at one point as I sat on a stool and she had her hands on my thigh while we talked. I felt intense attraction, but I did not intend to make any moves and I think she was able to pick up on that. I was hanging with a family member and I still had my heart with Alana. Also, she had a girlfriend and I do not support cheating. *I've been the cheated on by past girlfriends- I will not be the cheat-ee to others!*

I dance the way I want to, flowing and grooving and having fun. The rest of the room is trying to hook up and grind all over each other in the typical college way. I have no interest in this and they make fun of the way I am dancing. I feel bad for them because seeking sexual attention is the only way they seemed to know how to dance. I became discouraged rather quickly and return to the bar. I can't really be surprised that they made fun of me. I was like a highlighter in a sea of darkness. My white limbs could be spotted across the room doing something very different than everyone else. They grinded and I guess I just wiggled and jived.

This night was a night to change the rest of my life though, because this is the night I was introduced to the dance, 'The Waddle.' The music fades into another song that I have never heard before. *"Ohhh."* A deep male voice yells as a throbbing bass noise begins. *"Ohhh…"* My cousin and her friends shriek and run to the dance floor to form a line. *"Ohhh… all the shawties in* *zeeya clubba' letta' me see ya disco...*" All the girls obey the song's request and I laugh at how literal 'shawties in the clubba' actually became. They assemble into a formation and then all start doing the same movements at the same time. I was thrilled to see this! Everyone knew this dance, well, everyone except for me, but this was the beginning of my being obsessed with learning *"The Waddle". As silly as this sounds, it would prove to be a useful tool in many occasions for years to follow.

After that, we went to a frat house for a party where beer pong was king. We drink crappy free beer and wiggle around to music in a gorgeous library room with a huge, thick wooden bar. At one point, I overheard a guy say something about "not having enough pussy." and "all these fucking lesbians." And something about the way I watched people's interactions all night had me a little fired up. I climbed up and stomped into a ferocious stance on that bar like a crazed, feminist raccoon and pointed at the sex-less woman-hater as I angrily spoke an impromptu speech about women's rights and vagina power. Yes, I was that kind of aggressive, angry lesbian this night, scurrying around with my mask of night power, digging in the trash can of conversation for something to eat and throwing the lids at the local cats. The raccoon outfit was fun to wear for the evening, but it didn't fit correctly over the wings I was attempting to grow on this trip. I guess I am a caterpillar and sometimes one doesn't know if it's going to ever be a butterfly until it tries on another outfit only to realize that it doesn't fit quite right, nor could it fly in a costume. *I won't be a caterpillar forever, but right now it's hard to imagine that I will ever fly...*

I am not a raccoon, nor am I an angry lesbian needing to thrust my bulging, robust feminism into frat boys' faces. I am now completely certain of that. What I am not certain of is what the next day will be. *Anxiety rises slightly.* I try not to think of it as the evening fades into a blur and I fall asleep feeling very lonely on the couch in the basement. Little did I realize how important that absurd feminist raccoon understanding would be in just two days. *Yep, I was about to learn a lot about other life.*

***IMPORTANT AUTHOR'S NOTES- Those disapproving family members during the time of writing this are now all much, much nicer and open-minded than they used to be and couldn't greet me with a sweeter welcome every time I see them so please don't hold those prior actions anywhere to heart. They are loving and encouraging in all respects now.

*** Also, do you know how hard it is to write a truth based book and not offend people?

Chapter Six

"It is just as important to know WHY you are born as it is to even just be born. Dare we call that finding the passion of our destiny?"

Somehow the next day, I wander boldly south into West Virginia and decide to go into the woods on back roads toward something off the beaten path. I wanted unstructured exploration today and didn't want to even be on a highway if I didn't have to. After all, I had my trusty tablet to navigate the way. It rained and I kept driving, singing and smiling until I saw a sign for an old iron furnace. I pulled out my video camera and started filming my exploration of it. A 25 ft. beehive looking thing sat before me as I walked around, careful of my footsteps on the slippery, rocky path. In this moment, I decided to share historical information with the viewers of my YouTube channel as well as exciting things too. I walked around and talked to the camera stumbling over my words and feeling the familiar feeling of stage fright, which caught me off guard because I was alone in the woods in the rain, but still wasn't comfortable enough to be myself. *Strange*... I noticed that there was a hole in the bottom left of the base. I bent down and held the camera inside giving the spectators full view of the inside of an iron furnace, but I realized that if I lay down I could probably maneuver myself into it too. So, I wedged myself in there and scooted until I could stand up, feeling an intense exhilaration, the type of thrill I only ever receive from exploration. The echo, as I spoke, was so powerful inside and roared tremendously around my whole body, shaking me free from my own inner fear of the camera. When I returned to the car I was almost in tears at how powerful I felt I was becoming, even in such a simple action. Eventually I checked to see where I was, but the tablet did not turn on. Dread rose through my mind as visions of the worst scenarios approached. I started to cry.

Crying was rather new to me. I didn't cry for years. Now I could cry at something as simple as a kitten tripping over a baby chicken. All the studies I have been doing recently have been about how one's own personal power lies within the power of the mind. To control the thoughts and observe the emotions was the first step to freedom. I was so scattered internally, but I grabbed the harness of my thoughts and reevaluated the situation. Inside my glove box was a map of Pennsylvania and the border of the map shows a tiny chunk of the surrounding states, so I consider myself to be around a certain area of the green wilderness to the left of what appeared to be a major road heading south. So, that's what I did. I drove westward bound like an old pioneer settler following the occasional sun peeking through the clouds until I hit the first major road. I didn't pass one business for a very long time, but I did pass homesteads and farms that looked almost like what my expectation of Switzerland would be like, mountainous angles that rolled steeply into valleys with little cottages. Somehow the sun knew I needed it and it peaked out, giving me a smile as it set vibrantly into the horizon. Darkness approached and I felt my drive should be close to my destination, just a three hour drive to Columbus, Ohio where I had a SofaCruiser's response for the night. After the tablet turned off, I had been driving for about 2 hours so I figured I should arrive within a half hour or so.

Finally, I stop at the only business I have seen this whole time, a small dingy looking gas station that only had soda and chips available. I walk in and pathetically ask the guy where I am; almost crying again when he responds that I am nowhere close to where I thought I was. "Yerp, young lady, I'd say you are about three hours from Columbus." I blink confused. He pulled out a map and showed me where I was on it. Apparently, that south facing road I took earlier turned a sharp west after the edge of my map ended. And it kept going North West after the sun set. *Surprise*. So, when I turned right, thinking I was turning west a long time ago, I actually turned north. Tears fill my eyes. I see that I am about 40 minutes from Wheeling WV, a city right over the border from Pittsburgh. *Backtracking! Ah!* That is the opposite of what I wanted to do! I wanted to be as far away from Erie as possible and now I am in the car heading right back to where I started! I called Madison and asked her what she thought and she said she wasn't busy and would be more than happy to host me again.

I arrive back at her place after an hour of driving, which now felt like a warm arrival of friendship rather than a burden. She had prepared swordfish and kale for me when I got there, expecting me to arrive hungry, which I was. I knew it was exactly where I needed to be that night. We drank wine and I told her what happened. We laughed like old friends and it was so good to be around the type of non-sorority/frat energy. Just relaxed, fun vibes were all my soul requested. We went into her room and she began playing records and showing me some cool things she had and telling stories about music and travel. I started to get tired from my wine goggles and we realized it was past her bedtime since she had work in the morning. She offers to let me sleep in her bed. *Ya know, since the room was already so warm and the upstairs room was so very cold.* It was so nice of her. I happily accept. We lay next to each other not touching, like frozen corpses and I feel a huge tension rising between our skins, warming us and instigating a type of magnetism. The silence speaks depths for us, yet we are both frozen in shock. The darkness cradles our nervous little lesbian bodies, both feeling the same thing, yet both too nervous to make a move. After the tension to simply touch nearly suffocates me, I ask if she would like to cuddle and she lets out huge breath

26

saying "Yes" like an enormous relief swept over her as if she had been holding her breath too. I just needed to be close to someone, to have someone cradle me and hold me caringly. We kissed very passionately for several moments, our legs intertwining softly as our bodies pressed together lightly. Her hands wrapped around my neck and it raised emotions of tenderness inside of me. It felt so good to just be held, to just be gently touched in a compassionate manner. Deep down, neither of us wanted more than that this night and the truth of the moment rose into awareness. The tension settled as we both decided that this would go no further. We felt the relaxation of just simply being close and that was all either of us needed this night. The wine and her arms warmed my frozen spirit. I played little spoon (not my common position) as she cradled me, holding me tenderly and kissing the back of my neck as she whispered, "Goodnight". I looked out the window, over the glistening city, lights flickering in a way I had never seen before. From up here, the world below me was like the abundant night sky. *This world is so remarkable.* We fell asleep, cuddled tight, with gentle smiles on our faces.

Chapter Seven

"Follow your passion, your unending joy, and the universe will take the closed windows before you and present you with open doors you never before knew existed."

Callie throws her hands into the air exclaiming, "That's it! Lies! You guys had to do it!" I am surprised by her response. "How do two lesbians get into a bed together and not have sex?" She looks way more frustrated by this than I expected. I laugh nervously again and explain that it just happened like that and it was perfect as it was, but that isn't what she wants to hear.

We talk several minutes on the topic of lesbians and she doesn't seem pleased when I say, "Well, it doesn't really matter whether we had sex or not. It doesn't add or take away from the story. Let's get back to it now. What? I'm in Pittsburgh again, right?" She tells me that it isn't fair to hide the truth from her. I tell her I am not hiding anything. I ask her why she is so obsessed with lesbians.

"What? I am not obsessed with lesbians." She blushes unknowingly as she says this. "I just feel like you guys did it." I tell her that the truth is this time we didn't do anything, but that wasn't the last time I would see her. I ask her again why she is infatuated with lesbians and she explains that she has never been with a girl before. This makes sense. I am speaking of unknown territory. *Maybe she wants to go exploring...*

....

So I left Pittsburgh- Again. Before I left, I wrote several pages in my notebook and said out loud, "Today I will go south, not north, but south." So, I drove to West Virginia- Again. I stopped to take a picture of the sign as I reentered the state. My friend Candy and I took pictures of all the state signs on our way back from California the month before I left Erie. I thought flying out to California to drive back with her was going to end my travel craving. All it did was feed it and here I am now, passionately addicted to the open road. I stopped at the visitor's center in West Virginia so I could find things to do. The guy told me about Seneca Rocks which was roughly 2 hours east from the highway. I went because I was so ready for mountain top adventure! While stopped at a gas station that had Wi-Fi, I sent out some Sofa Cruisin' requests in Elkins which was the closest city to Seneca Rocks, about 45 minutes away. Then I went east to answer the mountain's call. As I pulled up, a cute couple with two small golden dogs park by me. I start up quick conversation then head up the mountain.

I'm basking in the glory of existence as I begin taking pictures as much as I'm taking my time, enjoying the freedom that my life has finally become. I pass a woman pushing a baby carriage up the trail. She was massively overweight and was just pushing and pushing. I knew there was no way she would make it, but smiled at her determination because it was very impressive. *I wonder how far she will get before she turns around.* As I hike, sweat starts to line my spine so I unzip my jacket, but that isn't enough so I battle the temperature the whole time. I am wearing a big green winter jacket and I wish I hadn't worn it then. But at the top of the mountain, where the winds were most likely close to 25 or 30 mph and freezing, I was very grateful to have lugged that heavy thing up that mountain.

I am eventually passed by the friendly couple with the dogs as we exchange some fun conversation again. Upon the top, I meet two military people, a woman, about 25 and a man, about 45. He's from Maine and she's from South Carolina. *I just love meeting people from so many places! There is so much life in this planet*! I nearly float off the mountain by a giant gust catching my bulky jacket. The entire mountain seemed to shift from the intensity of the wind. The view is so pale and naked, so winter brisk and yet, endlessly amazing. The thousands of trees were just dark toothpicks below, awaiting the opportunity for their buds to blossom. I smile as I imagine how different this view will look in about a month. Nothing stays stationary. Nothing is set forever. Even the trees that spend their whole lives planted stationary sway with the unseen force of the breeze. They grow and shed each season; even the evergreens refresh their needles. I breathe out a tension that I was unaware I was holding in my chest. It was something dealing with the concept of time and expiration. After many deep breaths, deep moments staring into the distance smiling, wind attempting to beat the smile off my face, I climb back down and feel my face sting. I have earned this - this crazy, cold happiness. Eyes watering, nose running, chest hurting thrill of mountain top chill, *yes, I am so deserving of this*! My blood surges with pride for having the strength to follow through with leaving Erie. This mountain proves that I have the power inside. I turn around to head back to the trail and see baby stroller pusher at the furthest portion of the trail before it becomes rocky. Her inspiring action fills me with hope as I tell her how awesome it is to see her at the top. Despite her obvious potential set-backs, she made it! *Determination! Persistence!*

When I return to the car, I open an old notebook of mine that I found in a bag that I designated to holding my travel papers. It reads *"Bike ride. It's amazing where you end up when your body and mind become one! Shuts out all distraction besides safety."*

I text Madison to talk about hiking and how I am going to set up on the streets and perform magic tricks for money when I get to temperatures warm enough. My great new heart-break distraction keeps texting me saying "Yeah, you can do it! Do that magic! Kill it!" The amount of cute that she embodies is very adorable. I don't know if I agree with her description of what to do with magic, to kill it, but there is something that excites me about her enthusiasm and belief in me. Both thrill and guilt flood me when I realize that this is how I feel, especially with Alana back at home with my cat daughters, but I am trying not to focus on Alana or any other girls. This trip should be only about Katie Trainer discovering who Katie Trainer is. Not girl chasing. Not female distractions. My heart feels broken and I need to mend it and fix the cracks, patch it up and move on. *But I miss her so much…*

The couple with the dogs comes over and talks to me. They offer me a place to sleep tonight in their family's cabin, but it is a half hour north. *No! North!* They plan to go out to a local bar with a $12 cover and watch a bluegrass dance band. Since I have been trying to go south, I decline and expect to get to Elkins and have a SofaCruisin request there. They give me their number in case I change my mind. I almost do.

I head back into town after trying to get to a giant overlook, but it was snowing at the top and getting stuck in the snow at the top of the mountain is not really where I put my intentions today. Also, a man in a rusted pickup truck drove up to a stop sign on the mountain roads and stared at me rigid before flipping me off as he drove slowly by me. *I bet he saw my gay sticker and short hair…* So, after a few hours exploring the friendly mountains around here, I decide to drive back over the way I initially came from to go to Elkins. It seemed that was the only way to Elkins. As I drive up the steep mountain road, the car comes to a stop at the top of one of the first hills. Blood is smeared all over and cars were skidded around. I notice that I have approached as one of the first vehicles to the scene of a bad deer accident. I turn around mid-road and go back down the hill to the tiny restaurant that was at the base of the incline. As I pull up, excited to go inside to get a hot tea or something while I wait to see if the traffic clears, a waitress runs to the front door quickly and looks at me as I turn the car off. She turns the open sign around and stares at me while she does it so I know that I am not welcome. Clock says quarter of 7. *Sigh…* She wanted to close early and didn't want anyone getting in her way of leaving at 7. I wrap myself up in a blanket, lean back and watch the cars go up the road, but none come back down, indicating that the road was still closed.

I decide after a short while that I am so tired; I probably can't drive the whole way there anyhow and I get mad at myself for declining the invitation to the cabin. I drive down the side road and find a relatively safe looking place near a light and I crawl into the back. I wake up around 10pm and decide to work my way over the mountain anyhow. Maybe something good will happen.

Something good always happens.

   Right?

Chapter Eight

"If life were to be a lake and you, a stone, you never really know how far the ripples can go from every single action."

Callie chimes in again asking more questions about homo life. "How long were you a lesbian? Like, how did you know?" Obviously, she's been thinking of this while I was speaking about other topics. She plays around with a pen while looking at the ground, a total indication of her being anxious. This charms me. I tell her about how I was a lesbian my whole life; I just didn't know I was until I was in high school. "I always knew I would never have sex with a man though. I just didn't know I had another option." She laughs and asks me about my last relationship with Alana and how that whole thing happened. I consider this to be a great introduction for the next day of my trip, a day that began in a great deal of fear based upon lack of health.

....

I awoke, freezing, multiple times that night and adjusted the blankets around me. I tucked myself in tightly and squeezed in as snug as I could possibly get. I could feel the air stinging spots of my body that weren't properly covered. A frozen, icy air drift would begin on my right thigh and I would try to ignore it, but that patch would begin to grow until my whole leg started feeling frozen. The air was damp from all the frozen rain. It was clammy and cold and it made me grow a slight anxiety of sickness threats. This fear had risen since I had a history of unhealthy spells nearly my whole entire life. I would often get sick for weeks at a time. I fall back asleep to thoughts of the first time I met Alana.

Too often in my past, I would lay in bed, barely able to move with a variety of things such as colds, fevers, achy joints, sinus infections and the recent thing I had been battling over the last two years was frequent strep throat. Last fall I went into the bathroom with a flashlight to investigate my mouth- a flood of white dots on the back of my raw throat indicating the fourth time I had strep throat that year. I broke out crying and collapsed onto the floor. I don't really remember how, but I did manage to get better. It took another week and a whole lot more salt water. This occurred during the first week that I met Alana. I met her just a few days before this last strep throat encounter. She really wanted to get together with me and hang out, but she worked night shift. I had school and worked during day hours so our schedules didn't align. She wanted to come visit me anyhow even though I was so sick. Lying in bed, I heard her enter the back door through the kitchen.

"Hey Alana, come on in. I am in the bedroom." She sits on the bed next to my limp body. She shows a slushy and reveals a giant smile as she shakes a bag of chocolate explaining that they fix everything. Her eyes shimmer as she tells me about her day. I can tell by the way she is looking at me that she is very concerned by how thin and sickly I really do look. If I even looked half as nice as I felt, I still could have passed as a corpse. And I was very embarrassed to have this new, beautiful lesbian come over and see me like this, but I was in no position to deny a positive flow of energy into my home.

I awake again, in my car, realizing that I am now too cold to be concerned with the sad memories flooding my head. I decide to climb into the driver's seat and turn on the engine. My hands shake as I select the wipers to turn on. I am disheartened when they turn on and scrape loudly over the tiny ice acne that has developed on the windshield. I grumble while I open the door to the frigid rain and I scrape off a good portion of the driver's side glass without ever having put on gloves. I slide into the driver's seat like a lumberjack and put the car into gear as I watch chunks slowly reveal a shimmering world of cold darkness, my home of the Walmart parking lot. If I wasn't so cold and damp I probably could have appreciated it, but the memories of sickness made me weak and the fear of illness made me fear my future in this cold, dark parking lot bedroom.

Survival instinct kicks in. I must find warmth. A car is just a large tent when it isn't turned on and the air outside is freezing. Now as I shake with both exhaustion and cold, I watch as the temperature gauge indicates cold air will come out if I turn on the heat. It is just too cold to sleep. *What have I gotten myself into?* I decide to drive to the next town and find something open to research and write in while I wait for the sun to come up. These West Virginia mountains will kill me if I try to crawl back into those frozen blankets. Heat has been my whole mission all along, the race to the border of Florida, but then somehow, I decided to take my time and enjoy my drive. Which I am doing, of course, but I want some heat. As I continue onward driving toward lights and what I can only assume to be a busy part of town, I pray that I will see that powerful yellow. I have never before felt like this, but without a smartphone there is only inner intuition and hope to rely upon. Come on world; please show me a *Yell-Glow! I laugh because this is the first time I have ever thought that.

And as I make a turn to the right toward town, I see those golden spirals of survival up on the next corner. I pull into the parking lot as I start to see the faint haze of light green/blue start from the eastern sky. I grab my maps, books, computer and tablet and I enter this establishment. My phone is down to one bar from having the life sucked out of it in the mountains so I am thrilled to charge that little guy up! I place all my stuff down on a booth with an outlet below it, ignoring the judging eyes around me. I proudly walk to the line and order myself a coffee. I see the steam rise off the top of the moist rim of that cup and I cringe at how cold I currently am. The haze rises and dances in the air fading out into a background of ice cream machines and milk coolers. My attention then moves to the girl's voice which is growing louder.

"Umm, hello? Do. You. Want. Any. Creamers. OR sugars?" I blink at her, for some reason confused by the words she is saying. A woman of color with a southern drawl. That isn't the reason I can't hear her. It's because I am mentally and physically exhausted.

"Oh, uh, yeah." She scowls at me. I wonder how it is that some people lack any sort of patience. I feel guilty breaking into her phone texting time.

"How many?"

I am dazed… "I don't know. I guess umm… two? Or maybe one?" I receive my cup of coffee, much darker than I desire. I ask for another two creams and then retreat to my safe cubby hole to plug in my electronic devices and figure out my next route of action. I then realize that my phone isn't charging. A strong panic surges throughout my whole system. How am I supposed to travel this country without my phone? Am I supposed to turn around and go back? Are these signs that I should retreat? Maybe Alana is waiting for me to come back into her arms! *Yes! This must be what that means*! All these thoughts flood my head like insanity flooding the mind of a murderer. *That is what I am! I am a relationship murderer! How could I give up on her so easily?* I settle myself down as I jiggle the cord and take out the battery and replace it several times, but to no different result. It is not helpful at all in fixing my phone, which is already on very short battery life. My mom is going to flip! What do I tell her about my sleeping arrangement last night? I certainly can't tell her that I got stuck in a mountain and could have frozen to death in my car. *I realize how dumb this sounds, but I just can't let them know I slept in the car.* At this point, I am convinced that dirty losers do that and I don't think I am that yet. *How will I even tell her what I am up to now? If this phone doesn't work she'll make me buy another and right now I must live to the absolute least. I just spent a thousand of my precious saved travel dollars to move to Erie. I need to save as much as I can and...* (Over the course of this trip, I would discover how limiting my own thoughts like this actually were. The phrase 'you are only as limited as you allow yourself to be' really does ring true.)

The mind has a way of continuously fooling itself into thinking that it is unable to do a lot of things, but I think back to my abundance mindset readings and about the lessons that I have been studying. The mind is only as weak as you allow it to be. Desire and believe; acquire and achieve! So, I relax and decide that maybe the phone needs a break. Maybe that is the problem. I'll just update my Facebook so my mom knows that I am ok and won't rush to call the cops. So, I allow my phone to sit there as I take out my computer and plug it into the outlet. I notice that the battery life on my laptop is also not responsive. My panic sets in. *How am I supposed to travel this country documenting my adventures, filming a web series and keeping in touch with loved ones without a phone or a computer!?!?* That's when I realize that maybe the problem isn't my crappy equipment. Maybe the problem is the outlet. I move my stuff to another outlet and that doesn't seem to work either. *Oh, god! It is my stuff!* All my stuff is broken I determine as I try yet another outlet! I reflect on the tablet situation that occurred the other day and think about the simple solution that I could find. It wasn't broken; it just lost its charge.

Calm yourself Katie; it is all part of the journey. Everything will work out if you have faith. You know that. Relax the mind and just imagine everything turning back on. Yes, of course I know that, but my brain becomes a highway of uncomfortable thoughts and ideas at the flick of a switch. This is all part of that mind control thing. Control the impulse response to the emotions that arise and understand why you feel like you do. Then let the emotion settle and see the situation from a different angle. It's sort of like encountering a rock wall or dangerous ravine full of thorns and panicking, feeling that it is impassable without injury, but then climbing up a hill to an overlook and realizing that there is a path around it. *Perspective.*

"Hey, just so you know, none of our outlets work out there." I hear a voice exclaim. "The manager was tired of how high the electric bill was from people using their electronic devices like free loaders."

"Janice!" a voice yelled. The girl turned, nearly knocking a stack of napkins and condiments to the floor, looked at her and waved her arms to the side frustrated. "You aren't supposed to tell the customers that! Tell them that there was a power surge and none of the restaurant outlets are working. Can you handle that?"

"Uh... yeah. I guess." Sassy Janice replies. I doubt she will have a job for long.

"Wait, so none of your outlets work?" I ask genuinely concerned with the politest, sad voice I could muster. *Since I had just bought a large coffee* and was expecting to sit for at least two hours until the sun started showing some light. I was going to enjoy it peacefully and charge up my stuff. I was even thinking of purchasing an egg sandwich half way through as collateral for using their electric. I see this girl's head perk up as she listens in on the conversation from across the room in a different booth.

"Well there is this one here." Janice points to her left at an outlet in a strange location. "You could put the cord over top of this wall to this booth." I walk back to gather up my things to move to my new nest. My papers get pushed back together. My computer closes and the cords get placed into my bag. I put my phone and camera where they need to be, in the front pouch and proceed to turn around and move to that booth. That's when I realized that the other girl raced me there and she already had her computer proudly plugged in the wall where she sat there using Facebook. She was a friend of one of the employees and I had gathered that she had dropped someone off at work and had a while until she had to leave for her job. My icy body shook in cold, unsympathetic anger now.

THAT BITCH!!!

No, Katie. Calm thyself... I breathe in deep and then realize how exhausted I am and how much I just did not want to deal with this situation right now. *Homeless territory activate...*

NO, THAT ABSOLUTE HORRIBLE BITCH! How dare she watch me struggle moving from station to station for the last 10 minutes, trying to determine the problem, then race to take the spot that I had been told about! She, Dragonbitch, in just one swift move has become my mortal enemy. Now I attack. *Sort of...*

"Hey," I say in a meek, pitiful voice. I have shrunken from an angry rat into a small, annoying mouse, not really disturbing anything, yet unwanted by all around me. "Could I at least plug my phone into the other outlet, please?" She tells me she doesn't mind without ever making eye contact with me. This pathetic, exhausted, frozen mouse could sense the guilt and shame of a rotten, raging Dragonbitch. It is time for me to strike subtly, but deadly.

"Thank you. I just need a little bit of battery in my phone." I do speak sincere in my thanks because at least she is letting me plug it in. I mean, she does have rights to the usage of the outlet since she's in the booth. This is the first of many homeless battles that I will face. When you are a beggar, you really cannot be a chooser and on the road, you sometimes will battle homeless people or other poor people for things that should normally be so simple. Crazy situations arise that are seemingly pointless, but in the moment, it is serious and feels life threatening, just like the loss of this electrical outlet. I reassess and tend to back down, take a deep breath, and give thanks for the things I have because nothing is really that important to get upset about in this world. *After all, you normally don't die.*

The peace of mind is the only real thing of value and if I allow others to scramble my emotions due to objects, well, then they have already taken the essence of my spirit. If they have disrupted my peace of mind and if nothing else is as valuable as peace of mind, then I have already lost the battle. So, I breathe deep, remind myself of the great value I feel of finally being warm, finally being in a safe place with food and a bathroom and I am at least able to charge my phone. I genuinely smile at her downturned face as I tell her "thanks". I plug my phone into the outlet and see the familiar glow of charging battery signs. *It felt like heaven to see that little guy light up!* "Yeah, it won't be in your way for long. I just slept in my car and was unable to charge it anywhere. And since I was stuck in the mountains last night, I forgot to turn it off so it drained the battery completely. Hey thanks, though, I will move out of you way as soon as it charges."

I retreat, knowing that I made a deathly stab into the heart of the greedy dragon. I saw her mouth fly open and look up at me out of the corner of my eyes as I turned back to my coffee. She was ashamed. I could see it in her facial reaction. I had succeeded in my silent, gentle attack. Patience and relaxation can drive an enemy insane if properly executed. It also can prove to be a beautiful practice in self-control. *Who knows? Maybe one day something will happen and the thought of me in this situation will influence her decision to help someone, rather than go for her own greedy desire. If life were to be a lake and you, a stone, you never really know how far the ripples can go in every single action.* This is a philosophy that I began to hold very close to my heart for the rest of my life. I think the better word to use for this would be proper patience can be an enemy's worst attack. It is unexpected, silent and gut wrenching to the consciously deviant. Nothing makes a rude person feel worse regret than to actively see the suffering of those they have engaged action against. I win this round. I pulled out the tablet, which isn't what I wanted to do, but I began logging into SofaCruisin.com to see where I should go next. *Hopefully I'll have better luck tonight.*

The sip of coffee makes my whole body warm up. Well, everything gets warm except my feet. The shoes were like frozen patties strapped to my feet when I got out of the car. Those still were not warm in the least bit. Yesterday my dad had told me about several places along the way that I should know about. One that he said I need to see was New River Gorge in West Virginia. "Yeah and your uncle Eli was out there and told me it's one of the biggest bridges in the world! It used to connect the two sides of the river to these two villages on either side of the gorge. There used to be only one bridge that would connect them and it was a tiny one all the way at the bottom so people had to zigzag back and forth, up and down the gorge to get across the river to the other side of the town."

"Oh, so they just built an absurdly large bridge?" I inquired. My dad confirmed and said that I need to see it because my uncle Eli, who is a pilot accustomed to very high altitude, drove over this bridge and said. "Wow... this thing is reeeeaaaally high." My dad is a history nut, fascinated by how things are created. So, a bridge that his pilot-brother claimed was high is extraordinary. My dad would often say interesting, relevant facts. Other times they were just kind of pointless stories to show off his intellect. I used to think it was strange how he seemed to know everything about everything when we took family vacations until I realized that he did research for months before we ever went on a vacation somewhere. A spark of gratitude formed in that moment for my father and his passion to learn. *Huh, I didn't think the open road would teach me to appreciate my family more...* He then puts me on the phone with my mom, who has nothing nice to say about what I am doing. She sounds frantic and frazzled. I can't listen to her now. *(Her fearful panic for my well-being would eventually turn into appreciation in years to come. Many years later...)* I won't tell her where I slept... Bye.

I scan my maps and see the various routes and decide that it makes sense to go to New River Gorge. I flipped through the magazines that I had picked up from the state entrance visitor's center. They are helpful in providing whatever you need to know about the area. That guy loaded me up with a stack of literature about the state of West Virginia. I scan the pictures and compare all the different maps together to try to assemble some rough outline of what I can expect to be doing or seeing today. I see so many options. Bridge walk advertising says: 851 feet above the ordinary. Experience stunning views from the 24-in. wide catwalk under the New River Gorge bridge- one of the top ten bridges in the world! It is a catwalk that follows below the bridge. I consider the possibility of doing it, but I have just begun my journey and I am uncertain as to if I will have enough money to get back up in the future. *After all, I am driving thousands of miles. I can't just throw money at everything that I desire. I need to travel with as little spending as possible.*

Limiting belief thoughts ring through my head...

It is true that I must practice self-control if this trip is to go smoothly and organized. I will do some hiking around the bridge trails, but I will probably not do this high-rise walk. I continue flipping through pages and see something else that intrigues me greatly. *Orb the Gorge-* it shows a picture of a giant clear ball with people inside of it flying down the side of a large hill. The caption is: Get Ready to Roll! Apparently, you climb into a 12-ft. inflatable orb ball made from transparent plastic and you then spill down the side of a steep hill into a tree. At least that is what I imagine could happen. It doesn't show the ending, but this picture shows a guided space for the ball to roll, but no nets or anything to confirm safety. So, you would fly along through this thick forest at whatever speed you reach and could possibly fall off track into the woods and smash into stuff and die.

"What the hell, Katie. Where did you grow this fear from?" I tell my internal fears to release and calm down. *I am so high anxiety right now!* I just need to get my gears in line and get my head in focus. F.E.A.R is best understood as Fake Experience Altering Realty. I can choose to be fearless. It does not have to be a part of my existence. I remind myself that the first thing is to catch myself when I slip into my false fears. If I can control my fear, I can control my life. I flip the pages and see many images of zip lining. That doesn't excite me much. It brings back memories of a South Park episode and I let a smile leak out. Then I spot a picture of a war reenactment. There was so much in this booklet - Lumberjack jamboree, jet skiing, beaches on the lakes, log cabins, horseback riding, campgrounds, fishing, golfing, mountain biking, hunting and the list went on and on. Unfortunately, this stuff all required what I assumed would be a lot of funding on my part. I just wasn't prepared to be spending any money on anything at this point. I didn't know what the road had in store for me. And besides, my special interest was in hiking anyhow. That is a very exciting and free form of adventure that I have grown to absolutely adore.

This day would be one chaotic blend of life unlike anything I ever would have expected. This day would, in fact, be forever more be known as the day of the hippie-hillbillies.

Chapter Nine

Day 4 – New River Gorge, West Virginia

"Only when you have the awareness and understanding of how these universal regulations reveal our life's purpose, will you find the true power behind mindful, consciously creative existence."

The sun had begun to come up and I could tell because I was starting to get my bizarre morning writing flow. My mental creativity flourishes at sunrise. It had stopped raining besides a light drizzle. I was finished with my coffee and filled with an extreme sense of determination. In two hours, I would be at New River Gorge. *I absolutely cannot wait*! I unplug my fully charged phone. A collection of old men have taken over the Yell-Gold restaurant area. I thought it was odd that these elders congregated here rather than going to a local family owned restaurant, but figured that maybe there weren't any around, but this shows how much I know about American culture. I make eye contact with one of them. He says a friendly hello while mentioning my stuff and we get into conversation about how I am not in school, I'm actually traveling.

"Well, where are you headed next?"

"Down to New River Gorge. I cannot wait to get there. Have you ever been there?"

"Honey, I am from those parts. Born n' raised. Ya' heard 'a Beckley? 'Bout a half hour south of Fayetteville. My hometown."

"Oh, yeah. OK. That is where the bridge is, right?"

"Yes, it is. I can tell you one thing, right George."

George turns around and shakes his head, "Yep, those cops out there are nasty as can be! Do not go a mile over that speed limit or they will get you. They are all over that area."

"Yeah, the moment you hop on 19 make sure you always drive the speed limit. They have it set as a tourist trap. They drop the speed limit down 10 miles an hour around some of the curves and they wait and prey on those unsuspecting tourists to glide right into their trap." After that incredibly helpful information, I go to the bathroom to wash my face and brush my teeth. Then I hop back on the road. The goal is to get to I-79 south and then right after Sutton, I will need to take the exit for 19 south toward Summersville and Fayetteville. I zoom the electronic map out and see where the dot is on my tablet indicating where I am. *I can't believe that I am really doing this! I feel so free, like the champion of champions right now!* I am feeling so incredible, which is rather amazing after the type of night that I had. *I feel like I can take on the world!* And that is exactly what I am doing, the world being expansive USA random roads in this case. As I drive, the valley is beginning to awaken with the sun and the trees begin to glimmer with morning cheer. A faint mist waves to my soul, feeling at peace with the world as I drive onward toward my semi-destination. I feel a great sense of longing for Alana as I continue on my way, but I know I cannot give in. *I am fulfilling my greatest dream!* This is amazing! Most people never get to live their biggest dream and here I am! I really am and I just need to be patient with myself. I snap a couple pictures of me driving the car to get the entirety of the mountains, my car, my gear and my genuine smile. *(Picture in Author Bio)*

I cannot believe that the sleeping bag provided such little warmth... Maybe if I reorganize it a little better and have the blankets more prepared and evened out then I wouldn't have such a difficult problem with it and I wouldn't wake up to frozen limbs. I recap the stress of the night and decide that I will find a place to sleep tonight. I don't know where I will end up or who I will end up with, but I know that I will end up finding a house to sleep in for sure. Somehow, someway I will. *This type of forceful thinking provides a very high level of stress that I wouldn't become aware of until years later.* I figure that I would run into the bridge somewhere on this route, but I enter a town and still can't find it. I scratch my head, frustrated and rather anxious to just get there since the sun has been shining so bright. I need to get some sunshine on my skin. I just absolutely need to feel the warmth of nature to warm my bones and my heart.

I stop at a gas station to use the restroom in Summersville, WV. I sit in my car for a moment and decide to buy a cheap veggie sub and put every condiment on it, so sloppy and wonderful, habanero sauce pouring down my hands. I receive info from a local group of kids that tell me to keep on driving and I will see signs for it. The feeling of pure freedom found may be the realest thing I have ever felt, but I am terrified of people around here finding out I am a lesbian. *That pickup truck man did subtly attack me yesterday...* I have short hair and they are starting to get southern accents. They might 'have their way with me' or 'show me how a real man does it." so as I encounter many people, I am very scared that they might kidnap and rape me. At this point, I can't stand country music because I relate it to a situation in 2010. We

41

were on our way to the Washington D.C. gay rights rally with two cars packed full of dancing homos. Rednecks in a massive truck bearing the confederate flag abruptly tried to run us off the road, while flipping us off. They sped up and slammed on their brakes, trying to make us crash into their truck, screaming at us while blaring country music. It was horrifying to watch our friend's car fly onto the shoulder of the road to avoid hitting them as the brave, confident Redneck-Rebels drove by us honking and swearing. That was my first ever official encounter with country music, a southern drawl and unexpected irrational hate. It's funny because the rednecks probably forgot all about it, but their simple action planted a seed of fear inside of me for over four years. Eventually I would fall in love with everything country, but from that day, country music triggered a sense of dread in me. So, to every person I meet 'round these parts, I am silent of my true self.

I arrive at the New River Gorge welcome center and talk to a man at the help desk. I check out a few of the papers and maps laying out on the desk as I continue to ask questions about the area. My enthusiasm must have been realized by all of the employees working there at the time because they flocked to me and all began expressing their passionate opinions about all of the hiking, sightseeing and history regions around the area.

"Oh and this spot is great for white water rafting. Or kayaking." The other argued "No. No, that isn't the best spot. Most people go here." Another chimed in, "What? That is most certainly not a good spot for her to go. That is too dangerous." And they debated and talked over each other, each trying to help me, but just making me more muddled. I tell them I am more interested in the hiking and views than anything else.

"Well you should do this trail that takes you to long point. It's a fabulous hike up the mountain to a great view of the valley and the bridge and..." They have a pile of information stacked in front of me, all of them battling to provide me with all the information they know about the area. I was now bombarded with too much. I decided to ignore it all and just follow the signs to the overlook. I walk to the left side of the parking lot and head down toward the woods which are not that thick. I cannot see the bridge through the woods at all, but I can see what appears to be a wide clearing where I assume is the gorge. The sun is shining and I push my sleeves up on my jacket. *It feels so good! Finally, some warmth!* I feel some of the tension of thoughts of Alana fade from my mind. *I am living my dream right now!* The surge of life pours into my bloodstream and I am so triumphant right now, here, in West Virginia alone!

Nothing could feel better than this! I think while marching down the path toward what I'm sure will be a wonderful day of exploration. Little did I realize how much I really was about to encounter. This day was the real beginning of the education process dealing with the cultural differences within this country. This was the day of the real start of my inner travels and growth.

I end up trotting along behind a large Asian family. The trees have very little on them besides a few buds here and there and the ground is nearly bare. Everything is slightly damp around the ground leaving the boards of the walk a bit slick at places. Wet leaves are the comical bananas of natural settings. This large Asian family must have consisted of at least four generations. There were a couple small children being pulled by their annoyed moms. There were a couple of older kids, then teenage kids sort of hopping along ahead of the rest of the group. The fathers were walking together and laughing alongside an elderly couple who helped each other hand-in-hand or hand-on-shoulder the whole way. I analyze the steps as I try to slide by. Between people ascending the stairs on the left side and the Asians all taking their time down the right side, I decide not to rush. I have no reason to. This is a good time to remember how to be in the present. I am the least in a rush out of anyone here today. It is time to relax, walk slow, and enjoy life. I also considered this to be a great opportunity to learn a bit of sociology from another culture. Since they all spoke their native language of non-American (as I've heard it described as in the past by culturally unsophisticated folks) I decide that I will just take my time and study something new. I want to rise above the small-minded world that I grew up in. The Dutch lands of Pennsylvania are not the most open minded lands one will encounter in life. I had assumed that the Deep South and Tennessee are much worse breeding grounds for close minded people, but I am determined to have my eyes widened. I know there is a world out there just waiting to be explored. There is so much so see and experience and I just long to do it all. There is a special calling to be here today and I know something great will be uncovered about these lands in relation to my life. For the time being, I will just gently stroll down these stairs and study Asians.

The one child must have been no older than two or three and was throwing a fit. He did not want to walk down those stairs at all and the mom was pulling him along and talking to the other mothers like nothing was going on. She was struggling and kind of just ignoring her annoying child situation while the mothers were holding a conversation that sounded stressful and high strung. I listen to the conversation patterns of the men who speak quickly and laugh together joyously. They all seem to be having a much better time than the women, which doesn't surprise me, but bothers me. Am I witnessing one of those cultural differences between American feminism versus other parts of the world? These men aren't up there caring about the children's behaviors. That is the mother's job. The men are just there to enjoy and laugh. I watch the body language of the genders as well. The women are tense, yet elegant moving and the men are fun and happy, yet firm and stiff moving. The ruggedness of the personality is the contrast to the actual happiness perceived factor of the individual. I wonder if it is like that for everyone in the country that they are from.

I realize one of the men is continuously watching me every few steps. That's when he whispers something to another man who turns around to look at me and quickly turns around again. *What are they saying about me? What on earth could they have said? Have they mistaken me for a boy again?* That hasn't happened in a while now. I have been told many times that I look like an anime character. Perhaps that is what they are talking about. They turn around again and I realize almost instantly that the problem is that I am way too close. I have almost blended into their group from studying too intensely and I have made them grow into a threatened stance. The man in the burgundy sweater is the king of the pride and he has determined me to be a predator. The woman protects the young. The men protect the herd.

I wave and say hello.

"Oh, hey-low. Eet ees beautiful at rivah!"

"Ah, yes." He nods and smiles in acceptance, "Yes, I am very excited to see the bridge!"

His smile is followed by a series of upraised eyebrows that confirm that he doesn't know what I said. "Yayes. Verrree nice!" He smiles and keeps on walking. I had a slight hope that he would offer to let me pass now since I had become rather embarrassed and I was sure that my cheeks had grown pink. But no, they just continue on their happy little Asian merry way. I slow my pace as to avoid any further odd situations. I focus now only on the nature around me. I can feel every beam of sun seep into my longing skin. It charges me to my root to just feel some warmth. Erie, PA was so dreadfully cold, both physically and emotionally and I just cannot wait to arrive in some t-shirt weather. At least that will thaw my frozen bodies. *Oh, even better would be to be at the beach swimming and sweating.* A flash of thrill bursts through my body and I almost skip with joy.

Finally, I arrive at the bottom of the platform and can see the full on view of the bridge. It is astoundingly large, so massive in fact that it is almost unreal. There are about 12 other people around the platform besides the group I had followed behind. I grab a seat on the bench and reach my arms out wide to fully breathe in the scenery. It is incredible! Several minutes pass and I offered to take a picture of the Asian group all together. I snap several pictures, but I am sure at least one person was looking away in every single one. *Well, maybe they can edit them together.*

Typically, when someone takes a picture of me and my group it is rather courteous to offer to take a picture of them. But they didn't offer. They just marched on out of there. I laughed at the silliness of this situation and decided there was no sense getting upset at something like that. This was right before selfies were a big thing so I decided to just wait for someone else to come down here to help me.

"Essxcuse?" I hear a voice from behind me and I turn around. "You wan me take?

"Oh, yes. Thank you. That would be great!" He must have heard my disappointed thoughts and turned around! I hand him my camera after making sure it is on. He snaps one then climbs up on top of a bench and snaps another, shooting me a thumbs up at the second shot.

"Hey thanks so much. I really appreciate it!" He waves and meets up with the rest of his group. *Keeping a positive mind is one of the most important parts of life's journey.* I am on a mission to weed out all of my negative influences that disrupt living harmoniously. There is so much I desire and to remain in a constant state of positivity has become not only one of my goals, but one of my passions as well. A positive mindset continuously seems to bring about good results. The moment I change my mind from a negative thought to a positive one, it always does seem to produce a greater outcome which is exactly what all these self-empowerment books I have been reading tell me. Trust the power of the mind. I am so greatly excited to learn more and to experience more of this power.

There seems to be an everlasting mist in the air surrounding the whole area. It almost has a defining silence, a permanent capability to cease anxiety. Even the humming of passing cars over top of it doesn't distract from the beauty of the river below. The flow of the New River is very peculiar because it flows south to north and is one of the only rivers in the world that does that, another being the Nile. I stare at the river below and hold the handrail for quite some time taking in the bit of sunlight and the sounds. I breathe deep and allow my chest to expand. Tightness reveals itself from within and I tighten up my lower stomach muscles and begin to do several repetitions of deep belly breathing.

Deep belly breathing is a type of breath that allows for a maximized air intake, therefore allowing the blood to circulate better through the lungs and body resulting in the elimination of toxins creating a very relaxed emotion.

Babies are born breathing this way and somehow we change this flow of air intake. Usually we breathe in and squeeze our stomach in at the same time. Then we breathe out and push our stomachs out, but that is inefficient breathing. We should be breathing in and expanding our upper stomach to allow for the lungs to expand. Then we should be breathing out and pushing the stomach in to use the muscles to press the air out of the lungs. It not only tightens up the mid-section, but it will also produce that greatly anticipated calming effect, which is exactly the feeling I desired now finally having made it to my destination for the day. I smile and feel the sensation of power around me. This place is super charged with positivity.

I look down again and see a tiny piece of a car at the bottom of the gorge. Its view is covered mostly by trees, rocks and foliage, but I see them and they don't look like park rangers. *Hot dog! I found where I want to be!* After my momentary meditation, I climb back up the hundred plus steps to the top again. I realized how tired and sore my muscles had become from the hike up Seneca Rocks yesterday. I guess the endless snow in Erie produced some fatty Katie muscles that I wasn't accustomed to. Nevertheless, I was in for the adventure!

I got back to my car and sat there for about a half hour studying the maps. The angle I had parked at provided me shelter from the impatient wind, yet was the perfect angle of sunlight so I was able to sit without a jacket or hat on for the first time in days. It felt so marvelous! I studied these maps and read about the different areas until I saw the trail that I was searching for. I had to go to Fayette Station Road and follow the path to wherever I ended up because I pushed the keys in the ignition so fast and sped out of there with a trail of enthusiasm following my car's exhaust. I found an odd residential area and turned around to take the other way which went around a very sharp bend. The cliff on the right side of my car was about 15 ft. high of just chiseled out rocks that could fall on any badly placed car at any moment. I ignored it. I was so excited to film something for my YouTube series, *The Everything Show* too. This was the perfect place to do it!

I follow the twisted road a few more yards and encounter another car going the other direction. If I am not mistaken, I could have sworn I saw a one-way sign. I could be wrong though and I swing my car all the way to the edge, the furthest I can squeeze without scraping up the side of my car on this mountain and then having it collapse on top of me because I caused enough force to create a landslide and then…*Man, oh, man. Where are these thoughts coming from? Calm the mind, Katie. Relax…*The car inched by, revealing a smiling man and woman that looked to be foreign. He has a large mustache and waves thank you as he passed. *Maybe they didn't know what 'One Way' meant. Positive thoughts, Katie…* I continue my mission down the hill to the base of one of the giant struts of the bridge. I park my car and snap a few shots of the astonishing massive structure before me. It's brilliantly large; so full of history and power. The bridge was constructed in 1978 and was so massive, in fact, that from the base of the river you could stack up two Statue of Liberties and a Washington Monument on top of each other and there would still be another 20 feet until you hit the bottom of the highest part of the arch. It is the third largest single arch bridge in the world! I walked around for a bit observing different angles and sat down on a large boulder intended to prevent cars from driving off the edge of the gorge. I position my camera on the tiny tripod that Alana had gotten me for Christmas. The stupid little thing broke right away. *Oh well...* I duck taped the bottom of it to hold the fragile little piece of plastic together. *Doesn't matter.* My selection of unprofessional equipment is so pathetic and my travel preparations are so sad. If I actually had extra time, I probably wouldn't have any better equipment. In all reality, I had years to get prepared and I never actually did prepare myself. So, it's my own lackluster fault that my equipment sucks. I am continually in a constant state of tardiness or procrastination. That is one of the things that Leopold Mountain speaks of in his book. He suggests that "Procrastination is a nasty habit of letting things go until tomorrow, which should have already been tended to yesterday."

I set up and record several versions of *The Everything Show.* "Hello, this is Katie Trainer and welcome to The Everything Show! I am sitting here today on day four of my road trip at New River Gorge Bridge in West Virginia..." And I filmed take after take of that and was not satisfied, but I figured oh well. I am not looking my best today nor am I really in the mood to look good so oh well. *I don't care. I have an Everything Show video and that's all I really needed.* I went over and examined the bridge from the bottom. It didn't even look real. It really did look like a giant alien structure up over head, like an absolutely massive spacecraft descending these long 15 ft. wide cement and metal spurs protruding from the ground to stabilize it. It is just a huge structure.

I drive down below to the base of the bridge and carefully take my car into this bumpy parking lot at the edge of the river. I get out and climb onto the big rocks along the water's edge, feeling the coolness of the current's flow. I sit down on a large flat rock for 10 minutes and listen to the current crashing against the rocks scattered about. It blocks out every single sound besides my own breathing, which I have once again become aware of. *It is just so beautiful out here...* This moment right here is everything I needed to recharge myself to get ready to go on a hike. I am becoming re-centered and relaxed, ready to take on the extreme landscape of a West Virginia gorge trail.

It is surprisingly warm in the gorge. The resilient winds apparently remained up at the top, leaving the bottom full of sincere sun. I decide to cross the tiny bridge, the historic bridge that connected the bottom of the gorge before they built the massive one up top. This bridge is small with a chipped blue faded paint coating the metal pillars mounted over a thick wooden base. I walk across it and as each car passes, I can feel the rumble in my feet all the way up to my shoulders. The whole bridge shakes with each car, not that a lot of cars drive this, but it is frequented by history buffs often.

I climb up a 12-ft. mound on the left side where the road connects and discover that it is a train track running along the edge of the river. The metal looks shiny and worn so I consider it to be a track still in use today. This is a great thing because this means that there is an absolutely amazing train picture to be taken, rolling down this track along this river with that great bridge in the background. I envisioned what it would look like and took some fun shots of the tracks with nothing on them besides their plain natural beauty. I sat there for a bit and took out my notebook to jot down some happenings of the day so far. I then decide to write a poem.

Eventually I decide that I have waited long enough. *If there was going to be a train I would have willed it into existence since I have desired it so badly... That's how this whole 'manifest things' works, right?*

I get up and take one long look at the tracks. Nothing. Then I see a van pull up on the road right down from where I climbed up from previously. There is a 6 ft. pull off space right there that has many specific signs that say no parking, yet this giant van pulls up without hesitation. The back door flings open and I see smoke pour out of the van as a collection of hippies climb out of this vehicle. I continue to watch them walk around and giggle. They wear shredded pants and hats and smell like incense. I watch from 12 ft. above on my train track altar. They laugh and begin to walk across the bridge. One is on the phone and seems to be having an important conversation and the others are laughing and cracking open beers. Two of them have book bags and I bet that I know exactly what the contents are. Another one has a plastic bag that seems to be dripping. They start to head over toward my car... *Great, here we go. Great timing, Katie. Now you have to talk to these stoners and all you want to do is go on a spiritual hike to reconnect with your inner self. Just walk across the bridge and ignore them.* I quickly slide down the steep slope from the tracks to the road. This involves a very quick footed maneuver because it is almost completely vertical drop off for about four feet.

As I come bouncing down through the bushes and rocks, the last hippie comes out of the van and becomes startled by me and the falling rocks around me. His eyes widen as he tries to make sense out of what he sees.

48

Uh oh...

    here we go.

Chapter Ten

"In each moment may we find the golden treasures of being here, now."

It was an accent I have never heard before. It was a blend of hippie mixed with country. *I didn't even know those ever merged.* We both stared at the other like we were senseless. "Whoa, dude! Ha! What are you doing? Wait. Dude, who are you? Ha! Where did yew come fra'hm?" He looks at me bewildered and cracks up, slapping his hands across his knees as he bends forward in laughter. "What are you doing here? Haha!" He just keeps laughing. I explain and don't go too into detail for obvious reasons. I figure if I keep it simple, then it will be simple. This was a very important lesson for me to learn though.

Lesson. A young lesbian on a road trip alone should never assume that any man is uninterested in getting with her at any point at all along the journey- especially if she never even openly says she's a lesbian.

Solution- Be upfront with nice men in safe situations. They will not be upset if you are forward and true in your intentions. Plus, you can make lifetime friends rather than make drunk, broken hearts. Unfortunately, it took until after this day to really learn that.

"Oh, I was just up there waiting for a train." I explain.

"Dude, why are you here?" He emphasizes the 'Why' laughs and looks around me with wide eyes as if there were more behind me waiting to come out to surprise him.

"Well, I am a big fan of hiking and rock climbing." I respond

"What? No way! Here, girl. What's your name?" He holds out his hand and puts on a hefty smile. He reminds me of a guy I met years ago that I used to skateboard with named Matt. He looks like him, sort of sounds like him, the same height and style. I tell him my name and he invites me to join them, but something about hiking with a bunch of stoner country speaking hippies from West Virginia doesn't seem like such a good idea. They seem friendly enough, but at the same time I have my mental knives out. No offer sounds better than keeping my life at this point and four hippies just doesn't cut it. Of course, hesitation provides the loss of opportunity... But then again they could rape and kill me. There would be many internal battles between the worlds of irrational fear vs. justified intuition vs. rational awareness vs. not allowing fear to take over my life. It's a very delicate balance without direct physical answers.

I walk over to meet his buds and he tells me that his name is Matt. I laugh so excited and explain how he looks, acts and sounds just like my friend Matt! What are the chances? *Ok, life. This is a synchronicity moment. I will pay attention. I may as well meet and greet some real West Virginian's since they are going on a hike.* They finish a beer and crack another and have this really interesting smell. It is like very floral incense; it is definitely not the smell of marijuana. Maybe an undertone of it in there somewhere, but they all just really smell like incense. I meet them, ragged, friendly with faded smiles, but Matt just seems more into me than anyone else. I start talking to the one guy who offers me a beer and I decline due to the fact that I am in unknown lands right now. I am so apprehensive about everything that I am experiencing yet. I just slept in my car for the first time in my life and I only woke up when I did because I was so cold! I am so scared of so many things! The travel hasn't really become part of me yet. I am still a travel baby.

Matt reaches up and grabs a hold of the metal rim of the bridge's upright strut. He begins to climb it like a confident acrobatic professional. None of the other guys seems to care, but he keeps climbing and I begin freaking out considering the fact that they are drinking, probably smoking and maybe even are on other drugs. I don't know, but all I do know is if he slips, I will not be alright because he will not be alright. I hold my bag tightly as I watch him get to the cross section of the bridge. I look around, expecting to see cops pulling up or something, but no one is around. This is good; I would hate for him to be arrested for public drunkenness or public disturbance or something.

"Yeah, we are from Fayetteville." (They pronounce it fay-yayet-veel) "It's sabout fiyyeve meenuts up the ro-ad hey-yere." A red haired man tells me. He smells strongly of whiskey.

"So you come here often?" I ask. I am trying to make some sense out of the circus act before me. It is an incredible amount of danger and awakening, all in one swift action.

"Yep, we cerm out here all thee tie-yem." He takes a big swig of his beer and crushes it in one giant squeeze, dumps it upside down to let the couple drips fall and places it in a plastic bag. "Yep, we be nature boys out here. Hiking, cay-yamping, kay-yakin' you name it." So these guys are local. They come here a lot. They are climbing on an old historic bridge in a national park where there are hundreds of tourists every day and drinking

51

beer? *What have I stumbled upon? Are they really doing this?* Just then, Red-Hair slides a full entire whiskey bottle out of his sweatshirt front pocket and takes a big swig of it and slides it back in his pocket…

Yes, that is exactly what they are doing. I figure if they are that comfortable with it, it means that they do this often. So the chances of anyone seeing them or caring are very minor. Maybe they even know the cops out in these parts, I reckon! But it still seems so foolish. Matt is 25 ft. in the air, walking from one side of the bridge to the other. Then he climbed down, grabbed another beer and chugged it. I was beginning to feel as if I missed out on a lot of fun life in my existence so far. These guys seem to have a great deal of fun together. I consider maybe accepting their invite. I could really explore a new perspective of culture, just like the Asian observations, but I still am hesitant. The mission of this trip is to not just be a tourist though. Anyone can go somewhere and take a picture of themselves at something, but to really indulge in the nature of the lands and the culture of the people, that is traveling. That is what I desire and am destined to do this trip and maybe even for the rest of my life.

"We've got some friends coming to meet us soon. Once they get here we are taking off up the mountain to the spot to hike."

"Who are they?"

"Just some of our buddies. Dude, I think the one is bringing his girlfriend. They all seem pretty cool. I only met them once." I take this fresh information and I decide to wait. I could rush to my car and hike alone in a place that I don't know to a place that I don't know and explore alone just like I did yesterday… Or I could view this as a possibility of incredible enjoyment and experience. I choose to wait it out. I think of everything I would have missed out on if I had given into my fear with Madison. I will base my judgement not off of a crew of hippies, but off of a crew of hippies and the other girls they bring with them.

The others arrive and they crawl out of their Jeep and hang out on the bridge. I say my hellos. "Dude, sheeyas traveling from Hershey chocolate!"

"Well, why are you here? The girl asks.

"To hike and explore."

"Well, come on! Let's go!" She seems genuinely nice and not quite to the same filthy standard as the rest of them. I guess she is slightly younger than them too, which I also assume her boyfriend to be. They both had sweet faces and very trustworthy energies so I suck up my scared feelings and decide to go with the group. We leave one car at the base of the mountain and drive my car up. A bunch hop in the other jeep and some sit on the roof. We go over 20 mph around these wet twists and treacherous ravines as the two of them sit on top bouncing around. I am driving behind them filming as I drive; it is absurd! If they fall off they will probably die! I cannot believe my eyes as these drunken hillbillies fly up this bendy, damp mountain road! We get to the top, park the cars and my heart is racing. There are signs that say no smoking, no alcoholic beverages, no dogs, and no glass. We at least followed one of those rules.

They loaded up their bags and pockets with goodies and whatever they needed for the hike. We followed the trail up the side of the murky ravine. Everything was wet and thick with ferns, rocks and rotten leaves. I end up talking to them about their lives for a bit and I get really intrigued. Never had I met people who actually do real rock climbing. They started talking about some of the places they had been before. Two years ago, they were out in Colorado doing some free-hand climbing and mountain scaling. They found a wall face here and started to compete in their abilities to climb it.

"Hey, check this out. Hand jam."

I laugh and repeat hand jam and he looks at me funny. I think it is a funny description of something until I realized that it is a real thing. They take a long thin crack in the rocks and reach up as high as they can and jam their hand in it. Then they rotate their hand until it becomes crammed in it tightly and from there they will pull their bodies up with just one tug upward. I couldn't believe it! I had never seen real climbing before and they seemed shocked at how surprised I was. Apparently, that is a common thing to do down there. Their accents are a lot of fun to listen to, a real blend of hippie-country.

They also have this odd obsession with pushing large rocks down the side of the hill. They would work together to pry a boulder from the ground and then they would try to lift it up in the air. Once they lifted it they would try their hardest to throw it off the edge, but it often just fell right in front of them and then crashed down through the woods. There were several times when they picked one up and had the entire group watching and cheering as they threw it. Then they would all be silent as it cascaded down the mountain cracking into other rocks and bashing into trees.

"Yep, that one was awesome!" They'd high five and laugh.

I didn't understand it. But then again, I don't follow a lot of sports.

They stop at this beautiful overlook on a curve of the mountain and they pull out their pipes. Apparently, they have some pretty harsh stuff because the way that I am sure that they smoke shouldn't have resulted in so many coughs. But they all were choking and giggling, smiling and laughing. That's when they passed it to me. Now I am very hesitant with marijuana, especially since I don't know these people. I don't know if they are accustomed to laced weed. Actually, I don't smoke anyhow really anymore, but they offer again. Then they start arguing over whether they are being polite by offering or offensive by seemingly forcing me to smoke.

"I tell you what, man. I am sick of you fiy'en with me all the time!"

"I don't fight with you! I'm just offering the girl a good time! It'd be rude if we didn't offer!"

"Yeah, but she said she didn't want any so leave her alone."

"Excuse me, miss. Do you want any of this?" I smiled hesitantly and shrugged and shook my head no. Something about nature always makes me want to say yes to one marijuana hit. After all, I am a one hit wonder.

"She said no!"

"Her eyes said yes! Here take it." He handed it to me. Fortunately, they never handed me the lighter so I just held it for a minute, wondering if it was laced with any additional drugs as they attempted to swing on these giant vines hanging from the tree branches above. I watched as they swung about 15 ft. back and forth along the path. Other Girl then grabbed a hold of the vine and they were trying to take a picture of her swinging on it. As she jumped, the rock she leapt from broke its connection with the earth and there was a terrible crash to the ground. All the guys raced to her side and picked her up. They discovered she was ok and laughter erupted all around. The one guy took a picture at the exact moment the rock fell and bashed her shoulder. Her face appeared to be in incredible agony in the picture, like a warped circus clown, which was funny because she really was very pretty. They ask for the weed and I handed it over like a bandit getting away with a robbery. Then they asked for the lighter and I pointed at the guy who I thought had it. So, I effectively skipped my turn! Cheers!

"Hey, sweetheart. Wahn' swig?" Red hands the whiskey from his sweatshirt pouch to me and I look at it. He smiles big and generously, revealing a full view of his deteriorating mouth. I've got this thing about germs, ya know, since I have been very sick for so much of my life and he says about how since its alcohol it shouldn't be a problem. But I have been

54

watching their teeth rot as I speak to them and I am more than certain there are some moldy tooth particles floating around in this bottle in my hands. I look at it. Then I look at him. He's got a raging grin on his face and I wonder if they slipped any pills into this. I heard of people purposely slipping drugs into a bottle to make everyone feel it better for a cheaper price. I felt the pressure rising like a scene in a movie where the crowd slowly comes in to surround the main character chanting *"Do it! Do it! Do it!"*

"Here, Hun." Matt pulls out a cheap light beer and hands it to me unopened. He even hands me a napkin to wipe off the top. *Classy n' fancy.* "Chug this'un I'll git cha 'nuther."

So, I did just that. Like a big ol' baby too.

"Come on! You couldn't even chug that whole thing?" My eyes burned and my throat was numb. I never was too great at chugging anything, but I am very good at avoiding being potentially drugged. And so we marched on, each of us with our own specific buzz out here in the sunny valley. We talked the entire time. In fact, I learned that most of them didn't have licenses and most of them were between the ages of 27 and 35. I could believe it by the way that they looked, but then again I couldn't believe their ages due to the fact that they act like a deranged group of stoned high schoolers. But this is the life that they know. And this is exactly the education of other cultures I had been seeking. A couple of them have been to jail for something ranging from really stupid to alcohol and drug abuse. I watched them all interact with each other and they were having such a good time. I considered what the value of life really was. Here were these people, brought up in the drug infested lands of mountainous region of West Virginia and they seemed like they were happy people on a hike together. That's more community than the adults I know back where I am from that only sit around and drink while watching TV.

"So, do you have a boyfriend back home?" Matt asks me as he holds my hand. I pull it away, not only because I do not want to lead him on, but because he doesn't seem like the cleanest person either.

"Umm… I actually am single, but…"

"Oh, but you're seeing someone. Ok. I get it. Is he in Pennsylvania?" Matt begins to stumble a bit. He is obviously really drunk now because his words are taking a long time to come out. I grab his arm as he stumbles over this rock and trips to the ground, scraping his elbow. I was too late to stabilize him. We were all beginning to work up a sweat as we neared the top of the trail. Up to our left was an old home built with mountain rocks many years before. They claimed it was the bunks for the workers, but another said it was the house for the original property owner. This place is a timeworn mine area. Littered through these historical woods are old coal cars, tracks and equipment everywhere. A couple and some kids walk by us and I don't like the way the man is looking at the group.

"Hey, sure smells nice and herbal out in these woods, eh?" The man shouts out and makes direct eye contact with every single one of us as he passes. I am not stoned, but I know that if I were, this would have freaked me out. I wonder if old stoners who get married and have kids do that to young stoners just to freak them out for fun. It's like he was looking for the faded stares or bursting red whites of their eyes. Suddenly I become concerned that maybe he is an undercover cop. I become alert of my surroundings and take note of all the people around. There is a military man up in front of an old abandoned welded up mine with two other people. I feel a drizzle begin to fall on us and look up to see the ugliest black clouds peeking out from behind the trees.

"Did any of you guys check the forecast to…" I ask, interrupted by Matt again.

"So, Katie, what kind of guys do you like?" I cannot stand the look of drunken love toward me in a man's eye. *Ugh… it grosses me out.* I wish it would not ever happen. I want men to look at me with the respect they initially give other men, not disgusting, drunken lust. *Gross.* I try to be honest at this point, but I was still a little scared to tell the truth of my 'Lesbianism' out in the woods. The image of the gang of them slowly closing in around me saying, "Here girl, let me show you how a real man does it…" flashed in my mind. I only wanted to reveal my lesbian secrets when were closer to civilization.

I was so thankful Matt disrupted this conversation. "Whoa, it's raining! Guys, let's get down this mountain!" The view was flawless as we began our descent. We could see far down the valley until the mist faded the background. We arrived at the top and were standing before an 800 step staircase and started walking as fast as we could down the stairs, the biggest stairs I have ever seen. They told me Olympians come here to train and something about that fact made me gallop in pride. After a few flights, it became a sort of happy gallop that shook the core of my thighs. But we were all laughing and smiling. The rain continued to hold off, but as I glanced into the sky, I knew it wouldn't be long. Those types of black clouds were always sure to produce rain and possibly lightening, but considering I have a slight fear of storms, especially storms while being out in nature, I was not focusing on that fact. The wind began to pick up as we passed by these old, antique chunks of metal being eaten by the forest. We climb through an aged series of buildings collapsed in the middle, but still proudly standing after all these years. Giant pillars and gears remain from the days of prominent forest work. At the bottom of the trail, we had to walk through the woods through abandoned factory buildings and rusted machinery. I didn't mind it one bit.

We finally made it down to the railroad tracks and it was still drizzling. We hoped that we could make it back to the car before it full on rained, but that only lasted about as long it took one of us to say that sentence. The streams of ice water had begun to fall at an almost horizontal angle on our backs. We were all singing and talking and enjoying the comical rain. It was so cold and we had a half mile to walk yet, so we just decided that we might as well enjoy because no matter what, we were going to get wet.

And oh, did we ever enjoy that rain storm. It was absolutely incredible walking on those railroad tracks in that valley except for the fact that Matt grew drunker and bloodier as he continually tripped into the hard, ridged railroad bed. We finally made it, piling into the remaining cars as we drove back to the top to get our other cars.

"So, can I take you to dinner?" Matt asks me, "I promise it'll be great. You must drive though, but we could get pizza or something like that."

"Umm…" *I didn't know how to respond to this. I didn't expect that. I thought the entire group was going together to get something to eat considering how we were all talking about how hungry we were now.* "I don't know. Why don't we all just get something together?"

"No, let's just go out. I'll buy. We can go back then and watch YouTube videos! Ha! I love to look up fat people falling and FAIL. We can do that then at my parents' house." The only way he could be striking out worse was if he was hitting on a lesbian. *Oh wait…*

"Let's just do what everyone wants to do. I'd rather be with the group." He did not want to hear that. He got so mad that I actually got a little scared. I was given Marcus's address as backup, but they told me to follow them to his house. Matt's car was parked there. He drove earlier. I found out that he doesn't have a license.

Things were beginning to look a little different to me now. I feel as if my caterpillar body was being pursued by some predator. I could feel an evolution ready to take hold, but it felt like something was about to attack before I ever was able to evolve… I haven't found the safe space to transform and I don't know if I ever will…

We arrive at Markus's house. *Thank god.* Matt crawls out of my car and hops in his car right away. I run upstairs quick and tell them about what happened and they run down and talk him into relaxing. Then the one guy grabs his keys and comes upstairs with them. Relief goes through me. I didn't want the drunken fool to hurt himself. Four of the guys live together in an apartment building, but not sharing apartments. They are all neighbors who hang out. Over time as we hung on the deck and talked, I realized that they all knew each other from parties long ago and Markus moved into that place and the others slowly moved in. On the far right, there was a very fat, unpleasant woman who kept coming outside and staring at us. Then I realized that she was the one guy's girlfriend (we shall call him Macho Man) and that he was ignoring her calls. *Wow, that is rude....*

The guys break out more whiskey at Markus's house. He's the one with sketchy tattoos all over his body, the quiet one I didn't trust at the beginning upon first meeting them. But he surprised me here in his domain. He has a son that he is very interested in providing for. I was very surprised when his eyes lit up as he talked about his little blonde haired rascal. He even pulled out a pile of pictures from the wallet he had chained to his pants. Markus begins to cook some rice and beans for me since I was starving and didn't eat meat. He comments on my crystal necklace and I say about how I'm into rocks and minerals for the metaphysical aspects. His eyes light up again and he says, "Well, wait till you see this." Somehow Matt's car starts up and pulls away and everyone tried to catch him, but he drives off fast. The one drummer guy jumps in his car to make sure that he gets back home safely.

Markus pulls out two briefcases and opens them up to show me an incredible collection of minerals and fossils. It is the best private collection I have ever seen! He starts telling me stories of how he acquired them through his travels then he hands me a Blue Kyanite to keep, telling me that he feels that it resonates with me. I tell him that it is my favorite stone. He says, "Well, look at that! Ha! What are the chances?" These people didn't have much, but they didn't need much. They all seemed to have learned from their previous errors and had evolved into decent people. At least, for the most part.

Meanwhile, Macho Man is talking bad about his girlfriend harassing him. She comes over and knocks on the door and walks away and waits for him to follow. He opens the door looks at her waves his hands in the air and yells a very aggressive "WHAT!"

I hear a slam and he comes back in and just starts talking about her again. *Uh oh... I feel that former, feminist raccoon rising... I want to fly with strength, but I still don't know how... I put the suit on.*

"Ok, I know it isn't my place to say this, but you should really respect your woman. Obviously, she is trying to tell you something important." I build up the confidence to stick up for her after hearing a lot of his women-hating negativity. I swallow hard, completely afraid of what could happen next, but determined to bring down the patriarchy! *Yah!*

"No, but it isn't important." He yells at me, waving his hands in the air. I gulp hard and build up the courage to properly stand up for women everywhere, digging through the verbal trash to find something earnest.

"Well, it seems to be to her. You should respect her opinion since you are her boyfriend." I stand up for all woman, speaking my, this time, apparently appropriate, but totally outsider feminist views. I watch the face of every single one of the guys cringe and look away. *Uh oh...*

"Ok. Here is what you need to know. I do respect women, but..." And he proceeds to tell me a story of how she's pregnant with another guy's kid because she was cheating on him. Everyone shakes their heads as he talks to me, signifying how effed up it truly is. They all take large swigs of beer and whiskey as I feel the guilt of assumption sit upon my shoulders. My rampaging raccoon costume sits back down. *I was digging in his recycling, not his trash...*

I apologized for asking, to which he completely understood. I explained how I couldn't just sit back and hear someone talk bad about his girlfriend in front of me like that if she was doing nothing visibly wrong. We all pour out onto the porch again, hanging out and really having a great time. It was as if my asking that opened the door for an even deeper level of friendship to flourish between all of us. His girlfriend opens her door and stares at us, then slams it shut twice. The phone rings three times. He cancels it all three times. Then she opens the door and holds her phone in the air and starts yelling to him about dinner. He yells back, "I don't care! I just don't care! Make whatever you want!"

To which she screams, "Well, fine! If you want to fuck the out of town girl, then just go ahead!" I had my head down until this time, trying to ignore the comments and jokes the guys were making because it was actually very funny and I was trying not to laugh. Also, I was trying not to listen to their domestic dispute. But then I realized it was me she was referring to. Everyone goes silent, like in a movie where two people are about to have a quick draw showdown in a western town. I look at her and blink, surprised. Then I look at the guys who are all glossy eyed and wide in shock, (probably too because they were all hoping I'd be their prize that night, but they never brought up the fact that I was gay and when I tried to tell them, I was continually interrupted.) These guys looked like a pile of scolded children all silent like, "Oh no, she didn't!"

I turn toward Cheater-Woman, still standing there with her hands on her hips, staring forward making direct eye contact with me. Her fury was entirely on me. *Its time...* I gently, yet triumphantly say, "Umm… I'm a lesbian."

There was a delicate moment, just a second when all time stopped. The guys all heard it and had the words sink into their heads. I swear that I heard several clicks as they all understood that I was off the market. This was a marvelous turning point in our friendship, because from here on out, they still competed for my attention, but it was mostly friendship attention. It no longer was possible love attention.

"Arrraaauugggggghh!" she screamed, stomping her feet as she stormed back into the apartment. This was followed up by a roar of celebration and applause from the guys! They cheered and hoorayed and slapped me on the shoulder. I was now, in their eyes, a bro. A pretty bro with big boobs, but still a bro. They made me feel like an NFL star making the final touchdown in the last few seconds. Katie-Coon defeated the unlikely beast.

After our question and answer session, we all got a nice little buzz and headed over to their favorite bar which was actually just a cabin on a campground. They were charging 8 bucks cover at the door which just seemed crazy to me out where we were. But all the guys went and Markus even paid for my door charge and bought me a drink. The rest of the night everyone was buying me drinks. I made sure to always be at the bar just in case of a date rape drug. I still had that thought in the back of my mind and ensured my safety in this foreign hillbilly hippie town. The bluegrass band was amazing. They had an upright bass player and I watched everyone in that place get up and dance; they were shuffling their feet and moving in all joyous ways I've never seen people dance before. And everyone was doing it! I jumped up and accepted the one guy's hand and we spun and twirled and locked arms and grooved all around that place. The shuffling of happy feet could be heard a mile away in them yonder hills, I reckon!

There was this sweet gal who went by the name of the sweetest name you could ever in your life imagine. And did she have a body and a face to match that little name. We shall call her Sweetie Honeyblossom. If you heard her name spoken anywhere across the country, she is the exact woman you would expect her to look like. And she held the attention of all the boys in that neck of the woods. They all knew her. They all wanted to be with her, but she toted along this strange friend, whom I had assumed to be her mother the whole night. But this friend, we'll call her Hilda, was mostly a caretaker for

Sweetie the whole time. It was a very strange friendship dynamic. For a moment, I wondered if they were together because no matter whom Sweetie talked to, Hilda would intervene. It was very bizarre.

Anyhow, the reason I started dancing in the first place was because Sweetie was out bouncing around on the floor having a blast with a group of her friends. She kept looking at me. I know those eyes when I see them and I was almost certain, somehow in this crazy world, that I had stumbled upon the cutest little lady ever to exist in West Virginia and she was definitely giving me the want eyes.

She reached out and grabbed my arm. It was as if we had taken elegance classes together, laughing jubilantly as if years had gone into our vibrantly choreographed dance rehearsals. We flowed and twirled, shredding up all hesitation on that bar-room dance floor. We swayed deliberately together as the music settled, one hand rested upon my shoulder as her other slid around my neck. We spoke sweetly into each other's ears about how much fun I was having here. We then did several more twirls as we ripped up the dance floor. I became aware that the guys were watching us, but the finest lady in the bar was giving me attention so I really didn't care what they were thinking. I also needed the optimism boost as well. I could tell that this recovery from Alana was going to take a very long time and nothing helps to pass the time and build up my confidence than the attention of a beautiful little sweetie.

Her arms graced down my neck and shoulder. I tried not to pay too much attention to how much attention she was giving me, but then her hip slid in between my thighs and pressed against me. My eyebrow lifted slightly as she glided back down my thigh. A confident, yet, nervous grin slid across my face that to my surprise, made her get a devious look. Heat rose through my body as she pressed against me more and I felt the eyes of a jealous crowd piercing knives into my back. I knew we were the center of attention and I could feel the unwanted masculine anger focused on us. I instantly grew nervous and broke into a dumb jig where we locked arms and spun in circles. Then her friend grabbed her arm and pulled Sweetie close to her. During her scolding, Sweetie looked back at me with a longing in her eyes and didn't take her eyes off me the entire time. I adjusted myself and decided that I needed a drink after whatever that was. I went the bar and started conversation with some people whom no longer held any interest in me. I scratched my head awkwardly feeling both aroused and nervous. I was still afraid that these here good ol' country folk might hate gay people and that a sexy lesbian dance may have sparked the wrong interest. So, I bought myself a two dollar beer and stood there, catching a few guys looking at me in a very uncomfortable manner.

Chapter Eleven

Day 6

"I appreciate all of my life much more sincerely when I live with optimism, but I live that optimism without expectation."

I awoke on a bed with stained sheets. I was afraid something like this would happen, except in entirely different circumstances. Keeping an eye on my drink constantly was on my mind last night. So was keeping an eye on how I felt. When buzzed became tired, I let it be known. The Sweet Red Haired Whiskey Pocket Guy offered me one of the 12 bunks in the cabin that they rented right down this hill from the bar. He then gave me his big bed, which was the best one in the building and he slept on a bunk in another room. They gave me the nicest bed in the whole place, a dirty bunk bed in an old cabin, but what could I complain about? It didn't smell bad and the bar was smoke free last night *(thank god)* so my eyes and sinuses are not puffy. After all, I could have been stuck without anything to sleep on besides a hard floor or an awkward guy trying to take me home.

From the living room, I can see the flickering glow of epic battles continuously playing day in and day out. There were battles and hobbit travels on that television- All. Night. Long. I heard hobbits wandering and epic music accompanying warrior battles and oark fight scenes all night long. Which was fine because I only woke up four or five times in the morning to try to go back to sleep. I didn't know what to do. I didn't know how late these guys slept in usually and I had no idea where I was in the world anyhow. I think town was out to the left when you walked past the barn/bar we were in last night, but I am not sure. I don't have my phone because it is now dead so I don't know the time. I get up and go to use the restroom, which is so disgusting that I am afraid to even enter.

Red Hair roomed with an older veteran that said that he needed to watch Lord of the Rings and smoke pot to survive. He claimed that was the only thing that settles his pain. Weed and Rings. He spoke eloquently, obviously very intelligent. He went on to tell me that he was subject to Agent Orange during his service in Vietnam and everyone who was part of that now has testicular cancer, prostate cancer, lymphatic cancers or has died. He told me that (in his exact words) *"every single man"* that he had known to be exposed to Agent Orange during their service has that type of cancer, even though the government and military claimed it was all 'harmless' at the time. Well, I guess at the time it was harmless. It took 15-30+ years for the cancers to develop. Weed-Vet didn't have a very optimistic view of the world, the government, or anything, but he was living 'proof' of potential deception by the military, living 'proof' to something I always felt could be true. He was drafted, exposed to poison and now lives life in great pain, living the same day, every day. He had a light in his eyes as he spoke to me and whether it was my presence, me being a young female actually excited to listen to his story, or just his weed infused splendor, his eyes, his truth as he spoke, made a lasting impact on me. In life, black and white isn't always just black and white. When you sign your name to a document, there is no such thing as just black and white print. There could be hidden pages attached so deep that one never knows exists, much less ever gets to read until 30 years later after something like cancer develops. Life is full of so much truth and often, so much deception. *In fact, over the course of travels he would not be the only Vietnam veteran who made this very controversial, very powerful claim.*

After I finally get back to my car, I decide to hop right back on the road. A strange feeling of stagnation or deterioration was setting in my body and I felt as if I were a full sponge from the water of education in Fayetteville. It was a wonderful stay, yes, but I've got places to be and things to do, even if there really are no places to be or things to actually accomplish that I know of right now. *The prime goal is intense travel on the open road and I must go on!* I could spend another day here and hike another trail, but I feel as if I have learned as much as I can manage to understand from these people in this time. I do consider staying another night, but something just told me to go and try out some more new life. My intuitive self had a lot to mentally digest from this past day. A lot has happened since I woke up freezing in my car.

I gave my farewell hug to Red Hair and he told me if ever I come back into town, just let him know. He told me to do anything I could to find him because he will take me out kayaking on the rivers and in the rapids and explore on all the best hikes in the area. He then smiled the deepest smile he could possibly give, which really meant a lot because I could see the sincerity in his eyes shine vibrant and true. It's been a long time since he had a deep friendship with a woman and I could really see how much he appreciated my company. He didn't have much in life- a microwave, some ramen noodles, microwave popcorn and pop tarts, but all he had, he offered genuinely. And for that I will never forget this man or any of these guys. Red Hair then said, "Kay-tee, Yew are always part of the Fayetteville famileee."

Sometimes the simplest phrases or the simplest gestures mean the most. I actually almost teared up; it was so wonderful to make such an impact on people I hadn't even known for 24 hours. The kindness was absolute and it hurt to say goodbye. I tell him that I will see him again, but there is no certainty to the words I speak. There is hidden doubtful hope. I say those optimistic words knowing as they slide from my lips, that I probably will never see any of them again. This emotion is an odd pain unlike anything I have ever really known before. No, it is actually rather similar to the experience of heartbreak, but with entirely different energetic make up. It's when you feel that the strong connection you had with someone is over and they have broken up with you. You feel as if you will never see them ever again and it is almost unbearable to breathe. Yes, that feeling is so very familiar. Only this happened with a very short amount of knowing and a very deep amount of impact. This is the moment that I realize I have no time to lose. I am going to change lives everywhere I go and in turn, they will change my life as well. I must make my presence aware to all who seek enlightenment and I have to live that freedom, to live that truth and that awareness in the representation of the beauty of this world.

I can make this creation a better place, one person or town at a time. Heck, why stop there? I can inspire many people and many towns at a time. Thoughts of my un-started YouTube channel flash into my head. Images of my future book and public speaking flash through my mind. I feel the direct force of my longing to share true life-experience fill my vision momentarily while I wave goodbye. I know several years from now they will talk about that random traveling lesbian who just showed up as a best friend in their lives for one day. I know my memory will bring smiles to their faces just as they do to mine. It's a beautifully blended swirled world of constantly rotating lives all over this planet. All around us are people flowing in and out of our lives and it is up to us to make these connections become real. For instance, if Matt hadn't said anything to me, I never would have had this experience. And as I drive through these West Virginia Mountains heading into the unknown, I recall the previous day's events and I smile. I know this world has so much to offer and my ambition increases as each mile separates me further from Pennsylvania and more importantly, further from my limiting, small mind. The distance creates room for me to breathe.

Chapter Twelve

West Virginia

"Where's the magic in life? It's everywhere. But it's also nowhere. You have to believe for it to even exist in your realm of awareness."

Callie bursts out. "Ok, Katie. This is so awesome. I just have so many questions to ask you. You should totally write a book."

"I should keep you around more often…" I respond while stretching my legs. "Ha, I have been trying to write a book, but I just keep getting stuck."

"Seriously. You really should write a book though. People should hear this. You could possibly help some people. I mean, I just want to hear all about your experiences because I haven't traveled." She stretches her legs long indicating how uncomfortable we've both become sitting.

"Yet." I say. She smiles and nods. We decide to take a walk and continue our discussion in a new environment. Fresh movement releases stagnation of conversation and of body functionality. The sun was alive, bursting behind the thick clouds. They didn't look like storm clouds, but more so like the ones painted by Michelangelo depicting imagery from the gods. They brought me what felt like a divine inner peace as we continued talking and walking. As we stroll, she teases me several times. I blush when I realize that I think she is starting to like me…

. . . .

I was told not to, but I drive through Beckley anyhow. It seems like a very charming little town at first glance, although the guy from the previous night did tell me about the meth or heroine culture that exists in this town. I have never had experiences with any kind of drug *(besides marijuana)* before. I've had plenty of friends that seemingly lost their minds for me to learn quickly that I don't need that in my life. I am sure that Beckley, WV is a great town in essence. Every city has its up and down citizens, but I wasn't in a position to deal with drug addicts today so I just drove around it to see it and look for a quick breakfast. I found a donut shop on the outskirts of the city in a place that looked pretty clean. "Do you serve real eggs on your sandwiches?" I asked in an optimistic tone although for the cheap price, I highly expected what they told me.

"Uh, it's from a bag."

"Ok, then. I'll take a Boston cream, a coconut and your finest cup of coffee please."

"All the coffee is the same." I laughed, kind of, and tilted my head to the side, curious at the response. No smile from her. Just a very unamused glare. I responded that I knew that all coffee was the same and that I was joking and she looked confused. It was an absolutely generic, not very good donut shop and that is all I knew in my time in Beckley.

From West Virginia I drove to Virginia, stopping several times along the way at various places to use Wi-Fi. I am beginning to see why having a smartphone is a necessity these days. The inconvenience of 1. needing to be at Wi-Fi to use my tablet to 2. Send messages out to find places to sleep and then 3. Get back on there again to check responses- is so absurd. But it is what I am committed to currently and it's also a fine additional mission. But I am seeing how having information at my fingertips would be helpful, such as going to some neat place that I stopped on the side of the road, doing quick research as I discover its online history or interesting facts. Then recording *The Everything Show* would be so much simpler. That would make the series just so stuffed with information. But the manner in which I am trying to represent sharing ideas and stories from all over the country just doesn't seem too practical if I don't come prepared first. This trip is more about the spontaneity of adventure. The plan is to experience freedom, to have no direct plan and so far, I guess I am doing a good job at that.

I continue my way down I-77, the West Virginia Turnpike. I had read about some little things along the way, but I was more focused on finding a place to stay for the night. I had sent out a couple requests, but there weren't many choices in the areas up ahead. I saw a few in Blacksburg which seemed to be a little further north than I'd like to make that night, but I'd go any way if I didn't get any more responses. So, I sent a few requests out around Wytheville, WV because I was told the world's largest pencil was there.

By the time, I made it into town it was about three or four. It had been raining all day and was beginning to downpour heavily. I was told that if I just drive through the city I will see the pencil sticking out of the side of a building. And it sure did. It stuck out at a 75-degree angle from the wall and was approximately 25 ft. long. It seriously was a big pencil sticking out of the Wytheville Office Supply building. They had built it as an attraction to draw people to the town. It worked to draw me in, but apparently not everyone because it appears that the local giant mosquito, *Shopinwalls and other massive corporations sucked the life dry, right out of this once thriving, now struggling downtown, unfortunately a common theme all across our country. It was actually kind of depressing walking through this overlooked town, but there is something so thrilling to me about seeing this world's largest stuff. The biggest in the world means that it is actually the biggest in the whole world! *Nothing is the larger than this*! And to be the most of something in the whole world really does mean a lot, especially in this day of mass production and uninformed consumerism. Nearly everything around us is a blend of unappreciated fabrication and wasteful plastic. To have something be original in this day and age, the biggest or best original in the world, is pretty special in my book. *Yes. In my book.*

I have skipped around several world's largest things this year so far. In February, I flew out to San Diego and spent several days walking around and sightseeing with a friend of mine named Mandy. My other friend Candy was moving back to Pennsylvania from L.A., so she came down and met me there. We drove back across the country together and stopped a bunch of times along the way and saw some amazing things- Montezuma's Castle, hiking in Sedona in the snow, climbed volcanoes, Petroglyph National Park, but more importantly, I discovered my craving of world's largest things.

The first one was a sign we saw along the road, just a tiny sign that said world's largest rocking chair in Cuba, Missouri. It is off Route 66 located right next to Fanning Route 66 Outpost, a general store where Candy purchased peach moonshine. The chair is over 42 ft. high and was awarded by Guinness World Records in 2008. Then the next was the world's largest Wind Chime, which actually worked! We could pull the thick rope and it would create a very low vibrational gong sound. It stands an impressive 55 ft. tall right in cute, downtown Casey, Illinois which is located right off I-70. This massive structure weighs just under 17,000 pounds. Casey also is home to the world's largest golf tee, knitting needle and crochet hook and they are looking to continue their expanding collection.

The next place that we stopped was in Ohio, which was supposed to be a grand endeavor of various world's biggest things too, but was a wild goose chase for a while. We intended to see the world's largest crystal ball in Westerville. I typed it in online and got an exact address saying it was in a store front. We went there and couldn't find it. I went online again and saw that it moved to a new address. When we arrived, we found ourselves in a pile of locked office buildings. We looked it up again and found out that it was moved to the second floor of an office building and was unable to be seen by the public anymore. Treasure hunt ended! So, we then went to the world's largest corn field, which we expected to be lame, but we ran into a security guard at the office who told us it was right in the next city, Dublin, Ohio. Off we went on our next excursion. When we found it, we were incredibly surprised to see 109 human sized ears of corn standing erect in a field. We saw them and burst out in laughter because it is just such a strange sight, cement cobs each 6 ft. high.

After that, we were told about this local park that had these giant dancing rabbits on the top of a hill. From that description, we expected something kind of stupid. We expected it to be both small and a waste of time, but we were pleasantly surprised. As we drove through Ballanetrea Park in Dublin, we rounded a few corners until in the distance, came the shapes of something enormous- giant dancing bunnies. Massive 20 ft. rabbits holding hands and prancing at the top of a grassy knoll. They seem to be celebrating something, perhaps it is Bunny Foo Foo's birthday or perhaps they are clubbin'. Either way, they are fascinating creations made from what appears to be recycled objects ranging from bicycle chains to old gloves. Giant, sculpted, weird recycled art. *I absolutely adore it.*

Snap back to Wytheville's pencil. Since it was raining viciously, I didn't find it practical to get out now considering I was already uncomfortably chilly. *Add some sad town rain into my already uncomfortable skin and who knows what would happen?* I continue onward exploring and eventually searching for some free Wi-Fi, hoping that I would be able to find a place to sleep. I had three messages denying my stay for the night, but all it takes is that one to say yes so I maintained a bit of optimism. I had a message from a girl named Mady who looked like a lot of fun. She said she was on her way back to Blacksburg from her hometown in Columbus, Ohio and would be back close to 8. So, I took my time getting to there, especially considering Blacksburg was about an hour north of where I currently was. *Ah, North again!* This is, yet, another prime example of how a smartphone would be assisting me better, but I am determined in my simplistic travel this time. *This travel will be plain and simple and that is all!* I remind myself, stroking my raging ego, dead set on this idea of increased difficulty while waving my paper map pride in the air.

So off toward Blacksburg I go! I scan my map and effectively plan my route. I've been on too many highways these last few days in the determination to finally get south and I can't stand highway driving. It's monotonous and repetitive, lifeless and draining and I need to shake it up a bit. Highways are like the robotic structure to hold humans in place, to follow the design, to skip the love of the travel for the underappreciated destination. There is a divine beauty in the how, not just in the arrival of how one gets where one is in life. To really appreciate the travel from destination to destination is what it is all about right now. Otherwise it isn't really travel, it's just kind of waiting while moving. And we've got plenty of time to wait for things in life.

The song comes on the radio *"Heck yes, life goes on… And it goes on long even when the thrill for living is over."* I have heard this a few times on this trip so far. I decide that thrill and enthusiasm is always something I want to have plenty of in my life and that no, life will never go on without thrill for me. I decide to take route 11 up through Pulaski and Dublin, WV, (a different Dublin), and then Radford and Christiansburg then I'll be in Blacksburg. I figure this route will be a nice distraction from the rain and will hopefully provide some small-town thrills. I did not expect to encounter what I saw next. I drove through shopping malls and business centers, amazed at how big this town must be considering its tiny letter size on my paper map, but it must be huge due to the massive amounts of corporate business! So, I absolutely couldn't wait to see what this downtown was like. I follow a sign toward the downtown district and I prepared myself for an intense amount of culture. I couldn't wait to stop at the local coffee shops and use their Wi-Fi, to order a nice, warm coffee to counteract this rainy day and nibble on a delightful treat made with small town love.

I take a sharp right where the streets diverge into two one-ways through the city. As I bear to the right, I see a mural chipped to almost indistinguishable features. I learned the true power of a ghost town created out of a beautiful city. The streets are decorated with the loveliness of plastic bags and soda cans. I slowly drive down this silent city. It's as if the zombie apocalypse has taken place here and I've stumbled into the aftermath. There are storefronts on every single block, on every single building and they are all closed. Just about every single one of them is boarded up. It's rather frightening, the death that was represented in this once thriving district. I drove around several blocks just letting it all sink in. The rain continues to fall in attempts to wipe away the sadness that took over this town, but this city developed a cancer that it just couldn't beat. 3-4 story beautifully engraved buildings from the early 1900's, all left for dead in the town of yesterday that couldn't hold itself in the arms of corporation uprising.

I turned off the main road and drove through some developments mainly composed of beautifully large, immaculate homes. Some were well taken care of while other looked like they were struggling to keep their heads up, just barely standing. *The zombie leftovers, I assume.* I drove through this city so slow and observed the crumbling sidewalks and allowed the history to leak into my mind. These granite walls were begging for someone to pay attention to them. They were pleading with me to listen to their story. I drove through every street and appreciated each piece of that place for what it was, what it is, and I prayed for what it will become. The echoes of a busy life's past ricochets songs of sorrow and longing and I felt deeply for this city. I really felt for this desperate city and I knew there was nothing that I or anyone else could do at this present moment to restore its youth.

Quite possibly, something reminded me of my hometown, a once bustlingly historic hub for steel production in central Pennsylvania. Something about observing this place through compassionate eyes made me understand where I came from. The need for immediate gratification and the growth of our culture to not appreciate quality or permanence has hurt our poor America in many ways, so many ways actually, that we are only now beginning to realize how much damage our mindless consumerism is causing. Most of us live with our eyes blind, eating with our fingertips engaged in our plastic. We feed each other's false beliefs and they feed ours too. And together we churn out this constant flow of buy and buy and want and want. And I just never understood ownership that way. *At least I didn't think I did.* Maybe I just didn't understand my own self-worth or the fact that I could acquire nice things that actually worked. It takes a lot of wasted energy to roam around a home as a hoarder. *Hmm…There is a lot of stuff in my house back in Erie…* I gave that city my all, but I was unfocused and I just couldn't make the woman I loved happy. Our dreams conflicted and she set me free and here I am now wandering around the country. The feeling of this town reminds me of the feeling of loneliness I drag with me across these states, the feeling of desperation chiming like tin cans clattering behind my cross-country, self- marriage ceremony, my fragmented search of true self. There is such a connection to this city's feeling of being lost. Having been strong and powerful at one time, full of so much energy, transformed into a shell of what once was. The only real difference between us is that I can transfer my physical position. This city is stationary.

So, I bid this place farewell and I thank it for the lessons that it taught me. It thanked me for listening to its stories and I continued my way with a new sense of purpose somehow. I was also filled with a fear of the future. This is just one town that I've been able to explore that corporations have devastated. How many more wonderful, small towns have been ripped limb from limb like this across this country, destroying all culture and local business around the area? *More than I'll probably ever know.* But it does remind me a lot of my hometown. I think about how precisely poetic that song is in relation to this city, * *"Gee, yeah. Life continues onward…"*

I depart, still northbound. I put on my Glenn Miller Orchestra cassette tape again and that gets me in a delightfully better mood. Eventually I see something so beautiful that it almost makes me cry: two large fenced in Volkswagen Vanagon fields. There are hundreds of them lined up in rows organized by color. The sky is beginning to darken and the rain prevents any quality pictures to be taken, but I walk around the lots in awe of the beauty of such fantastic condition. The paint jobs were perfect and they all looked to be in great shape. My dream car is to have a Volkswagen Vanagon pop top camper van. Preferably it would be top white, bottom orange or that pale lime aqua color they often came in. But I see these and consider them to be a great source of influence to my travel. It represents the furthering of my journey. It represents what I want and what I need. *I need to feel the freedom. I need to see the world through new eyes.*

I smile and hop back on the road.

I arrive in Blacksburg, Virginia and realize it is the home of Virginia Tech. I had no idea I was entering a college town, but I was kind of excited to be with fun, young people. I stop in a restaurant's parking lot to log into Wi-Fi. I don't want coffee. I think it would greatly counteract the sleepiness I feel and the rain, but I'm not in the mood and I need to save as much money as I can. It's why I eat only peanut butter and jelly on either bread or crackers right now. And of course, apples. I think about the books I am reading and how they suggest learning a positive mental attitude, one that observes abundance in all things. I realize this cheap mental capacity I have is very limiting, but I convince myself that it is important to think this way now. After all, I still have many more miles and many more days to explore.

Mady calls me and says that she just got home. I look up her address in the Wi-Fi using my tablet and realize that I am just around the corner (which is rather incredible considering all of the places around here that I could have randomly stopped.) I park two blocks over; her apartment is in a beautiful brick building, very similar to three other ones on that block. I hop over puddles and dodge raindrops as I arrive with my backpack and suitcase in tote. She has a hipster style with a very interesting hair style. It's interesting in the fact that she's got a lot of hair, but she doesn't brush it so it is matted and knotted on the top of her head; it was seriously just a giant knot. But she couldn't have been more hospitable. She was very friendly and offered me everything she had. I was actually taken off guard by this, considering she hadn't even known me for more than two minutes. She grabs a towel out of the closet and places it on her dresser. Then she grabs bed sheets and looks at me funny. "Oh, I got a bed. Well, a futon. It's nice, but it's new and in the car."

"Do you want me to help bring it in?"

"No, no. Well, unless you wanted to use it you definitely could. But my couch is there, too. But the futon is brand new and really cozy." So, we venture out in the rain to her car and remove what felt like a 300-pound futon from the back. The endless downpour fills our bodies with laughter as we become soaked. We place it at the top of the stairs as she tries to figure out what to do with it next. Her grip slips and our precious box falls down the flight of 7 steps into a large dirty puddle. I panic, but she practically falls over laughing. We race down to pick it up and the box begins to melt while we drag/pull it to the apartment. Just carrying it was a challenge enough and now we need to tug it up three flights of stairs! Why are there no strong college guys around when you need them on a college campus?

The two of us were not quiet in our futon fananza. We laughed and pushed it one step at a time, slamming it around, slipping all over the giant wooden staircase and into the freshly painted wall. Some of the other apartments must have heard it and I figured maybe one would come out and see if we needed help. Just one person to stabilize it while we pushed and pulled would have made a world of difference, but the doors never opened. So, the he-women within stepped in and conquered. We open her apartment door covered in a blend of sweat, cardboard chunks and rain.

She then offered me something that made me feel like Jesus upon his weathered arrival to a new city- a shower. *Or in his case, a foot wash, but I got that feeling of immense gratitude.* I haven't showered in days now and I have been constantly cold for the entire time. I had a hot meal the day before, but it was very basic- beans and rice with some spices. She offered me her sister's homemade vegetarian chili. *By golly, that stuff tasted incredible!* It was just an unbelievable flavor full of the flawless blend of spice and sweet, so many vegetables and herbs, just so much precious deliciousness and she offered it to a stranger so freely. I couldn't believe the treasure I was given. I couldn't believe the amount of happiness a hot bowl of soup could bring someone in my situation. After showing her my deepest gratitude, she tells a story about a few homeless people she knows.

She grabs a pipe and begins to smoke a big bowl of marijuana. She offers and I decline. After high school, my weed craving diminished, although I am considering it. She explained that a few friends of hers did the same thing that I am doing, but they did it very differently because they all did drugs. She said about how they lost everything and ended up on the streets, homeless and addicted with nothing. They managed to bring in a couple hundred dollars a week begging on the streets. She said about how the homeless don't get taxed so depending on where they stand and what they do there, they could usually bring in between $8-$50 an hour, all untaxed.

"Wow, really? I can see how the lifestyle of homeless can be of great interest to many."

"Yeah, but when you have a drug habit like most of the homeless do, you rarely ever have money by the end of the day." Good point. I was just thinking about the possibility of setting up on the street and how profitable it actually might be. Then I looked out the window at the rain and reconsidered. *Many future encounters with street kids would prove this to be a generally accurate conclusion that the vagabond traveler lifestyle often goes hand in hand with drug addiction. These encounters, however, would solidify my desire to prove that drugs and traveling don't have to go together and one could happily and soberly soul-seek across the country without developing a drug habit (or ever even trying anything).*

Chapter Thirteen

Blacksburg, Virginia

"A routine creates behavior and behavior creates a personality and a personality generates one's true destiny."

I wake up and drive north on back roads all the way up to the famous Natural Bridge. Around a bend and up a steep hill, I am greeted by a repetitive noise. I instantly know what it is and pull off onto the shoulder, barely getting my car by the white line. I get out and look to see a flat tire. *Great...* When I bought Felix, he didn't have a spare and I never bought one. Thankfully, I got AAA before I left Erie so I called; they told me it would be 20 minutes to an hour until they arrived. *Ok, I can handle that.* I pull out my camera and guitar and I set it up while sliding into the passenger's seat to begin filming a funny impromptu country style song about getting stuck in the hills of Virginia. I notice lights blinking through the rain and realize that I filmed a cop pulling up behind me as I was playing. I started to laugh and put my stuff away so I didn't look as crazy. He asks me what I am doing as he vigorously inspects my stuff, telling me that it is unsafe for me to stay there and I needed to go down the hill to the pull off on the other side of the street. He walks out in the middle of the street and stops traffic flying around this bend in the rain for me to turn around and go there. Doing that seemed even more dangerous than my staying, but I trusted him.

I was towed to Roanoke and had to buy a used tire since mine was completely blown. While there, I discover that it is home to the World's Largest Star so that was thrilling to me. It's a frozen, wet embark up a trail to the top of the hill where I could barely see anything at the lookout. I could hardly even see the 100-ft. star right in front of me, but anyone could see that I couldn't get the smile to leave my face the whole time.

I arrive at Natural Bridge; my family was here years ago, but I really wanted to experience it alone in here, to really be at the majesty of it all, see it and feel it, the reverse energy of powerful, pulsating rocks defying gravity. I arrive and there is no one around. Just three other cars are in the parking lot until a half bus pulls up beside me. Two girls and two guys come out, all mid 20's dressed very clean cut. Their accents indicated that they were not from this country so I asked what they are doing. They flew in from Spain to explore America. Then flew into Orlando and are driving up the country over the course of two weeks and stopping as many places as they can. Meeting people like this always makes me not feel so foolish in the world. It makes me feel justified and proud to be one of the few I know who currently craves to see the world and actually does so on their own terms. Next on their list of must-sees was Washington DC. The flight to depart New York City was in a week so they weren't at Natural Bridge for very long.

With my ticket in hand, I excitedly marched down the stairs to the entrance for the arch park. They had a lot of stuff that looked open during the season, but was closed now. It looked like a great place to go to have a family outing in the summer. *Not in the freezing rain mist weather.* Of course, I have been residually cold all day so what does it matter at this moment if I still am? I walk the pathway down past this man-made waterfall that follows the stairs. It winds around a giant tree and comes back around to head down to the base. The bottom is a gated area with a ranger station and lined with benches. I bear to the right of the path toward the sign that says arch. It seems simple enough so I keep on walking. The stream ripples beautifully and sounds graceful. I have heard falling water all day via rain, but this is stunning and I become totally entranced by it. Being the only person down here, I take my good ol' time walking around and looking at the rock walls. Then I see it, the giant arch right before me.

It is so unbelievably large. The authorities told me not to go under it because of the dangling icicles, knives waiting to fall upon my head. The Spain kids arrive and they had a lot to fit into their schedules, but they were perfect timing to trade pictures with me. They took several, which I greatly appreciated. It was dark and misty here and when I stood directly under the arch, I was unable to be seen in the picture. I was wearing my black winter jacket so there really wasn't much contrast at all. *I take note on what to wear for future travel pictures at dusk.* After I traded pics with them, I went under the arch because there was a whole other area out there- like an entire extra mile. I was told to stay on this side of the arch, but... the universe beckoned me. I walked along the river bed to this old representation of an Indian fort. Then I continued to where they have the old shelter built into this natural cave area. There was just such a powerful feeling in this place. I swear that I could see a few odd mists floating around so I snapped some pictures. Several orbs showed up. *Ghosties? Dust? Raindrops? Energy? After my unprofessional analysis, I pretend that it's everything until proven otherwise.* I then walk back to the river and continue following upstream where I get an urge to run. I look around and realize that I am most likely the only person in this park right now and I am in an area I was told not to be in. *So, that means that I can look as crazy if I want.* I grab my backpack and I hold it tightly securing all things into place before I begin. *A very important traveler awareness tool is to check your bags often.*

I start to run. I run hard and I run wildly. I run strong and the sweat and rain is once again building up all over my body. I run until I can't breathe and then I run more until the end. Each step seems to fill me with strength and power. I start talking aloud to myself, not caring if anyone can hear me or not. I say positive affirmations as I go and it becomes an enchanting symphony gliding into my every step. *"I am beautiful. I am strong. I am powerful. I can do anything. I can be anything. I am beautiful…"*

The key to positive affirmation (from what I've been learning) is that it is very important to not only think good things about yourself, but to also really invest your energy into believing it too. It says to identify what you consider to be your weaknesses and adapt those thoughts into a positive way, a believable vibration inside self. And when you believe the positivity, life really begins to fill with magic. Rather than saying "I don't like that I'm unorganized" just begin saying "I am organized." If you feel ugly, just begin saying "I am beautiful." Say it over and over and really feel the beauty inside yourself.

It's been said that "A routine creates behavior and behavior creates a personality and a personality generates one's true destiny." So, that is what I did as I ran. I created the routine of empowering myself. I felt my power growing and I felt my tension melting. I let the words flow from my mouth and into my ears and I let the negativity that was within me, just float on down the river. I released all of my tension. I felt so liberated and free as I reached the end. My joints cheered in contentment to the fact that they had grown so damp and cramped from being in the car, sitting and walking. They felt good being shaken up, getting that blood flowing through my body.

The waterfall was so peaceful. It flowed and I smiled. I breathed in the freshness, the brand-new start. Wave after wave of endless water surged over that edge just continuing and flowing over again. It seemed to dance beyond the edge of the earth and float down, interlacing the wavy fingers of droplets into each other. I felt my breath ease up as I stared at the natural beauty before me. It's as if this was all meant for me, which sounds greedy, but I allow myself to be not just a part of the universe, but to communicate with it. I appreciate every single thing happening. Therefore, I can acquire more in my life. I just continually ask for things and they happen, like this moment. I was trying to hike around before the sunset and find a waterfall at a park nearby, but since I lost time to the tire incident, I now have acquired one into my life anyhow! I smile at the irony as I whisper to the universe.

"What are the chances?"

I stand there alone, a human sponge, to the growth of wisdom from the universe's call. I examine that this may be the most incredible moment of my trip so far, the most spiritually enlightening moment yet. I can't stop smiling. I breathe deep and take in the swirling energy from around me, expanding my chest and stretch out my lungs; it's been a few days since I've done yoga to stretch my lungs. I take several deep breaths while I close my eyes, shutting off the visual to experience the other senses stronger. The river begins to surge, roaring with a deafening passion into my head. My breath continues to flow in and out, in and out until I am completely at rest in my mind. I smile and feel the tension melt from my entire being. It feels so good to just calmly explore the relaxation that my troubled mind so greatly needs, to relax into nature, especially in such a public place. Rarely does a person get to experience this revelation of tender calmness by themselves in this type public tourist attraction. I erupt into enormous smiles, breathing deep, appreciating every essence of these moments. I then open my eyes, realizing that I don't know what time this place closes and that I don't have my phone on me either. I also don't suspect that they have anyone else in this dark, wet park right now that I could ask. So, I say my goodbyes to the waterfall and I take off down the path again. I could have stayed there for hours, but I can't overstay my welcome in nature. I begin to run back.

There is a hole in the ground to the left that I ran by earlier. This time I stop to look at it. Scientists claim that it goes nowhere- The hole to nothing. The water flows into it and they have never been able to figure out where it goes. The scientists did these ball tests and color sample tests to try to figure out where it goes, but as far as I know here, the tests never concluded anything. Geologists assume it goes deep into the earth and comes out somewhere else incredibly far away. It's rather an interesting concept, making me think about the longevity of some life's results and the power of patience on a grander scale than self.

As I run, I think about my travels with Candy in Arizona. We stopped at Montezuma's Castle, an ancient Puebloan cliff dwelling, then continued over to Montezuma's Well, another ancient land with a mysterious water hole just down the road a little bit further. They claim that whatever you throw into the water will float back up to the surface due to an ancient organism that makes everything in the water incredibly buoyant. The interesting thing is that they do not know where this water comes from. They did the same monitoring process to figure out what continually fills this enormous hole, but they never did discover its source. And now I'm across the country at a separate, opposite one. I highly doubt they are flowing 2000 miles underground to meet each other, but it is an amusing concept to think of.

I make it back and I'm entirely out of breath. They told me earlier that a guard would be waiting for me at the ranger station so I didn't have to walk all the way back up the stairs, but I waited and waited. I knocked on the window and no one was responding although the door was open and the lights were on. So, I just decide to awkwardly walk all the way back up the stairs. It takes several minutes, but I get to the top and I'm trying to pretend that I'm not out of breath, but I really am. I then go to the door of the giant entrance and knock. "Hey I just wanted to let you know that I am out of there."

She says, "Oh, you walked up? He's down there searching for you." I explain my knocking and waiting. She calls down and tells him I'm leaving. He sounds frustrated; I thank her and let her know how much I enjoyed it. It closed at 8 and it was 8:02 when I sat down in the car. I had just enough time on my own natural instincts to be exactly on time without ever knowing. What are the chances?

I head back to Blacksburg, so thankful to have a destination in mind where I know I have my stuff already and a hot shower. This is such a simple concept, but when you live without it, having a returning location is such a magnificent thing. I arrive. Mady is stoned and I take one hit, a marvelous well-deserved shower and then she wants to go out to a bar. So, we do. We get calzones. This meal is so well earned: a new tire, two frozen adventures and a good friend to share the evening with me. She drives me around the downtown to see a bit of the not so happening life. We then go back and she is fascinated to hear that I made out with someone from the SofaCruisin website. She said she's been hosting SofaCruisers for years and has never ever hooked up with someone from the site. *Beginner's luck.*

The next day I wake up and take my time leaving the house. I use the computer and update pictures and my Facebook. I want to make sure to get them up just in case something happens to my camera. At this point, I fully intend to write a country exploration book and include pictures of my travels and for people to follow along online, so it's very important to back up my stuff. I do a little bit of research to see the next day's route and off into the world I go.

I explore the internal workings of my mind while reading several chapters of *Contemplate and Welcome Prosperity* on the top of a mountain in North Carolina. On the way to that mountain, I hit 200,000 miles on my car and pull over to film it and celebrate. *(As if I drove them all)* I get out at the base of the mountain road and take a picture of my triumphant car and realize that my tire is again almost flat. *Ah! Oh, no! Maybe I shouldn't go any further!* I step out of my fear filled thoughts and try to form a solution. I open the hatchback and find a tire repair spray; it inflates the tire with sealing fluid.

I drive to the closest gas station and fill it up the rest of the way like the directions suggest. I ride for about 15 minutes so that the fluid can properly cover the inside of the tire and decide to go to that mountain and hike anyhow. I also brought up a notebook and wrote a few poems and allowed the gushing river of my mind to spill onto the pages, welcoming a gentle, peaceful stream again. My thoughts flow through my fingertips and melt effortlessly onto the page

I write- *The good news is that every day I am standing at the beginning of the rest of my life. Hopefully, it is a lot warmer tomorrow. Hopefully my tire will stay inflated, but we will see.*

Hopefully, I also go south.

I guess, only the day will tell…

Chapter Fourteen

"Once in my life, clouds rushed in to formulate storms and tragedy. Now I see them as precursors to a soon to be miraculous sunrise or sunset. Patience holds the key."

C allie asks me a few more questions and I specify that these writings have been driving me crazy. "Ok. Imagine this. It's like you are sitting on a pile of gold, but you are lacking the organization skills to get it out to the people that it will benefit. That's how I feel. It's like I have this golden offering that I am sitting on and I know that by helping others, it will help me too, but I am lacking the ability to share it." I reach into my bag and pull out one of the three old travel notebooks I am carrying. "See, I carry them with me everywhere in hopes that I'll pull it out somewhere and go through them and mark them. But there are about 12 other notebooks just like this! They have my thoughts, my experiences, my wanting to do's, my directions, random things people say to me that I want to remember and so on! It is so much to go through!"

Callie reaches her hand out and flips through one, "Well, are you going through them?"

"Well, sort of. I mean, I am talking about it now, right? It's just there is so much! It's overwhelming. I'll tell ya, I've figured out 1001 ways how not to write a book by now." Callie smiles at me as she opens to a random page of the journal and begins reading aloud.

Journal entry from previous day 3-19-13

Today I am sitting on a mountain top overlooking a 360 view of a vast valley. It is North Carolina and I've got to say, North Carolina is remarkable up on top of Pilot Mountain. In the distance, I can see Winston Salem or some city to the South. I'm feeling much better than I did when I first started this trip. I am still emotionally stuck, but I have opened up my mind to be like I was before; happy and very much alive. I'm considering never living with a lover again. That's one of the things people tell everyone about relationships. Everything with Alana just confuses me so much. I thought I may be moving on, but then yesterday after my hike in Roanoke, she called me and the whole rest of the day became fuzzy. It was right after I got back to the car when my phone rang. I was soaked with frozen rain mist on the exterior and sweat

80

infiltration from my interior as I slumped into the seat of my car after having climbed to the top of the World's Largest Star, which sat at the top of a mountain in Roanoke, VA. I started making a peanut butter and jelly and then I heard my phone go off. Heart raced when I saw the name. She started talking about her new job at the pet store, which by the way, she will soon have three jobs that kind of go against my purification quest. 1. Working at a pet shop supports puppy mills and doesn't support animal shelters that are filled with loving animals already in need of homes. 2. Working at the massive corporation retailer supports the destruction of local economy/communities and it supports our culture's obsession with wasteful impermanence and lack of appreciation. 3. And she is going to soon work at a huge fast food chain which supports a great deal of negative things that I feel I don't need to list. Yes, I do support them for their absolute convenience and I do buy a coffee every time I use their bathroom or internet, but there isn't much that's sustainably healthy for our planet. And since I live on this planet, I feel some crazy dedication to honor it for some reason. Work is a large portion of one's life. If someone works a full time 40 hour a week job, that is nearly 1/3 of their adult life. So, if they then decided to be employed by something that goes against their spirit, they are fueling the monster that they don't support from within and that is a direct energy flow of negative energy being generated into 1/3 of their lives, thus forming an energy inconsistency or blockage. And in my case, I give a great deal of love and energy to the one with who I am in love. So, if that is a blend of energy from my whole life being channeled into someone who spends a large portion of their time working for things my soul does not support, that is then my energy being given to things I don't support.

Alana then asks me what I have been up to. I explain the wet mountain hike and the frost covering the ferns. I tell her about my flat tire and the cop and I mention how I am about to eat a peanut butter and jelly. She exclaims, "What! Oh, my god, no way! I am eating a peanut butter and jelly now too!" What are the chances? I consider for a moment how often I say that sentence lately. Behind every great rags-to-riches success story, there is almost always a struggle of misfortune. It's been said that one must first know bitter pain to learn how to fully appreciate life's journey. I just wonder how long this mental strain will affect my journey. The feeling of helplessness flows into my being as I take a deep breath and see the mountains' strata range in all directions.

Callie stops speaking momentarily, "I worked a job I hated… Actually, I worked a lot of jobs I hated. I mean, some of them I liked, but they weren't my dreams."

"Yeah, a lot of people do. Sometimes it is just what you have to do."

"Yeah, but you have a good point about time and life. Hmm…"

....

The next day I woke up in Mt. Aires, NC in a bed. Andy gave his bed to me last night. I couldn't believe how sweet these guys were, considering they were all in college, in the military or both. It was four guys sharing a one-bedroom apartment with their one other friend. The one on the lease was Andy, the one who had the bedroom. I met them yesterday when I was climbing barefoot up the wall facing south on Pilot Mountain. They came walking through the path, chatting and laughing like young lads freezing silently when they saw me there, barefoot, wedged between rocks several feet up by myself. They looked at each other, laughing before asking what I was doing. I explained my travels and they invited me to stay the night if I needed another place. It was a charming, cute, little apartment considering it was above an auto repair shop. The stairs were about 1 1/2 inches too high and made of solid steel that I could imagine would be very unforgiving if I slipped so I made sure to grasp the handrail every time I went out to my car. We stayed up until 3 am watching Black Swan, a strange movie for five frat guys to be thrilled to watch for the second time (although I think they may have been most excited for the lesbian scene.) Since it was my first time watching this movie that was the part I was most excited about too. *Yay, gay stuff!* Man, did these guys really know how to smoke marijuana! They had three bongs, two vaporizers, one hookah and two bowls. This seemed like a normal college guy life at first until I began to talking to them a bit. "Yeah, I'm in the Army National Guard. I have drill tomorrow."

"Umm… You are in the military and you are smoking weed?"

"Well, yeah. It's fine. Three of us are in the military. Brian and I are in the National Guard and Jeff is in the Navy." I ask how they are doing that if they are being drug tested frequently and they told me that they don't need to worry about it.

Now I am confused and curious. "Why don't you worry? Don't you get kicked out of the military if you get caught?"

"We won't get caught. The guy we buy from is a sergeant. He gets a paper with the upcoming drug test date on it."

"And he just tells you? Like hey, guys! There is a drug test coming up soon and you should stop smokin' the ganja!"

"Sort of. He usually says, "I think this would be a good time to study for the test." That means that the test is about a week away so we just need to exercise, drink a lot of water and some vinegar tablets and we are fine."

I helped them assemble a list of people to invite to their upcoming party. They are planning a raging party in a week and they want there to be a lot of girls, but not a lot of boys. They repeatedly mention this... *Well, duh.* I say that girls love themed parties. So, they say toga party. I laugh as I explain that they need to be more creative. Girls love getting ready for parties with other girls and they like having a mission to prepare for. I explained ABC (Anything, But Clothes) parties, which is pretty self-explanatory. I personally have never been to one, but I have always heard they are very artistic. We talk of zoo parties and of summer in winter parties and we start tossing out all sorts of crazy ideas. Michael Jackson Parties, Celeb Themed, Homeless, Cat, Zoo, Ocean and so on. The guys chose toga... I congratulate them on their creativity. I return my focus to the present moment and decide to go to Hanging Rock. It is approximately 30-40 minutes east. The guys all must head to class in the next two hours and John has 25 minutes left before he had to be in class. His drive is about a 20-minute drive, but he just keeps hanging out and talking. We end up getting into some great conversation and I realize another five minutes have passed. "John, you better get going soon!"

"Yeah, I'm not worried about it."

"Yeah, but if you leave now you can probably make it on time." He says ok, but stays and the guys start talking about Kevin Hart, quoting him in nearly every sentence. I say, "John, you are going to miss class."

"Yeah. Hey, Jeff. Can I have the Prof's number?" I ask why he has the professor's number. "Oh, we are really cool with him. He gave it to us if we ever need anything. Ok, let me text him. Hey... I... woke... up... with... a... sore... throat... What else should I write?" Andy tells him to write fever.

"I... am... burning...up." I started to feel guilty for being associated with lies. I was trying to keep this trip as honest as possible, as true as can be. So, I kept my delicate little angel thoughts to myself as these guys giggled and composed a not very convincing text to the prof saying how he is not making it to class, once again. And the professor ate it up. The goal was accomplished and comedy acts were enjoyed by all.

I eventually leave, not really wanting to spend my day indoors in front of a television. I say my farewells and head out toward my cliff top sanity. I see Pilot Mountain in the distance as I drive by it and toward Hanging Rocks. I had no idea what to expect as I arrived there. I follow signs as I generally do to the top of the mountain until it actually opened up into a parking lot which was kind of in the middle of nowhere. I could see a rock face in the distance, but the confusing thing about mountains and hiking is that it is always very difficult to determine how far of a distance it is to get to something. There have been many hikers I've met who are good at judging distance, but I just haven't acquired that skill yet. But those tannish-grey cliffs, ah yes, those glorious cliffs. They were begging me to be on top of them. I could see little dots up there, all little fluorescent people exploring in their multicolored outer wear gear. *I want to be somebody's little dot today. I want someone to look up there longingly and see my little dot body prancing around at the top.* As I begin walking I think about little dots and perspective.

I analyze how spacey my thoughts have become and realize how much I need that mountain top perspective today. I also hear my notebook and pen calling my name again too. *Nature, clear my mind!*

Chapter Fifteen

Day Tired- Becoming Exhausted

"Intention is everything."

Callie asks me about how I had the time to write so much. I explain that it's really easy when I take it everywhere with me. Every moment could be jotted down, but that is what makes the part I am in now so difficult. I try to explain the emotion of guiding intuition. "Did you ever have a feeling, an impulse like you should go somewhere or do something, but you don't and then nothing bad happens?"

Callie responds, "Yeah, that happens sometimes and I feel like I was about to encounter something bad, like an accident or a terrible situation, but then I didn't encounter anything bad. I always wondered what that feeling was trying to tell me though..."

My eyes light up, "Well, what about those times when you feel as if you should go somewhere, even though it doesn't make sense to, but then you actually do and something so absolutely amazing happens! Like, it is something you can barely believe that you stumbled into. Yeah, this happens a lot to me when I am feeling harmonious with my existence. I follow that same intuitive feeling to go somewhere, even if my head can't make sense of it and it almost always guides me to what feels like an answer that I have been seeking or an unbelievable situation I would have otherwise missed out on." She nods that she can understand that.

I then tell her, "Imagine if every time that you ignored that feeling, you miss something incredible. It could be something that could greatly impact your life forever. It could be the greatest thing you have never experienced before or the moment that you could meet someone to guide you on a journey you otherwise wouldn't have taken." Her eyes widen as she tells me a story of a moment with a celebrity that she almost missed, but she didn't miss and she's so happy to have that experience. I tell her "I have tried never to ignore this impulse. The impulse to engage in life is one of the most powerful things I have ever honored."

"You know; impulse isn't really the best word for what you are describing. You should call it a beckoning. Or like, the universe's summoning." I watch her as she speaks, hand casually slapping against the face of the notebook for dramatic expression. I can't help but to find her even more beautiful after every word. *Sigh...* "What is that?" She points toward my bag. I explain that they are a few more of my journals.

"Wait... you just carry your experiences around on your back like that? It's like carrying the weight of your life on your back." I try to explain that I carry one or two with me usually so I can pull them out and edit. Even as I say this to her I know the weight I am carrying of myself in my bag on my back is a massive life metaphor.

....

Journal Self- Conversation

*S*o as I write, what do I write about? Do I write about what I've done? What is it that I document- thoughts, research, events, and historical significance? So much is being experienced that I couldn't possibly document it all- visually, verbally, spiritually, educationally- through video recording, writing, poetry, photography and written conversations of golden moments representing incredible synchronicity- It's as if I can't both document and experience at the same time! And to experience it all as pure essence of being in the moment (which is essentially what I am trying to express) is impossible while thinking of remembering every detail. It's as if I either experience divinity and fully live in the moment and forget about documentation or I forget about really living it and I document it for later analysis. And how much truth do I share?*

Where do you cut the line on the truth?

That's the battle I am facing. I want to write a legacy of truth within traveling, but I am struggling with how to write this stuff. It is very challenging. I battled even as I was writing in these notebooks. I found myself having to edit some things out because of offending someone I met or because of exposing something about someone or myself. But then I realized that this is the unveiling of a time in the life of a young lesbian traveling the country. This started as truth and it must be consistent in truth. I cannot bear to expose gaps or falsities so I have decided to just reveal it all.

Fortunately, most of it is good. But to family and friends, you may not like to read some of the near death stories or crazy experiences that I have had that easily could have turned sour. Some of the days already could have switched in an instant, but I move through life on the good faith that keeping positivity consistently on my mind produces only the ability to dance in a

86

peaceful universe. Anyway, let's give a cheer to the truth because in the end, the truth is really what is of greatest value.

....

Today I hiked in the mountains of Hanging Rock, N.C. I climbed out to the edge at the beginning of the hike. I placed my hands upon the Earth to touch crumbly rock walls that were below the 200 ft. high overhanging pillars; I felt the surge of energy flow through me. There is such a churning of power in a space such as this. The weight of the Earth dangling over the gap of air and space I was standing in, not only has a force of pressure pushing down on it, but it has something else. Gravity is a formidable force, especially with millions of pounds of earth sitting above me now, but there is also another law to consider. The law of equal and opposites suggests that for every force there is an equal and opposite force.

Therefore, the pressure of gravity pulling down on these tons of rocks is matched by an opposite force, the force of stability in the structure reflecting gravity's pull. And within this tidal wave of surging force, tons above and tons below, I stand with my arms outstretched and a huge smile across my face. Life is too beautiful to only see it as surface level and when I really get to be alone in nature, I really tap into the metaphysical beauty of natural creation. From this perspective of science-based aesthetics, I can see millions of years of earth's evolution propel itself into my being, into my journey, into my life. I breathe in deeply many times and my body fills with the essence of the appreciated air. Everything inside of me releases into peace. As I hold my hand on that rock and feel its power and solidity, I float off into a vast world of gratitude for Mother Nature. It's as if my entire energetic being morphs into the power of the air and ground, feeling a great sense of understanding about balance. I feel a sense for the yin and yang, the sky and earth, the sun and moon. And its moments like this when I am so thankful to be alone because it's time for me to get weird.

I smile because I know this connectivity makes me a tree hugger and I laugh into the world around me because I know I look insane, but there is no judgement in nature for my pure happiness. Maybe I am insane, but it is moments of great joy in landscapes like this that just make me feel as if I were lighter than air, as if I were floating through space without anything holding me back. As I make my way up the cliffs and slanted rocks to the top of the mountain along the edge, I am reminded of the importance of maintaining a solid grounding while being in this physical form AKA a body. A large gust of wind can always trigger an unwanted perspective. Or maybe 'unwanted' is the improper description for what I mean. 'A necessary reminder' is a better way to describe it. It is treacherous to live with your head in the clouds without maintaining some form of grounding. One can easily *(in my case here)* literally slip into a dangerous situation, even a life-threatening position.

That gust catches me off guard and for a moment all of that joyous air is sucked from my being. I reach out and hold tightly to the flimsy tree rooted firmly into the rocks next to me, after getting my several-hundred-foot-drop-danger-selfie, when a strong gust grabs the mountain and all upon it. My breath gets stolen from me, just like that moment upon Seneca Rocks. I bend down on all fours and shakily return to sturdier rock. Surging excitement fills my body and I laugh nervously as I check to see if the picture came out. Yes, it's perfect! I look out across the tree-decorated valleys and my body trembles and quakes as a stupid grin grows across my face. It is that stupid grin which indicates I was just really close to making a colossal, stupid mistake. But I'm ok. My hands shake as I sit down, firmly connecting to solid rock to analyze where I actually am.

"So worth it." I smile huge into the sky. I suddenly feel as if I am scolded for that thought. I apologize to whatever just happened and thank it for not killing me for getting too 'high' off of nature. I laugh again because now I feel insane. I feel the cold rock beneath my palm. It's real. It's firm and true. I connect down into it and allow myself to be more present in the moment. *I am on a cliff and if I fall off I will die.* I laugh nervously at how easy it is to forget that sometimes. (*Things like this can and should be done way more intelligently and I don't suggest ever putting oneself in danger, especially for a picture. Yet once again, this is one of those lessons that took me over four years to really understand.*)

Small towns and coffee shops, good soups and crappy gas station breaks guide my day. I talk to some locals, two blond high school girls who rave about a cherry drink. She then with her sweet southern drawl, tells me about her ex-boyfriend's truck that is in music video called "Welcome to Welcome". I asked if Welcome was a city and they laughed because they thought it was funny that I didn't know I was in Welcome. I laughed because I had stopped here initially to figure out where I was, but when you are lost, you are always welcome in Welcome, N.C.

On day 9, I woke up on a brown couch. We drank a little whiskey last night. Granite cubes were used to keep the drinks cold without diluting the liquor. So I guess when you say I'll take my whiskey on the rocks, you are serious. After one painfully burning drink, I decide that I actually do like the ice though. But I drank it anyhow because it was pretty neat and I am fascinated with geology, rocks and crystals. The SofaCruiser (Ricky) who lived here said he would fix my computer today so he took it to work with him. He trusts me fully in his house and I trust him fully with my computer. It seems like a mutual exchange, but I am terrified deep down. I am very nervous because everything from my trip so far is on there and everything from Alana and I is on there as well. I don't have my stuff backed up anywhere *(Dumb)* and this is me having total faith in a stranger. I barely even know Ricky and I am trusting him with all of my memories and photo history. Why? I can't say other than they just feel like good humans and have many prior references to confirm that they mean well. References can go a long way in validating someone's integrity. Even stranger to me is the fact that I didn't know him and I trusted him and his roommate, two decent sized men that both seemed pretty strong and fit. I trusted them to not rape me or do harm to me in any way after meeting them and seeing that they were really sweet people. This was my first actual SofaCruisin experience with a man and due to accurate awareness and safe consideration combined with incredible trust, look what I got- A computer technician working on my computer for free, a beautiful house to stay in all day, all to myself to do yoga and stretch and do whatever it is I desire and access to the fridge and stove all day! How wonderful life works out sometimes when you have a little intelligent faith! He is copying all of my files to an external hard drive and then swiping my computer clean. He says he will remove all viruses and he is deleting Vista and installing Windows 7, which I am very excited about. I had French press coffee again- strong and stimulating. He also lives only a 25-minute walk to downtown Columbia N.C.

This morning I woke up with a whole bunch of gunk in my chest and I am pretty sure it was from smoking some of that hookah the night before and sleeping in that smoky house with those guys. I was just hacking out this junk. *Gross.* So I take my time relaxing and refreshing before taking off. *My body needs it.* I do some yoga which feels amazing after so many days of being in a vehicle or hiking. My body needed this so badly. As I breathe I realize that my soul needed to stretch too. Ricky has this really neat leg muscle massager, a foam cylinder approximately 2 ft. long with a diameter of 8 inches. He showed me how to use it the night before when I asked about it. So I laid on it and gently rolled until things inside my leg began hurting in a way that I didn't even know was possible. So much tension released and I felt as if the pain in my legs was connected up through my back and spine into my shoulders. Massaging all of those sore muscles gave me a full body refreshed feeling. *My travels in later years would guide me to study Qigong, yoga and anatomy that would teach me how accurate that observation really was. Everything is connected.*

If I was back in Erie, I would be driving meals on wheels right now. I keep trying to call for days, but no one picks up. And when I wanted to leave a voicemail it was full. I did call a little bit ago and could finally leave a voicemail, but now I feel very guilty and I am afraid to call back. I have good intentions, but I just cannot be there right now. I want to help, but my body is elsewhere. I hope they listened to my voicemail and found someone to fill in. In the meantime, guilt builds up inside of me. And maybe a little fear of confrontation as well. Fear comes in the face of many masks. Right now I am battling the fear of conversation with people. It is the same fear I have been battling my whole life though: This ridiculous fear of confrontation. I have become trapped within myself and I have been setting my own limitations. *Why? I do not know.* But I have identified this blemish for quite some time. I suppose that is one of the underlying reasons for this trip. When I am forced to use only myself, I have no one else to rely upon beside myself. So the fear either allows me to fail or I overcome it and it makes me stronger. I roll out all these thoughts into this little foam psychiatrist beneath my thighs, this foam cylinder body massager, bringing me such pain and such release.

So despite the wind chill, I venture out with my book bag. I fill my head with positive affirmations- *"Today I will go out on a fantastic walk all over Charlotte. It will be sunny and warm and I will have so many people to talk to. People will give me money for my journey. Actually, I will make back the entire cost of my tire today. $50.50. And I will make money for lunch and I will make an extra 30 for gas. I will advertise my magic and YouTube show and I will amaze and inspire people. I will be a beacon of light, a breath of fresh air! I will be open-minded and I will be creative with my surroundings. I will meet amazing people with amazing stories for my show. I will get some great footage for my show."* And on and on I spoke to myself. Every time I do positive affirmations as I walk, it puts me into a meditative trance and suddenly a great insight will pop up that could change my perspective on everything about my whole life.

I find a sunny spot and pull out my notebook to begin reading old passages, searching for some gold from the past. Affirmation, poem, story, Law of Attraction story, poem, song, magic show schedule, business model, poem… and I began to feel brilliant. I began to feel unstoppable. In that notebook, I found gold and it was just the feeling of worthiness. I was walking around the city and decided not to look at the map, but just kind of go out and search for things. An urge rose to find another quiet place with a block from the wind to sit alone to write in the sunshine. So I had the city within my eyesight to the left and I looked to my right and saw a small park. All the grass was crispy and yellow, to me, representing fluorescent death, but then I looked over and saw this giant sphere mirror sculpture. I immediately ran over to it. How could I possibly ignore something so bizarrely beautiful reflecting its 360 degree surroundings? I then felt myself drifting from normalcy as I sat on a bench and realized that it was so windy and cold that I couldn't stand it. In the reflection of that sphere, I felt perfect and normal in my blurred appearance, but in normal light on a normal bench right now, I just felt wrong. *All I wanted was to find the warmth! This whole trip, oh, that is all I want!*

So, I walked around a bit more and found this odd staircase that went up about 10 steps then had a large platform connected to another staircase to the right. I found a home in this corner space for a while. It protected me completely from the wind chill so that I could sit in the sunshine in a t-shirt *Yes! Thank God!* And enjoy the crisp, sunny air. There was a rock circle in the floor in a very interesting pattern. I wondered what it was for and I was sure it held some other meaning besides just being a random circle in the cement. I decided it was, in fact, just a random circle decoration. I used to consider embellishments just wasteful- jewelry, buildings, landscaping- I am not even sure where such a hideous perspective came from, but I have been growing a great appreciation for aesthetics and that little extra. What is more important in life than to enjoy it for all the beauty that life is? I look up to observe where I was in this world because in the background I could see the Charlotte skyline shimmering. It shone beautiful from this circular floor station I have been occupying. People would run by me. They walk by me. Some were riding bikes and others were casually walking their dogs. Most had fitness in mind and all looked at me as if I were crazy or something, sitting here in a t-shirt, eyes closed and not on a standard sitting protocol bench. *Such a bizarre world we have evolved into…* it is more expected to sit upon something manmade while frowning than to sit upon the earth with legs crossed and a big smile across my face.

At this point, I started to not care about being different. I had become fond of the word traveler. I even began to grow a fondness for the term 'professionally homeless' too. I mean, I was kicked out of my home and left all my belongings, so it's theoretically true. I see a brown clothed, tattered man with a bulky bag trudging in the distance. I am technically homeless, but as I watch him move through the day, I know that I am different kind. I am a truth seeker willing to sacrifice all earthly possessions to fulfill my deepest desire of enlightenment.

He lights up something in a corner where he thinks no one can see him. I watch as his body trembles and he spits. I know that there is a mountain of variance between that type of homeless and whatever it is that I am doing. Everything is intention.

My intention is to learn, to understand homelessness- not to become lost. I watch him scream something into the sky as he spits again, followed by a snort or gargled burp.

I hope that I remember to remember the difference…

Chapter Sixteen

Day 11 to Charleston S.C

"Nature is my chapel. Mother Earth is my connectivity to the divine."

L ife began to speed up after this day. The next day I drove through Columbia, but did not stop. I drove a bunch of streets to get a good look at it. The city has a lot of sculptures and art work and it looks like it could be a lot of fun or at least worth a stop in the future, but everyone I meet keeps telling me to go to Charleston. *'Don't stop until you hit Charleston".* I have a Sofa Cruisin' request from a guy who invited me to a campfire in Charleston with a bunch of other much more seasoned SofaCruisers. I cannot wait to have an outing with them! But I was also very intimidated since this was my first trip. This was my first official traveler group meeting and I was shaking in excitement as I pulled up to the address and parked on the side of the yard.

It was quiet as I approached the house. I knock on the door and a short guy wearing glasses answers. He doesn't seem too happy to see me, not like I expected anyhow. He is the roommate of Joey, the SofaCruisin host I am meeting and I'm the first to arrive and he looks at my bags and raises an eyebrow hesitantly, stating he didn't know anyone else was spending the night since the room was already full. I explain my situation and he says its fine, but they already had a German couple staying in the spare room. I don't care; I'd be more than grateful for a warm floor after some good company. I ask what they need and he said people will be bringing snacks, so there will most likely be plenty to share, but if I want to drink anything, then I would have to go out and grab some. Ten minutes and a six-pack later, I return and start to meet the voyagers. This night erupted into so much education, so much fun. I met a couple who was building their own tiny home on wheels so that they never have to pay property taxes for the rest of their lives. They explained it all to me and it was the first time I had ever heard of any of it. I met musicians and all sorts of interesting people that have been all over the world. I listened with wide eyes and an enthusiastic mind; I wanted to hear it all! As I listened to them and asked questions, they just shook off their experiences as something that has just happened. I couldn't believe it! They were at peace with whatever life had been. I was practically shaking every single moment that anyone mentioned the word 'travel'! One day I would have travel behind me and I would be able to be at peace with what I have done and where I have been, but now there was so much to see in this world and I had experienced hardly any of it. Living is easy with eyes closed, but when they start to open it is so hard to not want to see it all. Then Joey mentions that he is the ambassador of SofaCruisin in Charleston, South Carolina. I burst out laughing at this, but he expresses he has over 300 SofaCruisin references. *Wow. And I thought I was being extreme…*

There were two people in particular who held a block of intense memory this night- a man we shall refer to as Dancer and a gal we can call Symphony. Around the fire, Dancer became intrigued by my current life situation and was asking questions about why and how I was where I was mentally. He was interested in the fact that I was doing this alone at 22 as a woman. I explained that it might sound crazy, but I think that I willed my dream to happen, even though my life wasn't going in that direction. His eyebrows rise robustly as his questions intensify. I tell him about the Law of Attraction and he excitedly erupts, claiming that he always knows someone who is on the path! He started throwing out this lingo and these reference stories to things that I couldn't understand. Law of Attraction and abundance mindset ways of thinking aren't a language I am fluent in yet, although I really do intend to be soon.

He expresses a great deal of excitement when I pull out my *Contemplate and Welcome Prosperity* edition and tells me that this is the book that changed his life. *How many people across this country must tell me that before I grasp the true power of the unlimited imagination?* He suggested that this book gave him everything he wanted and now he is a professional ballroom dance instructor and is making all the right connections to get to where he wants to go next in life. It's so nice to talk to people with true ambition. It is quite the contrast from nearly everyone I have known my whole life. Then he tells about a book that he just finished from Leopold Mountain called 'Outsmarting Your Demons'. He explains how it's connected him to all kinds of amazing things and he insists that I just must find it and check it out. So I set my intentions to run into this book soon. *Let's see how long this takes…*

The next person to make a dramatic impact upon me was Symphony. Symphony is very beautiful and has a great personality. She wants to go to the car with me to smoke some weed and although I'd like to kiss her more than I'd like to smoke, I accept knowing that my chances are much greater if I do. She has been very touchy and flirty with me and I cannot tell if it is actually flirty of just her accepting me as another girl, a comrade of travel in a world of male explorers. But whatever it is, she wants me to go to the car and I'd be a fool to not figure out what her intentions are. We return from the car all giggly and happy, exchange numbers after she offers her couch to me whenever I need it and I hear everyone retiring for the night.

The group tells me that they are doing a marathon in the morning where they throw colors all over people as they run. My head nearly exploded. I had never heard of such a thing before. But I was also slightly high from one hit and as they talked about it, I visualized a rainbow world erupting over thousands of cheering, healthy people. I knew I had to go. I had to be a part of this. This is undoubtedly the reason I had to get to Charleston and not stop. This opportunity to be a part of something with a group is why I had to be here today, not tomorrow. If I had stopped in Charlotte today, tomorrow would have been too late for any of this. I followed the intuition to just go and now this incredible opportunity has come forth from the shadows of destination-less destination. They tell me that the wake up time to go is in five hours.

I am slightly drunk and stoned.

Bring it on, rainbow existence.

Chapter Seventeen

Day 12 - Charleston

"Experience will unravel the scrolls of the universe's wisdom. Appropriately lived experience will teach you how to read them."

C allie asks me. "What are you going to call your book?" I think for a moment.

"I really am not sure. I have been writing so much down, but I haven't had that title quite stick for me yet. I was thinking *Travel Truths* or *Open Road Soul Seeker*. Maybe *Traveling by Deck*."

"Traveling by Deck?" She asks curiously.

"Well, yeah, like a deck of cards because I made money doing that along the way. But it's not really the purpose of the book being written though. So I feel it won't do the book justice because the journey wasn't based solely upon my being a magician."

I watch her eyes perk up and know what happens after this. She follows suit with my expectation, asking me if I am a magician. I confirm and am instantly asked to do a trick. I agree to, but this is that type thing that people always warn you about. When you turn your passion into just a job, it stops being as much fun.

Her eyes flood with amazement, which is always amusing for me because I love that I give people this reaction, but my unenthusiastic response confirms that the book will 100% not be called anything dealing with magic.

"You are good with your hands…" Callie exclaims as she asks me to do another magic trick. "I like that. Hmm… you can probably do a lot of really awesome things with your hands." This proves again, true, of my theory that magic tricks are great pick-up lines.

....

We wake up bright and early. I actually woke up naturally a bit earlier than everyone else and my body was so tired that I just laid there like a lump of potatoes under the covers. His couch was so fluffy and I was wrapped up like a burrito. *A potato burrito.* I realized I was hungry. I am not sure when it happened, but somewhere after I turned 21 I acquired a delightful taste for waking up and not knowing where I am. I really do love getting up and stretching, looking around the room and analyzing where I am and then recapping the previous day's events. I pulled out my tablet and started wasting my time playing a game of solitaire, which I have never done before. I then made my way out to the kitchen and attempted to get a glass of water without disrupting anyone. Sometimes when I wake up early before anyone else, especially not in my own home, I feel as though I am a belligerent rooster destroying their sleepy time with my sunrise outbursts, crows of the wild animal resting gently within its caged fence, saluting the sun. I bang glasses by accident often. Every placement of a ceramic cup upon anything sounds like a fire alarm going off in the wee hours of the morning. So I chug my water and head back to the couch. I play about two minutes of the game and then I fall asleep again to be woken up by movement around me. It is 7:30 am and Joey is running around the house. I immediately get up and fold the blankets. Joey unloads his collection of Color Dash gear which consists of long rainbow socks, glasses, t shirts and bracelets, the perfect outfit for a vibrant, energetic rooster... I am jealous. When his friend arrives, they put everything on as I wash my face and layer up my non-vibrant clothes since its pretty chilly outside. Fortunately, this day would be so filled with color that it doesn't matter what I wear. He tops his wardrobe off with a thin, black jacket. His other friend arrives with camera ready and we take off toward the location of our destination.

On the drive there, we share stories of our travels and what we do in our normal life settings. It is misty and murky, but we are all ready to take on the day. *I cannot believe how excited I am for this!* I cannot imagine how many remarkable things are going to come from the experience of the day! *'Wait 'til you see Charleston' was true!* I have made connections that will further grow this experience as well. And just about 12 hours after I get into town to meet these people, I now will share a life changing event with them. I don't even know what to expect because I have never even been to a marathon before. This is my first one and I never would have guessed the incredible things that I was about to witness.

The traffic comes to a stop on the highway in an extremely dangerous manner. We are lucky enough to be stopped right after we pull onto the extra space next to the exit ramp and the cars just begin lining up. Tires are squealing and screeching and I get very nervous. *"Katie, calm thyself."* I try not to pay attention to what is going on, but we begin to check out all the cars around us. It appears that everyone is going to the Color Dash and the line for this exit flows down the highway, shutting off the outermost lane as far as the eye can see. Up ahead consists of a very busy cross road that has the right of way so the traffic coming off the ramp has not much opportunity to move. Hopefully this doesn't result in a massive color car pile-up. The amount of people arriving for this color run must have been way more than they expected to come out to this event. We sit for close to a half hour then look at the clock and realize that the run has begun. My smile diminishes. I really couldn't wait to see all the cheerful, healthy people unite at the starting line and take off together to run the 5k.

They explain the concept of a marathon. "They actually send them off in waves. There is a wave that goes every five minutes." *Waves. Hmm.* That is a very clever and interesting way to describe a collection of running people. We park. It takes so long and we start to see people running by our cars. Everyone is honking and smiling and yelling at each other. Women in funny costumes and men in bikinis and dresses. *Such great energy! Yes!* Joey takes off his jacket and I offer to hold it for him until he is finished with the race.

The experience I had at the event was unlike anything I ever could have expected my first marathon to be. Since I didn't have a registration number (which I was ok with because it would have cost me $40 to be part of), me and Cameraman ran beside everyone taking pictures the whole time just outside the fencing. We were cutting across fields and areas to get ahead so we could watch guns shoot out bursts of fluorescent paint clouds over the participants. Hundreds of volunteers were equipped with backpack squirt guns loaded with paint and boxes full of paint powder that was thrown at contestants as they ran by cheering and laughing. Everything everywhere was a vibrant world of rainbow and I don't think a smile left my face once that whole time.

The amount of love and happiness, children with their parents, friends pushing their handicapped friends, everyone dressed in now painted costumes, was the most liberating, free thing I have ever experienced in my whole life up to this point. Life is so very beautiful and had I not taken everyone's suggestion to not stop until Charleston, I would have missed out on all of this. At the finish line, everybody screams and laughs as a giant surge of color shoots 50 ft. into the air. Then Joey asked me for his jacket and I looked at my hands containing only a camera and said, "uh oh…"

I stayed another night at Joey's house after we watched a movie in theatres with some friends since it was raining. I went to pay for the ticket and they told me it was already paid for. I look around confused and Joey smiles and tells me not to worry about it. I laugh, hug him and say thank you as I consider the loss of the black jacket to have been forgiven. I would have taken this to be a form of him hitting on me if it hadn't been for the fact that he has a fiancé. They then take me to *The Relaxed Shroom, a place that will change my idea of pizza forever. This funky stop was loaded with happy hippies and those of the free spirited mindset. There were many organic eateries in this city and people really cared about what they put into their bodies. Nearly every eatery had fresh chopped vegetables, a concept I wasn't very familiar with in average restaurants in my life.

Wow! And this was just the first day in this city! I fell asleep stuffed, in that potato burrito bed excited to see what the next morning had to offer.

Chapter Eighteen

Day 13 - Charleston N.C

"Positive action almost always spawns from positive vision."

I woke up early and parked by the riverfront downtown. The historical buildings in this city would take years to fully appreciate in their entirety. Everyone told me that the thing to see in Charleston is the market. To my uncultured mind, this seemed to be a strange thing to be told as a must do. So I go out and find a free parking space, which I have decided may be the biggest waste of time in my entire trip. I spend so much time driving in circles looking for that Goldilocks space- just close enough, not expensive- just right.

The wind was blowing incessantly in my face and eyes, making them water and ferociously search for a coffee. As I near the market, I see the city flooded with tourists, all sporting their newest travel gear and destination titled shirts/ hats. The market, originally established in 1807, is its own brick block in the center of the city, a tiny fortress of creative stands and foods all lining the compact space on the inside. I walk through slowly, for slow is the only speed in a crowd of this manner, especially on a chilly morning such as this. The paintings glisten with historical representations of the city, many of which I am soon to experience such as Rainbow Row or the historical sea wall on the far south side where mansions meet the majestic ocean just several feet from one another.

I wanted only to find a coffee. That is all.

Oh, coffee, where art thou? I was in circles past beautiful shops full of old fashioned architecture. This city is absolutely phenomenal; unlike any other city I've ever been to. There isn't a single building any higher than three or four stories. They have managed to keep this place a quaint little gem away from all the infusion of corporation takeover. It really is beautiful.

But there was not a single place in this whole area that sold a charming little cup 'a joe! And that is all I wanted! It shouldn't be a rather strange request, for a traveler to just accidentally stumble upon a cup of coffee in a strange city full of tourists, but apparently it was. I finally saw one person carrying coffee with them and asked where they got it, stars in my eyes and hope in my heart.

"Our daughter went and got us coffee and donuts. I don't know where she found it." So, my journey continues onward for close to 20 minutes asking everyone who looked like they may be able to help me, but I was met mostly with unsure glances around and uncertain maybe here's.

Then finally, off the opposing side of the market sat a great little Indian coffee shop. It was very cute, walls decorated in deep reds, oranges and golds. I get in line, which was just me at the tiny white counter space as I observed my surroundings while waiting for the barista to come over. There were 8 little tables about 2x2ft, each seating 2-4 people all crammed close to each other. I wedged myself in the back corner where there was foot wide handsome granite counter that ran the length of the wall. There were a few benches smashed in the corner and stuff lined up along the counter indicating that it isn't the usual place people sit. But considering how small the place was, how rare coffee shops were in this town and how much I really wanted to read, I made myself a tiny space and went up to get my coffee. Just $2.09 for a large! *Well, sweet deal that is the cheapest coffee shop coffee I've had yet!*

The lady hands me my coffee and I grab it and there is nothing in it. She turns around. I look around as if there is something I was supposed to understand, but I see nothing around me. I rescan my surroundings, again looking for something that I missed, but do not see anything representing self-serve coffee. *Possibly she has something on her mind and just forgot to put the coffee in my cup before she gave it to me.* "Um... Excuse me. There is no coffee in here." I hold my cup up and politely smile as I asked.

"You get yourself!" She points on the far-left side of the counter beyond the breakfast desserts spot that was completely blocking any view of it. *Even inside of a coffee shop, the coffee is still nearly impossible to find in Charleston!* I felt dumb and sat down, finally feeling the well-deserved heat roar through my body. I pull out *Contemplate and Welcome Prosperity* and attempt to open the book on my current page, but instead its flops open onto a page about persistence. I read a quote of his, "Patience, determination and inspiration make a supreme combo for achievement." I look at my coffee and think about how true that sentence really is. There is nothing too big or in this case, too small that you cannot accomplish in life with true persistence.

I texted Alana today. It is the first time we communicated in about five days. She's doing well and sold another dog yesterday and started her job at The Sales Corporation. This morning she was there at 5:30 am and she said this whole multi jobs thing is becoming difficult, but she's going to continue. I think about persistence and sip my victorious coffee feeling proud of her. I ask her how her body's been and she said that she's been feeling a little sick, but she's been keeping active. *I still love her...*

A very nice Asian guy from the SofaCruisin gathering meets me downtown at night and walks me through all the districts. He knew so much about the whole place, all the streets, all the businesses and places of historical relevance. We laughed and talked for three hours as we walked around in the cold. He is a type of SofaCruiser that doesn't have a place to offer, but loves to meet up with travelers and share his city with them. That was just what I needed, because Symphony offered me her couch for the next few nights.

After I left the library with Symphony, where she was working on homework, we went to her friend's house and a bunch of her stoner friends were there. *Surprise, surprise.* It was super frigid so we are talking about anything just to keep ourselves from shaking. She mentions about how warm it was last week and I showed up as a cold front came through. *Yes. I know this. Every place I have stopped so far has told me that last week was great weather.* I tell her about the text I just received from a friend in Pennsylvania who reached out about something great that happened and I explain how it relates to my life and everything going on. I say about how I am applying the Law of Attraction into my life and am searching for the most scientific explanations for its existence.

"When you exert a force of sound, it is a vibration that we pick up as a verbal representation of thought meant to be transferred from one person to the next, but we really just release vibration. When a vibration is strong enough, which really doesn't take much, water can ripple. So you can physically see the water move from just a frequency! Now since our bodies are around 80% water, then of course our sounds will influence our bodies. Everything is vibration. Thought, light, sound, movement, heat, everything is vibration. I have been studying the incredibly high frequency of thought and how we can actively alter our surroundings using our minds. It's all about harnessing the power of vibration."

"Wow that is really cool. I like how you elaborate on your philosophies with believable science." She told me, her eyes shining at what I said.

Believable science... It took a while to understand what she meant by that, but after seeing her stoner friends, I remembered when I used to sit around with other pot smokers and create all sorts of fantasy possibilities that were all entirely possible, but we just kind of made up theory. Something about the way she said believable science really made me understand how far I have come mentally since high school. And lately I continually talk about personal strengthening philosophy and often I get caught up in a spiral of ideology and I forget that I have the attention of the other person. I just instantly really appreciate having the conversation appreciated. I guess I really never had that before, but I really want more of it.

Desire and believe; acquire and achieve!

They have dirt, filthy chips and sauce plates scattered around their apartment and so much more junk. There's three chairs, a television, one dirty couch with a blanket thrown on top of it, a coffee table and three skateboards, a bike, boxes and more dirt all lying about the room. I grab a seat on the edge of a chair and Symphony sits next to her friends and they all pack a bong, actually pack one of the many smoking devices laying all over the room. I just sit and observe their dirty little world and snap back into a life not long ago when I too lived this same way. I had no idea how disgusting my life had become. And I don't look at them with disgust; I look at them with interest. I was brought here to see, to learn and really understand how far I have already come in my life's journey. It's like my own version of Charles Dickens, A Christmas Carol where Ebenezer Katie is taken back in in time by the ghost of drunken past, to re-experience a world from a different angle. I appreciate my surroundings and relax. I listen to them talk and laugh. My observation moves from them to the objects on the table.

My heart nearly stops when I read the title of the book right in front of me. I even let out a way too excited "Oh my god" as I grab the small black book and place it upon my hands like I am displaying the little baby Jesus before God. "Symphony, this is it…" she looks at me confused.

"Yo, be careful with that! Let me see it quick." The kid grabs it and I am instantly shocked by how much he cares about the wellbeing of such a sacred book to me at this moment. "We were crushing up drugs on this! Ah, never mind I don't think there's any there. You are good." He hands it back and I look at it astonished as he goes back to grinding up herbs. To him, the gold was on the cover. I laugh so ridiculously hard at how they don't even realize the gold between the covers.

I whisper, "Symphony, this is Leopold Mountain's next book, the same book Dancer told me to read at the campfire – *Outsmarting Your Demons*… I can't believe it." She looks at me wide eyed and screams as she grabs it.

"Whose book is this?" I ask as the attention of stoners is not evident at all. I ask again and they all look at each other with dull, careless eyes.

No one knew. No one even knew why it was there or where it came from...

This is one of those times that I should have just followed my gut and asked if I could keep it, but I didn't get the best vibes from these kids and I felt like because I didn't smoke their weed, they didn't trust me. So I flipped through it reading a couple sections here and there before Symphony and I again ventured off into the world. There is so much more to see and do in a world than remain faded in trash. She looks over to me and expresses again how incredible it was to find that book there.

She says, "Seriously, though. What are the chances?"

I am beginning to think that the chances are pretty amazing when I let them be. The next day would prove this statement to be deliciously, flamboyantly correct.

Chapter Nineteen

Day 13 Charleston

"Often the shift of awareness, from a traumatic ending to the start of a fresh beginning, is everything."

I wake up and grab my books out of the bag. I was secretly hoping that I might wake up in a bed rather than on Symphony's couch, but whatever. I'm not about that straight girl life anymore anyway. Straight girls used to be fun to try to catch, like a fun game, but I definitely am not in the mood to get involved with anyone at all. It's fun to entertain the idea of waking in her bed, but a teasing idea is where that idea lives best. It's really nice to have a beautiful female companion right now and its very stress free having that be all it is. But honestly, if I woke up in her bed, I certainly wouldn't have been upset. Instead, I climb off that couch and prepare my bag for the day with warm clothing, my book and my notebook.

The house she lives in is an enormous colonial house. Just about every house in Charleston, South Carolina is historic and colonial so it really does make sense for the second floor apartments to be that way too. She and three other girls share the apartment and Symphony doesn't really talk to them very much. But as I am getting ready in the morning, her one roommate comes down and goes into the kitchen to get something to eat before class. This is that awkward traveler moment where you are in someone's home that may or may not know that you are there. I play it safe and make the first greeting.

"Hello, I am Katie." She looks at me surprised, then says hello. We talk about her life in Charleston and why I am here. I explain the site and she mentions how she would only expect creeps to be on the site and then I say "Well, what do you think I am?" which makes her giggle. "Thank you guys so much for letting me stay here by the way.

"Well you are welcome to stay here as long as you like, sweetheart." I am not trying to be overbearing by any means to anybody so I thank her and say how I will only be here one more night. On the enormous second story porch, I find a perfect wall to lean against where the sunlight hits me but blocks the battling wind. My body heats up a tiny bit as I write and read. Eventually Symphony wakes up and I see her crazy brown hair taking a hit from the bong. Joey texted me asking if I wanted to go to yoga with a SofaCruisin group tonight at 6. *Of course, I do!* Then Symphony told me we should go to an amazing park after her class today around 3:30. It wouldn't take long so I'd have plenty of time to get back in time for yoga. And the divine timing of life works again my favor! What are the chances?

I decide to head downtown to explore White Point Garden then walk from Oyster Point up East Battery Street, one of the most picturesque streets in the entire country. The perfectly detailed and preserved multimillion dollar mansions sat on my left and the ocean sat just a few feet below to my right along the sea wall. It is phenomenal to see the edge of civilization right beside the ocean. I walk around town and find another coffee shop to sit in when I get cold before heading out to Waterfront Park where I meet a girl who is in town performing with Cirque du Solei. I never actually met someone before like this, really living the life of their dreams and it is so fascinating to realize that this life is a real possibility. I say my farewells and continue exploring every place I can possibly find. I am drawn to this one particular building with columns. I stare at it for a moment until I realize I was staring as if almost in a trance. *Don't be weird, Katie.* I stop next at the very interesting looking bar/restaurant named *Chappychuchu where the hostess harasses me to look at the menu. Being cheap, I look, but decline to go inside, casually saying about how when I am hungry later I might come back to try it out because it looks good. In my head, I am laughing because I know that I will not go back to a nice bar like that. It's probably going to be another peanut butter and jelly day. *Yet, something about that place really struck me as a place I felt I needed to go inside... hmm...*

After her class, her two friends picked me up and we ended up going to Angel Oak Tree before she has to go to class. I was told it is a giant oak tree. Wrong. Not only is it just a giant tree, but respectably the largest oak tree in the country! *Mmm.. Delicious.* On the way there the GPS kept glitching. This was not good because the park closes at five. Exceptional trees line the path, flicking lights and shadows the whole way there. The entire drive is a very beautiful one, but when we first pulled up to the Angel Oak, I could not believe my eyes.

The unbelievably huge octopus-esque limbs stretched out 89ft wide and they stretch an impressive 65 ft. high. This tree is no joke. It is believed to be over 1,500 years old and is just remarkable to see. The best part is that to enjoy this massive, majestic life form you don't even need to pay a fee. They have a store and a donation box, but the park itself is free.

I just stared and walked all over the park, trying to understand this beautiful creature, but it just was so big. This tree has met so many people, so many celebrities and influential figures throughout history. This living thing was touched by so many people who have changed our world forever. It survived all the potential threats and dangers and is alive before me right now with 1,500 years of stories to share with me. Some of its limbs reach out 30 ft. and sink into the ground then come back out like a snake the width of a trashcan. I watched one of Symphony's friends run up to it, hug and not even get 1/10th of the way around the tree's trunk.

I walked to the shop, but must have arrived a few moments too late because it was closed. I wanted to buy something to support the tree. The glass feels cold against my forehead as I look in the window only to lock eyes with an angry woman glaring at me nodding her head. I spy the clock on the wall and it says 4:50. *What! She's mad at me because she closed the shop early! Jerk.* Oh well.

By the time we leave and they drop me off at my car, I am running about 20 minutes late for yoga. I am supposed to be across town now to be 20 minutes early to talk with everyone, but I have about a 20-minute drive. After calling Joey and having him say that there is no rush to get to the yoga class, I really don't feel any relief driving though this city in slow bumper to bumper traffic. Then the traffic comes to a halt and I look over and see two guys walking next to one another down the street. The heavyset balding man is pushing a baby stroller and I consider how sweet it is for men to hang out in a beautiful town like this together. I smile, thinking of how different friendships are and can vary in this world depending on cultural acceptance and familiarity. In my area of Pennsylvania, I don't think I have ever seen a dad walking with his baby downtown, just enjoying their stroll with another friend. Women do that all the time, but not necessarily men. Then I notice the baby has a tiny flag in its hands, waving it very rapidly and giggling. It's almost as if it just told a funny infant joke. Then I realize it isn't a joke. *Wait, is that a rainbow flag?*

That's when the world around me opens up and I see others holding flags and as I continue forward, wondering if there was a gay pride, but realizing that it is a Monday and there is no reason for there to be a gay pride celebration on a Monday. I go further up the road and I hear music, a live band with huge speakers! There must be something happening! Then off to the right I see the United States Custom House, a building very closely resembling the entrance to the white house with its enormous white pillars and multi leveled stair entrance- the exact same building that I was so drawn to earlier that day! This building is a solid representation of power and success just by itself, but today, right now at this very moment, it was the base of a civil rights movement, a gay rights rally taking place right next to me!

At the stop light I see a flock of older people jumping around and holding signs. This isn't the first time I have encountered these folks, the religious protesters sent forth to convert the "evil" gays to Christianity, to save us and make us follow in the steps of The Bible. The greys hop up and down waving signs at the cars and yelling all sorts of things that I couldn't even make out. I strain not to make eye contact with them since my faggin' wagon' is currently representing rainbow stickers on both the front and back. Also, I look like a little dyke myself and was trying not to cause a scene while driving by a bunch of bible thumpers. That's when I actually do look over and catch a glimpse of what their signs really did say- "Equal Means Everyone", "Love is Love" but the one that really caught my attention was the hand drawn rainbow sign "Marriage Equality". They weren't protesters at all; they were a group older people, mostly senior citizens vibrantly cheering for their rights. *Wait, my correction- Our rights.* This struck me so hard and I almost cried and immediately was determined to find a place to park. My eyes lit up, life empowerment exploding through my body as I saw hundreds gathered in front of the checkered marble floor in front of The Custom House, stretching up and across the steps, all holding rainbow flags and hand painted signs. There is no time to delay. I must park and get there ASAP!

I speed walk, wind slapping every portion of my body. I began feeling the strain in the front of my shins tighten, the thrill of the gay running through my veins. I ask what the occasion is for the rally and am told that the Proposition 8 case, an anti- anti-gay marriage ruling, was being heard today and the Defense of Marriage Act (DOMA), which allows states to refuse same-sex marriage, was being addressed in court tomorrow. Two enormous gay cases in two days is a great reason to rally to raise awareness! So I joined in, talking to everyone I could, gathering all the information that I could about anything. I listened to the speakers dramatically gain support from the crowd before them. I watched the American flag homo-edition flap tenderly in the winds, proudly displaying its rainbow stripes instead of the traditional red and white. I stood there and soaked up every bit of that moment. Yet again, one of those intense life moments where I cannot believe where I am. What are the chances that I would be going by right as it begins?

"So, you don't live in South Carolina? That's fine. Thanks for supporting anyhow. Why are you here?" asked an adorable gay man and his partner after I declined my ability to sign a petition because I wasn't from the area.
"I was just driving by and saw the rally!"

"You just drove by? You didn't plan to come to this?"

"No, I seriously was on my way to yoga and saw this instead."

"Oh my god, honey! What are the chances?" And this continued on the whole day.

"Oh, Katie it's nice to meet you. I see you got the memo to wear red."

I look around and notice that everyone is actually wearing bright red, including me. "No I didn't know that we were supposed to wear red. Ha-ha. This is the only red shirt I have in my car."

"Hey, that's amazing! What are the chances?" Sometimes I don't realize how interconnected and strange life can be until I catch someone else saying this, which they say to me increasingly frequently. I mean, I say it all the time, but when others say it to me, I really wake up and pay attention. Sometimes there is just a day or two in life that just seems enchanted; the synchronicity aligns in so many ways that if you were to plan a day like this with so many overlapping relations, you simply couldn't do it. There are just too many amazing interwoven connections to ever even consider planning, but when you really let life lead you where you need to go and you listen to your universe, it really does present wonderful opportunities that otherwise would have been missed. This was one of those days.

Actually, I never used to have days of divine synchronicity. There used to be beautiful moments here and there or a string of funny situations, but ever since I began studying and applying the Law of Attraction to my life, I really have seen engagement of incredible occurrences happen to me. Honestly, the chance of me driving past a gay rights rally in Charleston, South Carolina at the exact moment that it began is pretty phenomenal. I cannot stop smiling. The tingles of excitement flow through me. It amazes me how beautiful the world really is and is becoming more so every day. Today is day 14- *Two weeks...* Wow! It's been two weeks of freedom and personal liberation. Right now there is the music playing that sounds like my soul smiling and grabbing me, hugging me for giving it a chance to finally come alive.

It fills me with such a pure bliss as the energy of the world flows through me and it seems that when I feel like this, others can see it too. The two I was with last night told me things I have been telling myself consistently since I discovered there was a higher form of personality that exists to attract my dreams and desires- "they told me be powerful, be magnetic and be strong. They said that I was incredibly attractive and on a much deeper level than just externally. That is much more than just a compliment because it proves that I am growing stronger and also growing to be in tune with my world. The universe and I are becoming unified it seems and we are becoming one. The best part is that it is not just myself saying it. It is becoming a truth, a fact, a tangible concept that others can see and feel. It is no longer just words in my heart that I say, write, think and repeat. No, this is something that is attracting people to tell me that they see it within me, radiating from my pure essence. This is my evolution to the next step to success.

And this is a huge deal! After the rally, everyone filters out pretty quickly because it is cold. The television reporters ask us to stand in the background for television. I am more than thrilled to do this! After that, I go back and continue talking to people when I find out that there is a gay after party at the bar right around the corner.

"Yeah, it's just right over there. Oh I hope you go! I would love to hear some stories that you have!" said a group of very sweet gay men when I asked where to go. "It is right down that street by the water then on the left hand side. You really can't miss it." And I really couldn't miss it. I walk up to it and laugh hard as I approach *Chappychuchu, the only business in this whole town that grabbed my attention earlier today. I seize the doors knowing that I am where I am supposed to be right now and I enter into a very respectable gay atmosphere, not the usual gay after party I am accustomed to being invited to. I like this. It's not sloppy drunk dancing gay- this is a professional gay. And it isn't a gay bar either. It is just a nice atmosphere normal bar and tonight was what the older men told me is 'a gay takeover'. And I was a part of it.

Sort of. I look around and everyone knows at least one other person here to which they are deeply engaged in loud discussion. I am generally good at communication in public spaces, but this threw me off a little. I walk through the bar and realize that I don't recognize a single face or person from the rally. This is just fine. I just look around and observe the immense amount of happiness filling this room. Everyone is smiling and laughing, happy and chatting about great things in their lives or serious situations with a positive outlook. I just find a tiny chunk of the bar and slide in, absorbing all the goodness around me. This smile doesn't leave my face for a second.

Over the course of the night I end up meeting more gay men than I have ever talked to before in my life. There were a lot of lesbians there too. In fact, there was one young group sitting and watching me for a while as I danced with the gay boys, but I had absolutely no interest in meeting them or talking to them. I missed Alana and didn't even want to put myself in a situation where I could accidently get involved with someone. I met a very nice gay couple who lived on their boat for the last 15 years. They lived everywhere! I had never heard of such a thing before, but they acted like it wasn't a big deal, but to me it really opened up my eyes.

The limited mind structure I had been shown really never allowed me to see that there was no set way to live life. There wasn't a job you had to do to survive. There wasn't a house falling apart, smashed full of stuff you don't care about. Life didn't have to be stressful, wanting more and more until you die most likely full of debt from a heart attack. Life can be simple and these random gay men that I met were the first people in my life that let me understand that life really can be whatever it is that you want it to be. This is a huge lesson for anyone who wants more in life than what they were born knowing. Life is limitless.

I meet one woman who fascinated by the concept of SofaCruisin. She gets her friends to come over and hear my stories and they laugh and ask questions and really think I am fascinating. She buys me dinner and a few drinks and just continually compliments me, not in a creepy way, but in an absolutely supportive way. She really cared about me and in the time we talked she seemed to shine in a way that I think she hasn't felt in a very long time. And that is the feeling I want to give people everywhere I go. I want to be an escape from the clutches of normalcy. I want to inspire those around me to see life as beautifully inspirational in every moment.

This one gay boy keeps looking me up and down, almost in a judgmental way and I keep catching him watching me. *Oh my god... what is he thinking? He's totally judging my traveler style right now.* "Hey, how's it going, man?" I say nervously as I confront him because I cannot handle these looks any longer.

"Honey, you are beautiful." *Wait what?* I stare in disbelief. "You just have the body and mmm... the things I could do with those hips." His flamboyant verbal assault takes me by surprise. "I want to put you in a dress and walk you. Do that now. Do a runway walk. I want to see it." I stare.

"You want me to be a model?"

"Yes, walk like this." This makes sense now.

"I can't walk like that. Ha. Ok, I'll give it a try." He reaches out and grabs my hips and makes them sway side to side a little bit more. I was born with a pretty nice female body, but wasn't granted with the most feminine movements, especially in my hips. They just don't like to do that sexy female hip thing very much. It's more of an awkward Lego toy movement. He keeps trying to move them more and more before stepping back and telling me to do it again then continues to talk about my body and my eyes. He reaches out and feels my boobs momentarily, like a gay boy does, then continues to talk about how he'd love to put me in this and that and blah blah...

"I don't really like girl things. It doesn't make me feel comfortable."

"But you would look so good! It would be a shame to let a body like that go to waste." *Waste! What! I've got my own style and I like it!* We continue

110

talking for a long time and we gather a giant group together and all talk for hours occasionally getting up and doing dance moves. Someone said something about syringes and my opinion on what I just saw in New Mexico slipped out.

"Yeah I was just out west driving back from California last month and stopped at a casino to use the bathroom. In the bathroom, there was a baby changing station right under the syringe disposal box. I couldn't believe it. It is as common, if not more common out there, to have diabetes as it is to have a baby. But the box was in such a dangerous place!" Two overweight gay boys got very defensive and started to make rude comments on this topic about how 'ignorant" I was because it didn't matter because the baby wasn't going to get AIDS and I am stupid for thinking that. I spoke of nothing referencing AIDS. *Interesting... not at all where I was going with that, but ok... I was more so referring to the accidental contamination of an infant's changing station… or the accidental contamination of a diabetics healing station.* I decide to be quiet, apparently having hit a sensitive nerve.

The rest of the night was wild and crazy there until I started to get a little bit tired. Mr. Model Man invited me to go to another gay bar across town and I consider declining, but instead accepted. We walk to his car and as we do, a drunken motorcyclist just sprawls out across the road, bike slamming into a sign. The cops are on him instantly as if they had been following him. Model man mentions about how we need to be careful. I think about the motorcyclist rolling across the ground into the sign and how we may have just watched someone get arrested and pretty much destroy their life. That thought creeps through me and at the bar, I think about all the people ordering drinks and taking shots, hopping in taxis and blowing money everywhere. I don't understand how people make so much money that they can just waste it and not even think twice about it. *Limited mindset...* As I go on this journey I realize that I really don't understand anything about success and finances. I hardly even have an adult brain! Guess that's another reason why I am out here - to see a new life and to learn to think a different way.

We get there and he instantly hits the drunken switch and gets so crazy drunk that he can't even stand. He gets escorted out into a taxi after about twenty minutes and forgets about the lost gal that he leaves at the pool table looking confused as to why she is alone in a gay man's bar. I don't really know anyone in the place and there aren't any cute women in there that I could try to find a place to sleep for the night, so I leave. I ask the bouncer where to go to head back to town the he points me to the right. I keep walking a good 20 minutes until I realize that I am nowhere I recognize. At this point it is about 1:45 am, freezing cold out after having rained and I am carrying a giant palm tree branch with me, which I decided I needed for some reason. About 7 ft. tall, I found it lying on the ground and realized that I have never before held one so I picked it up and the stalk of it felt similar to bamboo, only rougher and triangular in shape. I proudly marched down those streets carrying my prize, expecting to eventually end up at Symphony's house where I would place it gingerly in a bush or somewhere funny.

Instead I am just marching in the wrong direction because the guy pointed the wrong way. So now I am in North Charleston, many blocks from my destination and my palm prize snaps. There is a convenience store that would allow me to navigate myself back to her house so I ask him where that is. He responds saying that it is probably a half hour walk so off I go, so cold that I can hardly keep going. My body is exhausted and I consider finding a place to sleep elsewhere, but there is not a great deal of life out around town at this point to ask. A cop drives by and I wave my stalk at him in hopes of getting some help, but he doesn't pay attention and keeps going, not even putting on his brake lights.

Finally, after an amazing day of all types of adventure, I make it back and go inside, collapse on the couch and fall into immediate sleep again being so very thankful for random couches and true trust from wonderful people all across this country.

Chapter Twenty

Leaving Charleston

"Our minds are a sacred capsule and nothing can truly enter without our conscious or unconscious authorization. Live intentionally and the world will open up in ways never before imagined."

I drove route 17 south with Savannah in my eyesight. Everyone told me that if I love Charleston, *"Just wait until you get to Savannah, Georgia."* This strategy worked before, so I was excited to have it work again. The energy of this day is so powerful. Sunlight floods the gaps between the giant oak trees and sends a glitter all over the landscape. Up ahead, I notice that I will be crossing a bridge over a river. I decide that before I get into Savannah, I am going to really experience some sunlight. I love the feel of the sun beating down on my arm in the car and I just cannot wait to feel it in nature. I search for a good spot to pull over and see the water's edge, but I cannot find one without going on some rich person's land. And I am in southern territory so there might be shot guns and redneck raping! *I have no idea what this land is like out here*! I do several U- Turns, seeking a safe solo haven to sit in the Georgia sun. I even follow down what I thought was a back path that takes me out to a dock at a very expensive used-to-be-island. It is covered by this dry marsh land in all directions beside the road I came down. Fibers of white, fluffy grass coat everything and flutter in the breeze. It's almost like a nuclear death site in this part- the expiry of this marsh.

So I drive and I am astonished at the massive mansions that line this odd, little land. There are children riding bikes and playing games in the street, which makes sense on this Near-Georgia Island considering why on Earth would anyone that doesn't belong here be driving out here? Well, this is exactly the odd type of place I had been searching for to see and learn about. I drive around and wave at the kids and toward houses that might be watching me. If they close off the only escape gate by the time I come back around, I will consider this to be one of those horror movie set ups and I'll be pedal to the metal flying toward them, dodging bullets if I have to! My imagination shoots heat through my body.

Fortunately, my fear doesn't ring true. I take an honest look at myself in the mirror and laugh at how crazy I felt back there. *Where did all this fear come from inside of me? I don't even watch horror movies!* I leave and drive across that bridge and pull off in the right side boat loading station. It connects under the bridge to the other side of the road and there is a parking lot big enough to suit hundreds of cars and boats between both sides. I couldn't be happier to be near the water though! The only car that is there is an old rusty pick up and there are two guys standing along the waterside. It looks to me that they are drinking beer and just talking.

I decide to park far away from them in the open for the main road to see. Open air protection. I get out and feel the sunbeams melt down my body. I grin and unwind, intoxicating breath filing my lungs. I am just about to be in Georgia for the first time! I cannot wait to see that sign indicating yet another giant step in my life's awakening! But since I drove a back road, this stop feels like I must be here because it just looks like Georgia! *Whatever that means...* There is a large pile of rocks that serve as a water barrier and I walk out on them and watch a pelican coated dock. This is the first time I have ever seen real pelicans hanging out. Mouths wide and eyes skeptical of me, I watch them just do their pelican thing. Such large royal looking birds, such big blue bodies. They trot around and fly about, land and go to the bathroom everywhere they want. Then they walk in it and lay in it and walk in each other's. *Ah, what a beautiful life for the majestic waterfowl.* So I watch these birds interact and I watch the water shimmer. There is a bit of trash scattered about and it kind of smells like musty fish, but I am very excited that it smells like water. *Musty stinky water, but still water. Ahh, such sovereignty, such freedom.*

I notice that as I make my way down along the water's edge, hopping from rock to rock, that the men are now no longer next to their truck. They have moved from being at my far right to having walked around behind me and are now standing to my far left. I consider it to be such a farfetched thing to be attacked here before I ever officially touch Georgia. But I have my stranger-danger sensors on high. I just haven't learned the skill of proper stranger trust yet. Especially when it comes to old hillbilly men drinking beer by the river. *I mean, in all seriousness, most people don't want to kill me.* I keep my eye on them anyway.

Now of course, they could be just men enjoying a beverage looking at the water. After all, that is no different than what I am doing here. But my problem is that I only brought one knife with me, where as I usually have three on me as I travel, one in the back right pocket, one in the front left and one in my bag. So I am a bit scared and decide to nonchalantly work my way to my right over closer to the cars. The dock looks like a neat spot to go anyhow. As I walk out, I realize that it is floating and moves with the water's waves, up and down along the cement posts. I go out to the edge and stare at the water, closing my eyes and feeling the movement of the earth beneath my feet. I am anti-gravity right now, connected to that which is not structurally stabilized on the earth. I am floating.

Why would I ever be here, right now? And yet, here I am! Here I am right now! I watch a boat pass and I see the people smiling and having a great time. I imagine what it must be like to be cruising along the water like that, at high speeds feeling relaxed and free. In this moment, I decide that I want to be on a boat. I set my intentions to be on a boat very, very soon. I want to feel the wind in my hair and the water splashing around me as the motor hums away my fears and the sunshine smiles upon my dreams. But for the present moment, I will settle for being on a floating dock, which is sort of like a boat a little bit. *I guess...*

I close my eyes again and breathe deep, deciding this is a good time to do a short meditation. I release all tension from my being and allow myself to experience the moment, feeling the sunshine, feeling the breeze, seeing with my other senses and listening to the sounds of the universe. I listen to the individual waves crashing about, birds squawking in all directions, cars passing up ahead creating a stabilized, low-resonance hum, and boats in the distance moving from one place to the next. I then notice subtle sounds that I did not previously hear, like a faint dog barking from what must be miles away, but its sound being carried across the waters. I hear wind howling gently in small spaces in the dock, chirping bugs each singing their own tune and then I hear a deep roar of blended water movement as an underlying tone holding it all. It makes me wonder if that underlying tone has a larger effect on the subconscious of the body. Perhaps, that underlying tone of water movement creates that white noise that makes everyone naturally drawn to water. Or perhaps, that sound is just a blend of everything we relate to when we get near water and it just has a wonderful feeling connected to it. Whatever the reason, it is a lot to smile about.

That's when I notice something strange. I hear this tiny popping sound. I can't put my finger on what it is. But there is this tiny, quick, guttural popping sound that resonates in everything around me. It is to my left. It's behind me. It's to my right. It's everywhere! I open my eyes and look around expecting to see bugs crawling all over me, but I can't find anything. Feeling gross and slightly disturbed, I then gaze to the cement pillars. *There! It's coming from there!* I bend down and look closely at the pillars to see these sharp little barnacles. (Although I had no idea what they were at the time) Inside the hard white edges, I see what looks like a tiny, white chicken's beak. It takes a moment to open, shakes a little bit then squeezes shut quickly. When it does this strange motion it creates a loud popping sound. That sound is everywhere! Absolutely everywhere! It makes such subtle, yet loud obstructive noise that I don't know what to do! I have never before seen something that appeared to be so alien to me. They are everywhere and I am right in the middle of them. I don't know if they are shooting things out or if they are reacting to a predator or if they are releasing a gas or mating. I don't know anything about these alien things! But I know they look like trapped chicken beaks in a hard shelled donut that are yelling. *Creepy.*

By this point, the men have made their way over to me and I realize that I am out on the dock. *Oh god, I am trapped on this dock with these popping alien species and two drunk old country boys are going to block the only exit to land! If I jump off the dock maybe that will show them how dedicated I am to surviving. But this leads to the ocean so there could be sharks!* I see large fish glistening below the dock. *There must be sharks!*

Ok, no panicking, Katie, until they actually get to the dock. I reach for my knife to prepare myself for battle. They would never expect a young solo lesbian to carry a knife.

Aha! They pass me as they talk and head up toward their truck. They are safe.

"Umm… excuse me." I yell to them after realizing that I am probably crazy for thinking the world is such a threat. They turn around and look at me. "What are these things on these pillars?"

"Whelp, those are barnacles." He exclaimed as I looked at them. "They spit out water and that's the noise of them doing so." I continue to watch these odd, little things as thousands of them continue to pop while I talk to these shrimp fisherman. They take their boat out on the water every day and return with loads of shrimp. What a very interesting way to live. I have never been around water much in my life and have never met a professional fisherman before. They tell me about how they can't believe these are the first pelicans I've ever seen up close and then tell me about all the dolphins and sharks they see here. *Whaaa?*

"I can't believe there are dolphins out there!" I say while I think about how fascinating the depths of rivers and ocean waters are.

The older man points, "Look, there is one right there behind you." I turn around and see its fin come up out of the water. My eyes sparkle like a fairy princess. "Yeah, we have this one trained to come up to our boat. It's illegal to feed dolphins, but unless you are the FED…" he points his finger at me and smiles as I shake my head no, "then you can know that we bang the side of the boat when we get off shore a bit. Doesn't matter where that dolphin is, she'll swim to us and we'll feed her. We can even pet the top of her head."

I have never heard of anything like this. I spent my days in the walls of a diner or in a school classroom. This was everyday life to them, just dolphin feeding while they work. They invited me to go out the next day since I was so shocked by everything they were telling me. I was still very cautious. It's a great opportunity to not only feed wild dolphins, but to also go on a boat! I realize then that within a few minutes of stating my desire, I have used the Law of Attraction to attract the boat opportunity I requested! What are the chances?

So I talk with these guys and I make up a quick story about how I'm not sure what my friend is doing tomorrow, but I'm going to call them to tell them if I can or cannot make it to the dock. The one gives me his number and tells me that if a woman answers, it's his wife so he will tell her that I would be calling. This made me feel much, much safer. It was about 20 miles away from Savannah, so it wasn't a long trip to get to where they were going.

I say my farewells and immediately begin on the road again headed for Savannah with so much light in my eyes. My head is filled with a great variety of emotion. I can't believe the opportunity that presented itself to me! At the same time, I can't believe the amount of risk that would go into being in a situation like that. I also can't believe I am considering getting on a fishing boat for hours tomorrow with a group of men that I don't know. That seems too foolish. But at the same time it is such a great opportunity to do something phenomenal! But just because I was able to manifest an opportunity, doesn't mean I have to take it.

I'll have to sleep on it and see how I feel in the morning.

Once I enter Savannah, it is already dark. It is 8:30 and I drive several times through the city to get a feel of it. For some reason, I see lesbians everywhere! What kind of town have I found myself in! Cute, lesbians walking hand in hand on every corner. *Oh what joy!* I see a restaurant tucked away in a street corner and I go around the block and park next to it so I can use their Wi-Fi to check my Sofa responses. As I excitedly back in, I accidentally back up gently into a very nice parked car. This guy is walking by and sees it happen and starts pointing and laughing at me. He walks by and I decide that I am not going to run, because what happens if there is a cop watching or the guy who owned the car is watching. So I park and sit in my car and compile an apology note for the owner of the car. I write one out and then I just sit there and turn on my tablet. I log in online and see that there are three Sofa responses!

All three of them are Sofa declines. My heart sinks; I panic. I quick send on a few emergency responses hoping that someone would take pity on a

117

sorry sap stuck in the city on a chilly night like tonight. The problem here is that I expected that someone would respond with a yes, but no one did. Then I researched gay bars because I figured that I would be able to find a place to sleep with a woman at a gay bar more easily than if I just walk into a bar and try to make friends and find one. There seem to be maybe one or two gay bars around. There are no clubs from what I gather. I basically waste an hour hoping for something that didn't happen and most likely wasn't going to happen. I decide to just park my car downtown somewhere that looked like a main street that didn't have any parking meters or permits. I then decide that I am going to sleep in my car, but first I will walk around sightseeing to make myself very tired so that I will just pass out by the time I find my way back to my car. *No problem...* I am walking and observing all the large, beautiful oak trees everywhere. I watch the architecture vary from house to house. Everything looks so old Victorian beautiful, another world before me, a European whisper from the 1700's. And I guess, to some extent, I am in another world.

So far I have been guided by my success studies and the Law of Attraction and I have been granted the gift of this land tonight. So I suck up my self-pity and say that I may as well enjoy it. I figure I will stop in for a beer at some point somewhere if I feel like it. But as I walked and watched smiling people and friendships all over this place, I began to feel very alone. I decided that I wasn't in a mood for a beer. Actually, as I walked I began to feel rather sad and pathetic. A deep depression began to invade my body, providing an uncomfortable restless mind that keeps the body from achieving slumber, but I needed to rest well tonight. A swirl of Alana begins to invade my apprehension, creating a dark funnel of worry and distress. It approaches me from down the street and I can see it approaching fast, flipping cars, shattering glass storefronts, ripping apart historic building facades, creating oncoming devastation headed straight for me. I turn to run, but can't seem to run fast enough as I am swept up into the vortex of worthlessness and pathetic despair. *I don't deserve this trip. I don't deserve Alana or a family. I should just give up...*

The hate-nado consumes me entirely as the black night coated sidewalks glide me into a mental hell, a turmoil glistening loneliness into every single step. I hear no happiness from the pedestrians passing. I hear no cheer erupting from bar rooms. My eyes tear up, but the key is that I don't stop walking. I keep walking, keep moving and eventually I begin realizing how disorderly these thoughts really are.

Things aren't really that bad...

And the tornado seems to let me go from its death grip.

That's when I take the reins of my emotions. *No, I am going to find a place to sleep tonight. I am worthy.* I put it out in the universe that I will find a safe place to sleep! I turn the next corner and see a girl step out of a doorway. Long, dark hair covers her face as she lights up a cigarette. I optimistically approach and I say a simple hello while I pass. I take a few steps and notice that she is on break while working at the hookah/smoke shop. *If anyone would know someone who uses SofaCruisin, then it would probably be someone like this. Please…*

So I ask her if she does, to which she responds a depressing 'no'. I say my 'thank you for your time…' and I begin to walk away a few steps. Something just pulled my energy back to her though, like a compulsive turn around. I stopped, turned and said, "By any chance, do you know anyone who would be fine allowing a traveler to sleep on their couch for the night?"

"Yeah, well I am actually getting off work here soon if you would like to meet me back here at 11. You can sleep on my couch for sure, but I do have plans to go to my friend's house for a while after work, so if you don't mind tagging along…" SCORE! Not only have I found a place to sleep, but I will most likely meet some interesting people too! "My name's Kalsey. Nice to meet you. See you at 11" Friendship*! So much yes!*

So I walk around, feeling way more in love with the faint glow of the historical buildings than previously and by the time I return with my car, she is just locking up the door to the shop. I follow her to her house where we park my car and then she drives me to her friend's house. And the night ended with good laughs, new friendship and most importantly safe slumber. Actually, the destruction of loneliness by friendship was the most important part this night. I gave thanks for all the good people with open minds that I have encountered thus far. This was all I needed tonight and that is exactly what I found. I mean, yes, again falling asleep in a gal's bed would have been a nice surprise, but this evening ended perfectly. And a good night's rest was very much needed for what the next day was about to be.

Unfortunately, there is no amount of sleep that would ever prepare me fully for the character I was about to meet.

Part Two

The Enchantment

Noun

1. *A feeling of great pleasure; delight.*

2. *The state of being under a spell; magic*

Chapter Twenty-One

Savannah, Georgia

"These dreams of love are some of the fondest and most painful emotions. But they sure have been the fondest and that is worth everything."

I get up and log in to see there is another SofaCruiser named RawkyMount who just got into town and is staying at his sister's house. He wants to meet up today. Apparently he is a big fan of just meeting other Cruisers and doing stuff together. So we plan to meet at this restaurant around 10 am. I am not a fan of paying for parking so I just end up taking a nice stroll and once again sightseeing from a morning light perspective. The place is packed! I wait in line and observe the incredible art work all over the walls. I spot a map of the local area as he enters. At first glance, something about him seems off. As we talk, I can't put my finger on it, but something seems just off. He didn't take off his sunglasses for a long time and when he finally did, his eyes looked strange.

He tells me that he owns his own construction company. When he was working once, he really hurt his spine because his entire crew drinks from the moment they started the job that day until they sleep at night. He emphasized "Every. Single. Day." And he was trying to quit drinking because he started to have issues where he would hurt himself and not even know it and would be out of work for weeks because of the injury. *Aha. So the mental problem he has is not from drugs. It is from alcohol.* We stroll downtown and stop in a costume shop and at other various stores. It's kind of neat to travel with people who do have a lot of money and who do have a far different outlook on finances than I do. They see the world very differently. I don't have an interest in things that aren't free because I have developed a habit of only being interested in things that I can afford. Since I have never had a very good job or a very financially free world, I have never developed an interest in spending money on anything I didn't absolutely need. He insists that we enter a fine salt shop that basically sells only salts and foreign spices. Our mouths fill with taste test samples and we talk to the owners for about 15 minutes about all of their products. Then he proceeds to not buy anything from them. I am uncomfortable with this because I realize it's rather rude since they had many other customers in the store that were requesting their attention. I purchase a small bag of salted popcorn and 2 chunks of 500-million-year old sea salt. They were chunks about as big as my palm that I had to grind with a metal grinder over top of my food, full of many vital minerals. I would then have the opportunity to make a piece of 500 million year aged ocean a part of me as I digest it. *Energetically thrilling to me!* But Rawky was busy taste testing more stuff again. I notice that he really lacks any type of appropriate human interaction skills. "Man, a woman like that. Watch her boobs shake when she walks." And I swear just about every time he would talk about someone, he would say it so loud that they had no option but to hear him.

"Oh yep. Hey, check out this black ghost pepper salt." I tried to change topics…

But the conversation wouldn't change. He would go right back to degrading women. I honestly couldn't stand it. It was painful to have to hang out with this guy at times, like digging a knife illuminated by worthless conversation into my temple. I missed companionship though. We then make our way down to the river front where there is so much going on. They have live bands playing at what seemed to be a collection of local high schools performing in a competition. That is when the dorky trumpet player started playing his solo. *Man could that kid play! What a surprise!* He held the bottom of a toilet plunger to produce altered sounds from the trumpet. I believe it worked as a muting device, but considering that I never have played a brass instrument, I really can't pretend like I know. I was just smiling and enjoying some sunshine, but when I had to go to the bathroom, I noticed a guy doing magic tricks. He was just about to start a set so I stood in the background and watched. This guy performed sleight of hand like such a professional. He wore a tan hat that he used for several effects. His vest was a prop to disappear and produce a magic wand. He then finished off his routine with a stunning cups and balls in which he produced a four oranges and a cantaloupe from under the cups and his hat. *Woah! This guy is fantastic!* I waited for the crowds to leave and then I went over and talked to him. His name was Ron Ronmond, a professional street magician from Cleveland, Ohio. He travels around and performs his show on streets all over the country. That is what he does for a living.

I am so mind blown at this point. This is what I have been trying to do! *I want to figure out a way to make money all along the country as I travel.* This guy does it! I know for a fact that I must collect his information immediately; I cannot lose communication with this guy. He has so much street knowledge in him. I can tell from the way he speaks that I can really learn a great deal. Rawky stands back as we talk our magic talk.

He then refers us to use the bathroom at a bar over on the riverfront that sells alcoholic slushies. After the bathroom sanctuary reset, I decided that I have never had an alcoholic slushy at a river and I am finally in Georgia for the first time so I may as well indulge. Then this is when Rawky actually for the first time confirms that he can't drink at all, not one sip, because he is a severe alcoholic. He explains that he actually cannot have one drink, which I have heard of, but have never at this point actually encountered a recovering alcoholic before. I say, "Oh, well. Umm... Good for you that you have the willpower to not." He orders a virgin strawberry light daiquiri. I get the blend of chocolate mixed with white Russian slush. My taste buds dance as I sip it and smile. *The sweet life of experience!*

We walk through a profound statue of a giant earth split in half by a walkway. It is a stunning WWII memorial, located on the less busy side of the riverfront and would be a great place to write. I decide to come back to it alone sometime. Rawky says that he needs to check on his car. He wants to make sure it isn't going to get a ticket. I ask him why he parked at a place he could get a ticket. He says that he just doesn't care. *He, once again, makes no sense to me.*

We are beginning to get hungry as we arrive at his car. He asks me to sit in his passenger seat as he pulls off his ticket attached to the window. I say "Um. Ok sure." We get in and he starts talking about stupid, stupid, stupid stuff, disrespectful blubber overloading my ears and I feel like I am being drained of life until he asks for a hug. *Excuse me?*

"What? No!"

"Why not?"

"Because I told you that I am a lesbian!"

"So. I'm not asking to have sex with you."

"Well, then why are you asking for a hug?"

"Because I don't know. I just want one."

"Well, I'm sorry." I cannot stand being pressured to lie, but I did lie. "I've got a problem with personal zones. I don't like when people touch me."

"Well, maybe I can help with that." His persistence is something that I could see a weak minded woman easily falling for as charm. Unfortunately, I am a heart broken lesbian who considers any form of affection to be a threat currently and I am ready to pounce and rip out a jugular of anything attacking, male or female at this point.

125

"Seriously, you are creeping me out." He leans back and looks offended. "Do not talk weird to me again or to say anything disrespectful." He tries to interrupt. "No, I don't want to talk about it anymore. I'm done. Let's go get food."

If there was anything I learned from Alana, it was to stick up for myself. She used to tell me that all that time. I allowed myself to grow only an exoskeleton for protection and when I was in a relationship, I would give the other full access to my gooey, boneless interior. Once that external skeleton was crushed, I had no other protection. But things are very different now. I have become an evolved species. I now have a skeleton growing within me to support me and situations like this no longer made me feel weak. I am growing stronger.

Before we leave the car, he reaches in his center console and pulls out a packet of tuna fish. The air fills will the stench of fish as he dips his two fingers inside forming a hook and pulls out a chunk of tuna and slips it in his mouth. I watch him, in disgust, as he digs deep in the pouch with his fingers to pull out another mouthful.

"Do you want some?" He angles the pouch to me. I laugh, absurdly repulsed, as I decline the offer. I try to leave, making up an excuse, but he is so lonely that he hops up instantly and gets ready to come with me. We then go to this new Asian restaurant and Rawky orders a second helping of food. We walk around town a bit more and I try to tell him that I don't want him to come with me to Kalsey's house. He just doesn't seem to take the hint that I am not interested in hanging out with him. He is so frustratingly awkward; I don't know how to handle it.

I make up lies to try to get rid of him. Then he asks why I was getting so strange and awkward. I tell him that I just don't want to bring people over to her house. I just met this girl and I don't even really know Rawky, nor do I like much of that which I already know. I can't invite him to her house.

He gets mad and says, "Well, why can't I just stop and say hi and then she can decide if she likes me or not." *I know she won't like you, you ass.* So his persistence persists and we get to her house and she has a few friends over. They are all going downtown and walk around and drink. *This is when I hear some of the most glorious things I've ever heard before.* "Savannah has an open container policy." After I ask what that means, they explain that you are allowed to walk around on the streets with an open alcoholic beverage. People are allowed to publically drink! *So thrilled about this!* Of course, here I am hanging out with a bunch of underagers with fake ids and a recovering alcoholic, but here I am in Savannah Georgia none-the-less! And I have a crew! I have homies! So let's see what this city is all about.

They smoke up incredible amounts of marijuana and we pregame with a bottle of liquor. The girls are chasing with wine. I decide that it may be wise to chase with water since I am not trying to get sick in a downtown in Georgia. We fill up our cups and the boys load beers in their pockets and we head out on the town. The world is a handsome kind of fuzzy while we dance down the streets. They have no concern for the amount of noise they are displaying. It is just all about pure fun and since they all had legit fake ids, we could bar hop without any hesitation.

They do this often. The stories they tell of going out are unbelievable. There are all sorts of people that come to Savannah for all types of reasons from all over the world. Mostly the girls had wild stories about men attempting to capture them for the night or drunken people doing absurd actions like hopping on police cars and trying to run away. This brings back a memory of the drunken motorcycle in Charleston and I laugh to myself. *So much life has happened in such a short time!* My thought is disrupted by something senseless that Rawky uttered. Whenever he speaks everyone seems to get uneasy. They seem to not understand a word that comes from his mouth. He's just got that way about him that makes everyone uncomfortable. It's kind of a horrifying gift at how good he is at destroying the serenity of a group. It's like popping a balloon in a roomful of sleeping babies.

We bop around a few bars and try to squeeze in here and there. The girls just mostly want to say hello to people they know from school. It amazes me how busy it is on a Thursday night, folks in every establishment, spilling out all over the street. I learned that most of the young folks don't go down to the riverfront that I walked around the night before. Apparently that is where a lot of crime and dangerous activity goes on in the dark hours. I should have guessed by the lack of light in the area. And I call this lucky, strategic learning. *Also, stupid, lucky traveler. Be smarter.*

We mosey from bar to bar and my eyes gleam with happiness. I am elated to be submerged in a large group of people from a city again that I just entered and I am already a part of a group of friends. It feels so great to be just simply part of a group. Then I look at Rawky and I feel bad for him. He just wants to belong, but he just doesn't fit in. Whereas with me, besides my lack of smoking incredible amounts of weed, I do fit in very well and everyone seems to like me. These are my type of people and I am having a blast, but I see Rawky just looking around uncomfortably. He's got women on the mind all the time and not much else and he isn't content just being friends; he's always got to feel sexual stimulation and I do honestly feel bad

127

for him because he does try, he just is trapped in his own mind and that is all he knows. He sees more, maybe even wants more, but that is all he seems to know right now.

The crew I am with knows nearly everyone everywhere we go! It is remarkable to feel such a friendly vibe from so many different types of people. I smile and say hello, shake hands and start to chat. Unfortunately, Rawky cannot blend quite as well. He goes to the bathroom, but he returns with a beer. I ask if he is going to be alright and he says that he has thought about it enough and one is ok. *I hope one is ok.* The bar is packed with young college students. Everyone around us is fit and thin, smiling and happy and Rawky is just not any of that. He is tall and large and awkward and not artsy in the least bit and doesn't wear a smile much. But he is out here and he is trying and that is the important part. He really does want to fit in. He just doesn't though.

I start chatting to this beautiful girl who recognized me from somewhere within the last day. She is gorgeous and we end up talking and she tells me how cute she thinks I am. *Confidence boosted!* Then Rawky returns and I introduce him to her. She kind of looks uncomfortable and he starts to say something dumb again. A plaid, clothed arm slides in behind her shoulder as a big, dark bearded guy slides a kiss upon her cheek. She turns and plants a big kiss on his lips and she says to him, "Isn't she so cute?"

I blush a bit because I always blush when I get a compliment. I do get very shy around women. It's funny because it never used to be like that, but it is now. I've lost all women skills after having been bonded by 'lesbian move-in marriage' for the last nearly two years, but I know what this type of thing is. This is a straight girl who thinks I am sexy and is either looking to make out with me, most likely in front of her boyfriend to turn him on, or she is bi and wants some fun with me on the side and wants his permission first.

Either way, I am not interested. At all… I shudder at the thought.

It's a tough world in the lesbian realm of existence sometimes. There are all sorts of different types of situations you find yourself in constantly. For instance, I am asked just about once every 3- 4 weeks if I want to join a straight couple for a threesome. Even more exciting is when I say that I am not interested in that type of thing and the girl says something along the lines of, "Well, you and I can do stuff and he can watch." *No thank you, ma'am. I'd much rather get my arm stuck in an elevator shaft.* It's a shame because all these girls really are gorgeous. But I was more than certain this girl was something along those lines, so I said my farewells as I headed up the stairs to see what lies beyond the first floor. We find there to be another bar and a bunch of tables. There is a balcony that has one large circular table upon it and then there is a set of stairs that leads down to a smoking spot outside in a separate portion of the building. As we go out, Rawky and I stand there and talk for a minute. There isn't much room to do anything so we talk about how uncomfortable he feels in this atmosphere. He is a burly man, beer and sports- not artsy, creative musician atmosphere. Kalsey shows up with two other girls and stand next to us. They talk as I notice that the group is leaving this one, specific balcony table, the only table up there on this levitating hang out space. I spot it and tell Rawky hold on. I climb over a plant and fill in the space around the side that the group is leaving I yell to Kalsey. Her eyes open wide! She pushes Rawky out of the way and squeezes by the exiting people to give me the biggest, full swinging hug. The walkway is narrow and it is so difficult to get to the table, but we get it! *Simple celebrations!*

"Oh, my god! How did you get this table! Hurry! Everyone fill in the seats quick before other people try to!" She hugs me and motions to others to pile in around her. "I can't believe we got this table!" It was the holy grail of spots to sit in Savannah apparently. Horns blew for me and trumpets wailed in excitement for my success. Whenever Kalsey spotted friends of hers she shouted for them to join us and everyone was so shocked that we were sitting at this table.

I showed up just at the right moment of the night at the spot to take hold of the most desired throne in all the land. *What are the chances? I was king. At least in my head, I pretended I was.* It felt good to be at the best seat. We could look down and watch people below. We had stacks of cups and cans piling up on our circular table as we continued to share stories and drink. This was more of a friendship group than anything I have had since I first turned 21! It's almost as if the world stopped spinning and everyone started talking in slow motion, really loving each other. All around me there were people, good friends, close encounters that I just made, but people that I could trust with my life for at least this night. We were a pride right now and we all watched each other's backs. I watched everyone smiling and laughing. I became so filled with happiness that I could barely contain myself. Then my thoughts sparked up from the previous days of traveling.

Oh, so much life I have lived in just two weeks. Two Weeks! So much glorious, flamboyant life!

There is so much to experience in this world and this feeling of absolute friendship has been a lost chunk missing from my soul. I felt that gap being filled. And the strangest part was that it was filled by people I had just met. Nearly absolute strangers all mended together by even just semi- interests, but we were all linked by just unity and it was a cherished emotion. I snapped back into the regular world with a new appreciation for all the people surrounding me. I cheers Rawky and Kalsey and we all did a group cheers.

"Cheers to life!" I shout in absolute certainty.

"Cheers to this fucking table!" shouted a guy who went by the name of Scraps. *I don't know why they called him that.*

"Cheers to everyone here! Woo!" yelled Green Skirt. *I called her that.*

"Cheers to hopefully getting laid by some hotties!" yelled some guy who didn't have a seat, but was hovering next to this blonde across the table from me. She didn't look amused, but he ignored her apprehension, making eyes toward her and clinked his glass with his buddy next to him. She took a sip of alcohol and I was sure that he most likely was getting laid tonight.

"Cheers to Cheersing! Cheers to beers! And Cheers to Queers!" shouted another guy and then realized that I was sitting there. "Oh, sorry. I didn't mean it like that."

"Yes! Cheers to queers!" shouted the girl next to me as she planted a kiss on my lips and grabbed my head while climbing on top me to make out.

Actually, that didn't happen... What really happened was I responded with a laugh to that guy and said, "Ha ha. It's cool man I like women kissing women as much as you do! Cheers to queers!" I yelled and everyone smiled and cheered.

We all walk back to the apartment and they immediately start smoking out of the bong. I figure, hey what the heck. I might as well take one hit. There's no harm in that, except that I choke my brains out. It was way too big. I don't usually smoke in the first place, nor do I usually use a bong. So combine those two together and I have no idea how on earth to smoke a bong properly. I choke endlessly and actually feel the burning rising from the back of my throat into my brain. I am pretty sure that the smoke was actually entering my brain and spinal column. I excuse myself and go to the kitchen, attempting with all of my strength to not choke anymore. Things are starting to get weird. I fill up one glass and chug it. I fill up a second and chug it and I am still coughing. I stand in the kitchen alone and start to hear the voices of each person separate from my own distinction of reality. The thoughts in my head begin to grow stronger and my eyes stop tearing so much. Their words flow beyond my mind and I become very focused on the darkness of this dingy kitchen. I know not why I entered this room and have yet to put on a light. I stand alone in the dark and I begin to laugh at how funny this really is. I recap in a deeply spiritual manner about what I am.

I then think of where I am. I then realize who I am with during this time.

And I think about what I have done and how miraculous it is that I have lived a great deal of life so far. *It's just incredible.* I am so absolutely content with where I am in the world right now, it's ridiculous. I can't do anything except smile as I think of everything I have gone through. I was certain there were more amazing/devastating things to happen on this adventure, but I was so ready to experience it all. The passion that roars within me is the equivalent in strength to a volcano waiting to burst. I can't wait to be where I am right now. And the best part is that I am already here, right now!

I leaned up against the wall and made love to my own thoughts of my previous experiences this whole year. I slid to the floor and thought about how amazing everything was. Well, everything besides the painful, burning sensation in the back of my throat. Somehow eventually I must return to the group, but I have no recollection of this.

Chapter Twenty-Two

Day 18 Friday 3-29-13

"Find your truth and live it fully in every breath."

Callie and I stop to sit upon a large grey boulder holding the shape of millions of years of Earth's shifting. I observe its deep creases and melted appearance and find a great respect for the unfathomable power of pressure, composition and time.

"I'm just curious. Why do you like women?" This question caught me off guard because I was entirely on other topics. I want to tell her about how sweet they are when they kiss, how gentle their lips are, how delicate their swaying bodies are as we dance, their graceful arms wrapped around my neck and waist, our breasts delicately touching and the way their hair carries an aroma of heaven in it. A macho-man inside of me wants to take her in my arms right now and show her exactly why I like women, but considering we are in a public place during the daytime, I keep my gentlemanly composure.

I instead just laugh as I say, "How could I not like women?" An elderly woman in a pink hood from across a bench looks over, eyes widened. I see her adjust her sitting position to try to listen to our conversation a little better. I then explain to Callie that ever since I had been a toddler, I knew that I would never be with a man. "I was never checking the boys out in school." She asks me more questions about my struggles growing up and I respond as honestly as I can. *She seems to be studying my lips…*

"Getting changed in front of other women during gym class was seriously hell for me. I knew I wasn't feeling the same way other women were feeling and it felt wrong to be near them, like I was infiltrating their locker room. I kept my head down and my eyes on the ground. This eventually produced lack of confidence which then guided me to a deep 10th grade depression, but I naturally grew up loving the female form. Looking at a man just didn't ever make sense to me." I shudder as I explain. "I would tell people I was waiting until I was married to have sex, because the thought of a man's winkie anywhere near me absolutely repulsed me to no end. Ha. It still does. But later when I realized that I had another option, to date women, everything in my life began to make sense." Her lips open slightly indicating she said a silent wow.

She laughs and repeats the word 'winkie'.

We continue talking slightly quieter, fully aware that I have become Elderly Pink Hood's next great gossip story at bingo.

....

I wake up. Fuzzy eyes blur my surroundings momentarily.

I roll around and do my personal inventory. *Clothes on- check. Bookbag- check. Wallet and money- check.* Not that I had any doubt that things would be wrong, but it is important to check. I don't know where I am. The funny thing about it is that it happens even when I do not drink. It is just a natural thing that I crave to wake up and look around the room and not know where I am. I scan the room and realize that I am in a living room. Then I get a foggy memory of the evening before as I pull the blankets off of me to make sure that my clothes are on properly. *Good. Nothing seems out of place. Nothing has ever been out of place in my life, but I know plenty of women who have been taken advantage of and I do not wish to be that.*

I hear something that sounds like a large, stupid bear rumble from across the room. It scares me slightly as I look up in horror and see exactly what I didn't want to see. Rawky...

Rawky is sleeping on her couch. His big, dumb, oaf self is sleeping on Kalsey's couch. A fire burns inside of me briefly until I consider that maybe she let him stay the night. *Nope, I know that is wishful thinking.* He has pulled the blankets covering the couch out from under him revealing the giant tear and stains on the actual couch and has himself covered with those covers. So no, he did not ask to stay because if he did, she would have been kind enough to provide him with either a blanket or a pillow.

I don't want to be that rude traveler you always hear about in stories or see in comic strips that shows up, is given a ride, shower and safe place to sleep then sneaks another traveler in to stay the night. I did not invite him. He is a trespasser in my life and in my spiritual advancement of positivity. I do not take advantage of anyone, especially while on this trip. I wake him up by throwing a pillow hard at him. He snorts loudly as he wakes up startled and alarmed.

"What are you doing here?" I yell-whisper at him and make direct eye contact at his hands rubbing his eyes to try to make sense of the day.

"What?" He tries to blink awake.

"Did you ask her if you could stay?" I knew his answer before I asked. "You can't just show up at people's houses and just assume you can stay. Everyone else left and they all drank more than you did. Man, she was just so nice to allow me to stay over and now I just show up with this guy and expect that he can stay too."

"Dude, chill. It's not that big of a deal." Maybe I should take his advice to chill.

"Yes it is! I can't just invite people over to stay at this person's house who just welcomed me, Rawky. I don't do that."

"Ok. Ok, sorry."

I figure that I need to waste some time because Kalsey doesn't work until 10 and I offered to drop her off and pick her up from work today. It was only 8:15 and I wanted to get out of Rawky's air space. I could taste the ignorance, wafting in airborne slumber. Kalsey won't be up until 9:30 so I head upstairs as quietly as I can and grab a shower. There are two reasons for this shower being so significant. 1. I am dirty and need one. 2. I really need to relax. Steam presses against my body, heating up my muscles and tendons. My eyes close and I let the water glide down my face and skin, shedding the negativity from my form. I visualize it flowing down me, extracting all the negative darkness held inside and flowing right down the drain and away, leaving me purified and cleansed. I come out of that shower almost a new person. I look at myself in the mirror and decide that I need to do something about these eyebrows. They've begun to look like stalker mustaches on my forehead. My massive brow could possibly connect my hair lines together if I let it free flow across my face. And it's been countless days since I took care of it so it is in the high priority level. After this painful, forehead war is over, I feel like I can take on the world!

Kalsey is up and looks beautiful as she stumbles into the shower. She doesn't seem to mind that her hair is wet on her way to work either. In the car I apologize for Rawky and she says it isn't a problem. She understands that it was not me, but just an innocent mistake made by a lost person. Hippie minded people seem to understand life as not being just situational, but they see life as an expansive energetic growth that sometimes results in unwanted situations. We chat about our hopes and dreams. I tell her that I feel slightly out of place everywhere I go lately. It's almost as if there is a fundamental something inside of me that feels off and I have been trying to distract myself from it by constantly doing things. I like to be alone and let others flow in and out of my life and I am ambitious about nature and exploration, but I also enjoy relaxing and floating down that life river sometimes without paddling

134

so hard. She then told me a sentence that would change my whole life. *'Savannah is a great place to relax and float in this majestic life river.'* This was comforting to hear at the time, but the actual truth of this statement was to make itself known to me on a very sincere level within a few days.

It's very nice to share the companionship of a beautiful woman. I expect nothing other than friendship from her, nor do I want anything anyhow. She fulfills some gap inside of me. Like Symphony, she boosts my heartbroken spirit and shines light from the darkness. I swing by her work and smile sincerely as she says thank you. She hops out and I drive around wondering *"where to next?"* This city is so handsome this morning that I just cannot help but to want to see it all. I drive around and sight see again. I decide to call my dad and tell him about some of the local attractions because I thought he could appreciate the history of this place. Mom gives her standard freak out conversation, which I still haven't grown accustomed to. I then call Alana and I explain the previous day's events to her. The moment I hear that voice, my heart melts. She doesn't want to talk to me long though and it leaves me with a solid dread in my chest. I hear myself shrivel up; I want to cry when she says she misses me. Thankfully right away I get an incoming message from Kalsey so I tell Alana that I'll call her back in a minute. I hate having to lie to her, but I tell her my dad is calling anyhow.

"Hey Kals. What's up?"

"I don't work today. Those jackasses changed the schedule and never told me."

"Well, isn't that a good thing? Did you not just say to me about how much you wanted to spend time together and go to the park?"

"Yeah, I guess. Hey, can you pick me up?"

And I am back there again. She hops in and mentions swinging by this little gas station called Preachers on the way back through. It's like that local place, the type in the old days of soda jerks and malts where everyone used to listen to juke boxes while they hand jive. It is a locally owned gas station converted into a convenience store that has made-to-order food and all sorts of goodies to buy. We both get a cup of coffee to-go and head back to her house. We get in the door about 11 and Rawky is still sleeping. We talk and hang out a bit while we get ready for the park.

The car gets loaded up with my guitar, blankets, hula hoops, friends and her friend's dog. We actually stopped by her friends' house for the sole purpose of picking up a dog. The girl complained how her dog gets more dates than she does. There are several groups lounging around all over this park and the ground is slightly wet, but the sun is so hot that I can't imagine it will be wet for long. This heat, the sunshine, it is all I wanted when I left Erie. It is all that I have desired to have and now I sit surrounded by friends who were a day ago, just strangers in a new city. We dance and laugh and I observe the hippie arts culture of this place. It is incredible what these local kids get away with out in the public eye. They are selling weed openly and not even caring who sees. I got a little nervous when the shirtless guy who goes by the name of Mack pulls out a large pillow sized Ziploc bag of herb and a scale and lays it out right in front of him. He just starts dipping his hand in the bag and gently tugging it out and weighing it. I cannot believe what is going on in front of me and I start to sweat nervously as I look around and pray to god that cops aren't watching.

It's the same feeling I got with the West Virginia hillbillies. I remember to set aside my misconceived judgement of others to properly analyze what it is that I am actually feeling. Am I sensing danger? Or am I sensing my own inner fear of liberating my spirit further? I realize it could be a little of both so I need to find out if there is any danger of cops arresting us. I ask Kalsey if all of this is ok and she looks at me funny as I watch over my shoulder like a paranoid sweetheart. She confirms that this happens every single day in this park and the cops don't care. She explains that as long as no one's personal business is bothering anyone, no one's personal business here gets bothered. I look up and that thought settles in deep as I accept one hit of marijuana and allow the smoke to filter away all my fear. The grinning ocean of joy welcomed me and the animated laughs carried me away into a world of external peace, a world of cops being friends, not enemies. The people here didn't fear the cops for just enjoying their lives. They lived and they loved and the cops patrolled the park in the distance, creating a safe environment of coexistence, not a separation of authority force vs. blissful life. There coexisted a state of peace between the higher and lower rankings in this park and I had never witnessed something so simply peaceful in a public setting in my life. I asked the others if they trust the police and they told me absolutely and that they wouldn't be afraid to ask them for help. They don't live in fear of police here. They don't live in fear of being themselves and enjoying what they love like I did my whole life. High School was an odd time for me. I never smoked a lot to get high, but when I was coming out and terrified to be myself, I did smoke frequently, a lot of one-hits to release tension and stress, a sort of medicine for myself that I carried with me like a tiny bag of fear these last few years. One curious Pennsylvania cop could instantly ruin my life for taking a hit of weed. That fear dragged itself into my entire state of being everywhere I went, always looking over my shoulder. And here in this place no one lives with that underlying fear. I breathe out and let go of that residual tension in my head, my heart, my chest and I let go of feeling inferior. A cop even waved and smiled from a distance at one point, kind of securing the feeling of liberty.

Let me set the stage for this park. There are two main fields, each about a football field in length, divided by a straight walking path lined with very scenic, massive, old growth oaks coated with neon Spanish moss dangling over the branches. Many photographers have used these majestic beasts to their advantage over the years. The fields are occupied with every type of person you could imagine to meet, just living and enjoying life together. All races, weddings, hula hoopers, drum circles, daycares, families, sports, birthday parties; absolutely anything you could imagine is in this park every single day. The front of it has an amphitheater and a stage; the middle has a famous statue fountain and the back has a few paths through more old oaks waving their energetic moss just above our heads. It's a majestic, simple park that apparently the cops just allow to thrive as a culturally diverse destination. This is an absolute art city and I was about to get an education on the art/homeless culture in Savannah, Georgia. Some guys show up with beers and crack them open and drink in full view of anyone. They offer me one and I decline. I brought a tiny bottle of whiskey if I want to sip anything. They crack out their own bottle of whiskey and start taking shots right out of the bottle in the middle of the park. The hula hoops are swinging and the girls are looking fine as they start to strip off their unnecessary layers. Everyone in the park is having a fantastic time. A guy shows up, pulls out his laptop and begins playing obnoxiously loud reggae music. Another fellow shows up with this portable speaker stereo system and starts playing music even louder. So many people are smoking bowls and joints right there in the open sunshine of that historic park. In the distance, parents freely allow their children to run and play games and don't even think twice about this giant festival growing before my eyes. This is just what happens here and there is no fear necessary. I could cry at how beautiful this life is. Our circle keeps growing until it combines with another circle of what I consider to look like gross, grungy, hooded kids wearing mostly faded black. When we combine our groups, we form giant circle of so much diverse life: Everyone is drinking, smoking, laughing, dancing, swaying, living and most of all, smiling. There are several dogs running around and having fun together with people throwing Frisbees and people dancing. A few drums start playing and we continue to grow in our variety of life, our flourishing coexistence. I can't believe how disruptive these people are to the gentle, historical scene here, but this is their life and everyone allows it to be. They live and enjoy it daily. They leap around joyously and dance however they feel. The cops let them live and don't harass them for literally dancing to the beat of their own drum.

This whole time, however, Rawky is silently sitting there with a bandana on his head and sunglasses on, leaned back in an awkward stance that is as

137

uncomfortable to see as he must be feeling. He sits Indian style at first and then lays down to take a nap. It's a hard life walking around streets, fighting off alcoholism at night with a bunch of underagers. *I guess.* He was supposed to spend the day with his sister after staying at her house last night, but instead tagged along with me to Kalsey's and now is feeling awkward in a field instead of honoring visiting his family. I breathe deep and when I breathe out I release all the toxicity of his energy in my presence. *Let it go. Let him grow as he needs to.* This girl shows up with a cage and I see her place it down at the edge of the group several yards away. It's a colossal bird cage, but I see people picking things up and girls are making really cute noises at something. My kitten senses are going off and I rush across the field to discover that, yes, a girl did, in fact, bring a cage of tiny kittens to Forsyth Park and was passing them around to everyone. The group of girls slides over to join our group and everyone starts holding the kittens. They are so sweet and adorable and just barely the size of a palm. It's been so long since I held a tiny life form like this and I put its little face up to mine. It's soft, tiny body was shaking until I placed it against my cheek and slowly pet it. This must be an incredible amount of sensory overload for such small bodies all at once. I feel a bizarre mix of emotions for these sweet little fluff balls. Everyone is holding them in such a sensitive manner, loving them in the middle of all of this festive madness. Actually, this will probably make these cats wonderful little pets in the future. Rawky holds one and I snap a few pictures of everyone. It is just absolute insanity to my unknowingly semi-conservative, Dutch lands of small-town-Pennsylvania-raised mind! I try to get a good picture of the kitten's face, but it is just so tiny and adorable that I think the cuteness freezes that camera into a blur. I walk around and take in the amazing beauty of life everywhere. So many happy people are doing so many enjoyable things. I desired a situation like this and I have now acquired it! *Desire and believe; acquire and achieve!* The girls try to teach me to hula hoop decently, but I am kind of a doofus with a hoop at this moment. Growing up, I resented anything feminine, like hula hoops, as a way to show that I was not like other little girls. As a child, I felt I was different and despised anything feminine to prove it such as Barbie, Hansen, Spice Girls, Lisa Frank, stickers, the color pink, ponies, jump roping, those hand games when you chant with your friends, and all sorts of little girl stuff similar to hula hooping.

But now that I have been 'out of the closet' for years and am becoming more comfortable with who I am, I have decided that I am open to reevaluate my interests. I grew very crooked from childhood after realizing that I was not like the other little girls around me. I was not like the teachers told me I should be. I didn't like the boys the same way the other girls did. I didn't have crushes on them or think they were hot. As we grew older, this contradictory feeling crafted a deeper valley between me and my peers forming me into a quiet, awkward child. I had secret crushes on my girlfriends that I was unaware of and when that thought flashed into my mind for the first time in second grade on the playground in elementary school, things were never the same. I scolded my second grade self for thinking that little girl was cute. *Girls can't like girls!* This thought was planted in my mind at some unidentified moment, but that was the transition instant when I began to shut down. This was the point things about me started to shift. I began to hide who I was deep down because I was made fun of when I dressed like I wanted to or acted like I wanted to. Coming to terms with my inner truth was incredibly difficult for me and I received very little support from my home life. Not that my family wasn't nice to me, but they were not supportive in the way I needed. I wasn't nurtured in the way that could allow me to thrive and I just grew crooked. Not all plants grow in full sunlight and not all plants require constant water to survive, the same goes with people. We are not standardized build-a-bear-kid creation with assembly instructions and one size fits all mentality. I was sensitive and growing afraid of what I was inside because whenever I showed my true self, I was horribly made fun of. The only real support I received was in 10th grade after my first girlfriend helped me realize that I had another option than to like boys. After a girl ripped my heart from my rib cage, the only support I received was from marijuana. I could release all this pain, this aggravation, this tension I had been carrying my whole life with just one small hit of marijuana. I could have the freedom to be who I felt I was inside because if I received criticism, the same painful criticism I used to receive on the playground years prior, I could just blame it on me being high. *I was finally free to be me and if people didn't like it, then I could just blame it on me being stoned!* Brilliant! I could laugh it off and be confident in myself just as I was! But I secretly normally wasn't ever high. I actually didn't even like being high. I smoked one hit every day before school and one or two after school, but I honestly didn't like being high at all. But I sure did play the part of a high-school stoner to its fullest so that I could finally have the subtle experience of being myself for the first time in my life. I took the hippie thing a little far, though. I barely passed high school due to poor grades and attendance, but like I said, I am a true one-hit wonder. The thing that I was attracted to most of all was that through marijuana, I could finally release this inner turmoil- the pain from hiding my inner truth my whole life. I found a supportive family in the falsity of an illegal substance and it was so wonderful to just finally grow into feeling comfortable in my own skin! Honestly, through marijuana I went from pretending/hating/hiding my true self to throwing my deeply hidden /alive/excited/tree-hugging/lesbian/ hippie/magician/happy true self out to such an extreme. Neither approach fully honored the true essence of Katie. And now I am finding the balance between those two extreme 'Katies'. Now I am out here finding my truth and the truth has never tasted or looked so good.

And now, here I am a thousand miles away, surrounded by that same exact scent of freedom. I sit, smiling in this sunny field and I just watch everyone around me vibrate to their own divine frequency. I don't feel anyone here knows how much I genuinely appreciate each and every one of them in this moment right now. The sunshine animates such a whimsical emotion of really being alive and true and I really don't feel I could be any happier than I am right now. Right here, right now, I am so in love with life- all of it. And not just the good things! All of it! I spiral into a growing appreciation for everything I've ever experienced. All the pain I went through, all the hidden existence and inner hate, all of it has blossomed me into this moment of gratitude and I swear that this freedom feeling must be what heaven feels like. And I am more than certain this happiness has nothing to do with the three shots I just had and the 1 warm beer I just drank. This feeling has been evolving my whole life.

That homeless guitar player I saw the first night that I got into town is over there to my left. I could recognize that raspy voice anywhere. It's such a terrible raspy grumble, like a pterodactyl flying into a tyrannosaurus' eye. His voice really sounds like that. He is not wearing a shirt and he has a bag of fluid taped to his hip/stomach part. I ask a hippie next to me who Bag Guy is and he tells me that they call him Sparks.

"Yeah, Sparks is technically homeless, but he finds places to stay usually. He's dying actually." The guy I asked just said it like it is no big deal and went back to playing his guitar.

"He's dying?" I watch Sparks talking to everyone. He is holding two beers in his hands. One gets chugged and crunched up and thrown to the ground as he heads over to the book bag and puts down his beer. He pulls out not one, but two beers and cracks them open. He is just hopping around and singing the only way he knows how with the only voice that he has. He doesn't care whether he sounds good; he just sings anyhow. It makes me feel kind of ashamed that I get so embarrassed about singing in front of people. I have no reason in the world to be embarrassed of anything I do. I just watch this man, this dirty, filthy, dying man marching around with his half toothed smile talking to everyone in the circle. There are many different colors of the human rainbow that I have never seen before. It's like my eyes are opening up to these new, assorted characters who are teaching me deeper insights on a daily basis. Several times a day I have this awakening, but there is just something about Sparks that stirs up something inside my chest at the lower center of my ribcage. Something is activated in me and as I watch this man freely flow, I appreciate everything he is right now. He's got quite a story and he is willing to go all out and share his momentum of life if I just watch. He's literally got nothing left to lose except to be himself. One of his favorite songs comes on and he starts dancing and swinging all sorts of silly ways. He holds a tight grip on his three beers as he hops around, his smile never once leaving his face. He throws his hands up toward the heavens and rhythmically stomps to the beat of his own chaotic drum. He closes his eyes as he embraces the skies and he dances. Some others join him, all bouncing around. They are having an absolute blast, really living how they feel they want to live at this present moment. They are here. They are now. I sit there stuck, wanting to join, but feeling a little nervous to bounce around. I am lucky enough to be able to watch this, whatever this is. *It makes me wonder, though.* I began on this trip as a trip of great hopes and experience and it has become a sort of business endeavor. I study my power and success book every single morning. I write about the day's events. I focus my energy on these principles that I am told will provide absolute happiness- *eventually*. I just have to stay focused on my idea of success. But I watch these homeless, filthy men linked arm-in-arm, dancing in the middle of a field in the middle of the day amongst a great deal of wonderful friends and it really does make me wonder, *"What is the price of true happiness? And who is anyone to judge true happiness?"*

My thoughts are interrupted by a girl asking where Cat Cage Girl went. We looked around and didn't see her anywhere, which seemed very strange. I was confused and stood up very concerned because it was as if she just vanished and scattered kittens around this field like that of Johnny Appleseed, except with kittens. *Cagey Kittentoss*. These two girls held a kitten up and said they could not keep it and needed to find the girl to give it back. They just asked her if they could hold it. I investigated, seemingly the only person around here who really cares about these abandoned babies. I discover that someone overheard Cage Girl say how happy she was that she found them all homes so fast.

Oh no... She left. These girls and I kind of panic as this grungy, hippy guy, Shaggy grabs hold of it and kisses it saying how he was thinking about getting one anyhow because tourists tip better if there is a pet next to the homeless sign. Homeless animals usually eat better than the homeless people because passerby people usually bring the pet food before they bring the homeless person food. The girls seemed to know Shaggy and seemed to trust him so I trusted that the cat was safe. Once again, I look around with slightly different eyes and think, *"What is the price of true happiness? And who is anyone to judge true happiness? What is true happiness? But more importantly, what is the truth here?"*

I smile, laugh and dance in my rose-tinted glasses until the sun goes down.

141

Chapter Twenty-Three

3-30-13 Saturday

"To appreciate the highs, we must first understand the power of the lows so we have comparison to live always in gratitude."

I woke up at Kalsey's again and went out to get some coffee to do my reading and writing. I am starting to see people around town who know me already and call out my name! It's lovely how people remember my name in every city. *I wonder if it is my strikingly unforgettable personality or if it is my distinct lesbian haircut and my persistent wandering. (It's probably the gay thing.)* Across from Forsyth Park is a cute, little coffee shop that serves only organic coffee and the place is packed. There is a line all the way to the door when I enter, but that is always a good sign. A guy named Jeff is sitting next to me and tells me that he has traveled all over the world and has just returned from South America not too long ago. He lives in Savannah, but frequently travels. I have acquired a new conversation strategy since being on this trip and communicating with people that live all kinds of different lives so I ask him one of my favorite new questions, one that people have begun asking me. "So what is one of the most interesting things about a recent place that you have gone?" I've started to ask about a 'recent place' because I figure that eventually the juicy details fade from the mind and I love hearing fresh detailed perspective. It's as if they are no longer in front of me talking, but rather have traveled back in time in their mind- to that place they describe. Their eyes glimmer so bright when people talk about great places they have been that have made a lasting impact on them. It's as if I can see them re-experiencing the situation in their mind while still being physically existent in front of me. To see someone shift into a state of inspired memory absolutely instigates me to make as many positive impacts in this life as possible.

He begins telling me about this bus to Nicaragua. "They do anything to swindle Americans out of their money and will purposefully tell Americans the incorrect charge for transportation because they know we don't speak the language. But I watched how much the locals paid before me to get on and it was about 1/8th of what he was charging me so I called him on it. And he said it was final. So, I said well fine and paid it anyhow. That money to them is so much, but to me it's just pennies. What do I care if I give a homeless person in America a buck or I give a bus driver in a third world country a dollar? There's not much difference…" Often times I do engage older men in a very vivid manner. It's not in the way that most mid 20's women would engage men. It is on an intellectual level, an encouraged outlook level. I want to hear how they got to do what they do and how they have what they have. I want to learn from them and they are often very happy to talk to me about all of it. I want to hear about lives and I crave experience. I crave knowledge and this guy sure has a whole lot of it.

"On the bus, there were no signs to tell you where to go. We didn't know where to go, but to get to the next city we had to just kind of guess. A large group of passengers got off the bus at a dirt path with nothing around. No one spoke English and our butchered attempt at their language was not anything to be proud of so no one would tell us how to get to the next city. The spot honestly looked like a small dirt path leading into the jungle. But there was only one other person on the bus after the crowd got off so we took a leap of faith and decided that we probably should get off too. They can't all just be getting off to be eaten by lions or whatever. And it's good we did because as we walked a quarter of a mile up a hill, we finally saw the town we had to be in! There were no signs at the bus though. Hell, you can get lost in Nicaragua without ever even knowing you are lost!" I am so fascinated by his stories. They flow through my blood and embed in my head. I would like that someday. I want to feel the broad perspective he feels and I want to share it with eager explorers too.

"And it's everywhere. The signs are terrible in other countries. They don't tell you where roads go and they don't tell you where you are or when you get there. Let me tell you about Italy..." And I listened and held every word tight in my grip until he finished his coffee and told me that it had been a pleasure talking to me. "Remember, just keep on keepin' on. There is so much in this world. Now I'm not telling you to be dumb about it. Don't be foolish, but never be afraid of it because this world is amazing. I wish you well on your travels and your book."

I see Chakra Guitar Guy. I swear he is everywhere. I ask him a variety of questions about his lifestyle and he tells me that he basically plays guitar for a living. *That is what he does?* He walks around all day long and makes a living playing guitar on the streets of Savannah, Georgia. I can't even begin to think this is a way of life yet. People actually live like this as professional street performers. *What a crazy concept*! But is that really any different than what I am doing right now? I guess not, but I am not making that much yet either. He finished eating on the street and then he sets up on a bench and puts his guitar case out to reveal several dollars already inside. I listen to him sing and play and when a large crowd is approaching I walk by and throw a dollar in. He smiles and gives a wink as he keeps playing. I decide that I need to fill my brain with power. I need to give my mind some strength and read a bit. I've been doing several nights of damage to my brain and I need to give it a break and send it some Leopold Mountain nutrients.

My blanket crumples upon the rocky grass, strategically laid out half shade-half sun so that I can read and remain warm. I flip several pages and read as I watch people pass by. At this point Chakra Guitar is no more than a faint hum in the distance, hardly audible. It's just me and the trees. Oh, how mighty they have all grown together. These trees are best friends; they have lived together like a royal family admired by millions. They are staples, historical markers of this city and now I am lying under them, on top of their roots, interwoven like a blanket, webbed below the soil that I lie upon. They are an entire world below that which I can already see, the invisible support that holds tight to this fabric of growth into this massive creature, this tree, so beautiful and powerful. It stands tall among all of its brothers to create this lovely domain of Forsyth Park. I spot a group of black hooded kids hanging out again in the middle of the field. *Not black kids in hoods, but dirty kids in black hoods. Very big difference.* Every time I would see them an uncomfortable feeling of unease would wash my body as I would continually think, 'Oh no…it's the black hooded kids…' They are sitting around and I can only assume smoking and drinking already. These were the dirty kids I didn't really care for too much. They don't have much positive energy around them, nor do they really have much personality, but I figure they must have something if interesting people like Chakra Guitar and Kalsey hang out with them. Then again, maybe they could just be hanging out with the crowds that are around. And these people are always around. I figure eventually I will go over there when the group starts to expand beyond just the grease rats. I continue to read, filling my head with an assortment of positive affirmations. *I am powerful. I am beautiful…*

This flamboyant glittering guy, Randy, walks over to the circle and I figure now is a good time to go on over there. He talks about this drum circle they are hosting on Sunday in the park. The guy, Shaggy, that kept the one little kitten the day before, is walking back and forth and talking to people, telling this story about this crazy time he had a few nights ago and this and that. I kind of tune him out because he is nice, yes, but there's something about him that I don't care for. Two very pretty girls in dresses show up and ask Shaggy how his kitten is. He says "Aw yeah, he's sleeping right here." He points then to his hood and pulls the kitten out of there. They named him Sonny. I pray that this bright name is a good sign of good care. Sonny is such a little, tired sweetheart. Shaggy says that he slept all night and he fed him kitten formula all morning. He stays curled up in a tired little kitten ball and he nuzzles up next to Shaggy's hands.

Just then this girl shows up in riot mode and pushes Shaggy back, screaming outrageously. "Who do you think you are? Where is my money, Shaggy? Where is it?" He denies knowing what she is talking about, but she keeps accusing him and screaming and doesn't seem to care who is watching. The scene is growing and people are beginning to watch from a distance. He pops the kitten back up in his hood and starts to retaliate against her. A bad feeling rises inside my stomach and I feel as if I knew something would happen before I even got here. They scream and fight increasingly physically; her belly rolls are as aggressive as her words and I run up to save the kitten just as another girl pulls it from Shaggy's hood. He gets slap-punched in the face and falls over backwards. People are jumping in trying to break it up and I step back now trying to understand what I am seeing. I wait until it's all over, openly express my disappointment for them and their disregard for such a small life form, threaten to take the kitten and then leave. The decent looking girls who grabbed Sonny from the hood promised me they would ensure Sonny's safety. I sure hope so. I breathe in trust.

I swing by my car and grab a tank top. I figure if I am going to head down to the riverfront to perform and make some money then I am going to want to get some sunshine in my break time. It is funny to think of how little I have now when I return to my car in search for a tank top. I go through my inventory, two shirts, three tank tops, two pairs of pants, two pairs of shorts, I have about 10 socks. I have three bras and one sports bra and I also have five pairs of underwear. I am down to my last pair of clean undies and realize that I either need to find a place to sleep where I can wash everything, wash them in the sink or go to the laundromat. It's funny how my car has begun to feel like my safe-haven or my home. It contains my possessions and my dreams, my safety and my backup home. I have become a hermit crab and it has become my shell. I curl up inside of it when things get dangerous and wait for the danger to pass. Then I emerge and crawl around trying to make sense out of where I am- a Katie-crab of coexistence in this present reality. That visual makes me laugh. My creative magic energy must be ready to perform.

On the way to the river, I decide to walk down the whole waterfront starting from the far right. There are two famous statues, a large statue that represents the US 1996 Olympics and the even more famed Waving Girl Statue. It is so beautiful that I am cautious not to walk by too quickly. I really want to feel the history of this landscape; this old, invigorated city has such majestic charm. There are shops lining the cobblestone road that I walk upon and a row of shops on the right side as well. I kind of walk through everything and browse a lot. I don't intend to buy anything. I don't need anything nor do I have any money to spend on anything, but I do love to look at this ocean style stuff. There are these old artifacts for sale- old bullets, bottles, shark teeth, utensils, thimbles, buttons, and all sorts of old things from the historical war era. I arrive at the riverfront park area again and watch Ron perform another show. Then I head out to talk to visitors and hopefully make some magic money. This grungy dirty kid feeling needs to be scrubbed from my energy now and the creation of cash seems to be a justified way to separate myself from whatever felt as if it were lingering on my being. I just need to fill my head with some type of sanity and a great way to do that is to make people smile. I trade a collection of smiles for a few bucks and a release of tension from my head. It seems like a fair trade.

That night I end up sleeping in an apartment on a couch with 4 dogs. 4 guys live there, all travelers themselves, each having a dog. They were so nice to talk to, having hitchhiked and caught trains across the country. I felt (after hearing some of their stories) that I don't ever need to do that. I hopped on a train once just for fun when we had our bicycles parked under it as we hiked, but it let out a huge pressure whistle sound, indicating that I would soon move so we ran back, threw our bikes into the woods, climbed on and rode it for a few minutes. It was very exhilarating as it sped up, but we hopped off fairly quickly. But what they did is like the Wild West dangerous, an underground existence of vagabond travelers and bandits hopping trains and encountering incredibly treacherous circumstances just to get from one city to the next. The rush of freedom on the tracks is exhilarating, but the outcome for most that do that seems to be pain and life-threatening situations. Many have hopped trains, tripped and had limbs cut off. Most who hop the trains are addicted to heavy drugs and if a train-hopper isn't addicted to drugs, chances are they will encounter a highly addicted person in a dangerously intimate location at some point. One guy explained that he hopped on train once in the middle of the night and as he got himself safely into position, a homeless man hit him on the head with a blunt object, took his stuff and threw him out of the car. He woke up in terrible pain at the side of the tracks and had to figure out his way back into town without anything in the middle of the night. Train hopping is also incredibly illegal so there are train hopping maps and secret times that have been developed as an underground travel guide, but some of the information has been sabotaged and is incorrect and can lead train hoppers into very dangerous situations where they can be robbed, killed by thieves or caught by the cops. One girl I knew was caught train-hopping in Arizona and spent a few months locked up behind bars where she was granted the freedom of being later released into the streets without any money or anyone at all except a hefty fine on her name.

As far as I am concerned, train hopping is like a reverse gamble, where rather than gambling to win, one gambles not to lose. But the experience of the power of that much metal weight moving below you, carrying you robustly into the cosmic night's sovereignty and not a soul in the world knowing where you are as you venture into the wild existence of wherever the tracks lead, is absolutely astonishing and very addicting if all goes well. The feeling is a high of divine existence. After experiencing so much universal openness and trust for life, I can imagine how hard it is to come back and live a normal life. I really don't need to live the type of extreme chaotic presence they described at all, but as I watch these guys talk to each other, I wonder how different I really am from them. I am kind of doing the same thing, but spending more money to ensure a backup station wagon safe zone. I listen to them some more and realize that it is really a very different thing than what I am doing. Something about that both relaxes me, yet frightens me. The one guy that had invited me to stay the night, we can refer to him Wed-Train, told me he had an ex-wife and he was only 20 years old. I looked astonished and he explained that he and his gf were traveling together, standing on the road with a sign asking for money as cars passed. A priest stopped and handed them a small bible, which they denied (not because they disrespected it, but because when you carry everything on your back, you don't need extra weight that you can't wear, eat or drink) The priest then asked if they were married. Of course, they weren't. So the priest then asked if they had sex. Of course, they did. So the priest told them to get married. So they did. That priest married them within the hour. For the next few weeks they set up at a busy intersection with their hands tied together and held a sign that said "Just married". He said they made close to $300-400 a day for that. So far all I have been able to get was a couple bucks, some free drinks and food in exchange for magic tricks. Maybe I could create some type of situation like that to promote better results. I am not trying to just sit around and fly signs though. I've got big dreams and I have great skills that I am looking to develop.

I continually have to keep in mind the difference between beaten down and dirty homeless and the truth I am seeking through understanding what it's like to have nothing. At least I have my backup money for emergency, but I have been meeting so many people that simply have nothing. The next few days would be a dive into the pool of real homelessness unlike anything I have ever experienced before. Unfortunately, as disturbing and traumatic as these next few days become, it would be a long time until I really felt that my intensifying homeless understanding would be satisfied.

Chapter Twenty-Four

Savannah, GA

"As above, so below, as within, so without, as the universe, so the soul."
Hermes Trismegistus

An artistically, fuzzy day in the field of hippie haze greets me without any negativity, but with plenty of dancing and hula hoops to fill its space. It was then followed by Ron Ronmond meeting me outside of a dueling pianos bar. There are two guys on two pianos on opposite sides of the stage facing toward each other, both dressed well, a professional style and jamming out to a familiar Elton John tune. A giggling woman rises as she approaches the pianos and turns back to her friends to smile. They watch her come up to the stage and she puts a grimy looking dollar and a piece of paper into a bowl on the stage. The guy says thanks and I ask Ron what that was all about. He says that this is a bar where the entertainers are comedians and they take song requests from the audience. They write whatever they desire on a piece of paper and then take a dollar up to the pianos and place it in a jar and the guys will play it. They just seem to have a complete collection of songs: they seem to know it all. I can't believe how well they play together, having just come in from two different parts of the country to collaborate here and now. It still blows my mind that people are able to make a living doing something that they love so much. The rhythm is incredible and the vocals are astounding. They play happy birthday for a group of young kids that came out to celebrate someone's 21st birthday. The family sat beside them and they laughed as the comics made jokes.

"Pssst…" the one guy whispered loudly to the group while pointing at the dad "Don't let thaaaat guy get any of the cake. He'll eat it all." And he points at the guy's belly as the crowd laughs. The other comic stands up and says about how the other comic is fat and is just using the father as a distraction so he can get it all. The audience goes wild after every pun. They play on each other over and over, having fun the whole time. I watch and think about how delicious that type of life would be. They run out of drinks and ask the crowd to buy them a drink. Suddenly a drinks shows up. They get paid great money to hang out in a nice bar with a bunch of fun people and make people laugh. I am sitting with a man who loves performing while watching two men who love performing. Their skills create their dollars and they are having a great time being at work.

To me, it has no comparison to working in a restaurant or in a kitchen like I've grown up knowing. This world is new. I decide here and now that I don't want monotonous again. *Ever. My whole life so far has been that until recently. I want to enjoy the rest of my life and I want to make money helping others enjoy their lives too.* Here I am having drinks with a professional traveling magician, watching professional traveling musicians. I would be just absolutely crazy to not learn anything from watching these unlimited people live delightfully successful lives. *I am so close to understanding so much about happiness, abundance and prosperity thinking.* There are so many great ways to live in this world.

Ron and I talk about magic and we have a wonderful time hanging out. He shows me some new sleights that I have never seen before and shows me the proper handling for them. I think it is pretty neat and I decided that I wasn't spending any money while out. I shouldn't anyhow. If I am on a budget then there is no reason that I should spend money to poison myself with alcohol. This trip is about true values and real life and if I indulge in using my little cash to fund the slow poisoning of myself then I am doing no real good at all. I became determined to find free drinks and the thing about this business study that I have learned is that my mind has absolute power potential. Once I become determined to do something it really does just happen. *Money will come.* Soon I will be able to buy drinks and not have it be a big deal. I know it. *But for now, I'll try to score some free ones.*

Ron bought each of us two drinks over the course of our time here. He did one trick for the waitress then I did one as well, his was much better, but she brought us each a free drink. *Score! I just thought about getting a free drink! Awesome!* Just as we finished those, the pianists grabbed the mic and mentioned how there were hidden Easter eggs all over the place in the bar and if you found one you could get a free shot from the bar. I had just been in the bathroom and saw one on the stall and I raced back in there to find that it was gone. I even looked at it and thought, *'hmm. How odd. Nothing inside'*, but now I know! *The truth shall set drinks free!*

It's not often that I grab random eggs while in a strange bathroom. I walked around and looked under the bar and I spotted a green oval! At the bar I stand next to a guy and we end up chatting about something stupid. *Bar room chats extraordinaire, right here.* You never know who you are standing next to. They could be that person from that hilarious online video you loved 7 years ago. They could be the person that once saved someone's life or the Olympic athlete that competed 20 years before. They could have swum the English Channel, written a book, been a backup dancer for Britney Spears, invented the scooter, rescued a puppy, or set a world record! Anywhere you go, everyone has a story. I want to hear it all. *I just cannot seem to get over how much life there is to be lived in this world.*

I end up next to a business consultant. He made a lot of money and he used it to drink beer heavily and eat fried food, due to the representation of his belly. His smile was nearly perfect and his hair was slicked back and short. His glass was held in his right hand as he leaned over and asked me about my prized egg.

I told him it was a shot and he looked at me like I was insane. I laughed. I love when people give that look. Some people do not really care about free things that much. They have more money than they even know what to do with and that was the story for this guy. He has no family. He has no wife and traveled alone drinking in bars with other strangers almost every night of his life. This is what America's schools are told success is. Get the high paying job and you win. But I saw the damage in his eyes as we spoke about life. There is nothing negative that he said other than the emotion he put into his words. He was a hurting man and in that instance, I could see the pain of a misguided child within this grown man's pupils. He was just a lost soul who found a soul-less job and was making the best of it. We kept talking and he was thrilled to talk to me about what I am doing. His eyes lit up like a child at Christmas. Often, this is the case when I speak to people who live life on repeat every day. I am very surprised by how frequently I make people's eyes sparkle with excitement. They ask me questions and the most common words that I hear when I speak to people are, "I wish I could do that."

I hear it over and over from nearly everyone I meet! It's always those 6 exact words in those 6 exact spaces and they mean so much to so many people. It's the possibility that never was, the heartbreak of a broken desire, and the pain of longing, reaching out from their souls to keep them from following their dreams. So many people want to just quit their jobs and see what this life is really about.

Nearly everyone I meet has said the sentence. "I wish I could do that."

So I started saying, "Do it! "

And they usually respond, "No. No. I have this or that in my way." Or "I am no spring chicken" or "I have this job or children" and just keep overlapping their dreams with a variety of self-blocking 'truths' (some relevant, some not) that I could not persuade. Eventually I learned to not try to persuade the overbearing self-blocking mind because nothing that I could say could free anyone from their own mental prison.

The same went for me as well. And then I also think of myself and my wavering longing to see the world, my tortured pain that birthed my dreams of travel, the lands, the people, the sights to behold, the world to experience alone or with strangers, friends that I had just met that day, but will impact me for the rest of my life. I think about how I used to say those words when I met thru-hikers on the Appalachian Trail, when I was just up there to do just a few overlook miles myself.

"I wish I could do that…" I, too, know those words so very well.

Those hikers always held such wisdom, such power. They always seemed so certain and sure of their world. They had their determination and their eyes seemed brighter than anyone else. All that I knew for sure back then was that I was going to travel and it took me five years to give myself the opportunity. I had saved up money for five years to be able to just go. I got a black Volkswagen station wagon so I could get good mileage and still have a place to sleep if I needed to. I never used it until this year in the way that I intended.

And the saddest thing is that it wasn't even my doing. A river began to flow over my world as I saw clear certain truths behind Alana's existence in my life. She helped me escape. I fell in love, oh, how I fell in love with that gal. She moved me out of that town and placed me down in a new place. I quit my job and disconnected all my influences and we left together. Once I landed 6 hours away, she released me into a new world. I tried to make Erie my home, but it just didn't accept me and so I adapted to the changing climate in my life and I left. I left because I was forced to. It's what I secretly needed, but I was forced because I wouldn't open the doors myself.

Suddenly, I see in this random man's eyes, a million words of gratitude to Alana.

"I've gotta say, Kate, I wish you weren't a lesbian. You are one of the most alive, genuine people that I've met. You really have a great spirit and I wish you well in all you do." For some reason there is never a more genuine compliment than that which comes from a very sincere older man in a bar referring to my energy. I get that so often and every time it charges me up. "You've got a beautiful aura. This whole place lit up the moment you walked in and I'm not just saying that. You are absolutely beautiful. Promise me you will never change who you are and where you are going. You are amazing."

These compliments aren't something I brag about. They pour in from people all across the country, those I have just met or those I engage with in long conversations. They are picking up on something metaphysical, an inner light that is glowing from within and it is such a great compliment when they do. I appreciate these energy compliments. I mean seriously, if they are saying my soul is beautiful, then I am absolutely doing the right thing in my life.

I return to Ron after a free shot of whiskey and Ron is talking with two guys about something that he seems very excited about. Suddenly, I am tackle/hugged tightly from behind, a thin body pressed against me and a scent of perfume floods my senses. These non-threatening arms squeeze tight around my chest and neck as I hear, "Oh, my god! Katie!"

How on Earth does it make sense for anyone to recognize me in a random piano bar in Savannah, Georgia? I turn to see a beautiful face that I recognize from days before. It was Jenna and Paul, a couple I had met at the campfire in Charleston! They had come down for the evening to go to this piano bar and were driving back up Charleston again tonight. Never before had they been here, but they decided to go out tonight on a crazy whim. *What are the chances?* I notice she is wearing a shirt that reads *'As above, so below. As within, so without.'* I mention to her about how much I like it and she expresses that out of any shirt she wears, that is the one she gets the most compliments. To top it all off, it's a thrift store treasure! *As above, so below... Hmm...*

She introduces me to her friends which were conveniently sitting next to the lesbian table. It seems that everywhere I go there are lesbians in corners, watching, waiting to attack me in my gently grazing gazelle outfit. Luckily, I have my lesbian radar deception device on at all times because they never actually attack. I put off that 'uninterested in anyone because I am married' vibe I guess. Either that or they think I am a bitch and old men think I'm awesome. Whatever. My soul wants compliments more than my body now anyhow.

I walk around the bar and am surprised by how many people are dressed up in Easter costumes. Apparently this Easter/Halloween is a normal thing here. I ask this man where he found a rainbow Easter egg costume. His pale, hairy legs entirely exposed from the base of his suit, junk barely staying in, must mean he is a homosexual man. So I approached this beautiful blonde haired man and start talking to him about why all his friends were dressed up as characters from Alice in Wonderland and rabbits and eggs, oh my!

He explains that they are on a beer crawl. I hear beer crawl and I think back to my first one in San Diego last month, joining a group of nearly 300 people on the streets at Pacific Beach. We all sported our purple shirts and drank all night. I was very thankful that drink prices in Georgia are much less than those in California. I meet and greet the whole crew then take a picture with them because they look like a moment I want to remember. I look underneath the bar stools in that area and spot another pot of liquor gold! I rush over and get under this table and grab the egg as a lady turns around and says, "What do you think you are doing?"

I instinctively back up and hit my head against a post behind me where a bunch of bar stools are elevated on the second step level. "I was just grabbing an egg. Need not worry!"

She looks at my hand and says, "Oh, well I have two already." I explain about how the egg for liquor exchange rate works and she comes up to me to the bar and takes a shot with me. We cheers and laugh and the world is grand again. She's an older, yet very attractive woman. The cougar then hands me her second egg and I now have yet, another free drink. Oh, what a wonderful world this is when I open myself up for opportunity! All I had to do was think about wanting free drinks so I didn't spend money and four free drinks showed up in an hour! At this point, words are getting sloppy and confidence is rising. I start dancing and laughing with the people around me. We start our own dance party in the upper area in front of the bar and disturb the official business men that are around us. It's ok because I think that they were just excited to be looking miserable in public and now we disrupted their unhappy lonesomeness.

*"I enjoy rock and roll. Place another quarter in the music box baby!" They sing and we dance and sing along. *"Cha-ra-ra ah ahh! Chama ro mama gaya ooh ta ta! I'd like your corrupt adoration."

Then Ron left and I decided to hang with the people from Charleston until they left. I left when they did because it was already about 1 am at this point and I was getting pretty tired from a long day of constantly walking-hooping-dancing. I had been all over this town talking to people all day and I was just beat. I walk past this club that is jamming right next to the piano bar and I watch gangster looking people and people who don't make eye contact with me go in, but it sounds like dubstep is playing and at this point, I am invincible. I can do anything. *Ego rises…* so I walk up and start conversation with the bouncer. $5 cover. I don't believe him.

This instantly became a famous scene from Star Wars about death sticks and mind control. In my case, it was a cover charge. The creature walks up to the main character and says in a growly, rumbly voice, "Hey, want to pay $5?"

Our hero, Jedi-Katie waves her hand in front of her and says, "Oh…five dollars… You do not want me to pay $5."

Grumble Door Man blips into a trance, "I do not want you to pay $5."

"You want me to just come into this club for free and rethink your life." Jedi-Katie's story unfolds as he asks why I am there anyhow. His eyes fill with excitement as he explains that it is his biggest dream to travel too, but he feels too old now. I tell him he is never too old to fulfill his dreams of travel. I wobble back and forth in ambitious happiness over everything that my life is becoming. He lets me in for free after I hopefully plant the seed of possibility in his mind for his dream. He did not want to sell me death sticks. He went home to rethink his life.

Inside I am grotesquely greeted by people practically humping in the corner. I felt very uncomfortable and was surprised that the bouncer let me in there for free knowing he was putting a small, white lesbian in heavy territory. There is nothing brute about me other than the fact that I carry knives for protection. That's it. I don't fit in and there doesn't seem to be much safe opportunity here right now so I leave. *Now I want to go home to rethink my life…* Actually it wasn't really that bad, but I was increasingly tired as the minutes rolled by and I had about 15 blocks to walk back to… *Wait… Back to where? I never told anyone that I would be staying over.* I quickly dig for my phone and text Kalsey's number. She is across town staying at her one friend's house tonight and says we can meet in the morning.

Uh oh… There is a fine line between ego and confidence. Ego subsides. I text another guy who told me they were going to a party and that he was sleeping on a couch at this guy's house but that I could sleep on the other couch no problem. He messages me back a moment later and says about how the party was lame and they actually just went to another party and are all going to sleep now.

Oh no! A quick panic spreads across my face and I realize that I have nowhere to go tonight. I remember that a guy named Snoopy had given me his number and told me that he had a place to sleep if I ever needed it. Thank goddess for the general random acts of kindness that exist in the world! I text him and he says that I am more than welcome to stay, but I would want to bring some blankets and a pillow. I walk back to my car, every step adding an additional weight of pounds to my shoes. I can barely walk straight, not that I can do anything straight, but I am staggering back and forth and I realize it isn't from the alcohol. I was almost too tired to function. I make it to my car and grab a sleeping bag and a pillow, my toothbrush, a towel and a new shirt. I carry it all over to the address he had given me and I stand before a giant massive doorway with a beautiful wrap around porch. It is a gorgeous building that they have converted into apartments. It really is a wonderful building. So I knock and the door is opened by a long haired hippie that smells like incense and weed. I am not surprised in the least bit.

He then looks at me confused and I see his eyes focus in on me as I explain that I am looking for Snoopy. He says, "Naw, man. He isn't here."

"Well, where is he?" I ask fatigued, yet hopeful.

"I don't know. He's not around here that much." I am so confused. Was I sent to a wrong location? I had walked about 15 blocks to the car and now 7 blocks from my car to here because I didn't want to risk driving and getting a DUI. I didn't think I could walk any further. My body was depleted of energy at this point and the concern rising within me was just straining the last fragments of it out.

"Oh, wait. Uh… Yeah, he's here. Ha, I forgot. Come in." *Foolish stoner.* I hang with Snoopy and his girl for as long as I can until I can't keep my eyes open anymore. I didn't want to be rude and not talk a bit and just show up to sleep, but I think they could tell by the way that I was slouched up against their doorframe holding onto the hole in the door to keep myself from falling over that I was ready for bed. He explains about the sleeping situation and that we can carry the couch into the hallway from the porch if I want, but after feeling how heavy it was I decide that the couch is just fine on the porch where it is.

I don't even have the energy to check for bugs. I brush my teeth and spit into the flower bushes. I lay out my sleeping bag on the couch and crawl into it while tucking my bag under my legs to secure that it wouldn't get stolen in my slumber. I wrapped the one strap around my leg just in case and felt my bones sink down into my skin. Each portion of my body was chilly and heating up and melting into itself while the night slowly wrapped its arms around me and cradled me into the stars. In this place, I felt my internal harmony meet the external calm world.

My last thought as I drifted off into the night sky was of peace, both within and without.

"As above, So below.
As within, So without.
As the Universe,
So the soul…"

Chapter Twenty-Five

"Enthusiasm, have you ever seen anyone with it?
Isn't it a powerful force?"

Callie looks at me with very serious eyes, as if she had been thinking it for a while before speaking. "You say that a lot." I ask her what she means. *Golly, she's beautiful...* I try not to think about the eyes she's giving me, but I am pretty sure I know what they mean.

"You say 'What are the chances?' a lot." I think about it and realize that it's true.

"Huh. You are right. I do. It's like all this amazing stuff happens constantly in my life and I can't help but to say it. Seriously, what are the chances that all this stuff would line up in such extreme instances? I mean, it feels like destiny is just unfolding before me."

She responds with some of the strongest words I have ever heard in my life. "Maybe that should be the title of your book then. What are the chances?"

I think about it momentarily as I look at the clouds, their expression almost that of a boat or a horse. A horse in a boat? No, it's kind of both a horse and a boat. I breathe as I allow the images to settle in while the words roll through my mind. Down across the field, I notice a boat softly floating on the lake. It leisurely rotated sideways, swaying with the delicacy of the reflective surface, showing a blurred dance of the dark contrasting trees in the background. Just beyond that I noticed a horse emerged from a path in the trees carrying a policeman upon its mighty back. I always thought it was funny, these progressive colonial arts cities with horse-riding authority. Many times though, I have thought about how much scarier it would be to be chased by a cop on horse than in a car. But as I watch them trot by the fisherman in his boat, I realize that they both look identical to that which I was just staring at in the clouds.

"Whoa, what are the chances? As above, so below!" She looks at me rather puzzled when I say this, but that's certainly not the first time I received this reaction. *I know exactly what I mean.* In the world around me I see intense clarity. "As within, so without." *I am getting it!* She mentions that I am kind of cute when I sound a little crazy.

Something gently startled me awake. That's the only way I could describe it. I faintly open my eyes to take in my surroundings to figure out where I was. The rain was pouring down; the thunder was playing games in the distance. The mist from the rain was drifting close to me, splashing in on the porch and splattering toward my position. I was just getting a slight haze from it so I didn't care. 'Katerpillar' found a safe haven, the perfect temperature, to build my little cocoon, nestled in the corner of a couch on a porch, gently awaiting oncoming transformation, a future flight of endless fluttering beauty to burst from the seams of this sleeping bag cocoon upon morning. Nothing was able to bother me here. The world around me glistened like a little parade of flawlessness, a gift just for me. Anyone else up at that time would either be too drunk to appreciate it or getting up to grind the gears of work. *But this was my moment.* This world was my beauty and I laid there watching and dreaming about the next great experiences to take place. What would be my next amazing situation? There were so many things that could happen- Limitless Potential! But I had no idea how personally revolutionary this next day really would turn out to be. This day would change my life forever and sometimes change comes in an uncomfortable package and unfortunately my Katie-butterfly would emerge from this chrysalis, wings like gelatin, into a world full of leaches spewing from a toxic river.

I woke up to the darkness under my sleeping bag. The birds chirped from every direction and I pulled the cover from my eyes to show off the morning sunshine, allowing the world to vividly illuminate. I really had to go to the bathroom, but I was afraid to go inside and use it. I always have a fear of waking up people. It often makes me awkward for no reason. I hear some commotion from inside and a guy emerges from the large door. He slams it shut and turns to close the screen door and sees me. I wave a sweet hello and his eyebrows show his confusion as he pauses in his steps to realize that there is a lost little Katie sleeping on his porch.

"Hi. I'm Katie. Snoopy said I could stay here." His stare at me made me realize this was still an awkward morning awakening.

"Oh, I'm Vince. Um, do you need anything?"

"Nope, I'm just laying here enjoying the beauty of the world. Have a great day!" He started to walk away and then I realized that I was about to let a bathroom opportunity slip away. "Wait, can I just go in and use the bathroom?"

Turning around and laughing he replies, "Of course! Ha. Why would you not be able to? Go ahead. You look honest. The house is yours." I can't believe how many people allow a stranger to just have full access to their belongings. It's unbelievable when I think of how many different types of people show absolute trust in a traveler from a distant land. I laugh to myself at this world's opportunities. Of course, maybe the opportunities are presenting themselves to me because I am honest.

I go to the bathroom and open up the curtain to the shower. It looks kind of filthy, but I have grown very used to places of cleaning being places of filth in the last few weeks. It sort of bothers me how much dirty bathrooms don't bother me anymore. Life on the road changes one's perception of clean. It does so in ways one could never imagine. This filthy, hairy tub lined with mold, stained with many rust spots, was just the clean kingdom I needed right now. I dig through a drawer and find a washrag. I was hoping they would have a pile of them and they did! I wet it and wipe down the floor so at least my feet aren't stepping in anything gross. The water, slick across my body, felt so uninhibited, so fantastic that I swear I was being massaged by naked vixens smearing coconut oil all over my body. This relaxing shower was so well deserved after the night of experience I had.

I get out and put on my capris, a shirt and I dry my hair. I notice that my eyebrows are looking a bit Neanderthalish again. I grab a razor and shave 'em up as a quick fix and I edge my hair line. The minor details are the things that separate me from feeling like a dirty homeless kid vs. a professional traveler on a valiant life mission. I take notice to the fact that my skin is rather pink today and I don't want to peel. I left my coconut oil in the car so I go to the kitchen and pray that they have some olive oil to soothe my skin. I have a firm belief that the soaking of skin in oil provides skin with great nourishment and vitality. Anything that goes on the skin begins to absorb into the blood steam in just about 28 seconds. The theory is that putting oils with high vitamin content, like olive or coconut, keeps skin looking youthful and vibrant all throughout life. If I am sunburnt, then hopefully it will soak in and help to reduce the damage. As I take off my shirt for about two minutes to smear oil on my body in the kitchen, I hear a noise. I look up to see a shadow walking down the hall. My slippery fingers try quickly to hold the edge of my shirt to slide on over my head without getting oil marks on it, but I am too late. A man looks in the kitchen and sees me standing there in my bra.

I laugh and suck up my nervousness because the timing of this is just too funny. I explain why I am standing shirtless in his kitchen, smearing oil on myself with a paper towel and he laughs and says that it's totally fine. He goes to the bathroom and comes out and we get into a discussion about traveling. He's been on the music festival circuit for a few years and has seen a lot. I notice he is drinking something odd, a gourd with a metal straw. He explains that it is yerba mate, a South American tree with the heightening effect of coffee, but without the crash.

After I leave to drop my things off in the car, I see the guy that was hosting the drum circle sitting at a restaurant. Sparkling glitter boy looks like he is talking to official people so I don't interrupt, but I feel very compelled to talk to him. Then around the next corner, I saw him on a magazine cover. I grab a couple copies and turn around to find him. I interrupt; this time feeling justified and showed him. He leapt in the air like a winged fairy since he hadn't seen this since he had been interviewed about it! It inspired me to see how happy it made him. He just wasn't sure when it would be published! At the field, there are these horrible little biting flies. They look like gnats, sort of, but appear to be tiny black dots that really sting. I wonder how large their fangs are in relation to their bodies. The locals call them chiggers. I accidentally referred to them at jiggers and everyone thought it was incredibly funny, even though I didn't see why it was so hysterical.

There are guys with guitars and drums hanging out all day long every day. I considered this to be an interesting concept for the local kids. They could just go downtown and hang out with their friends in such a beautiful environment in the same exact way that people in my area of Pennsylvania do. But these kids would have the opportunity to meet all sorts of people visiting from all over the world. They can make all sorts of connections if they desire, just hanging out in their backyard. They sat there and started racking up dollars as people passed. Some would stand momentarily and listen, maybe bobbing their head back and forth to the familiar songs the guys played. Some would greet them and comment on how good they are.

An older man walked by and tossed in three five dollar bills and looked them each in the eye while he gave thumbs up. His plaid pants held as much positivity as his smile and while he walked away, he seemed to take pride in the happiness he had caused in those young whipper snappers.

Something about generating happiness in others also generates happiness in that which had initially given it. It's as if love is a perpetual energy machine, erupting from nowhere and continually expanding exponentially.

As I watch this man walk away, my eyes shift from him to someone in the distance. My stomach turns for some peculiar reason and I feel almost as if I hate the person I am viewing. *What the hell, Katie? Where is this judgement coming from?* But that intuitive concentrated emotional shift would be more than vindicated in a few short hours.

Chapter Twenty-Six

Day 22

"Music is vibration and when it is played loud enough, we can see water respond. If thoughts are vibration and if we are approximately 80% water then what do our thought's vibrations do to ourselves and to each other?"

This whole time I did not like River. River was a guy that stank, was a rude alcoholic junkie with no respect for anyone or anything, burnt out stoner loser who would probably shoot his own mother for 20 bucks. His grumbly shouts of forceful ignorance rained over the lands occasionally the last few days and I tried my best to ignore him. I did not like him from the beginning, from the very first moment I met his stinky, rotten face and grimy hands, but I thought, *"No Katie, don't be judgmental. There are all sorts of people in this world and you are being rude and judgmental over appearance and circumstance. Don't be that person."* But today would be a lesson in trusting my inner intuition vs. remaining in a state of non-judgment. I initially did not like him for a reason, although the reason was initially unknown to me. And I honestly should have just allowed that emotion to guide my actions to stay away from him. But I overpowered my initial heart-based feelings with my mind's reasoning for openness. No, I knew he was not intended for my life flow from the first moment I met him. I did not give myself the full honor or confidence to trust that which I was feeling. I told my gut instinct that it was wrong and that I shouldn't judge a book by its cover. Usually a book shouldn't be judged, but if the book contains black mold and rot inside of it and I pick it up anyhow and accidentally breathe in some of the spores, I could die or get very ill. That book should have been judged by its toxic cover, same with people who are rotting on the inside sometimes. *Listen to your emotions.*

So I opened my mind to embrace some diversity. This was fine, as long as he stayed at a distance like he had all week, but somehow he had weaseled his way into my car to the beach this day and even though there was not a single seat left, he not only brought in a bottle of opened whiskey, but he also was sitting on top of everything and everyone without ever even asking if he could join. *(What a jackass!)* Underneath him to the right side of the car was Shaggy who revealed that he brought the kitten into the car too. I freaked out saying he shouldn't even have it in the first place and the girl next to him told me that she is foster mom and was taking care of it. So I allowed it to stay, but only because they used some of the sign-flying money they had made on the street earlier to buy it organic goat's milk and it was just too cute curled up sleeping in their arms. My senses were highly attentive as River positioned himself on those two and Blond Haired Guy, whom offered us all to stay the night in his apartment. The guy in the passenger seat had been traveling the country for two years, hitchhiking and walking city to city while playing his accordion on the street for money. He had it thrown in the back and Felix was very happy to be carrying such a tool for creative brilliance inside his station wagon trunk. I take note of my newly evolved, rubbery wings emerging from my Katie-coon spine, unsure of how to move pressed against my seat. I wished I could be strong and fly above this situation, but I am still weak. I rubbed Felix nervously saying, "Alright, buddy. Here we go. Tybee Island!"

We had a really great time walking barefoot down the beach and playing in the water; River wasn't even near us the whole time! We ran around and created drawn-out patterns in the sand with our feet as we paraded down the coast, the sweet Georgia Ocean kissing our bodies with its flickering reflection. Kitten-mom mentioned how she has been in Savannah for two months and hasn't been able to get out to the beach yet. She stared passionately into the ocean waves and held that kitten in her arms so gently and I could see so much appreciation in her eyes. This beach trip was truly for her and her spirit. She said she had two kids somewhere in Florida and hasn't seen them in almost a year. She stared into the water as she told me a little about herself. She longed to be able to share these types of experiences with them one day and even though she didn't look at me once, she looked at the ocean therapeutically as she spoke and I could feel her resonating with her desires. I told her that if she really believes it is possible, then it one day will be. She turned to look at me and had tears in her eyes. She was as thankful to have Sonny as he was thankful to purr into her big, black sweatshirt this day. When we were going to leave, River told us he and Shaggy would stay at the beach and they were going to find a place to party. Kitten-mom kept Sonny thankfully.

The five of us, Accordion, Blond-Hat, Kitten-mom, K-Train *(that's me)* and Sonny were all able to return back to an apartment, which I could hardly even consider an apartment, but I and two other travelers were offered basically a large box to sleep in. We arrived there to discover that Blond-Hat had no electricity or running water. There was an extension cord coming up from downstairs apartment which had a computer attached to. This is the setting for how the devil's theatre went down.

……………………………………………………………………..

I pick up one of my journals from my book bag.

161

Journal Entry-

As I write this, it is 7:15 am and I am swearing and yelling all sorts of insanities at what just happened. I cannot believe it and I am fuming and shoving things around in my car, trying desperately to make space for a traveler's accordion. I promised him that I would drop him off downtown by the river to meet his baby for the first time. He met a girl while traveling last year and they were in love, but he hit the road to see the country again. While he was out West, she got in contact with him to tell him that she had his son. He had been hitchhiking his way across the country to meet his child and we both slept at the same place last night. I was going to drop him off down there to meet his baby's mama and his baby for the first time and then I could already hear myself saying, "Fair-the-fuck-well, Savannah-fucking-Georgia."

Earlier, I awoke to several loud bangs on the door somewhere in the building. They were followed by raspy yells, "Hey, open up. Open up." *Bang bang bang.* We all were shocked from our slumber. My dream was a very odd dream in which I was sitting in a stream and I felt something on my leg. I looked down and saw a black leech stuck to the side of my knee. I could feel its prickles in my veins, draining me of my vital juices and I panicked while I rose from my seat and I ripped it out of my leg, revealing a bloody wound that hurt. I then felt the painful prickle elsewhere. It was on the backs of my legs and I arched my back and turned sideways and saw a bunch of them on the backs of my knees. Then I started ripping them off and I realized there were some on my thighs and up my back. I had rested in this beautiful stream, but became a dinner for the horrid creatures that were unknown to me. They were sucking my blood from my back and behind my ears all over in the places that I don't normally look and I couldn't believe how much they hurt as I ripped them from my skin. *BOOM... Boom...*

....

I wake from that dream into what is about to be a reality of equivalent representation. Sonny looks up, mewing from foster mom's arms. I walk out hesitantly into the hallway and Accordion, who was sleeping on the ground of the second story porch looks at my glossy, exhausted eyes and as confused as I am and says, "Yo, it is River." I reach in my pocket and pull out my phone. The time is 5:45 am.

Bang bang bang even louder than before. "Yooooo... let me the fuck in! Shaggy got arrested!" River's croaky, sludge-infused, toxic voice spews into my ears. *Ugh...already?*

Somehow I am not surprised, but all is still such an exhausted daze that I make my way down the crumbly, curved stairs and unlock the deadbolt on the door. As I do this, I consider what it was that I was really doing. These doors have deadlocks on them to keep out those who you do not want to have enter. I don't think that any of us want him in there and my hand pauses on the lock. He bangs again, startling me and I undid the lock anyhow, once again having faith that this River guy isn't such a worthless chunk of trash. I give a silent thanks to the bolt for at least trying to do its job in our protection from insane people entering at the wee hours of the morning. The door bursts open to reveal an even smellier, even stinkier, filthier River than before. *How is that even possible?*

"Shaggy was arrested." He runs by me and up the stairs, stench still lingering several feet behind him. He smells like a mix between moldy milk, a lidless trash can that has been sitting in the sun for days with maggots billowing out of it, a dirty, sweaty diaper and the most incredible aroma of burnt cigarettes and warm day old beer. *Delightful.* I was actually impressed by how awful he smelled right now in comparison to the day before because I really didn't think it could be worse, but it is.

He comes up the stairs which, by now all of us are standing around in awe at how stupid this guy is. He passionately explains, "We stayed up all night, man! Weeoow! We found a fridge in a backyard and drank all the beer. Someone heard us, though, so we ran and hopped fences. Bro, cops were everywhere, heh." From there they tried to sleep on benches, but were almost arrested for the attempt. They fled into some yards to escape the cops and then ended up stealing little girl's bikes and riding the 14-mile stretch from Tybee Island (where we all enjoyed a wonderful beach day yesterday) back to downtown Savannah. Apparently they were doing really well riding for a long time, having only been almost hit 10 or 15 times considering they had no lights and black clothes. About half way through their journey, flashing lights showed up behind them. River was such a victorious champion that he ditched his friend, who had been too drunk to even begin this trip in the first place. "Man, he was just riding like a zig zag, man. I was like, 'yo, stop doing that, man.', but he just kept on it". It sounds like if a cop hadn't shown up, he would be dead from being hit by an early morning commuter, but River screamed, "Yes, Shaggy is in jail, bro." He burped, mouth jutting sideways as he slammed down on a chair. "Fuck, Dude. I would have been too, but I threw that piece of shit bike into a swampy field by the road. I ducked down in the swamp, dude." In the high marsh grasses, from a brave distance, while his

163

friend was slammed against the cop car and handcuffed for public drunkenness, theft and a DUI, our brave warrior waited it out and then heroically rode the little, pink girl bike all the way back here. He plopped down in front of the computer and began playing games and making snorting grunts as he cracked another beer. We all just went back to sleep, except River who continued to do what he does best... *Whatever that may be.*

The little kitten is meowing and crying now. Other Girl Traveler staying on the couch next to me had claimed title as co-parent to the kitten yesterday after Shaggy told us he was staying behind to hang with River at Tybee Island. I grab Sonny and hold him as he starts purring so soft and gentle. *Poor little thing.* I feel so sad for him. I try to make him content as we both doze off to the sweet sound of tiny marbles rolling across a wooden floor, such a sweet kitten purr to relax my worried mind. Yesterday River asked me if he could ride with me to Jacksonville tomorrow because I said I was leaving that way. I told him a no, but he begged and told me he'd split gas. So I said a hesitant maybe. I still did not want to drive River to Jacksonville tomorrow and had grown very excited about the idea of him being left at Tybee Island. For now, I'll just settle for the peace of a sweet kitten in my shoulder purring my worries away. *I do feel like he isn't ever getting in my car again though.*

I wake up to a strange sound of something that sounded almost like a woman yelling, but it faded hastily. I actually couldn't tell what it was, but I just ignored it, reached for the kitten to ensure its safety and went right back to bed. Then again, I wake up to another odd sound, but this time it was a little yelling kitten. I leaned over and she was in the middle of the floor meowing. I focused my eyes on her and tried to reach out and grab her, but I couldn't quite reach. Just then, my eyes focused on the screen and I realized that there was porn on the computer. Then I realized that although River's back was to me and the room, I could see some movement. *Oh my god...* "What the fuck do you think you are doing?" I blurt out, natural instinct ignoring all civility from this point on.

"Eeewwoohhh." is the sound that he made, signifying that he had just been caught. "I didn't think you were awake…" He starts to shuffle around messing with his clothing and quickly changing the computer screen back to a game as if nothing had happened. I am in shock. He sips a beer and starts playing a game again.

"No! No! What the fuck? What the absolute fuck? Ah! That is fucked up and disgusting! You! You are disgusting and the fact that you even think that was ok is just… UGH! I am done. Fuck you. You are not coming with me. Find your own ride to J-ville because you are not coming with me." I stand up in utter disgust and begin gathering my things.

"Damn, chill out." He tried to brush me off, but outraged, warranted feminism rises. The feminism raccoon is justifiably released and thrashing.

"What!?!" I am fuming by this response. I respond in the most inappropriately appropriate way I can with a big ol' eff you. "Accordion, I am going. I will be back to get you and drive you downtown, but this is bullshit and I will not put up with this any longer."

Accordion responds right away, "Nah, I am ready to go downtown. I'm just laying here thinking anyhow; at least down there I can relax by the river with a hot drink and prepare for this. This is a very big day." He starts wrapping up his sleeping bag and I check with the girl to ensure that the kitten will be safe. I don't want to have a kitten on the road, but I will if I have to. She promises me she will take care of it from here on and that this kitten is now hers, not Shaggy's. The way she held it at the ocean gives me some sense of hope that she will truly care for Sonny. I march out of that crack house with more pride for feminism than I ever had before. *Fuck that.*

We arrive on the cobblestone road, downtown by the river and I say my farewells to this beautiful, traveling man. He is such a skilled musician and I am so happy to have been able to know him. Even out of the poisoned dirt filled cracks occasionally grows a beautiful flower and I will never forget Accordion. I wish him the best and I hope he finds the respect for his accordion playing that he deserves because he is the best street performer I've ever heard. I race out of that city and give it my last angry exhale- forget you, ya lovely, sexy city, full of bittersweet beauty and twisted grotesque life.

I head south again finally. Today I will finally hit Florida! A triumph fills my eyes while I drive and I know I will have inner fireworks to celebrate my finally making it to Florida. Sometimes it takes the dark's contrast to be able to see the light. Today I am so alive and knowing of my worth.

Back to that life analogy poem from a few days prior… Kalsey had told me that it's ok to stop paddling for a bit and just enjoy a float in the Savannah river of life. And I did that for a few days, but the problem with floating is that so many people do that here and they all seem to jam up on each other in the river. I got stuck behind a few of them, but grabbed my paddle and pushed them out of the way. And the problem with a water current that stops flowing is that it gets stagnant and begins growing fungus and algae. I need fresh, flowing water. *No Leaches.*

I feel those butterfly wings that I have been growing start to shake of the growth exhaustion. They begin to stretch and elongate, excited to begin to fly.

I need a fresh current of vibration and the freshest, purest water I could possibly imagine was just beyond that state line. And the fresh water I could feel in my mind isn't even fresh water; it is salt water. And I can already taste its cleansing properties, its salty purification releasing me from the stagnation of poisons gathered in the cesspool I just woke up in. *Florida, I absolutely cannot wait to taste you and your cleansing, salty water.*

Chapter Twenty-Seven

Day 22 to Florida- Finally

"Let go or be dragged." -Zen proverb

A parking lot greets me as I stop to take a break. Driving hours at a time is not my favorite way to travel. I prefer to make stops everywhere I can to explore the different types of cultures across the country and take as long as I can to get anywhere, mostly because there is so much to see and experience between the normal tourist driven destinations loaded with cookie cutter corporations and pamphlets telling me where to go. Pamphlets to guide to attractions are helpful, but they aren't the culture of the locals most of the time. And corporations that exist mile after mile are not a place I want to spend my time or hard earned money. I want to see the local home designs and talk with the local good-hearted people. It's very subtle, but if I put on my open-minded-culture-goggles, this majestic, beautiful country opens up in a very interesting way. The wide expanse of local restaurants and diners become sanctuaries for locals who have nowhere to hang besides churches or their homes, but they don't like the other locals enough to invite them over. They may have lived in these small towns their whole lives, speaking to mostly the same people so they get enthusiastic to tell someone about the world they know, have always known and will probably always know. Who better to learn about a true location than a true local?

Entire lives of people I have never known unfold before me, their daily ins and outs on repeat and I float by their timeline momentarily, included in their world for just a blink of moments. The diversity in this country is just magnificent, a treasure of experience unlocked beyond the invisible walls of humanity's need to be separate, our desire to live in learned solitude, yet in the right place at the right time, even the most solemn elderly man, cane in hand, bent over looking up to meet my eyes from below his worn Veteran hat, opens up his world to me, telling me stories from his childhood over that sunny hill where they used to hop the fence to play with lambs. His eyes glow with new life as he explains that he married his school sweetie and he spent his life as a farmer, watching the sun rise and set each day, an artist creating his artistic landscape, his palette was his time, his paint was his passion and his finished portrait was the pride of his work in those fields. And before me, he opens up for the first time in years, crawling out of the shadow that our generation has placed him in; and he shares with me his gallery of his life's work verbally. But I can see it in his eyes. Its moments of crystal, genuine existence like this that one will usually never encounter at the corporation guided country trip. We can ride around, pull up and take pictures of ourselves in a location or by a sign proving that we were physically at that location. *Yeah, that's cool that I can prove I sat by something.* Or we can climb into that landscape, dive into that culture and really be in that place entirely. A photograph will never capture the true essence of a culture being experienced while traveling. This indulgence in cultural experience is the difference between tourism vs. traveling. When I really am in a place, there is no rushing. My internal life experience sensors turn on and they replace the on switch of my camera. Life is best experienced through really living, not preserving possibility.

I pull in at one gas station right as my car hits empty. I buy an ice cream cone so I can use their Wi-Fi to send out a Sofa -request to the upcoming cities. I then go to the gas pump and fill up my car, but the pump denies my card. Fear floods my mind as I realize that maybe I have used up all of my money! *Oh no!* I don't know how much I really started with, but I do know that I spent a great deal to move out to Erie and then the few months' rent and electric bills without my having a job at that time. I panic and realize that oops... I may have to beg people at this gas station. My mind fills with creative ways to ask and I decide that this is the time to make a sign and do magic tricks. "Hmm... I just used this card yesterday for gas." I tell the gas station attendant.

"Why don't you call your bank and see why it declined then come back up here."

"Brilliant idea!" Then I remember that I didn't call this card to say that I would be out of the state so they probably blocked my card thinking it was stolen. Right now I suppose I do live a rather odd life that could resemble a theft. "Hello... yes, I think you guys may have blocked my card. Yes, my number is..." and I give her all the info just to hear back some dreaded words.

"No, your card isn't blocked. It should work." Hearing this just reinforces the fact that I am out of money. *No, there is no way I am out. I had plenty of money to start! I know I did!*

"Hmm... well this puts me in a tough spot. I need to get gas and we tried it several times already and it does not work." I then realize that someone probably did steal my card information and drained my account. An angry fire is ignited within as I talk back and forth with this very sweet, yet so far disappointing lady. "Well, maybe someone stole my card numbers and drained it."

"No… no you have… (Let's just say it was something close to $1800) left so you shouldn't have an issue with your card."

A confused comfort slides through me and releases some tension in my neck and shoulders. I breathe deep and feel a calm flow over me. "Well, I do. I can't use it and I am about to be in Florida and I need gas to get there."

"Oh, are you in Georgia?" she asks. I confirm. "Oh, well that makes sense. We have a strict no card usage in Georgia rule. There is just too much theft in that state so we just do not use anything in that state at all." Ok, so I understand the complexities behind theft and stealing, but I feel like knowing that this card is worthless in a few states, even just one state is a really big deal when unexpected.

"So what do you suggest I do…?"

"Do you have cash?"

I think back to my luggage and remember about my bag of change and a few hidden dollars left in pouches here and there. I often think of myself as being the victim of identity theft the moment something goes wrong monetarily, but establishing a basis of sanity in a situation is step one to conquering panic. I believe that is the basis of the annihilation of fear- the overcoming of the situation in the mind. This is all part of it that acronym for *F.E.A.R- Fake Experience Altering Reality* and that the only validation to the existence of this fear is within my own mind. On the other hand, Leopold Mountain talks about fear in a very similar, yet slightly different way. *"Fear is little more than your imagination creating blockages in accessing your dreams."* He speaks of the Six Haunts of Fearfulness in *Contemplate and Welcome Prosperity: Impoverished/ Longing, Criticism/ Blame/ Insecurities, Poor Health/Fitness/Wellness, Vanished Love, Aging /Weakening, Death/The End.* He states that all fears are blends of these six haunts that cling to everyone's mind from time to time. Personal power comes in the form of identifying our fears and not allowing them to stop our progression or peace of mind. It basically comes down to mind over matter; that is why I now am able to catch myself before I spiral off on this insane tantrum of false beliefs about my current situations. For instance, rather than allowing my mind to become frantic, like I used to, I take control of the situation calmly and identify the problems to seek out a desired solution. All I need now is enough money to make it to Florida's border and I probably have that. I just have to make it to Florida!

I can definitely do that. I hope… I check my maps to try to choose a new destination and I see Jacksonville. With a pile of pennies in my gas tank, nothing can stop me! At least nothing can stop me until these pennies run out. First though, I want to get to the beach as soon as possible which means I'll already be in Florida and able to access my account. *The beach. Yes... That's all I care about.* I slide over Florida's border without problem.

I was so excited to take a picture with the 'Welcome to Florida' sign, but they don't allow it! Those highway designers must anticipate that many individuals drive to Florida and want to take a picture with the sign so they have it mounted to the bridge so that the only way to see it is to drive under it. Therefore no crazies will be pulling off on the side of a busy highway, risking not only their lives, but the lives of every car passing. Those mega-lane highways can be very tricky to pull off and pull on.

So I rush to get over to the right lane to pull into the tourism welcome center. Usually they have a large 'Welcome To This State' sign. They better have a sign this time because I am so excited that I may light something on fire with my happiness if there is no way to represent this journey I am about to complete! It's been so many days, so many diverse experiences and I am finally about to be in the place that I sought out over three weeks ago! Heck, this journey began in my mind 6 years ago! *I deserve to have celebratory sign documentation!*

As I pull in I see old people crossing and little dogs dancing. *They aren't really dancing, but I kind of feel that little dogs are always dancing.* I see the *Welcome to Florida* sign, shimmering gloriously, an 18 ft. tall badge, my victory platform! A giant group of Asians are taking a picture in front of it, holding up peace signs and wearing Mickey Mouse ears and shirts. I laugh at stereotypes, but not in a bad way. I am such a happy appreciator of life's comedy in normal situations. People are lined up and growing impatient as I dance like all the tiny dogs around me, happy to be free and happy to be alive, slobbering in the gentle breeze, in the salty air kissing sunlight on the salty trees. The sun is baking my pale north-eastern skin and my eyes can't believe how beautiful the sway of a palm tree is here. It's as if I slipped into a tropical buzz, as if I slurped a big sip of some giant spiritual margarita. A lady behind me complains about how long the Asians are taking to get their picture. I turn around with glowing stars in my eyes and mention how lucky we are that we get to stand here longer observing how happy everyone is. She looks at the ground as her semi-crippled husband mentions how they could go faster to which I respond how much I'd love them to go before me so I could take their picture because they looked so cute in their matching outfits. They looked at each other curiously, and then blushed as they realized they did actually exactly match. They laughed while the husband said, *(yep you guessed it),* "What are the chances of that?"

By the time they left that visitors' center they couldn't have been in a better mood and all it took was me holding my space to be happy and not allowing their darkness to overtake my light. *A single candle can cast light onto all the walls of a dark room.* I go inside and I start to check out a bunch of the Florida pamphlets; every page I touch, I handle like an ancient Mesopotamian manuscript, a delicate doctrine guiding me to the Fountain of Youth. I see the massive map of this beloved state, the elongated angled phallic shaped state that penetrates all forms of success in my life at this very moment. *I have made it to my destination*! I am stunned as it really sinks in.

I cannot believe it!

All that time, all that wonder, all those frozen moments and crazy situations, all of that was pulled together for this moment. *Here I am! Now!* Right now I am in Florida and my smile couldn't be any bigger. I realize that they have an orange juice and grapefruit juice stand offering free juice samples. I film a sweet lady talking about the free orange juice samples for The Everything Show. Suddenly, she goes into a strange reenactment of some traumatic event that has happened in her recent past with her ex-husband. I keep recording, hoping she'll stop, but she keeps going and I can see in her eyes that she is no longer present in front of me, but she has teleported. The previously cheerful message has been vomited on by this point, so I stop recording although I make it look like I still am so she isn't thrown off. I guess she really needed to talk and maybe the camera gave her enough confidence to unravel something deep inside herself. If that's the case, then I am happy to be the mirror for her in this moment. I figure that instead of being a rude individual, I can just let this part kind of delete from the filming. No one needs to see a middle aged woman have a mental breakdown right as I have my spiritual breakthrough, right?

I consider that maybe some viewers would like to see that considering how much people watch reality television… Nah. That's not what my soul is about. I am about truth and purity, especially on this quest. She apologizes with tears in her eyes and exclaims that she didn't know where it all came from. I tell her that it's all ok and I was more than happy to help her rid her body of that tension, especially since I am full of so much light right in this moment. I may have been the perfect person to swoop into her life now. She wiped her eyes and explained how she felt so much lighter and I genuinely smiled as I hit the delete button.

Getting close to the beach, I see two hefty power plants and I also see a colossal shaft of black smoke billowing out of somewhere. I try not to freak myself out, but apparently that has become another job for me. I try to breathe deep to calm myself, but the smoke thickens and I can see debris flying around on the highway. White ashy flakes, burnt snow was raining all over, becoming so thick that it is nearly impassable in the front so I get off of an exit and I call SkyFly, a SofaCruiser in Jacksonville, because I fear that not only was this my destination, but maybe this was my final destination because a bomb went off in the nuclear plant and is now spreading toxic radiation into my lungs and everyone's bodies! It would be a pretty poetic fitting if the best moment in my life would result in the end of my life.

But that would be too ironic. That isn't possible... Right?

SkyFly Gypsy tells me that she does not see it anywhere and she checked the internet and didn't see any recent posts about it so that it is probably not a big deal. *Or it could be the biggest deal in the world! The total annihilation of Florida with me in it!* Or it may not be a big deal which is what I prayed for. I am happy where I am and I became way too perturbed by this. As I describe the increasingly difficult driving conditions she does tell me that this is not normal. I ask her to go inside and check the internet and see what it says and to call me right back. In the meantime, I turn around alarmed and am driving the opposite direction away from the danger, toward the clear skies. I call my mom and tell her about the white ash everywhere and the smell of burning and smoking. Both of her daughters are in Florida so I wish not to frighten her, but this is kind of scary for me, my tender mind ignoring toxins and radiation exposure on it.

SkyFly Gypsy calls back and tells me that it is just a controlled burn in a state park that is out of control. That seems to be a common theme among parks apparently. I stop after the skies clear to sit on the first beach I can find. There are people that invite me to play volleyball, but all I want to do is sit in absolute silence with the sunshine soaking me. Some of the best things in life spawn from completely unplanned events. It is always good to be prepared for any situation, but it is also very good to allow for positivity to take hold of your spirit and just go for the ride. Sometimes I end up at the top of a mountain overlooking an incredible view that I never would have seen otherwise. In this case, on this day, this unplanned opportunity happened with a gal named SkyFly Gypsy.

This was my only slightly negative SofaCruisin situation this whole entire trip. That site, if used properly, is very amazing. I contacted a guy named Skip in Jacksonville, Florida. I posted a Sofa request in the general location of people and he had commented on it offering me a place to stay. He had several references that looked pretty legit so I decided that I could trust it as a safe place to stay. The comments stated that he and his mother were so hospitable and helpful. They cooked for the travelers that they hosted and they offered them everything in their homes so I considered this to be the perfect place for the night. Especially after the night I had before, this sounded like heaven. I then noticed that I had a personal message from a girl named SkyFly Gypsy and I had never before received a message similar to this.

The message read:

"Hey, Katie. Do not stay with Skip." *Dread gulped down my throat.* "I stayed with him two nights ago and he was really weird. There is something wrong with him and I don't trust him. He didn't do anything in particular, but I just felt so uncomfortable by the things that he said and the way that he talked and looked at me. I eventually just pretended to be so exhausted that I went to the room and locked the door. I did not trust him at all and I would feel terrible not telling you that. You are welcome to stay with me at this guy's Sofa in Jacksonville. His name is Arnold and he has two Sofas. I stayed here last night and I'm just staying the night again. Here is my number…"

Wow…That is the complete opposite of what the reviews said. I don't take warnings such as this lightly. Unfortunately, I had read her message after I had already given Skippy boy my number and told him I was going to stay. My phone text signal went off and I flipped it open to see a text from a new number that I didn't recognize. Fear invaded my eyes as I opened the text to see the message, "Hey, Katie. It's Skip. I have a very nice Sofa for you tonight. Also, we could eat dinner together. Let me know when you get into town." That was a pretty standard message from people, to be honest. It wasn't creepy. I just decided not to respond yet. I'd much rather stay with a girl and young guy. Then the text signal went off again.

"It would be really nice if you came early. My mom is out of town for the week and I don't want to eat alone. I could pick up a bottle of wine and we could talk about travels. Let me know your ETA."

Wow. That explains it. He is a 40+ year old man who lives with his mom and as long as she is there, everything is fine. But when she is out of town, he's got an open house to lure in young, sexy, traveling chicks. I make up an excuse about getting stuck in Savannah another night or that I was picked up by a hot motorcycle broad and ditched my car in the ocean or something. I don't remember what I said, but it was a couple days before he stopped messaging me.

Since I had taken the back roads to the sunshine state and I had stopped several times at random places to see unplanned things and to get a different perspective on old decrepit towns, I arrived at the beach much later than I anticipated, but it was still perfect. I take a dip in the ocean to cleanse the

173

weirdness from my soul. As I step in, shivers churn up my toes. I step back and observe the open beach before me. I watch the tide go back into the ocean and I run full force into the surf, laughing outrageously as my legs blend into my thighs, into my hips, and I trip/dive into the sandy current while the ocean holds my whole body. I laugh and blink, unbelieving of the world I have found myself in. *I am here!* This burst of water is my initiation ceremony welcoming me to the other side of life. The water is so crisp and refreshing, flooding my being with sparkling presence, powerful divinity gushing all around my quickly numbing body. The wind chills my skin to the bone as I wade through it, but I sink back and just keep swimming, entirely in love with this pure moment. This is the immersion into my own personal power, cleansing everything from the previous days' stagnation; this crisp ocean current is my purification sanctuary, my sacred baptism. I swim as far as I can go without stopping until I feel I am sweating from every frozen pore in my body. I allow myself to fully relax, feeling both internal breath-heat blend with the frigid cold water caressing me. I then check my phone to discover that Rawky has messaged me.

"Hey, Katie. I will be in Jacksonville soon. I think you said you were going to be around here so let me know. Maybe we can get together for dinner or something. I have two other SofaCruisers meeting up at *Relaxed Shroom at 8 if you would like to."

So after texting SkyFly Gypsy and Rawky both back and forth, I realize that I have a good window of time to meet up with Rawky and the other surfers before I went to stay the night with SkyFly Gypsy. I sit out and watch the surf for a while, allowing the gentle ocean breeze to dry my salt lined hair. My head becomes a dusted mop of anime character styled semi-spikes and I realize here how awesomely textured my short hair looks when it dries in salty water. Nature is my best hair gel. I moved the car in an angle as to pop the hatchback open so I could stack my blankets in a pile behind my back and lean against them while I snack on crackers. The sun was alive on my skin as I smiled at the exquisite world I had found myself in. *I just cannot believe I am here and apparently neither can others.* It's as if it is so rare to just see a young woman smiling and being happy alone in her car just being. People drive by and stare at me as if I am doing naked somersaults, but really all I am doing is just sitting and being one with the purifying world. Some glance over and smile at the acceptance of seeing a young gal enjoying her solo time. A man walks by and is surprised to see me lounging in the back of my wagon.

"You've got the best seat in the house." He calls at me while he passes.

"Yeah, I know it's just so perfect in this spot."

174

He smiles and keeps on walking by. Several minutes pass and I realize he is sitting on the back of his truck bed drinking water out of a large container. Eventually we continue our conversations and he tells me that he hated his life the last few years working 9-5 for a corporation, just retired and immediately sold his house and converted his truck into a small traveling apartment. He lives on the road and lives how he wants to live. This caught my eye. I couldn't believe there were older people, even retired people who just broke away from the grips of common society like that after having lived an entire life in the restrictions of cultural expectation. I am not alone!

"Wow! That is so amazing!" *If only I was paid for how many times I uttered these words this trip already...* There is so much astonishing life to be experienced in this world! He then continues to show me the conversion he has done to his car. He has battery chargers and solar kits, a computer and a water filtration system. The batteries are in an external flap he installed on the right side of the back of the motor home. On the right is where he kept his spare water jugs and other equipment. Inside he can sit completely upright with inches to spare above his head. There were shelves he created, each for separate purposes. The one was to hold his laptop and that was a swivel arm on an angle so he could comfortably watch shows on his laptop at night and the batteries would hold a charge for a couple days. I forget how much power he said they could generate, but it was very impressive, the amount they would be able to output when needed. I have never seen such a display in a car before and this was the first of many car conversions I would encounter. This encounter watered some of my 'idea seeds' that I had planted years before in my mind. And thus, the sweet little sprouts of creation began to grow.

I have no idea how to find Relaxed Shroom, but for some reason I assume that I can find it if I drive to the right so I do just that. After driving for several minutes into increasingly suburban housing, I realize how senseless it is to assume that I can just stumble upon a dining establishment in such a large city like this. I have no idea where I am. *The ego vs. intuition struggle inside of me is resilient...* I decide to turn left at the next available cross over to do a U-turn to head back into the main business district to ask someone for directions. As I spot the next left opening, I realize it is right next to a very industrial and kind of boring looking grey building that says on it in bright shining letters, *Relaxed Shroom.* I freak out. "Whoa! No way! Seriously, what are the chances?" I yell to myself exhilarated at the exact accuracy of my intuitive actions. That same old smile develops across my face and I can sense my eyes animate with all sorts of wild happiness. I park in the parking lot right at the closest spot and realize that I am still wearing a wet swimsuit and now it has gotten a bit colder. I kind of feel the need to take it off. So I put a towel over me and I quickly do a wardrobe switch which takes

175

about 25 seconds. I step into pants and pull them up as the towel falls off my shoulders revealing a bra. I don't see a bra as being a big deal any longer at this point considering I walk around constantly with a swimsuit top on when I can. So I slide on a shirt and close the door and look over to see an old man open the restaurant door for me, greeting me with a very excited and pleased expression, "Well, that was a quick change if I ever saw one."

Rawky meets me instantly and we grab a seat with the two girls, Charlotte and Megs. They are dressed in very odd outfits and tell us about how they have a group that gets together and drinks and runs around the city doing laps all over the place. Apparently I could have been invited to this if I had arrived earlier…But oh well. After they describe it, I talk to them about the Law of Attraction and explain how it's been working for me. I say, "I am deciding right now that I want to be a part of one of these drunk run games with a group of friends soon!" *This statement of purpose is important because the opportunity really does reveal itself on the second last night of this trip.*

The crowd is playing a game of trivia, but we are so behind in the game at this point that we do nothing other than laugh and talk like old friends reuniting. SofaCruisin people all just seem to get along, like a global community that instantly links friendships with people from any region of the world. It's a bond that goes beyond that fact that we've never met before. It's instant friendship. Our food takes much longer to get to us than we expect, which is fine because we were having such a grand time anyhow. But I did still have to get to the other house later to meet SkyFly Gypsy and the guy that has the apartment. He wakes up at 6 am for work so I want to get there in a timely matter, but by the time our pizza had arrived, we had each downed at least two beers and were just in absolute jubilation over this life and the wonderful things to see in it. Rawky keeps elbowing me and pointing at their tits. *Uggghhh...* It's similar to a caveman grunting and pointing at women. Often I feel like men who see women as being just objects for their pleasure are being nothing higher than a standard animal from the jungle. It's as if he sees nothing more than just biological instincts to reproduce. He's seriously like a robust Neanderthal. I punch him in the shoulder and glare indicating that I am done with his caveman judgements. But there is something about Rawky I do kind of like, despite all the things I don't care for. He is a damaged man looking to make his life better and he is really putting himself out there as his true self to find a better life. And in that respect, I do like him because I am doing the same thing. Would I trust him to sleep next to me in a tent and travel with him?

Heck, No! Absolutely not.

But I do like him because I do feel like he is at least genuine. At least he is upfront with his obsession of getting laid and not closeting his creepy perversion. He is true to me in who he is and even if I don't want to stare at beautiful boobs with him right now, I respect the fact that he is real. He isn't pretending to be a gentleman. I feel as if he would not spike a woman's drink to get laid. He would much rather try and fail and try and fail ungracefully until he finally succeeds. There is no deception in this man. He is what he is. Maybe that is what I like about him, his unending persistence. Too often in my life I meet a wall of difficulties and just give up. I have personally done this over and over in many endeavors in my life. But Rawky keeps on going and doesn't get fazed by defeat often. And that is most likely the reason he owns his own construction company and is still being paid while on the road traveling the country for two months. *Persistence- That is definitely something I would like to know about more. Only a little differently…*

After our drinks, Chelsea invites us over to her house. I feel like I should go to the other house, but Rawky really wants me to go and Chelsea really wants me to go as well. Oh well. I can swing by for like 20 minutes or so. They have a nice apartment in a beautiful, simple neighborhood. The house is so clean and the walls are white. She makes us mixed drinks and immediately pulls out papers to roll a joint.

"I'm not very good at this. Does someone else want to try?" Immediately Rawky jumps up in a heroic stance. He fumbles around for several minutes, using not just one, but three papers to try to cram the weed into the roll, but he is so clumsy and goofy and ends up sticking the whole thing in his mouth making it soaking wet. The other girls just kind of watch him in disgust as he keeps smooshing it and denying the fact that he is just absolutely terrible at rolling anything apparently. The papers rip in half and he throws it down angry that he now has failed in his valiant attempt to win the hearts of the women in this marijuana effort

"Damn, I wish I had a bowl, but I broke mine last week…"

I am not the best at rolling anything, by any means, but I offer my services for them. I have no intention of smoking any of that stuff. Rawky pulls the dry contents out of his sticky paper mess and slides it over to me. As I squeeze as much as I can into it, I try to imitate the stuff at the apartment in North Carolina two weeks ago. They rolled it like the most beautiful Bob Marley joint and that is exactly what I created for these folks before me. I secured the seal and then handed it over. Smoking weed is such a strange thing. The person who rolls the joint or blunt really does slobber all over the thing. It's pretty disgusting when you think about it and where their mouths may have been. They moisten it to seal it and then use a lighter to dry it, but it is sealed with whatever was in their saliva contents, whether it be a sickness or a person they kissed or a cigarette they half smoked. I can't tell you how many times in high school I saw people pick up a partially used cigarette on the side of the road and then offer to smoke weed with my friends. I never caught onto that 'fad'. It disgusted me every single time I saw it. Anyhow, every time I see someone rolling something I think of these things. Not to mention that I don't think I've ever seen a stoner wash their hands before they rolled anything either and after watching Rawky's tuna fish escapade the other day, I am not too certain anything he touches is clean anymore. They all smoked and I finished my drink and looked at the clock to see that it had been almost an hour.

"Whoa, I've got to go!" There really was no reason why I was leaving a SofaCruisin house to go to another SofaCruisin house at 9 pm. Logic reasons that I really should have just stayed. They offered me their couch and I really should have just accepted it, but there was something that compelled me to go to the other house. I can't explain the feeling other than it felt like destiny. It was more than just a desire to meet new people or the fact that I felt I had made an obligation to them. There was just something else begging me to listen. And at the time I felt chaotic for feeling that I needed to go elsewhere. It is actually rude of me to arrive now because this guy was going to be up late waiting for me. But something was telling me to go so I left that house in a hurry and realized that I had almost a half hour drive to the next place. But I needed to do it! I needed to make it there!

And I did arrive as quickly as I could. I was greeted by a very good looking, clean cut guy and a very pretty gal hanging around in his even cleaner apartment than the last place. Everything was as orderly as this guy's clean cut shave and hair line. They couldn't have been any friendlier as I apologized for being so late. Sometimes it's as if the world just makes it that way and even though I could have made better decisions to be timely, the universe called and at least I answered. I can't stand being that straggly time-conflicted traveler, but sometimes I guess I just can't help but to be that. We talked and got to know each other a bit. I was honestly so exhausted from the previous night of not sleeping and I explain the story to them and they cannot believe it. "Whoa, that's got to be the craziest night you've had!" At this point, this statement was true. But over the course of the next few weeks, that night would be beaten many times in the crazy category. I explain the magic thing and they follow suit with asking me to do a trick. I make one up quick, because Clean-Cut has to work early and goes to bed after the trick.

We say our goodnights and head off to sleep. *I have no idea what tomorrow will be exactly, but something feels like it's going to be amazing.* I drift off immediately.

Chapter Twenty-Eight

Day 23

"The life lived as poetry is magical."

Callie sips her lemon water while watching me. "So is that how you afforded it?" I ask her what she means and she mentions magic.

"Well sort of. I had money saved up, but I didn't want to allow myself to touch my savings account. So I decided that everything that I did was cash, cash which I had saved up and cash which I had made along the way. Traveling with my car was expensive because of gas, but the plus side was that I always had a place to sleep. In later travels, when I traveled on foot, it was way less expensive, but then I absolutely had to carry everything and I absolutely had to find a place to sleep every night."

"I should learn magic." She smiles. "Then I could make money anywhere too."

I look her up and down momentarily, observing her delicious figure and thick, toned thighs. "You could always be a stripper. That's good money, I hear."

....

I think about how outgoing SofaCruisers are. This guy met me for a half hour last night and assumed I not only wouldn't kill him in his sleep, but wouldn't spend the whole day looting his house while he left for work at 7 am, leaving two random girls sleeping in his living room. But he did tell me to help myself to coffee so the first thing on this morning routine was just that. He had gone out special yesterday to buy a bag of bagels for us so I helped myself to the fattest everything bagel I could find. I try my hardest to be as quiet as possible as to not wake SkyFly Gypsy on the couch, but that proves to be a failed attempt because I hear the cushions move and I turn to see her eyes meeting mine. She rubs them and stretches big as I greet her with a jolly hello. Over the course of the morning, we end up talking about what we are doing and what it is that we are trying to accomplish. It's pretty amazing to encounter another young woman doing something so similar. She pulls out her tiny laptop and tells me about how she was mugged in Detroit and they stole her entire bag, including everything that she was writing. So she learned her lesson and now immediately posts her stories to her blog every day so if anything were to ever happen, at least she wouldn't lose all of her hard work.

I had never considered this before. I always thought that if I kept my stuff on me I would be safe, but a mugging is something I never really thought about. Yes, I always keep three knives on me, but I never really considered having that insurance fail before. She types her previous day's adventures into the tablet as we make coffee and talk about our lives. I tell a few stories of here and there and she combats my stories with her crazy adventures. My eyes glisten at what she is trying to do. SkyFly Gypsy is an amazing person with incredible determination. She tells me, "Yeah, I always thought hitch hiking was interesting, but there are so many people who have done it. It's just a ride from one place to the next so it's not a big deal. So I thought, 'Well, what about catching rides on boats?' but then I read some stories about how that has already been done before by several people."

"Yeah I just met some guys who live on their boat!" I exclaim excitedly.

"So the boat thing has been done. I wanted to do something that no one else has ever done in the world before. Something brand new." I watch her as she talks and she glows that type of glow that only true happiness, true ambition can bring. She is exactly where she needs to be in the world doing what she needs to be doing and everything about her shimmers. I think of this as a very important lesson to learn from someone else. I found it very inspirational how she used that experience as a way of motivating herself, rather than limiting herself. Perspective holds so much power over a human's mind and actions. She holds such a powerful charm about her and I cannot possibly begin to express how fascinating this girl is. She's really living life on the edge, similar to what I am doing, but with much more decisiveness and constructed planning. She excuses herself into the shower noticing the time and leaves me hanging in question. When she gets out of the shower, she starts to pack up her massive book bag.

"So what are your plans today?" She asks me, but my head is in the clouds.

"Oh, umm…Well, I don't know quite yet. I guess I'll head south, drive the A1A to Saint Augustine. Why? Do you need something? "

"Well, Clean-Cut was going to get out of work to take me to the airport at 12, but if you could do it that would save him the trouble of having to leave work."

I stare at her. "You need a ride to the airport? Where are you going next?" She begins to tell me about how for the last 8 months she has been traveling the country hitchhiking by airplane. She explains then in detail how it isn't just hitchhiking.

Ah... that explains her shirt. It reads "Quit Thumbing Around." It is much more of a connection, of a mission than anything else. She has had radio interviews and online glorification and magazine articles written about her. She actively goes out and engages her surroundings to produce her reality. And then suddenly I realized something. I realized that the pride I held in personally just helping Accordion Player or a SkyFly Gypsy is the same feeling that people receive when they help me. They really do just appreciate the opportunity to give. This lesson is what I need to learn from her. This world presents gifts continually and I am willing to accept all of the gifts I can get. It's rather amazing because when I met Car Converter Man yesterday, I wondered if there are any other young women out here doing something similar to what I am doing too.

And voila! Just like magic, she reaches out in a much more extreme way than me! In fact, I couldn't be more thrilled to help and be a part of the great life she is living. Pure willingness to provide for such a wonderful goal is all that I desired; just to be a part of her life's achievement. It made me step back and look through the eyes of all of those that have helped me so far. *Huh, being a part of someone else's adventure really is exciting after all!* The clouds cleared and the world opened up. Natural kindness still exists among humans. I can 100% declare that I have seen it and know pure desire to help others is still embedded in millions across this country. I have only been gone 22 days from Erie, but between driving across the country in February and all the different types of people who want nothing more than just to help, I can say that America is still genuinely beautiful. On the surface, we can be lonely and cruel, broken and downright malicious, but underneath the layers of humanity, a fine fiber of everlasting authenticity really does exist. I listen and ask questions about everything I can while we drive to the airport. Apparently she contacts guys that own their own private planes. They fly from one airport to the next and then back again to their hangars for fun and usually just fly solo. So they are more than happy to be part of her adventure in exchange for helping her out. It's a mutual exchange of sorts. This is how I've been trying to look at my trip so far. I have wanted to fill everyone's reality with inspiration for following their dreams in exchange for everything they have been doing for me, a mutual trade off from many different types of enjoyment.

And truthfully, this is really how life should be viewed all the time. There are so many lonely people out there. If they could provide someone an

181

amazing opportunity for just one day, only one day, they absolutely would create a snowball effect of good vibes in their everyday living. Life can become very monotonous to a lot of people and there is nothing wrong with monotony because it is safe and that is what people are drawn to, but there is so much vibrancy in diverse living. There is always a vivid beauty behind the breaking of monotony that gives a new freshness to those involved. The chains of daily expectation fall off, even if just for that moment.

It's sort of like when I perform a magic trick. When I do magic for older people (especially older men who don't often get surprised by anything anymore) and I see their eyes glow with curiosity as they stare at me and grab the cards yelling, "Now, what did you do?" I couldn't be more satisfied. It isn't about the fact that I can do something cool or amazing. It isn't about the money I make from doing illusions. It isn't about the fact that people recognize me as the magic girl. It is about the moment- that feeling. It is about the shredding of all reality, even if just for a moment to create a tear in the fabric of this standard life they have been living in. It's about the moment of utter astonishment that comes after their wet folded card is pulled from my mouth and revealed to be correct. It is that moment of absolute uncertainty when they grab the deck after a trick and shuffle through the cards determined to find a double, but ending up with nothing. It's the raw effect of a really good illusion. And this raw emotion can be applied to anything in life and nearly anyone in life. When I can get an absolute stranger to step outside their average routine to assist in my life, it can be a positive inspirational moment for them too. To me, there is no greater exchange than sharing inspiration.

We enter the airport for some free coffee. I am not sure if I am actually allowed to be here and I chat with a few pilots while she prepares her bags. "Well, if I had known something so beautiful was out here, I would have worn my nice suit today, whewwwiee!" waltzes out a pilot as he holds his hand before him. I reach out assuming that I should just kind of blend into the rest of this place the best I can and shake his hand. His big, meaty mitt grabs mine and pulls it close to his face as he gently kisses the back of my palm. "And what is it that you are doing here today?" he says while still holding my hand strong, forcing me close to his face.

Shoot… Busted. I wonder if I am in trouble. SkyFly Gypsy has just gone to the bathroom and now here I am caught getting a cup of coffee around the corner in an airport that I don't belong in. I'm busted! Before I get to open my mouth to say something stupid, he says, "Are you a pilot?" I laugh and tell him no. He is so quick to keep on talking about how pretty I am that I don't even need to explain what I am doing there. He just keeps on talking. "I would love to have you be my pilot mmm…mmm. Girl you could fly me anywhere." He still hasn't let go of my hand and it is starting to sweat.

"Hey! You old dog, get back on your leash." Another pilot says to him as he passes between us, "I don't think your wife would approve of you flirting with such a looker."

Ha! *He called me a looker!* Ha-ha! I don't think I have ever been referred to as a looker before. He shoots the other pilot nasty eyes and he jokingly says, "Aww Bill, now you went and told her I have a wife! Now my shots are shot!" he sends me up and down eyebrows signaling that he was joking, but from the response of all the other people that kept walking around, I can only assume that he does that all the time.

"Ha-ha. Katie, you causing trouble out here?" SkyFly Gypsy shows up laughing at the scene.

"Oh, Lordy! Bless my heart! There is another goddess in the building!" Flattery Pilot says dramatically while shooting me a wink. Men don't really flatter women like this anymore in our culture. I mean, it could be looked at as harassment by some, sort of, but no matter what, it makes you smile because it is an outward compliment. You see this flattery in the old movies. You see it in the old shows. Nowadays its uncultured bumping and grinding in a club or a "What up, ma?" There needs to be a gentleman revival in this country. *Hmm… Maybe lesbians are the new-age gentleman…*

We headed outside and entertained ourselves with some small lizards or geckos or whatever they are called that crawl all over everything in the south. We try to touch them for several minutes before she spotted her flight coming in for a landing. I had never observed one of these small personal planes move close up before. It kind of looks like a toy as it rolls in. At first glance, it doesn't look like a thing that could take people up into the air. It isn't big at all. I am not sure what I expected, but this tiny, pretty tin can wasn't it.

They meet and we all say our hellos and then she climbed in. He showed her the proper foot placement and explained that if she stepped to the side it would crack the wing. Something about this concept of foot placement being the determining factor as to if this thing would break midair or not kind of freaked me out. As she stepped down, the entire plane shifted a good 8 inches to the side due to what I assume to be a hydraulic pressure thing. Like I said, I have never seen one of these close up so I am just kind of examining how all of this is working. She slid her bag into the small compartment behind the tan, leather seat and then took her place while putting on the goggles, ear covers and microphone. He climbed into the pilot's seat and prepared himself as he pulled the hatch down over them. They gave a last goodbye before closing the airtight capsule.

I took out my camera in hopes of getting a good picture of them taking off so that I could put it on her website for her. I really do want to support other like-minded souls with a determination to accomplish more in life than the standard expectation. And within two minutes, they take off into the sky. I watch them as they disappear into the distance after doing a large circle overhead. *Wow. I decide in this moment, as I see them dissolve into the Florida clouds that I want to be in an airplane.* After all of the Law of Attraction reading that claims that if you believe it, then you can achieve it, I must be able to figure out a way! I say to myself, "I will be in an airplane soon." and I smile at the new strange new world I was just part of.

I go back and take a seat as another plane comes in for a landing. It is two young guys, not much older than I am, that climb out of the plane at rest. They come over, light up a few cigs and sit on the chairs beside me and start talking. I can't stop smiling. I just love to absorb all the culture I can and believe me, plane culture is entirely new in my eyes. I end up disrupting them due to something they said and I ask how? The one says that he always just wanted to be a pilot so he took classes, bought his own plane and now he can go whenever he wants to on his own terms. His friend was just along for the ride. I would have talked to them longer, but they didn't speak English very well, which I am fine with because I saw a sense of determination in his eyes and that is all that I needed to get from that encounter. I keep saying this, but there really is so much life to be lived in this world. My notebook guides my senses as I watch those guys take off and I take notes on what I am feeling at the time. It's rather difficult to continually keep updated on every event unless I make absolute time to document all the time. But I guess constantly being engaged in amazing activities so that I can't find time to write is nothing to complain about.

Two deep voiced pilots exit the doors next to me each holding a cup of coffee. They are talking and send me a polite hello when we make eye contact before standing next to me. This is the type of thing I really do like to see, two people just enjoying their lives and taking a break outside without the excuse of a cigarette. I don't see a great deal of that up in Pennsylvania, especially right now in the frigid cold. We end up talking and I, once again, tell my story about why I am sitting here in this local plane station alone with no reason to be here in Jacksonville, Florida. The guys think I am fascinating. They want to know more and they ask questions about me and about SkyFly Gypsy. Since I have talked about myself so much in the last few weeks, I am very happy to talk about another person's life and travels.

"Yeah, I think I may have read an article about her!" They tell me. These guys cannot believe that SofaCruisin exists. So John tells me that he is a pilot who does small flights from local places to other local places all over Florida.

That is what he does now. He told me his plane seats 12 and he just flies people from one local airport to the next. He used to be a pilot instructor and that is how he ended up getting his hours in so he could get his pilot's license. Apparently that is what most personal plane pilots do when they begin their training.

"Would you like to see the plane?"

"Yeah, I'd love to." *Wow, what are the chances! I just said how badly I wanted to be inside of a plane after seeing SkyFly Gypsy take off like 10 minutes ago! It took 10 minutes for that thought to manifest into a real situation!* He pulls the tiny door handle latch and the door folds down from above into steps, mentioning about how the sky's the limit, but I know now that even the sky is limitless. I grab onto the railing of the plane and think, *"As above, so below…"* and I climb up the stairs.

We went inside, watching our heads as we climb in and he shows me all the hidden compartments that are inside the backs of the seats and arm rests. Secret drink holding stations appear and I noticed that everything became a dual purpose storage container/ functional furniture. Then he tells me to take a seat in the copilot's seat and he slides in next to me in the other seat and pokes a whole lot of buttons and nozzles. He shows me the exact maneuvers and things that must be done in order to fly a plane. The panel before me is a buffet of knobs and buttons, gauges and whistles all serving their exact purpose. It was astounding how many buttons were on the walls and ceiling, lining the entire window of the front of the plane. We sit and hang out in there for a while. He gets out tiny waters from the cooler fridge located next to us and we look out the window and talk about what it's like for him to fly through the clouds on a daily basis. I take a few pictures of us together because this is just too awesome to not document. He explains that he has to prepare for his next flight as he escorts me back inside

I immediately go straight, *(well, gay)* to the beach and as I lay out my blanket, I think of how amazing that opportunity just was. I asked for an airplane and I got one almost instantly! I say out loud as I walk across the cool sand, "Thank you, Universe, for that opportunity! It was exactly what I said, but I would like to actually ride in an airplane next time, not just be in one. I know that I said I wanted to be in an airplane and I was given that chance, but now I want to ride in one!" I laugh at how precise the manifestation was. Being descriptive in asking what I am wanting is very important. They say 'know what you are wanting'. Being precise is crucial in vibrational emotional creation. This is a small, fun lesson in that.

I put my stuff down quickly and strip off my clothes. I've been wearing my swimsuit for hours now and it is about time I put that preparation to good use! I run in full speed, unaware of how nuts I must look arriving alone and sprinting to trip in the first few waves that catch my feet, but I don't care! *If the crazy are the ones really living life, then I would trade a sane mind for the craziest label any day!*

The chilly ice surge floods all of my skin, invading even the toughest to reach warm spots on me and chilling me immediately. The renaissance of me is taking place.

This I what my life is about... I burst through the surface and this salty realm tastes incredible; *I have worked so hard to get here.* I have learned and endured have so much in these last 22 days. I almost start to cry, but instead, I just start swimming. It startles me that I can't feel the bottom, but I don't care; this feeling of floating freedom is the most important thing in the world to me. And here I really am just floating, not even connected to physical Earth. I am swaying in the gentle infrastructure of non-solidity. I am a ship upon the sea and I flow with the currents. In this case, I do flow quickly and I swim my absolute hardest, stretching my body to its limit. Impaling the waves with my strides, I push myself down the coast of the beach. I swim until my body has reached its maximum amount of output, which by this time I feel as if I could be sweating if the water wasn't so chilled. It isn't even cold anymore and I look at the beach and all the people on it, mostly high school and college kids there for spring break and I think about how they are looking for everything besides the feelings I am experiencing now. They are searching for imitation life, a wasted party world faded reality, smashing bodies together in the dark. I remember that feeling, a pressure of the peers. I compare it to where I am right now. There is just no comparison.

I catch a few waves on my venture back to land. The gritty earth crunches beneath each arched step and I smile. Desperate sunrays beam down on my pasty, sun deprived skin begging, just begging for warm intervention. I really whole heartedly appreciate the beauty of this moment more than ever before. *The smell, the feel, the sounds of the ocean, ah, it's just the most therapeutic thing I can imagine.* I see the flakes of dead animals and dirt floating all around me in the thick, deep green shadowy, murky waters rolling in and rolling back out and I can't imagine a more serene world right now. I have been told that the gulf is so clear that you can practically see the ground all the way down! Until the day when I see the west coast of the Florida state, I shall wait, but until then this is perfection for me.

I collapse on the blanket and my bones sink into place. Until this moment, they had become gelatin, suspended such as the water suspended me. No one here knows me nor do I know them. It is entirely me here and right now. It's amazing how sick of people one can become while soul searching. I should have left Savannah two days ago, but oh well. Lesson learned. Trust my instincts. Don't get me wrong, though. I really did have an amazing time at the beach with all those Georgia kids and the kitten, but I really needed some solo beach time. And this ocean is most certainly the perfect therapy for a River rescue. I listen to the waves and I am continually interrupted by the kids next to me. Definite high school spring breakers, maybe college kids chilling with bottles and beers. I can't believe it. Right out in the open like that. They are sitting on each other's laps and making out and spanking each other while playing games.

Hmm… when did I become such a mean old lady sitting on the beach alone, yet not lonely? 10 maybe 15 minutes ago? I distantly pay attention to them and my reaction and I realize that I may be kind of jealous of their fun, especially after the giant group of field rompers in Savannah that I was a part of. I decide to interact with these kids in hopes that maybe they would invite me to their group. I go over there and ask if one of them will take a picture of me and the guys immediately line up and ask for my number. This isn't just college kids. This is college kids looking to get funky and do it with everyone. I decide that I think I'll pass on the invite and I am glad I did, because several minutes after I returned to my blanket home, the cops rolled up. Frenzy breaks out as everyone tries to hide the bottles under blankets and bodies. They all pose awkwardly, obviously not having been sitting in the positions they were pretending to be in and none of them even talk. They all freeze like awkwardly placed silent statues. It's the most hilarious attempt at being nonchalant that I have ever seen and I laugh as the cop comes up and scans over them. I smile and wish them the best and of course, the best does happen. The cops get off their seashore kart and grab two flags and take off down the beach to grab more flags.

The kids cheer when the cops get out of sight and I cheer for them. College kids are foolish and senseless. That's why they are in college though, to learn. And being dumb includes drinking and making bad decisions, but hopefully learning from them. But the thing is that these kids are at the beach. They somehow gathered enough money to go to the beach and bring alcohol and they didn't even have to drive back to their hotel. They were being what all college kids so aspire to be, drunken idiots having a blast on a beach in Florida. I smile as the kids turn down their vocal volume and I wish that I had the opportunity to be dumb somewhere beautiful with my friends before I moved. I never ever considered that to be an option though because I never knew anyone who actually lived that life. I smile and watch them while considering the power of my limited thinking my whole life and wonder what life would be like had I considered myself worthy of such experiences right out of high school. *Oh well. I'm here doing it now.*

I then realized that I may be getting too much sun. I was drying off from my first time really out in the sun for an extended period when I realized that I didn't bring any sunscreen down here with me and I didn't know where I left it in the car. It was packed up somewhere so I figured that I may as well ask someone nearby if I could use some.

"Hey, could I borrow some sunscreen?" As I say this, I realize how inaccurate borrow is. *As if I am going to scrape it off of me with a knife and smear it on a rag and give it back to them. Gross.* The young couple hands me their sunscreen and I spray a bit in my hands and rub it on my neck, shoulders, face and chest. I sit at the beach and enjoy the scenes all over. I listen to the beat of the earth's heart represented by the waves.

After that, I take off down the A1A, one of America's most famous drives. It is a nice two lane road that travels down the coast past beautiful ocean front properties sitting proudly on stilts surrounded by dunes and flowing grasses. Then, of course, you do enter the areas where it is sad, boarded up homes on stilts that look like they haven't been occupied for years. There is actually a great deal of them surprisingly and I can only assume that this wasn't the case before the 2008 recession hit. *Or maybe this is hurricane residue.*

But I enjoyed the drive and had the sunroof open basking me with all the Vitamin D I could possibly get. I didn't know what I was doing or where I was going, but I did know one thing for sure: I loved every single moment of it. Several hundred yards up, I see cars putting on their brake lights. I realize that the fog I thought I was driving into is actually smoke. There is just something about me entering Jacksonville and leaving Jacksonville that involves a lot of fire. I approach very cautiously in curiosity as to whether this is dangerous or not. I guess if worst came to worse, then I could just ditch the car and run a couple hundred yards to the ocean. I start to imagine a giant fire blossoming across the sands, catching fire to the giant dry prairie lands in northern Florida and southern Georgia. But since this was at the beach, I was developing strategies to go out and search for natural fire made beach glass. Then I realized I am planning this thing way too much and I should really see what is going on before getting too crazy in my head like I seem to like to do. I can hear sirens in the distance, although I cannot tell where it is that they are coming from.

The road becomes a big whirl of smoke, vision dissolved a couple feet in front of the car. It's become a trusting line of cars following each other through this smoky haze and I double check that all the windows are closed, realizing that I must have subconsciously done that awhile back. Pale yellow fills the air while I pass a brush fire off the road only a couple of feet. Two SUVs are parked there with guys on phones. It is rather foolish to park right in front of the fire and not behind or before it, but they are probably trained emergency crews that know what they are doing so I don't question it. I hear the sirens coming from behind me, but I am already passing the fire by the time they arrive. *First one on the crime scene!* It is really funny how everyone wants to be part of everything so badly. I watch the faces of the people driving by; everyone has their eyes pasted on whatever it is that they can see. Phones and cameras are out to catch any footage of mysterious Florida fires that they can. I smile as the air begins to clear, feeling like I was embracing a state of mental clarity too, that there is so much tragedy in this world that we become obsessed with it. I decide not to photograph it.

We are an under-appreciation nation. The natural beauty in this world seems to mostly be overlooked until something bad happens. Yes, all these cars are out here on the A1A mostly for only one reason- to enjoy. But I would bet that these people didn't pay that intense amount of focus to any other part of the trip. The part that they saw and will remember is the cigarette discarded from a window that caught a field on fire. The general natural beauty of every inch of the landscape will probably be overlooked in the memories of all those passing tourists, eyes starving for danger. *I guess I am guilty of this as well…*

Actually, when I look back at the world that I have lived in thus far, the most memorable days of my life have been those where I have been closest to danger. The threat of death always makes you feel more alive, but it's really just a stimulated physiological response to give your body an extra boost to survive, if needed. But it is also as if the thrill invested in yourself produces an additional zest for life that was forgotten about until you realize that, *"Hey, I might actually die."* And suddenly the burst of awareness flows through your veins and into your eyes and makes you strive to persist. It makes you strain every muscle to do what you must to retain that valuable precious thing that you have- your life. It makes you rise up to the threshold of your being, to a place where power radiates from your soul and the body shakes with enthusiasm to continue on. Maybe that is why we are obsessed with tragedy; it's the yin to our yang. It's the little reminder to keep on trying, to keep on living the best we can in every moment. It is that little bird that lands on your shoulder and tells you to get back on track before it's too late.

They do say that the best way to learn is to learn from experience, but I have discovered that this isn't entirely so. Negative experiences are not just painful, but they can either be a compost to grow from or it can be trash and damaging for many years. I felt that I needed to experience all; in fact, at this point of the trip, I sort of still feel the need to struggle, to feel pain and to live in the world of having nothing. I feel like I need to really hit the absolute bottom for some reason. Rock bottom is relative for everyone and not everyone needs to hit it. Eventually you need to wake up, but you never need to hit the bottom to do so. You can always watch other people experience misfortune and from their experiences, you can just learn without the consequences. It's kind of amazing how much everyone likes to talk about themselves. (*I wrote a book about myself...*) But give a negative person a simple introductory sentence and they will tell you everything about their struggles. They will say it with such vivid description and such agony that it can pour over you in their verbal waterfall. You can sip the tragedy from the look in their eyes and then you can realize that you do not need to struggle. You do not need to force pain into your life to learn from it.

Unfortunately for me, the feeling of the need to suffer manifested at the end of this day. *Not just basic suffering, ha. No, no.* But that special kind of education that jerks tears out of your gut, the emotional, educational kind of suffering rooted in your solar plexus, begging your soul to observe and learn something essential to your entire expanded reality.

Yeah, that's what is about to happen.

Chapter Twenty-nine

St. Augustine

May we find glory in even our deepest tribulations: alas, it is they that produce strength and patience and it is patience that creates durability and it is these raw experiences that create hope."

I drive out of the smoke and into the clear road. This is both metaphorical and real. *The Life Poem Extended.* I don't remember the clouds looking as appealing before I entered that fire, but the view of this world really is incredible right now. Eventually the gas light turns on and I have no idea how long it has been on because sometimes I fall in love with ideas that I have when I drive and I lose track of the fact that I am driving. I enter the next city and find gas instantly. I then begin the game of parking lot roulette. I drive in a few circles trying to find a parking spot, racing one car down narrow roads, but I lose. Then I observe another space while circling the block vigorously just to lose, once again. I drive a few blocks down and spot a great space directly in front of a large, brightly painted red porch. Tables and chairs lined the patio and the interior as I looked in the large, bay windows. It appeared super inviting and welcoming! *This spot must the parking space gold to me!* I can sleep in my portable hotel room, then wake up and go over to this place for breakfast. It must be a morning coffee shop or something. I can get something to eat and drink before heading out! *Wonderful! This is just perfect!* It's kind of funny how totally wrong I was to assume this to be a coffee shop, but only a few hours would reveal its truth.

I end up putting on a nice button up shirt and get my magic hat and my magic bag ready with my juggling sticks. I dig around through my props, deciding that two decks are better than one. I usually always carry a deck on me because it is very important to have a variety of tricks at any given moment and a deck of cards can become millions of routines and tricks. The opportunity of the world seriously is at a magician's fingertips with a deck of cards. The reason for my grabbing two is that oftentimes I will rely on one deck for standard tricks to allow spectators to shuffle it or put the cards on the ground, table or bench. But as one may imagine, constant usage creates wear and tear on the edges of the cards and a festival of germs and dirt. A card placed on a tiny bit of water will absorb it and warp slightly throwing off the entire deck's proportions. The tiny buildup of filth on the face of the cards increases with every touch of a hand and eventually the cards stick slightly to each other or don't slide properly. The subtle details in magic flourishes are

191

what make the effects so amazing and doing a trick that requires a good deck, but not having clean cards can entirely destroy an illusion instantly. A good magician can do amazing things with any deck of cards, but there are certain types of tricks that require not just a good magician, but a good deck of cards as well. Without the clean deck of cards, it is impossible to accomplish it accurately. I place several coins in my pockets for small close up impromptu illusions like switching pennies for dimes or transferring them from one hand to the other.

First thing on my agenda is to go to the bathroom. I walk the waterfront for a while, dipping into art galleries and local shops. I find it very difficult for me to just dive into performing on the street without first getting a feel for the culture of a place and the type of people I'll be interacting with while I am out. I then figure out a good place with a nice flow of people through it that doesn't seem to be patrolled by cops too much. I spot a large park with a statue and benches on the next block. There seems to be a solid flow of foot traffic through it, eager eyes for historical relevance rolling along the landscape. I sit on a bench and start coloring in a sign stating my purpose and my goals. The main feature on it is MAGIC. As I am finishing the sign, I see two moms with disgruntled children, one that had begun to cry slightly. I adjust my hat, put on my performer mask and I attack.

"Would you guys like to see a magic trick?'

The moms are immediately interested in the kids wanting to see a trick. As strange as it sounds, there are many times that children don't even know what a magic trick is. I show them something disappears and they really have no idea what they are looking at. It's rather challenging for me to think that so many children across the country have never been introduced to so many simple concepts. There are a lot of kids who are not encouraged to do art or music and there are so many that don't even know what juggling is. But even worse is the lack of mysticism in the current day kid's mind, which seems so outlandish to me considering the outburst of celebrity magic shows in the last five years. Criss Angel, David Blaine, Penn and Teller, David Copperfield, masked magicians, live talent shows and still there are so many children who just do not know what a magic trick is. *Surprising, right?* Don't get me wrong, though, there are a great deal of children who are very familiar with magic, but as a performer I am continually stunned by the amount of children ages 3-10 that have never encountered a magician once in their memorable lives. I guess that non-experience is the outcome when parents plop their kids down in front of babysitter television instead of attending festivals and events together. Anyhow, whenever I meet a kid that's never seen magic before I make sure to really take my time because I may be the first thing to ever shift their perspective to a different, creative realm. I could hold a place in their memory for the rest of their life and I want to ensure that I am a good, valid memory. I did a few cut and restored ropes and made some objects disappear and then reappear somewhere silly and the children started to smile and have a great time. The tears dried up after a few minutes and were replaced with smiles. I was handed a small donation toward my travels after discussing them with the women. They were very impressed by my illusions and I handed the kids each a playing card to take with them as a souvenir. I really do love the glitter that arises in a person's eyes when I perform something stounding. Zap the normal out of life and insert a mystical moment to separate the day between standard and bewildered. I then shuffle the cards in a bizarre manner. Extreme Card manipulation (XCM) is something that I had worked on a lot in high school. We studied various methods of shuffling to do some miraculous things with a plain deck of cards. Sometimes the shuffles were illusions in themselves, causing cards to either change or disappear right in front of the spectator's face.

I continue to do tricks and a man comes up to me. "So what's all this about?"

"Oh, I am just working on my sign. "

"You do magic?"

"Yes I do. Would you like to see something?" To me right now, it's a lot more fun to perform for kids with parents than just for adults on street shows. The parents appreciate the experience that the kids have and then tip not just for your performance, but for the kid's education too. It's like they get a double service, whereas when I talk to just adults sometimes I encounter rude drunk men just looking to make a fool of me. Sometimes it is people just asking questions out of curiosity and I waste my time talking to them and hearing their criticizing and questioning. They usually don't even tip and if they do, it is just a dollar. And when I am spending a lot of time talking, using up my performance energy, considering entertaining is my only source of income now, a dollar for an extended performance/conversation is a massive insult. It's like getting a $50 meal and giving the waitress a buck for her 'troubles'. Right now, this is my job. Making people smile and shaking up the average existence is my job. This is how I choose to make my money currently and I don't want to exert a great deal of energy into an unappreciative customer. And I do not want to be rude to anyone by any means. So yes, I do answer all questions people ask currently because I am so passionate about my journey and sharing it with anyone who wants to be a part of it. But wasting energy when money is needed is unwise. Fortunately, that first man treated me very well. He spoke with me for 10 minutes and gave me $25. "What? I only showed you two tricks! I cannot accept this for just two illusions."

"No, I insist. The tricks were good, but I like what you are about and I want to support your cause. You have a lot of dreams and I want to see you succeed because you have a great spirit. Keep strong and don't lose your focus." He turned around and started walking away. "And hey, thanks for the magic tricks." Before he left the park he turned around and waved. *Wow... This world is just such a beautiful place sometimes. He really believes in me... Wow. It's amazing how much support I can receive from strangers, yet feel so little from myself.* I am sure much of the population feels similar to this as well, but strangers provide so much more comfort, sincerity and kinship than anyone else I know currently. It's like I have more of a home on the open road than I do anywhere else in the country. Something about that thought stirred up deep sensations inside. As the day wears on, Saint Augustine is proving not to be very profitable, but it's probably my own feelings of inadequacy getting in my own way. I'd say about 1/15 families that approaches tips me, but they all greatly engage me in conversation and laughter. I just decide to not focus on the money anymore, but to focus instead on the happiness I bring. I brighten moments for a lot of people when I show them magic and this day is here on out dedicated to sharing happiness wherever I go.

Just then I see a strange woman hobbling through the park. She holds a cane in one hand, a book bag on her back and a dog's leash in her other hand. She seems distressed and I look down and decide that my sign isn't looking the best anymore and I start to color it. I have the contents of my book bag just lying out on this bench while this woman gets closer. After the experience with people who look like this in Savannah, I am not ready to be in close quarters with more crazy homeless people.

"Help! Help! Someone help me!" I hear this and look up and realize the lady is just spinning in circles yelling and screaming. I get very nervous and she just wanders back and forth. Then she gets closer and closer and I stand up. I have been in mental training for attacks since I first started hiking alone four years ago. It's time to find out what is going on.

"Hey, are you ok?" Her head darts to the side as if there were a string attached to her ear that was yanked and she almost stares in my direction, but not quite. It creeps me out like some type of twitchy stop-motion film from 70 years ago.

"Oh, yes. I need help!" She starts toward me, stumbling over a lump of twigs and leaves mixed with dirt and sidewalk. "I really, really need someone." A collection of semi-concerned individuals are inspecting from around. Most glance, watch for a moment and then continue on their way, attempting not to see. If they don't engage in the act, then they don't have to feel bad if something happens I guess. Human Psychology 101. *I think I missed the class on learning how to be afraid of everyone I encounter.*

"Well, what do you need?" I ask and she waves the stick back and forth and holds both hands forward as if she's combating something invisible. *Great... another homeless drug addict seeing stuff.* Then I notice that her stick isn't just swinging randomly. It is swinging with strategy, almost as if it's guiding her to something. This is the moment I realize that she can't see. This yelling woman is blind.

"My husband is gone. I can't find him since this morning." I can't believe this is a real situation right now. I hesitantly look in all directions to see if there were people about to jump me. They could use this blind, homeless woman with a dog as a distraction and then take all my possessions. I see nothing suspicious, so I continue to talk to her. She explains to me about how her husband wasn't there when she woke up in the morning and he usually comes back by 8 or so with coffee. She was really worried about him and was scared that he is either hurt or left her. I asked what he looked like.

"Oh, well he's about two inches taller than me and is pretty skinny, but has a beer belly. He has a beard and usually wears a beanie. He also has a teardrop tattoo below his left eye."

Oh god... Something about this whole arrangement of things seemed at first to be some crazy scam. It is almost too much. But there was something so sincere about her and her concern appeared to be real. But a lot of things in life appear to be real, yet aren't. This trip is really about a lot of things, one of them being about learning how other people live. I want the raw truth of life. So I decide to be open-minded about this whole crazy ordeal and just go along with whatever she needs. She tells me her name is Elaine.

"Well, if I see him I will let you know." Her panic begins to rise. She is scared and lonely and has been wandering around all day alone. He has her wallet and identification so she has nothing. Once again, I check around me to ensure that no one is about to jump me. I tell her that I can get the cops if she wants and she says that is a good idea.

But first she needs to go to the bathroom. "Can you watch my dog?" I look down at his filthy, sweet face and the gentle eyes and I sigh and tell her sure. The layers of darkened dirt on this leash make me instantly cringe as the scent of urine flows through the air.

"Uh, do you know how to get to the bathroom?" I ask as she turns around and starts to hobble-walk across the park.

"Yeah, I'll just use this shop over here." She points. *Interesting...*

His coat is thick with grime and I wonder how long it has been since he had a bath. After just a few pets on his neck my hand was coated with a film of dirt. I figured, well I am already dirty; I may as well give this poor guy some attention. He probably doesn't get too much, being a homeless blind woman's dog.

"Do you need help crossing the road? It seems kind of dangerous." I start to pack up my stuff in anticipation of her needing help. Really what I wanted to do was to not be left in a park with an orphaned dog.

"No." She stares straight ahead as she adjusts her backpack and her jacket. "I can do this. They won't hit me." Her determination is really impressive if she is real. If she is serious, then she has her blind homelessness all figured out in this town. As I watch her walk away from the bench I consider what will happen if I never see her again. The scent of urine disappears as she fades away.

That is not the right way to think. Think positive. You are helping this woman who really needs help.

And so there I sat, magic tricks sprawled out and a dog in my hand. I pet him and start talking to him, calling him a good boy and a sweet guy rubbing his head.

Oh god.... I hope she comes back. I notice that the dog is a girl and apologize to her for calling her a him. I hold this leash and pray that Elaine returns. *What if she left me with her dog because she didn't want it anymore? Whatever am I to do with a dog on a road trip? How am I going to be able to make money with a dog next to me?* I can't perform in bars for food and drinks and I cannot perform in clubs or stay at some people's houses. If I have a dog, I am immediately incredibly limited in my options.

Fortunately, after ten fearful minutes, she does return and all is well.

I get a local shop owner to call the cops and they come over to talk to her. I wish her well, then I make my way around Saint Augustine spreading the magic and making some travel dollars. All is going very well. Smiles are in the air as thick as the scent of chocolate outside of the candy shop I perform in front of. I consider this to be one of the best places I have been to so far. I hadn't encountered any street cops to kick me out yet either, so I have been lucky. I don't know the rules of the street here.

I actually don't know the rules of the street anywhere that I go, but I don't let that stop me. I just pray for the best and the best usually comes. I decide to stroll through the town all over to really explore before taking off a bit more south. I take streets here and there, crossing cobble stone roads, seeing parks and beautiful landscaping surrounding entirely lovely properties. Everything around here looked loved. These places are so historically beautiful, a masterpiece representing a time that never again will be.

I end up spotting a pizza shop sign that had a beer and two slices of pizza or a glass of wine for $5. I don't hesitate to make the turn down the back alley toward this shop. Pizza is in my vision and a drink will soon be in my worthy hand. I take a seat at the counter and place my cruddy book bag at my feet in my general secure location. When a book bag contains all the important contents in your life, it is very easy to never lose sight of it. Ever. It becomes your main focus, your responsibility, your baby. Sort of. You tend to its needs, mend it when it's sick and fill it up everywhere you go. You try to be as gentle with it as possible and keep it near you at all times, hoping that you never bump it too hard at the delicate spots as to destroy the camera or expensive contents inside, just like a delicate baby brain. *Or something.* So I sit and I wait. I wait a while.

I get my wine, a delicious surprisingly full glass of wine considering the price. It's well accepted.

A lady sits next to me. I begin casual conversation with her and we start to joke around. I then ask her where she is from and she says Lancaster, Pennsylvania. "What? I am from Lebanon! What are the chances?" I exclaim, almost surprising myself at how loud I yelled, yet how faint I sounded in this joyous, elegant building. It was the type of place that had hard cherry colored wood decor, but wasn't strictly too classy for tourists.

We talk and she orders me another glass of wine and orders herself one too. She is about 55 and owns a horse stable and riding club just outside of Lancaster, Pennsylvania. She is slightly interested in my coming out there to perform magic tricks for the kids at an event sometime this upcoming summer, but I tell her that I have no idea where I will be or what I will be doing, but that I would contact her if I was around at all. This summer would prove to be nowhere near Pennsylvania though.

"Aw darling, I would offer you a place to stay, but you see, I am down here with my daughter and friends. My husband was just diagnosed with cancer and it is really hard for me to deal with so they sent me down to relax." *Whenever I hear the C word I can't help, but offer the knowledge that I have found.* Having dated a gal who claimed to have a brain tumor when I was 21, made me do a lot of research at a young age on cancer and what I discovered is a whole different type of thinking than what I was normally taught to think about. I never did figure out the truth about her, but I spent horrible nights and days awake researching constantly until my eyes were red and my mind exhausted, learning all I could about holistic/alternative health. I spent every moment of every day researching how to save my ex-girlfriend's life, just to have it all kind of fall apart as a joke on me. A castle of lies constructed before my eyes and I never even saw the construction crew working.

But it's perfectly fine now, though, because I could apply the energy of shock that I would have faced with Alana's circumstance in a much more suitable way. I had already experienced the deep shock of a lover with disease and I had learned a basis of health education. From that base of understanding, I could share with her and build upon my own expanding knowledge. For this I am ever grateful. *There is divine beauty and truth in all experience and we have the choice to learn from it or let it weaken us.*

....

Callie chimes in, "Wait, you never told me what happened. So, what happened to Alana? You never explained how you were guided to that book either."

"Let me finish this part of the story and I will definably come back to that."

Chapter Thirty

"Integration of collaboration with nature and culture is powerful."

I scribble things down on a paper. I tell Horse Woman to research- *alkalinity and cancer, baking soda and cancer, gmo vegetables and cancer, microwaves and cancer, dead food, alternative health documentaries, holistic health, yoga and meditation and cancer, reiki and cancer, biofeedback machine, tongue and fingernail analysis, etc...*These are the things I write on paper whenever I encounter someone who either has or knows someone with cancer.

Tears guide her appreciations while she asks me how I know all of this. I tell her, "Please, take this. I knew someone very close to me and ended up doing a whole lot of research on alternative matters. I am not a doctor. I am not a nurse. I am just a random person in the world who has learned different things that I was not taught, but I have seen it work on someone with Lupus. I cannot promise you results, but I can promise that you will learn about another way of thinking about dis-ease." I intentionally split the word into two, the opposite of ease emphasized. "Take this and research it and do with the information what you will. I hope it will help you."

I always hand the paper over with this disclaimer, but it usually always brings tears to whoever I am speaking to. They are usually at the edge of reason, the brink of losing a loved one and are desperate for answers. I cannot withhold information from those who could benefit from it, even if it makes me look crazy. It would be morally wrong for me to withhold info that may save someone's life or at least offer an optimistic alternative approach to healing.

....

Callie looks at me and cocks her head to the side with a firm lipped semi-smile indicating that she wants to know what happened. "Ok, Callie. Ha-ha, I will tell you what happened with Alana." After a deep breath, I tell her that just a month after we started dating, Alana was diagnosed with Lupus, an autoimmune disorder. "Her joints were incredibly swollen constantly and the entire right side of her body would go numb daily. She'd wake up crying in the middle of the night because her feet were so painfully inflamed. I would prop them up on my shoulders and massage her thighs and knees until the swelling went down. She told me one day that I either need to be dedicated to her fully or I needed to leave now. She told me to take my time to decide what I really wanted because her body wouldn't be able to handle me leaving her later. I was head over heels in love with everything about her and decided that I would endure everything with her. So, everything she went through, I went through."

Some thoughts flood my eyes momentarily, but I continue, "I drove her to many doctor appointments in Hershey and tried to keep her from passing out from all the blood work. They expected her to have Lyme's disease, but we were surprised to learn that she had Lupus. Both have similar characteristics, but Lupus meant that her immune system was basically attacking her body. The mental hell endured to watch a lover suffer like that is practically unbearable, but it taught me key lessons in life." I glance in the distance and see a young couple holding hands and walking together.

"The harshest situation, however, was when we were driving in Lancaster, PA and she became fully paralyzed. Her body became firm and she couldn't talk or move. She was frozen stiff. She glanced at me, petrified, as a tear formed in the corner of her beautiful, blue eyes. I didn't know if she was dying. I didn't know anything because this was the first time this had ever happened. I hopped into hero mode, trying to navigate to the hospital with her phone, which I was terrible at using, while driving her stick shift car, which I was terrible at driving, while keeping one hand on her to keep her awake, which I was at least good at. I cried as I spoke with a smile on my face because underneath my inspirational talk to her, I thought this could be the last moment I ever saw her alive. I knew that in all those movies where someone is injured, they say, "Look here, look at me" to keep the person alert, to keep them from slipping away. *So, that's what I did.* I talked to her and held her tightly clenched hand and tried to get her to focus on me, remembering good times. When I pulled up to the hospital, they couldn't get her body out the car because it was so firmly paralyzed. Her joints were frozen and she was immovable."

"That's so scary!" I realize that I have been holding my breath the whole time I am talking. *Remember to breathe...*

"So, as you can imagine, when she wanted to live with her family in Erie, I was certainly not going to deny her that opportunity. And away we went, two lesbians, three cats, a turtle and a U-Haul."

"What happened then?" Callie asked in a comforting voice.

"Well, when we first met, her diet was a muddled blend of fast food, high sugar lattes, cigarettes and soda. After some of these traumatic health events, she decided to try out my diet, which was dramatically different than hers. She eventually developed an appetite for wellbeing foods. I researched holistic health information to make daily tests for her to learn so she could have better reasons to quit her 'bad' habits. Over time, with the introduction of a healthier lifestyle, her symptoms did practically altogether disappear, which was remarkable from my perspective as a young, unguided-besides-my-own-intuition health nut. But watching her progress really opened a new world of inspiration in my health fascination. I became obsessed with learning everything I could about alternative health and holistic healing. *This is where life began to get, well, different."*

"What do you mean by that?"

"See, Callie. This is where my life changed forever. In Erie, we lived a few blocks from the local health food cooperative and they hosted local educational classes in the back room which was converted into a classroom. They held classes about cooking, eating healthier, the benefits of Tibetan singing bowls, yoga, meditation and alternative wellness practices. There is a holistic practitioner, *Holy-Health, who did a speech about fingernail and tongue analysis. He studied under *Dr. Choochoo, a man who brought this version of Eastern medicine to America. They claim that any disease, malnutrition or inconsistency in the body can be determined based solely upon the fingernails and tongue. It sounds insane, right?"

Callie nodded, throwing her hands up, exclaiming, "Yeah, it does!"

I continued, "Yes, I know it really sounds crazy, but he suggested that cancer, heart disease and really any dis-ease, doesn't usually just suddenly pop up and surprise a person. He suggests that the disease's progress in the different parts of the body over years can be seen and identified growth, patterns, colors, lines, shapes of the tongue and nails. *Holy Health explained that being diagnosed doesn't actually mean anything other than there is now a title on something that most likely has been there for years.* The only difference with a diagnosis is that the patient is now aware of it. He said dis-ease can often be identified as lack of nutrition and can therefore be cured before it ever actually even becomes a disease. This concept was startling, shocking and beautiful, especially after my experience with Alana. I watched passionately as he individually did an analysis of all the people in the audience and told them what was imbalanced in their bodies."

Callie mouths a wow as she leans forward. "This is unbelievable! I have never heard this either! Is it even real though?"

"Yeah, I really do believe so. I overheard him say to a large, eager woman, "You have a deficiency in your liver because of this bump in your nail here, you may be developing something with your right lung as well and there are severe heart issues." Her and her husband began crying because they spent thousands of dollars/ hours in the hospitals to have them tell them that exact same thing. He then, after offering his professional medical 'opinion', suggests for people to take a variety of Chinese herbs to help stimulate healing rather than prescribe pharmaceuticals that just eclipse the problem, usually causing others. It fascinated me and I talked with him afterwards. This was a world that I have never ever heard of. He told me to meet him in his office in a week to really talk since we were out of time that day. So I did. We talked for two hours and after he detected my passion, he told me about the dangers of pursuing a holistic health career because it isn't in alignment with corporate agendas. He really explained so much about how the body works and how he uses a biofeedback machine to scan the electromagnetic fields of people's bodies and through that, he can actually see the frequency disturbance which indicates dis-ease in a particular area.

"What? He can actually see where someone is sick? What is it called again? I have to write it down." Callie exclaims.

"He said that if I was passionate about this, he would train me to use a biofeedback machine. I wanted so badly to learn holistic health after Alana's diagnosis *(dare we say that I made it a burning desire)* and I energetically was brought 6 hours across the state right to one of the only practitioners in the country that specializes in this type of alternative medicine. I explained how I used the Law of Attraction to meet him. *"The fact that you are teaching me all of this just is blowing my mind."* I told him of the recent influence on my life by '*The Secret*' and he proceeded to tell me about Leopold Mountain's book, *Contemplate and Welcome Prosperity.* This pivotal moment, this little bit of information, would lead me on a sort of treasure hunt of truth for years to come. This was the first time I had ever heard about this book and I became obsessed with attaining this knowledge. I told Alana that I would soon hold that book, feeling its rich weight pressed into my fingertips. The city library didn't have it, but I told her it would soon be mine."

"So did you end up attracting it?" Callie asks.

"Well, yeah. I researched and studied all sorts of stuff on these topics for the next week until a day when my Craigslist ad about looking for part time work had a good hit. A guy named Stevie hired me to come help him clean his house and do some side work for his business. I arrived at his place, a beautifully new, massive home that he designed himself to look like an old barn. He and his dog lived there on a large piece of property 15 minutes from downtown Erie. As I was polishing his floor by hand, I looked on his end table and saw the daily inspiration 365-day calendar of 'The Secret'. My jaw dropped. He was surprised I knew what it was. He leaned back on his chair and stared at me through different eyes than before, really studying this strange, awkward, short haired girl, knees down, scrubbing his floor. He then said those golden laced words, *"The Law of Attraction is the only reason I have anything that I do."* I began telling him about Holy Health and asked if he knew of the author he had mentioned."

"Did he know of Leopold Mountain?" Callie asks eagerly.

"Yes! He stood up exhilarated and told me that Leopold Mountain and that book changed his life! He explained that while reading that book, he started his own company and his whole world began to unfold. He was 28 years old and had taken control over just about every aspect of his life. As we talked, I learned that everything he had was because of the Law of Attraction being implemented in his life. He had me follow him to his back office, which had a huge shelf lined with motivational books and inspirational speakers on business strategy, self-empowerment, meditation and mind control. He pulled a thick purple book off the shelf and handed it to me. When I read the title, I almost cried." *Contemplate and Welcome Prosperity by Leopold Mountain.*

"No way! That's amazing!" Callie practically springs up.

"I know! I asked him if I could borrow it. He told me yes, but only if I returned it with more written in it. *Deal!* He told me he doesn't actually read much, but often listens to these books on audio book in his personal sauna. He then showed me the sauna and explained how he used the Law of Attraction to acquire that too. He toured me around and I discovered that the same goes for almost everything in his immaculate house. I held that book in my hands and felt the weight of it open channels of desire within my body. I still cannot believe that it took me less than a week to acquire this book. It was as if a mystical quest had just been completed only to open up another large treasure map. *I remember how proud Alana was of me and my new trophy...* Anyhow, if ever there is a lesson to be learned in life, it is that no matter what you focus on, if you really believe it, you can have it. Like I stated earlier, even if it is an old book in the tundra of the Great Lakes snow region in January, it is possible. Everything is possible." I make another note again to live life limitless.

Chapter Thirty-One

"Motivation lasts, but only if you cultivate it daily. It's like eating. I don't just eat my whole month's food in one day and expect to live for a month."

T hankfully, out of all of the hundreds of various educational-scribble shreds of paper that I have handed out all over the country, I cannot say that anyone has actually looked at me like I was nuts in the moment of discussion. They may have looked at me initially like that, but I think people see in my eyes that I really believed what I wrote despite its initial appearance. I really believed it could help them because I saw it happen first hand. And I offer these concepts with no exchange desired on my part other than to just help if I can.

I hope it's making a difference…

Horse Woman and I talk for an hour at least, and then she explains how her daughter will soon be picking her up. She calls her on the phone and complains about some 'doohickey' in it that doesn't make a sound when she wants it to. I ask her to hand the phone to me and I find it in the settings, adjust it and she thanks me over and over for helping her. She is now obviously drunk. We go out the double doors and stand at the deck. I notice that not only is it raining, but it is pouring. It is pouring and it has been for some time now. She's trying to explain to her daughter where to get her. "I am with my new friend, Katie. She's from Pennsylvania too! We are hanging out and drinking."

Her daughter finally arrives and pulls the car up, gets out and tries to dart through the raindrops, nearly sliding off the first step almost knocking down an old couple as she comes up. She seems surprised by her mother's drunken giggles and smiles as she grabs my hand and looks at me confused. She said hello, but her eyes said, "What the fluff are you doing with my mother?"

No, lady. I am a 23-year-old lesbian and I am definitely not trying to make your mother my sugar momma. I hardly consider sharing a drink to be opening the gateways to that. Then she looked at her mom and in a hesitant half/happy half/glare, nervously laughed asking why we were hanging out. I can honestly understand a daughter's concerned worries considering the situation, but at the same time I was drinking and was thinking *"Dayyyyum girl, chill!"*

"She does magic!" The mother exclaims. Every time someone initiates conversation between me and another person that is in relation to magic or traveling, I must then explain myself to them. Usually it is pretty much the same conversation between everyone and is very repetitive for me.

"Yes, I'm traveling. Yep. Over three weeks now. Yes. From Hershey, Pennsylvania. No, it's not scary. Yep. I just find places to sleep. I saved a bit of money, but I make money on the road doing magic tricks. Tip money. Well, yes food and drinks too. I'm writing a book about it. Yeah, I have a lot of goals…" It was the same conversation resulting in the asking to see a magic trick. Usually this would result in no tip, but a profound "Wow, that's amazing." So it's very repetitive. *Sometimes I forget how much I have really experienced in these last few weeks.* This solo journey is something that almost every soul seems to crave.

I also love that they buy me drinks and things too, as a means of either keeping me around to hear more stories, or just out of kindness. But every single thing that I have been given on this trip has been appreciated greatly. I always make sure to pray before a meal or anything charitable at all- to give thanks to the sun for growing it, the earth for embracing it and the people for their energy producing it. *If you really do think about it, a lot of life goes into a meal before we actually consume it.*

I hop back and forth between tables the entire night doing magic tricks for my insta-audience. I received incredible praise that eventually became foggy with alcohol vision. The amount of free drinks I was being given was just incredible. This family gave me $10 and told me to go perform at this cigar lounge at the open mic that they had going on that night. He says that I have a drink of my choice waiting at the bar after they leave.

I have decided that I am definitely sleeping in my car this night. At least I am in pretty warm weather, even if it is raining powerfully for the last few hours. I leave from the outside deck and go back inside and take a seat at the bar. I figure by the time I trot on over to my car, I will be so exhausted that I will not care where I sleep and I will pass out almost immediately.

This sounds just wonderful to me. I was fading for a long time. I can tell by the way I feel that this will be one of those nights. The bartender comes up and I tell him to make me something interesting with a kick. He looks surprised by my response and we continue to talk while he concocts this drink that he created several years ago. Then he reveals that his father owns the place and that is why he is allowed to share a drink with me. A lady comes up, obviously drunk and slides in on next to me, orders a white Russian and a tiramisu pie.

"You have never had one before! Oh, honey! You need to try this."

Bartender hands me a spoon and I dip into the interesting textured pastry and place a spoonful into my mouth. *Drunken deliciousness.*

We talk until I realize that it is about 11:15. I probably should be getting to bed soon so I can get up at sunrise. When the sun begins to bake on the car it is pretty impossible to stay asleep, especially on nights that it is raining because everything is so musty.

I say my farewells and then promptly put on my jacket and reach in my pocket to get my keys.

Which are…? Wait… then I realize I left them in my jacket pocket, *duh...* So I promptly reach into my pockets to remember that I actually left my keys in the front part of my purse. Stuff always slides into there. *Ha-ha! Of course! I confuse myself all the time with that.* And I realize that they are not there either.

And unfortunately, since I had been hiking, I had the key just simply on a carabineer key hook with nothing else so it could easily clip into my pocket. So I often lost it in my bag somewhere. It was slipping and sliding all the time everywhere. I begin to pull out the contents of my purse and search in everything. My cards, notebooks, pens, papers, magic props, coins, ropes, rubber bands, my wallet, camera, phone and…

There is no key…

"Is something wrong sweetheart?"

I look around and don't even make eye contact as I say, "My keys… I can't find them"

Eyebrows rise around the room as everyone goes, "Ohhh…"

Yes. Yes, this is me, the traveling lesbian magician, who just talked to all of you for hours about my goals and dreams and I know what I am doing. Yes, I am so incredibly focused in my journey that I can't even keep track of my keys. Yes! Believe me; I have it all together… What a joke! I can't even practice what I preach? Oh, my golly… What am I? Fraudulent? Fake?

They have to be here… I convince myself as I check time and time again, but with no new results. *"Oh no… I was all over this town today."* I think

206

back to all the streets I walked, all the places that I reached into my bag to pull out magic supplies. I thought about every place and realized they could have fallen out at about 20 different locations at any moment of the day. To replace my Volkswagen key would be to spend $400 and I just didn't have that much to spend. I had so much more to travel in this country that I could not possibly expect myself to just spend $400 to replace a missing car key. *Absurd!* "I have to find it!"

"I will help you!" Tiramisu Lady finishes her last gulp and starts to put on her jacket. I can't believe she wants to go out and walk around this town with me in this storm searching the ground for a shimmering chunk of very important metal that most likely has already been picked up by someone.

"No, I cannot ask you to walk with me. You are going to get soaked." I tell her as I gather up my possessions into my purse, this time ensuring that nothing goes missing.

"No, honey. I will walk with you. You can sleep on my sofa if you need to. I have extra clothes you can wear if you like also." I can't believe the generosity of this world sometimes.

We follow my steps backwards in time through my memory, reenacting the past day's events and praying that I would just see it somewhere. I even check flower pots, benches, and window sills, light posts, gates, anywhere that someone could have found them and just picked them up and placed them somewhere. But there is no luck. We eventually go back to my car because now my clothing is soaking wet, just to see if maybe there is a door unlocked. I notice that my windows are down a bit more than an inch. I remember this old trick that I used to do with my dodge neon when I locked my keys inside.

I reach my arm inside and I wiggle it back and forth, sliding barely lower and lower. It began to hurt as I kept wedging it down further until I was able to grab the handle and I pull. The locking mechanism shifts and I feel the door tremble as it unlatches. I smile and relax while I hear her cheer from behind me. We got it unlocked.

The passionate raining silence is disrupted immediately by thousands of marching bands and loud honks, roaring through these midnight streets, pulsing worry into the ears of those sleeping soundly in their houses around me. My car alarm continues shouting for all to hear. I panic and try to get my arm out of the window, because attempted theft of my own car is just an absolutely crazy thing to be arrested for and who knows where the cops in this city are patrolling. My arm has become swollen and tight and I wiggle it back and forth in the window of the car door that is now moving back and forth because it is no longer connected to the car, which causes deep black and blues that really do hurt a lot. I have to gently press my body firmly against the door to hold it in place, car blinking and honking, me wiggling and pulling and I finally release it. I don't know what to do. I climb inside the car and pretend like I am hitting buttons and pressing things that matter, but I know I am not.

Turning the car alarm off is useless without the key. I know this, but I frantically pretend not to know that as I turn every knob and poke every button I can find. This proves to be just wasted effort. I start to laugh, because of course, this somehow made sense to happen right now. Then I remember the homeless lady. "Oh, my god. The homeless lady has my keys!"

"What?" Tiramisu Woman squints as she tries to hear me speak through the honks.

"This homeless lady! She has my keys! I helped her today and she took my car keys!" Then I realize what this situation really is. Here I am at midnight, stuck outside my car, keys stolen by a blind homeless woman in a foreign city, thousands of miles from home with a dead phone and no way to turn off my car's horrid screams, soaking wet from wandering all over this city in a thunderstorm and drunk from all the free drinks I received from doing magic tricks. At least one of these things is a positive thing so I just laugh.

I laugh and laugh at how crazy this is. Then the car stops honking and the alarm stops. We both look at each other in that same tender emotion that one experiences the moment they get a baby to stop crying. "Grab what you need and lock your car and let's go to my place. We'll figure this out in the morning." She says from my passenger seat. I told her to climb in to get out of the rain while I open my doors and start rummaging through my stuff for dry clothes, shoes and my phone charger. I grab what I need, throw it in a book bag and try to lock the car. At least I have a nice dry place to stay tonight so that is another positive outcome to the night.

I press the button on the door which engages all the other locked doors and I close the door while still in the car to see if it will lock. Everything locks except the driver's side. I press it again and the same thing happens. "I don't think my driver's door will lock without the key…"

"Oh, no. You can't lock the car?" She looks back at all my stuff, my guitar, my computer and everything and makes a very uncertain face.

"Unfortunately I don't think so. Maybe I can just hope that no one will see it is open and that will be ok for one night."

"Honey, do you really want to take that gamble? Besides you are parked at probably the worst place you could be to leave your doors unlocked. This is the homeless shelter right there. Those small apartments over there are free housing for the local homeless people and this place is the food center where they can get free meals. "

"I thought this was a little coffee shop cafe…" I look at the deceiving red porch.

"Nope. Wrong, honey. If I were you…"

"Yeah, I know. I need to stay with my stuff. This is all I have right now and I really need to just stay with it.

"Well, here's my number if you need anything. Good luck, sweetheart. I'll be praying for you." And she opened the door to get out of the car, the alarm went off again. I forgot to disengage the lock on that side of the door. We look at each other like this is the worst nightmare… But I just start laughing. I don't know what else to do. I am currently creating enemies with all the homeless people next to me and all the rich people with homes all over this block.

I get out and give her a hug and I feel her sympathy radiate from her chest into mine. Sometimes I feel like such a pathetic soul and I can't stand it, but I keep on getting into these dumb situations all the time! I try very hard to focus on the positives in life, but it just seems that I always attract chaos and I really don't know why. Especially after these Leopold Mountain readings, I just don't know why. The rain is finally slowing up as we say our anything, but silent farewell. I turn back to face my circus car. I climb inside and strip off the wet sweatshirt and I pull on a jacket over my damp shirt. The alarm stops ringing as I pull off my pants and throw on the first thing I can find which is a pair of black, baggy capris. I arrange the back seat into a crooked bed and shove several blankets into the cracked windows to block the rain from coming in. I collapse, ignoring the wetness of my hair and my whole body, into an anxious state of sleep while I think of what on earth I am to do now.

Chapter Thirty-Two

"Optimism can restore one's faith in one's self
despite all downfalls, fears and doubts."

I awake to darkness, steamy, dreary darkness in the backseat lit by the droplets of water running down the car. The splatter of rain has pushed the blanket down and it now splashes small fragments of rain into my car and chillingly mists my face and neck. I am so very frustrated that I reach up over my head aggressively and try to adjust it back into place, but I only make it worse and now rain is dripping drops onto my face, only making my frustration grow. In a fury, I slam my hand against the small hole I've created and the blanket flops out of the car opening a hole about three inches wide, releasing a lot of rain onto my sleeping space, soaking my sleeping bag and my head. I sit up and grab the blankets and shove them in deeper. I even pull one off of me and shove it in, now having a total of three blankets and 1 towel shoved in my three windows. The rain has picked up and it is dancing on the roof of the car, a repetitive pattern that sends my mind into an anxious state of worry. *Will I ever find my keys? I don't have that much money in my account. Maybe I will have to activate my card and use the money. It isn't what I wanted to do, but I'll do what I must.*

I engage in an internal discussion. *No! I don't need to do that! I can make the money. $400! I can make that here in this city. Well, $400 is a lot of money... maybe I should just buy the key and move on... No! I can make that money! People make lots of money performing music and shows on the street. They can do it; I can do it!* And I have this internal conflict boiling troubles into my mind. The worst part is that they were all justified troubles.

What are the chances of waking up and finding a blind homeless swine in this city? She may not even really be blind. She could do this type of thing all the time to unsuspecting people. I could have just been one of her scammed contestants for the day. I fall asleep exhausted again. *Suddenly, in a foggy blur, I am running through these doors and hallways, grabbing for things and trying to get to the coast of the beach. I have been here many times before in my mind and every time the place develops even more. I walk the streets and search for Alana. I keep almost seeing her, but by the time I get to that spot that I had seen her, she is gone. She is always gone and I keep trying to reach. I keep trying my hardest to get to her, but the difficulty increases as each moment passes. Nothing I do to cut corners or break the path makes up for any time because she is always gone. I see her in the room sitting at an old wooden bar, upon a stool with her hair shimmering gold like it always does. I open the door to have her turn around and make eye contact with me. I tried so hard to get to her and I finally did. And she looks deep into my eyes and I see a sorry, disturbing look. It is just this doomsday color and I know she is about to say something awful and...*

I have dribbles on my face again. I have sprinkles splattering in my ear and I hate it. I hate this feeling, this completely lost without a cause feeling. I am pathetic and alone, sleeping in a wet, broken car with no means of getting home. I don't even have a home to get to...

This is when I break down. I begin to cry. I was strong until I saw Alana again. I could hold my own stance of strength until I saw her about to tell me something I didn't want to hear. I have dreams of chasing her almost every night. I try my hardest to get to her in my dreams, but I just can't. And now, she has gotten to me and I am suddenly wet with tears and rain and I pull the cover over my head. I don't care if my blanket gets wet. I don't care about anything anymore. I somehow fall asleep again.

And I wake up most likely not long after. My body feels strangely different than before. Something has changed inside of me. I have hit my absolute point of giving up. It's a point I have become familiar within my life, especially in the last few months. It happens quite frequently. It is the point where I can take no more and then suddenly the clouds clear and the sun shines through to dry up the rains. The fog leaves the valleys of my mind and my inner world goes through a renaissance.

I decide right then that I will hold my keys again. I imagine the way that black chunk of plastic felt, embedded with the tiny stud of metal. I imagined pressing the stud and having the Volkswagen key spring out from its hiding place. The weight, the shape, the engraved lines, the chips on the right side from having dropped it, I feel it all and when I press the lock button I hear my Felix give a happy little chirp. I see my keys in my hands again, providing assurance and I force myself to know that I will hold them again. "Desire and believe; acquire and achieve!" I fall asleep with a renewed sense of certainty. Somehow, someway, they would come back to me again.

I wake up again and think of the homeless woman. I retrace the events in my mind. *Ok, she came back and threw down her stuff. As I went to leave, I noticed my black book peeking out from under her scarf. I grabbed it before I left. Maybe my keys were under there too!*

Anger filled my eyes. I'll bet she did that on purpose, collecting tiny objects just to have something because she has so little. I shouldn't have helped her. *This is what I get for helping a homeless woman. Just makes me technically homeless now too.*

Then I thought about the picture of the dog that I took while I was watching her. I held the camera up and took a picture of me and the dog sitting on the bench because I didn't want to forget about that sweet, little pup. I'll bet my keys are in that picture! I grab my camera quickly and scroll through the images. Sure enough, there they are sitting right next to the black notebook. *OH NO! NO!!!* The swelling anger surging in my chest sizzled upon each raindrop hitting me in that back seat.

Then something different happened inside of me again and I realized that if she really is blind, this is her life all the time. It's just a major feeling right now, but an actual minor inconvenience to me. Her life is really like this all the time. I come up with clever ways of getting her to trade me if I can find her. If I offer her money, maybe she'll return these souvenir keys! *What did she say her name was again? Leila? Oh yeah, Elaine! Maybe if I treat her like a respected human and call her by her name, she will treat me like a respected human too and return my keys! It has to work!*

I wake up again to the sound of men's voices. There are two men standing on the porch of the homeless shelter, *not coffee shop.* I reach up, stretch and crawl out of the driver's side door. There is a funny emotion that goes on in one's head when you start to live a life out of the ordinary. Not that it is something that happens to make one extraordinary by any means, but doing something that not many people will often see. And the fact that I am a young female makes even more of an impact. This impact is one that I used to be afraid of. People watch and people judge. It happens everywhere. There will always be judgement, but there comes a point in time where judgement just no longer matters. You just begin to not care, to not be concerned with anyone else's view because their lives are by no means perfect either. Everyone has something to deal with in life. Mine is just obviously very visual right this moment.

I used to hide in my car until I thought no one was watching. Then I would get up and stretch. I used to be afraid to run, afraid to stretch, afraid to do anything out of the ordinary and then suddenly ordinary seemed so sad. It seems to be such a weak lifeless way to live, to consider the circumstance of the American standard to be a way for my mind to control my habits. I am beyond that at this point. I see through the drapery of expectancy, to be a proper woman living a standard life.

To be extraordinary, one must be different; otherwise one will just blend into the ordinary population never making a hiccup or impact in society. If I want to live a different life than I know, I have to live a different life than I know. *It's plain and simple.* So I crawl out of my car in pride and glory, determined to find some coffee and even more determined to find a blind, homeless lady. *Uh, I mean Elaine.*

The men stop chatting as they realize that I am emerging for my station wagon. I look over at them and give a big early morning smile as I stretch upward, even I am surprised at how calm and relaxed I have become at this point. They look puzzled and wave slightly frozen in confusion as they both watch me shake off the sleep and walk over to them.

"Hey, I've got two questions for you. "

"Well, hopefully we've got two answers for you. Was that comfortable in there?" the one asks while he studies me up and down, looking confused at my appearance and placement in this world. "What were you doing in there?"

"Ha-ha. Well, I didn't expect to sleep in my car last night. It's actually part of my questions. Do you have some coffee by the way…" and I follow them inside while they introduce me to all of the people who volunteer their time there. They share my story with each other and they all talk about current events.

One at a time I get a no response for anyone knowing a sightless, houseless woman named Elaine with a dog in this town. They seem bothered by the story I tell, since they have never seen her or her husband with the tattoo at his eye either. I am at least able to charge my phone momentarily and use the bathroom. So much gratitude for those two simple things this morning! *But they don't know Homeless Elaine… Great…*

I give my thanks and I take the gamble to leave my car there with the driver's door unlocked. I take my laptop, tablet, and any electronic devices that I can. I bury my guitar under my blankets and make the car look like it is filled with trash, which was easy because it was filled with trash. But it also was my home now. *My little traveling nest. My safety net hermit crab shell to protect my fragile body and belongings.*

I pray that no one will enter my car as I'm gone. I take off into the city with as many of my valuables as I could stuff into my bag. I put that aside and decide to just have faith in whatever this situation was supposed to teach me.

I know I will find that key again. Elaine has to be somewhere…

I walk several streets and figure that I might as well enjoy myself while I am here. The rain has stopped. It's not freezing, but it's a slight chill in the air. The sun looks like it will come out soon and the world is beautiful in this new city. So what if I don't have my key. I've got a pretty beautiful life that I am living right now and that is all that really matters after all. I venture around and realize that most of this city doesn't wake up until noon. Being that it is only 7:15 and my phone is half alive, I make my way down to the river and decide to just enjoy the morning air.

Ahhh... yess. The morning air is so fresh in Saint Augustine, America's oldest city, a handsome city, an old time city ticking with the newfound day. There is a certain charm about this moment and I breathe deep into the world and allow myself to just fully relax. I journey past the park I performed in yesterday. I see something burgundy at the pavilion, like a giant, fluffy caterpillar. Then from behind the one post I see a figure move. *Could that be...? No... No way... There's no way...*

"Elaine!" I yell and the figure moves a bit. It sits up and begins looking toward my direction. I see the familiar face and she seems just as surprised to hear her name as I was to see her again! I yelled. "Elaine, Hey! It's Katie!"

She squints harshly as if she were trying to see me as I run toward her, feet flopping in the wet ground. I didn't care how wet I was anymore. The world was a misty mess today and I was a cold part of it now. I see her dog rise from the sleeping bag, confirming that, yes, this is definitely the right homeless person. I have never before been so happy and angry at the same time to see a homeless woman.

I decide that if she just wanted to keep a shiny thing that I'll bribe her with money to just give it to me. I know she's a crazy homeless woman who just likes to keep anything she can find along the road so maybe she'll be able to depart with the object if she gets money for it. And if she doesn't want to depart with it then I'll just call the cops and have them search her! *I know she has my key! I win!*

"Hey I met you yesterday." I say as I get up the stairs of the patio. "Do you remember me? I helped you with the cops and stuff."

"Oh yes. Of course, I remember you. What are you doing out here?" She asks while she stares beyond me. She obviously is actually blind.

"Well, I have a question for you. Do you have my key? If you took it, I'll..." I begin to say, but she interrupts me very fast.

"Oh, yes! That was yours?" She responds instantly sounding excited.

"You have my key!" I smile big knowing that puzzle pieces are nearly becoming a full picture! She has my key!

"Well, no I don't." She says while she shakes her head back and forth. The smell of mildew mixed with pee fills the air and I can't tell if it is this patio or if it is her that smells like that. If it is the sleeping bag, then that might be even grosser because that means that she sleeps in dog pee most likely. *Or her own which isn't any better.* I am pretty sure blind means you can't see, not that you can't smell, but as I get closer, the stench makes me wonder…

"You don't have my key! But you had it? What did you do with it?" I yell accusingly, trying to figure out what on Earth she could have done with it. My heart sinks right back down again and the anxiety waves begin to roll on shore.

"Oh," she speaks so softly. "Well, I sat on that bench waiting for my husband to hopefully come back. He didn't yet. And then it started to rain so I got up to go somewhere and realized that I heard something fall off the bench. I bent down and picked it up and it was a key."

"Yes that was mine." I distress again accusingly. I can't imagine what she would have done with it. Hopefully she didn't just throw it away or place it somewhere and someone else took it. *Oh god, it could be anywhere by this point!*

"Yes, it was a key and I didn't know where it came from." She speaks with such a gentle manner and it really catches me off guard. She is so relaxed and calm while she tells me her story.

"What did you do with it?" I adjust my demeanor to reflect hers. *Whoa, is a homeless lady more Zen than I?*

"Well, I walked it to the closest store and gave it to the girl at the counter. I figured if someone lost it, they would check the closest shops nearby before doing anything else."

My jaw drops and I stare at her, mystified by the words she has spoken. My head tilts sideways and my eyes sort of tear up as a strand of sympathy and absolute shame washes over my entire being. She sees no reaction in me, but my whole soul feels split apart, like a rotten prejudice has been hacked open and exposed to myself in a worldly mirror. I am disgusted at how I felt just a second before that sentence. *All my worry and anger toward her all night long... I just can't believe it.* She has no idea I am shocked, disgusted at myself and completely energetically shifted. This is such a contrasting situation from that Savannah leech, River. She shuffles her feet over and pets her dog while she continues talking.

"If I knew it was yours I would have held it for you, but I didn't know who lost it." Her sincerity breaks my heart. An inner light from within her soul shines bright and I realize that I was the pathetic person who was so full of judgement now. *Who do I think I am?*

"Which shop did you take it to?" I ask, stunned by this woman's honesty. She has nothing in this world. She has even less than I do and she is lacking a very important thing in life- the sense of sight. She has so much less than I and yet, even I did her the mistreatment of judgement. She is pure and beautiful in a much different way than I have ever seen before. *I look at my hands and wonder when they became so filthy.* I didn't used to think the worst about people, but somehow I have become a black thunderstorm of disgust. *Or maybe I have always had this secret prejudice lurking unconsciously behind my eyes. I can't believe myself.*

"Will you take me there?" I ask her while she points to the cute side alley just across from the welcome center where I got the cops for her the day prior. We walk and share stories and each step I take brings me closer to my keys and closer to the light. She talks about her husband and how worried she is that he is hurt or in jail. She is so worried that he may have also taken her debit card and has robbed her of everything. Apparently, she receives money from the government for her disability, but I realize rather quickly that it is practically pennies, thus resulting in her living on the streets.

She did live in the backyard of some people who lived a mile away. They had tents set up, but when Elaine found this dog two weeks ago, they didn't want the dog on the property and they all got in a huge fight and Elaine and her husband have been banned from the property for the last two weeks. So she really is fully homeless right now.

She tells me again about how worried she is that her husband took her money. I am still hesitant that the key possibly might not be in the shop, so as a type of thank you and collateral, I offer to drive her to her bank after I get my key back. She looks so surprised by my offer.

"Oh my god! That would be great! I could walk there, but I always get so lost. It's pretty far away and down a few angled streets."

As we walk, she says hello to all the local homeless individuals out and about. There are a startling number of them here and I realize that it is a hidden community within a community. These people live these lives as homeless people, but they take care of each other. A man asked about how she's doing in reference to a previous event. Several other encounters allowed me to see something new. They are family to one another. They watch out for each other. They are a street bound clan. She alerts them that her husband is missing and they look very concerned also that he hasn't returned. They chat a bit and I smile and stand tall next to her as she tells them the story of his disappearance. I watch them interact and I see the sparkle in their eyes. This is the life they live. They don't wake up to television sets blaring repetitive pop-culture rubbish. They don't live nestled up in the cozy, simple, climate controlled structure of four walls. They live the night and live the morning in its entirety. They breathe each sunset and swim in each sunrise. They soak in the natural creation and don't turn off the weather with walls. They experience the world for what it really is and see all parts of the transition of day, the light, the dark and the ugly. They dream of better things than what they have, but they all get what they need to survive usually and they actually seem very happy where they are, right here hanging out at sunrise.

"Do you two want some?" This homeless man offers me one of a dozen donuts that he was given. These people have so little, but they are so generous. It is just really beautiful. A donut has never made me want to cry before. It's such a different way to live than anything I have seen so far.

We then arrive at the shop and I notice that it only opens at 10am. Currently it is only 8:09 so we've got close to two hours to wait. She said that she gave it to the person at the counter. I look in the window and spot a tiny counter where my treasure hopefully awaits! It is so close, just beyond that glass. I know I will have that key back in my hand again.

"Hey, Elaine. We've got two hours to wait. Why don't you come have breakfast with me? It would be my treat. I'd love to hear some stories."

She tells me about this cute coffee shop right up the way called *The Bun-Bun*. We arrive and I have to figure out a way to tie up the dog outside. Her leash is only about 5 ft. long so I reach into my bag and see what I have. I know immediately what to do.

I explain to her that I have these ropes in my bag for a few magic tricks and I tell her that I made some money last night so I can use that to buy her breakfast and I can use the ropes to tie up the dog outside. She's such a good pup, obeys and relaxes upon request. I don't mind sacrificing a few tricks to get her tied up just under the overhang by the window so we can keep an eye

217

on her so she won't be in the morning drizzle. The sky has become a bit hazy again and I would feel bad letting her in the rain while we dine warm inside.

I tell her to order whatever she wants, it doesn't matter. I get us big coffees and I make it the way she likes it. We talk for a very long time and I ask her if she would mind if I took some notes about our encounter. She agrees and instantly says that she wasn't born blind. She used to be able to see, but when she was young it started to disappear around the time she was getting her license. She got her driver's license and can remember how free she felt. She describes that red car and how quickly that emotion faded along with her eyesight. She can make out figures sort of, but it is mostly black. I ask the waitress if we could get any of the food scraps people leave on their plate for the dog. I explain the story and the waitress comes back with a full packet of turkey and sausage.

Elaine and I continue talking and she states about how this woman was giving her a hard time once so Elaine told her, "Put a bag over your head, spin yourself around and try to figure out where you are."

The woman laughed as she replied, "I can't do that."

Elaine said, "Well, *'Can't'* isn't in my vocabulary."

The moment she said that sentence, something inside of me broke. It was something rough and ridged, black and loud that I had been containing in a glass vase. It wasn't part of me, but it was in me and I could see it. And the way she said that sentence just shattered that and released that black vile from my delicate grasp. I didn't need it. I never needed to hold it. I never needed to preserve it and yet for years I did. But it filtered out from inside of me and released my attention on its dark contents. My eyes filled with unobserved tears at her stories. This is how she lives. This is how people all over the world live every day. *And I let whatever I was holding onto go. It's as if speaking to her was cleansing my soul.*

After our deliciously filling breakfast, we arrive at the shop a few minutes early and the lady enters from the backroom. I wave excitedly and she opens the door. I explain my key situation. She goes behind the sales counter and I hold my breath and cross my fingers as she reaches down and moves things around. *Please, please, please pull my key out!* She reaches her hand up from the counter and I see it glowing like a vivid ray of sunlight from God. She handed it to me and was breathless as I felt its weight drop into my palm. I hold it and feel it and I know the feeling is real this time. I imagined it appearing again in my hand, a visual imagination from the wet, backseat of the car and now I hold it triumphantly, pressing that tiny, metal, spring-loaded trigger. The key pops out. Relaxation fills me and I almost begin to cry... I grasp it like Excalibur, my sword to freedom. I look at Elaine, staring toward me, but not quite at me. *Wow, all I had to do was believe it was possible and take proper action.*

What are the chances?

My endless thank you's become joyous gallops, "Hey, Elaine. Let's drive you and your pup to the bank to see what's going on with your money so you at least have that figured out. Maybe they can help you find some clarity."

We find out her account is safe and she cancels her current card and reorders another. There is no word on her husband's whereabouts as she gets back to downtown center, but she feels confident that everything will be ok now that she is fully in control of her funds. I say goodbye to her as she and her pup slowly walk down the street to the park she spends most of her time in. She told me that is where she wants to go and being there will give her the best chance of finding out what happened to her husband. She ensures that her community will tend to her needs tonight as she wishes me well on my journey too.

Helping a blind person find clarity while helping myself find inner clarity as well? Check. I feel those butterfly wings that I have been growing start to flutter, shaking off the exhausted state of short, transformative evolution.

Now, time to get rowdy.

Chapter Thirty-Three

Day 26

"Incredible things are produced through a vastly interwoven series of beautiful, intimate little things."

S o I leave Saint Augustine, full of strange emotions that I know I will need to process. I drive south then east to Kissimmee, FL where my friend Krispop from Lancaster, PA is currently staying. I haven't seen a single person that I know in over four weeks. *Yes, I have memorable experiences with people I will know for the rest of my life, but I've just met them all.* There is a deep bond between anyone who has a previous current life experience with another person. It's like that initial 'figure out who you are' thing is already figured out. And I am very, very excited to be around a person from my past. But Florida has several people I know and I am so excited to see all of them.

First of all, my sister, Kris, is here in Orlando too. She goes to Penn State main campus and is in Florida on an internship with Disney. She is staying at some dorm like facility just south of Orlando, which is great for me because the place I am staying tonight is in Kissimmee, which is just a little bit further south of Orlando. I really only know two Kris's in my life and they are both an hour from each other in Florida right now so we will refer to my sister as Krissy and to my friend as Krispop.

I drive onward to Krissy's house. She leaves for work at 2:30 pm so I am already running late to meet her. I expected to leave Saint Augustine by sunrise. But after, yet again, another chaotic evening, I am feeling both disgusting and exhausted. I cleaned up and washed my face in a bathroom so I'm not 100% filthy. I am just that crazed, sleepless, soaking wet for hours, stayed in car, hanging with homeless all morning, type of filthy. So if you know what that's like, then you understand how much a dip in some warm water would mean. But unfortunately, I am very late due to my key quest morning and I was hoping to really spend some time with Krissy before she had to go to work. It should be just a two hour drive, but I sit in traffic for almost an hour, just blocks from her place. The design to her neighborhood from the highway is phenomenally badly planned. I cannot believe how terrible the road planning crew was; it's as if the foreman put on blindfolds and played pin the tail on the highway with strings attached to pegs so when they placed the tails, they drew road patterns around the random strings dangling and Tada!- called it Orlando. The traffic is stopped up on the highway, cars swerving around them, just to get off this exit to sit at the world's most inefficient stop light. They have it placed so that the cars can never get through because the next light has the line of traffic already blocked off. So I sit, wasting valuable sister time at this light. I put on some jams and try to relax while I am receiving texts from the only two Kris's that I know in my life asking me where I am.

Krissy- "Where are you? I have to leave soon!"

Krispop- "Katie! Huge lesbo party tonight! Hope you make it out here girl! Can't wait to see you! It's been too long!"

I tell my sister that I am in traffic, just right down the road. Once I get through it should go quickly. I arrive at her building at 1:53pm. Just enough time to give hugs, say hello and have her leave for work. But I was determined to get there and not let my sister down. So far this internship has been frustrating for her. She doesn't get full time hours and spends an hour commuting each way.

I arrive at the gate and pull into a parking space, waiting for her to come down to give the guards our licenses. They are super strict at this place. I guess that is why they won't allow me to sleep over. Lord knows that I could be a killer sister or something, causing all sorts of ruckus. Frankly, this place seems more like an internship prison than anything else. You have visiting hours, you are kind of stuck in this place, especially if you didn't have a car like my sister. And if you did have a car, the traffic was so terrible that you were stuck anyhow. And they transport the residents from this place to their jobs and then back again. There were no local restaurants so everyone ate the same standard meals and bought the same standard crap. It's kind of freaky in a way, in a twisted thank-god-this-is-just-a-movie-and-not-real-life sort of way. Except it was real life.

But here I was entering the gates with my sister next to me and I was very excited to see this new place, her home. But we really didn't have much time to spend together so we hung out as she ate her oatmeal, then got ready for work and that was it. I explained what happened the night before and asked if she would allow me to stay a bit and take a shower. She said she wouldn't mind at all and that I could help myself to whatever I needed. Krissy says, "So are there any days on your trip that you could have lived without?" I give her a funny look, suggesting her to elaborate. "Like are there any days that didn't matter if they existed or not?"

I think for a moment and consider what the worst day would have been. I have had some rough moments of hopelessness and near misery, but I can't even think of one day in particular that I could have lived without. I tell her, "No, actually all of the days have been really great. Well, there are the ups and downs of traveling and people, but the worst days still had great positives."

Krissy studies my face momentarily, "Wow, that's great. You've had 26 consecutively good days. That's wonderful." Interesting to view it that way, but it very much is true. *Was I ever able to say that I have had 26 mind-blowingly incredible days all in a row before?* I don't think I have ever said that. These days have been packed full of so much life and experience that one bad event didn't disqualify the day as a bad one. It just became a moment. And maybe that is what life should be viewed as, a collection of moments, some good, some bad, but the days shouldn't be collectively viewed as bad. She leaves and I jump in the shower. The heat feels like heaven sloshing down my body and I just let the water splash all over my face. It just feels so good. I scrub, shave and clean myself all over, feeling a whole world of worry and homeless stress flow down the drain. After I get dressed, I decide to go to downtown Disney because it is free before heading over to Kissimmee.

I arrive and see the giant Disney signs everywhere and I park and make myself a peanut butter and jelly. I pull up in the back of the lot because I wanted to spread my doors open wide and relax for a bit outdoors. The patrol keeps watching me. *How dare someone just simply relish sitting in the parking lot eating and enjoying the weather?* They drive by three more times to make sure I wasn't doing anything weird. *Everything I do is weird.* I finish my relaxation and go in and set up to perform magic and get kicked out right away. I was actually really impressed at how fast I was kicked out. *Oh well, I didn't feel like performing anyhow.* I walk around there for a bit, admiring the buildings and sculptures. *Awesome in every direction.* I leave and drive right to Kissimmee and when I get there, Krispop gives me a huge hug. She had been staying at her grandmother's house, helping to take care of her, but was staying the weekend down here at her lady friend, Tish's house. Krispop has been seeing Tish the entire summer and they have great energy together. Tish and her roommate lived on a huge property next to a small pond and fields. It was so private and beautiful, like living on a prairie. There was a large, wrap around porch and people were arriving with boatloads of alcohol. Beer pong begins and everyone is laughing. I am both very cautious to talk to lesbians and very excited. I do keep my distance whenever one starts talking to me too much because I really am just not ready to move on yet. But there is one or two that seem pretty fond of me. As I was explaining my recent life to one of them, the fire spinning began. Tish apparently was a stripper and hula hooper. She took off her shirt and lit up a couple of wicks extending from the edge of the hoop that she dipped in a combustible solution. Then she started hooping. The sound was incredible, a deep and powerful whooshing circling her whole body. She spun it up over her head and jumped through it in one swift motion. I was mesmerized. This was the first time I had ever seen fire spinning up close. It certainly wouldn't be the last.

I trade numbers with this one girl who offered me a place to sleep if I needed it. Out of all names in the whole universe, of course, she is named Alana also. *What a surprise*! She said that I can stay the next night if I want to. This is great because I don't like to take advantage of anyone's place for more than a day or two and I didn't want to have to stay another night at Tish's house if I can help it. Not that I don't want to. I don't think she would mind, but I only want to stay here when Krispop is here because I feel Tish has wandering eyes and non-discretely has been giving me 'the eyes'. I certainly don't want to get caught up in whatever that is.

The next morning I wake up bright and early, almost before the sun and stretch in the yard to do some yoga. I breathe deeply and work out. Then I sit on a massive, fluffy pillow sofa thing that they have on the porch and I watch the world evolve. I sit and smile into the warmth around me and then close my eyes. *So much consecutive happiness.* I have never, so often, sat with my whole body feeling peaceful and rested, eyes closed, just smiling at my life. And the fact that I realized this just filled me with even more happiness.

I am joined by her roommate, who the night before, told me that she has never been with a woman, but hears Tish all the time and kind of wants to try it. She is absolutely beautiful, long blonde hair, model type, but she has a kid. *Cute, but I am so in a different world than this right now.* But she makes a coffee and brings it out to me. As I sip it, I realize she added whiskey and baileys. This gal sure knows some good morning style. This day follows along that path. A little bit of alcohol all day, hula hoops, walks, exploring and I then realize that there is an art event happening in the downtown during the evening. So I convinced them to later go out, but none of them are into walking around the street and seeing what's going on like I am, so they go into a nice bar and order drinks as I walk around and create my playground. I perform for several tables and rack up $20 in a few minutes. I then go in to join them and they are impressed by my ability to just create money off the street. I didn't think it was such a big deal since I have been doing it for a while now, but I guess it is different than the normal way to do things. The night fades and I fall asleep rather early.

I wake up on a thick, fluffy sofa. It's actually the same one I woke up on yesterday morning, but facing the opposite direction so it confused me at first.

There is also a snuggling dog with me. The dog shifted and I woke up from its large movements. I open my eyes slightly and stretched high into the air, elongating my spine, bones and joints, entirely stretching my whole body as much as I can. My eyes are closed and I can really feel the relaxation kicking in. Then when my eyes open, feeling renewed and refreshed, I see a gorgeous, naked woman walking across the room toward me. The morning light glistens along the left side of her figure, showing off hundreds of dollars' worth of exquisite tattoos, spiraling in all fashions around her hips and stomach. The dark, curly hair was disorderly, indicating a very wild night and waving all over, as if greeting me as it graced across her bare collarbone and down her shoulders.

I blink because apparently something is wrong with my vision. I open my eyes again expecting it to be just a figment of my own mental creation. It can't be possible that a naked woman is in the living room right now. But I open my eyes and see the same thing. There she is, naked, glorious and beaming. *Yep, that's actually happening.* I gasp in shock and instantly apologize for disrupting Tish's naked stroll to the kitchen to retrieve a glass of water. I look away and cover my eyes while I say this, although she laughs and says that it's fine. I am stunned. Although, I suppose it would be out of character for a stripper to be uncomfortable walking around her own living room naked. Laughter fills my gut and I get up and decide to figure out what to do next. The next thing would be to fold the blankets. I guess that's what I do next... I awkwardly sit back down and take my notebook out to write.

I decide to unclog my thoughts first by doing a meditation until this rising sound, like a *Woooo Aahhhh* coming from somewhere beyond this room takes a hold of my ears. I realize then that a naked girl just walked by me to crawl into bed with another naked girl. I laugh and feel slightly uncomfortable at how loud they are being with me just in the other room. *Woooo Ahhhh...* I look over and see that the door isn't even closed, which makes me slightly more uncomfortable as I hear that sound over and over. *Woooo Ahhhh...*

Ah! A rapid, excited panic flies over me when I realize that if the bedroom door isn't closed, it is almost like an invite for others to come in and join! *I mean she did just flaunt herself in front of me!* I quickly grab my notebook and slide to the front door and unlatch it gently so that no one can hear me sneak out. If I do this appropriately and silently, they won't know that I was in the room if they come out to try to seduce me! I step out gently and hear a slight creak as I put my weight down on the floorboards. *Shoot. I hope they didn't hear that.* I close the door swiftly as I step into the patio to take refuge on the giant puffy couch thing that I wasn't even sure what to call it, but now I call it an effective escape. The couch was like a sun baked muffin top spilling over a platform, but it was snug and served its purpose as my shelter. I laugh as I consider how crazy things have become in every direction of my experiences since the first day I left Pennsylvania. *Wooo Ahhh…* I begin to write and I hear that noise again, only it's even louder and even more uncomfortable because it is coming from outside. *Wait… What?*

I bend down and look into the distance, but I can't see anything. *Wooo Ahhh…* It stops, then begins again rhythmically until it stops momentarily again. At least I know it's not coming from inside the house. *What the…* so I walk out across the yard, tip-toeing to secure silence in my bare feet until I get to the fence line. The sound starts up again. I freeze. I look just beyond the weeping willow and see two thick, long sticks yelling and squawking. *Wooo Ahhh…* I laugh so hard because they are so loud that I too, screamed slightly as my body bent down for cover. Through the high grasses in the field about 50 yards out, stood massive 5 ft. birds happily screaming into the morning sun. I watch these whooping cranes curiously as I try to go around the fence and get closer to them. They must be holding megaphones. They hear my steps and stop yelling as they walk to the other direction, all eyes on me.

I retreat to the muffin refuge laughing at my thoughts of that sound being a mating call of overly-friendly lesbians. I guess I have been out of practice for a while. I've forgotten what the lesbian mating call sounds like. I've almost forgotten what a naked woman even looked like until this morning. The good news is that in the next few days I would have the opportunity to refresh my memory. And what a surprise it would be.

Chapter Thirty-Four

"You are a masterpiece just as you are right now. Don't look at each individual brushstroke for answers. You just need to step back to see the whole piece and come to understand it."

I arrive in Venice, Florida a little later than I would have liked to. It was just about sunset when I pulled into the retirement community. The fine cut grass edges every property in such perfect formation that I consider this to be what suburban heaven's fine-tuned landscaping resembles. I make a left turn and pass a small perfect looking pond that lies before a beautiful building filled with elders, all smiling and laughing. They are walking around and hanging out like school kids. I assume that church has just left out, but these people look genuinely happy, like laughing hanging out happy. As I observe, I see that it's just a room with games and other fun things. *These elders were just hanging out enjoying each other? Whoa…* Something about this moment taught me, yet again, a lot about a world of happiness I have never before been witness to.

As I drive through the community, I go around a beautiful arrangement of shrubs trimmed down to their finest cut, the flower beds rainbowing blossoms next to another lake. One left turn, then another and I am face to face with Nina's new home. Everything around here has such a wonderful charm to it. It's all well-kept and clean and I see why these communities have such relaxed circumstances in such strict guidelines: It cleans out the trash. I look at my disheveled car-home and laugh. Nina greets me with another familiar smile and shows me around the house. After explaining the incredible deal they got on the property, she told me about the history of the kids who received it from the passing of a parent and didn't want to deal with the stress any longer and were just looking to get rid of it. I can understand that concept of 'delete this place from my life' by thinking of my mom and her two sisters with the property of my grandfather after his passing. He had a solid battle with cancer, actually the third form that he had in his life and after a three year fight with this one, he lost. And there was a property loaded with collectibles and mostly junk he had accumulated throughout his life. My family just wanted to get rid of it. I can almost apply that feeling to my life and the amount of things I will need to dispose of when I go back to Erie. *A sharp shudder rolls through me while I consider the grotesque thought of Alana and I not working out when I return.* Thankfully this thought is disrupted by Nina introducing me to her beautiful dog, Pierre. He is a golden doodle, which I thought was a joke of a name, but he is a blend of a golden retriever mixed with a poodle. He is so gentle and calm and is dressed in a little bowtie and makes him look like such a charmer. Nina says that we should go out to eat at this restaurant downtown that has outdoor seating. We hop in her car and get going. The windows are down and the world is looking beautiful. A stop light greets us as an SUV pulls up. There is a bulldog sitting in it looking over at us and then spots Pierre. Barks fly constantly from that moment on as this dog is trying to get the attention of Pierre. Pierre gives no response to this dog other than to just simply glance over at him and then he looks front again. "I can't believe how relaxed he is with that dog screaming next to him. It's crazy how behaved he is!" The other dog is barking and the owner is yelling and apologizing and commenting on how good Nina's dog is. He looks over with his sweet little eyes. *What a gentleman. They say that the clothes make the man and I guess the collar makes the dog.* Nina, Pierre and I arrive at the restaurant. This would be the beginning of my education with dogs along this trip. They are a fantastic way to start conversation with anyone and a great way to meet people everywhere. He gets tied up to the pole next to the table and the waitress greets us with a smile, two menus and a bowl of water for the pup. "This is one of the most dog friendly places I have ever been. This city just loves their dogs!" *Oh, Venice Florida, I feel like you could make my dreams come true.* At this point, I had no idea how true that statement would be.

I wake up alone in a bed and look around, confused by where I am. As I reach for the glass of water on the bedside stand, I realize that I am in Venice and I am about to go to a yoga class. A smile spreads across my face as I get up and go into the kitchen to make a coffee. *So many choices!* I choose something like a hazelnut moonlit surge of caffeine in the mouth and hear the celestial sound of fresh brew being delivered as I observed the organic foods in her pantry. When I first met her in Lancaster, PA at HACC, Harrisburg Area Community College, we shared a geography class together. She sat behind me and thought I was such a neat person. She would bring me goodies, usually health snacks similar to granola bars or chunks of compressed nuts that she got from Trader Jims. She always treated me so well and now here I am in her new Florida house.

This cup of coffee reflects my inner happiness in the moment. I couldn't be more grateful for anything else in the world at this moment. I am falling in love with America's coffee culture. I get on my shorts and a fresh pair of undies. I hope they don't stick out, but you never know during a yoga class in shorts. *Whatever.* I hop in my car and head over to the beach. The fire in my heart is growing robust as I get closer and closer to that gleaming water.

I arrive at the yoga spot and there are several people standing around and a bunch laying out their mats. I choose a spot on the back corner because I consider it to be less noticeable if I am not directly in line with everything. I nearly erupt with happiness: my first time on the gulf coast! I listen to the small waves while I do some pre-yoga stretches. After the amount of driving that I have been doing lately, I deserve to have a nice relaxing morning of yoga to reconnect me to my divine self and spirit. The class begins with a peaceful looking older woman on a large blanket in the center. She greets everyone and talks about the beauty of the sunrise flowing into our hearts and minds, erasing all negativity that we have. Many yoga instructors I've encountered so far are ages 40 and up and I have never seen an older woman look better than one who does yoga. They are always so at peace with all they encounter and it is kind of incredible to see the variation of yoga middle agers vs. non-yoga middle agers.

I cannot get the smile off my face, even for one minute. *The world is remarkable and I feel like I am where I need to be right now: that galactic alignment of perfection.* We contort, breathe and smile, all in tune with one another. I have never been to a class like this before. The teacher is patient, simply relaxed and the class is cheerful. Everyone seems to be having a lot of fun. She makes small jokes and creates little stories to enhance unity. I'm kind of surprised to see the variety of people here. A high percentage of older men out here are by themselves or with their buddies. *How great lives are in this place, along this Florida coast, smiling in the sunshine, getting deep inner stretches, shaking up their souls together.* The idea of a collection of older male-friends hanging out and doing something like yoga together is not a real thing in the world I grew up in. Most of the people I have ever known only hang out in bars and disintegrate together, bonded over malnutrition and lack of care. There is little to no combined self-improvement in the community I have spawned from. *Born n' raised! Yep, I know what I like and I like what I know! I observe my own personal pessimism of my past and I breathe into it to let it go, filling my mind with white light and peace...* "Namaste" The whole class chants and we breathe together. I release all the negative tension from the world I used to know, a world gone from my life forever. *There are so many ways to live...*

The class is completed a little earlier than I would have liked, but it's a free class and a half hour is a good amount of time for most of these people. I go alone to the edge of the water, walking barefoot in the sand while I feel the sun beginning to gain strength in the day. I arrive at the water's peaceful edge and I feel the gritty ground morph around my toes, holding my feet as the water comes over my ankles, I sink down a bit and that famous smile spreads across my lips. This is the first time I have ever touched the Gulf of Mexico and it couldn't have felt more perfect.

Step after gentle, mindful step, I watch the waves roll in sweetly, the sun gleaming like a rarity I couldn't even begin to imagine on my own. *This is what life is all about, this feeling right here.* I return to my pile of shoes and collect everything together. I lay out my blanket and hide my camera and belongings underneath. *Faith.* At this time in life that camera means everything to me. Those pictures represent my hopes and my dreams and hold a certain complexity of truth that I need to produce a life changing book or website. I pull my legs up one at a time to stretch them and take a few hops as I start to run down the coast. Barefoot on the beach, I sink in deep and guide my feet further. I expand my chest with every skip to take in more oxygen to promote my power. I run wildly.

I run with force. I run with such power.

Sweat begins to streak across my whole being, but I use it to represent my desire to be in the water. I feel so influential and resilient in this salty creation, so much larger than what I am, almost as if nothing can hold me back. *And nothing can hold me back!* I speed up until I run full speed, each step increasing in difficulty and in effort, but never growing any weaker. There is no time for weakness here. I see a line of rocks extending out into the ocean up ahead and I decide that is my current destination. I continue running and breathing, running and breathing until every breath strengthens my inner being and I smile as sweat pours down my face and my hair flops into my eyes. I slick it back and almost trip over a deep division of sand that sank down much further than I expected.

There is no time to trip up. I laugh and keep going, feeling the droplets of freedom sprinkle the backs of my legs with every step into the water. I splash it up everywhere and I don't care that my shorts are getting soaked. I want to be part of the Gulf of Mexico because it is already a part of me. I finally reach the palm tree line where I stop and begin my progressive relaxation breathing, but I am so tired. Running a mile in sand is not the simplest task, especially for someone who is so unpracticed at running.

I say hello to two random older gentlemen while I pass by them, a big goofy grin across my face grows as I catch my breath. They have some kind of interesting machines lying next to the grass, but I keep walking until I make it out to my rock destination, a channel boulder pile extending into the ocean. I start up small conversation with random people, some who are from Venice, but none that are from there originally. This is a place of peace for many people who fall in love with the lands in their later years. They retire here and live beautiful lives, never having to risk the fear of cold weather injuries or achy joints.

I smile and continue walking to the end of the dock, but there is a large 4 ft. bird that stands next to me. Its eyes watch in all directions as people pass by close enough to touch him. I have never been this close to a crane before. It stood firm, eyes widespread and it watched the world around. *Did he look at us with curiosity in the way that we look at him in fascination? I wondered if quite possibly, he was observing his universe. I wondered if maybe he was pondering thoughts of the cosmos and nature and questioned whether god existed to create this vast ocean before him.*

"He's a hungry little guy, ain't he?" A man says as he walks up from the path in the direction of the ocean. He holds, in his hand, a cup of coffee and a small jacket that he had recently taken off.

"I guess so." I consider that a strange way to start a conversation because I am not sure how to tell if a crane is hungry or not. It kind of scared me because maybe when they grow hungry they attack people. "I don't know. He didn't tell me if he ate breakfast or not."

The man laughs. Well, sort of laughs. It really wasn't funny, but he replies, "Well, why do you think he is standing here like that? He wants you to give him fish. The fisherman here must toss him their little guys all the time." I watch the glowing eye shift up and down my body, searching for some seafood movement and I understood that this bird wasn't just here to be a neat thing for me to look at. He probably wasn't contemplating universal existence. He is probably just contemplating breakfast. I watch the water and the waves for a bit before I consider myself cooled off enough to head back down the shore.

I pass those men with the odd watercrafts which I had passed earlier and I notice they have them up on stilts similar to a bench. They explain that they are ocean kayaks made exclusively in Australia and are rare to see in the US. They tell me how they try to take them out three or four times a week on the ocean early before the sun heats up too much. I realize, in this moment, that people from Florida do their best to protect themselves from the sun whereas everyone up north does everything they can to be in the sun. The sun exists in abundance. It's a very different world down here and with a different world comes a different mindset. I explain that I am on a trip and am running back down the beach to gather my things. We keep talking and the one guy with the moustache had mentioned something about the skies and clouds.

"What do you mean by that?" I ask genuinely interested by the strange sentence.

He points at his buddy next to him and says, "Well, Ronnie here. Yeah, he is a pilot." Ronnie looks shy and waves his hands in front of him while being certain to say that he is not a commercial pilot, but just flies for the enjoyment alone. I ask him what he means.

"Well, I have a plane I built and I try to take it up once a week."

The sparks start flying in my head. I think of SkyFly Gypsy. *What if I...*

"That's incredible! I just gave a ride to a girl who has been hitchhiking by airplanes for the last 8 months." I tell the guys more about my experience with her and they mention having seen her in a piloting magazine before. *I can see the world of opportunity opening up.* I see the trees clearing and the rain dissipating in my mind. The law of attraction seems to have proven itself an interesting candidate for the most influential thing I have ever known. *And this is just the start.*

They ask me how she goes about doing it. I explain that she catches rides to other states with guys that have an extra seat. "Yeah, I know what you mean... it always is a shame spending that 50 or 75 bucks to go up and then just having that extra seat go to waste. I've talked with my pilot buddies at the hanger about it before."

A colossal torpedo of incredible opportunity shoots me in the face. All fabric of sensibility rips apart as the windows open for the exact thing that I had desired since meeting SkyFly Gypsy.

"So..." I say in a very prolonged high to low tone of voice. I know I must word this in the proper manner as to not scare away a random older man who has the key to changing all objections to the book that I have been faithfully reading. "Do you know anyone that wants to fill a seat and take anyone up in the next few days?"

He looks at me kind of funny and gets a bit nervous. "Umm... Well..." I can feel the links of life connecting one by one in perfect harmony. I am so scared I can barely move, but I do not let go of eye contact with this man. I hold my ground, full of confidence and keep my head up high, my posture straight in hopes of showing I am worthy and strong enough to trust. "Well, I guess that I am going up. Umm..." He looks to his friend for help with a shaky expression on his face. I do not step down and retreat. All armies within my being firmly hold their positions.

"I guess you could ride with me." The bells of victory ring and the sirens start to squeal in the streets of my mind as the super bowl of life is won by my team! Yes!

"Wow! That's wonderful! When are you going?" *Keep your composure steady...*

"Today I'm taking it up... umm say around two." He looks at the sun. "Yeah, meet me at the gates of the small airport at two and I'll take you up."

My head practically explodes! *I cannot even grasp how incredible this is.* My mind is so shocked by these words. In just four hours I will be in an airplane. Unbelievable! Or rather, very believable! After all, that is the purpose of my studies, to believe that anything is possible.

I run back happier than anything I have ever accomplished in my life. I have successfully presented the opportunity of an airplane in my life. Desire and believe; acquire and achieve! What are the chances? I run down the beach galloping in a small Pennsylvania lesbian's pride, so incredibly happy that I start to tear up and become covered in various forms of wet, salty water. I continue repeating positive affirmations to myself and I cannot believe what this world has offered me. There is so much opportunity out there in this life if you let yourself experience it. The floodgates to my life have been uncovered. I return, grab my things and rush to the car. I play the radio loud and sing my heart out, * *"Well, yes! Life keeps going on- way after the thrill of living has ended."*

But my life has just blossomed and the living has begun. Believe me, I am beyond thrilled. I almost cry/smile at how irrelevant this song feels to my life right now. *Just four hours...*

Chapter Thirty-Five

A law of attraction philosophy spoken by Jesus.
"Therefore I say unto you, What things soever ye desire, when ye pray,
believe that ye receive them and ye shall have them."
- Mark 11:24 (KJV)

I arrive back at Nina's house and I spill through the door excitedly, telling her what happened. She is so sweet with her motherly concerns. I understand the risks, but I am not about to indulge in the acceptance of uncertain fear. I will be in a very official place. I tell her that I will text her the guy's name, plane and hangar number just in case. I know nothing bad will take place though. I change into my swimsuit and follow her over to the dog beach as we had planned.

I had no idea a dog beach was so much fun! We throw balls into the water and several dogs race each other, so blissful to be in community. They run and hop, roaming free in this place. Well, free behind a gated fence and all the way up to the signs that say no dogs allowed. But in these 50 yards of space, these dogs are in paradise. I wonder about all of the dogs in my life, cats too, that are obese. I consider the cats that long to live a life outdoors, but instead, end up with owners who forbid that. Or potentially they live in an area that's too dangerous so the cats live their lives in windows, always watching, always dreaming. No matter what they do, this will remain their life forever, never really knowing the outdoors.

That is… unless they do something extreme. Unless they do something bold, something outrageous, running beyond the legs and outstretched hands of the owners, to the door, into the wilderness to discover that which they have always desired. They may not have the skills and abilities to defend themselves, but they have escaped on the first step to fulfilling their dreams. They may be apprehensive and afraid. They might stop; the owners may catch them, smack or kick them and throw them back inside, securing that the pet may never again even consider the outdoors to be an option. *A happy windowsill decoration.* Some may escape, running, learning to live in the wild. Others may find new homes where they can be free to be indoor/ outdoor cats. Others may decide that they don't like it and come back days later, sick and hungry, happily entering the arms of their owners. They tried it and have decided that it isn't for them. Of course, some of the unlucky ones will be hit by cars or killed in other ways. *There are those that never get the opportunity to try. I can relate to these window locked animals.* I hope that I find an indoor/ outdoor home somewhere, someday. *Or many places...* But what it comes down to is that finally I am not a windowsill kitty, pondering existence beyond the borders of my confined mind. I'm escaped. I think of this while I watch these dogs gallop, sharing this moment of joy with their owners and many of them consistently come back to the owners to check in, to say hello, maybe shake some water and sand on them cheerfully before running off again to play. *A life poem enhancing bliss sparkling in the sunlight...* Every living creature is happy here. *Well, except for that one angry, old woman who apparently doesn't realize this is a dog beach and just got sand sprayed on her by a galloping pooch.*

I swim with the dogs while continuously digging in the sand for shark teeth. There are people walking around with fancy metal poles that scoop up the gravel. They then shake it in the water, releasing all of the sand and tiny rubble from the piles to sort through. I found that just using my hands to scoop and look was just as fun. I find three of them and think of myself as a treasure hunting master. The water is so clear and warm. *How have I never seen it before? Oh, such worlds I have missed out on!*

I begin getting nervous to go in the plane... My stomach churns.

The hanger is about a three minute drive away and at about 1:45, I leave the dog beach and walk to my car to get a change of clothes. I figure that I can change quickly and then hop over there just in time to meet him. As I walk toward my car, I see a strikingly gorgeous brown haired woman walking with a golden retriever to the left of the bathrooms toward her car. *Whoa... I am strangely drawn to her for some reason, almost in a sense that my soul was hurting that I didn't reach out...* It felt as if a craving detonated within me and I was just intrigued by her as she walked. I had no idea why I could not take my eyes off of her. *I have a plane mission that I had to be on.* That is the only time in my life that I was able to say that and I was determined not to make Ronnie wait.

So I grab my stuff and quickly rush to the bathrooms. I was unhappy to find that there was a line of one woman in front of me, but I figured that I could just change and go. No hassle, no worries. I hadn't been wearing make up for days so that wasn't an issue. I am bouncing from heel to toe as I stand in line, moments before destiny takes hold. The door opens behind me and I turn and glance at whoever it is. I see a golden retriever slide up next to me and I look over and see that woman standing there. The pooch tries to walk in the bathroom further and she scolds him gently, using only words, "No, Reno."

He sits down and I take notice to his rather flashy hair-do. "I like your dog's Mohawk." I was so thankful that I had a good reason to talk to her. She looks up at me and smiles. Her hair is long and dark brown and her skin is nearly perfect. We make direct eye contact and I cannot help but to wonder if she is a goddess. Then I notice her black band t shirt and black wavy pants and try to figure out what kind of person she is. She's got a very interesting vibe about her and I don't know why I am so intrigued.

"Oh, thanks!" She says and looks down at him. I have already broken the conversation barrier; I must keep it going before I let the opportunity pass.

"He's a sweet guy. What's his name? Reno?"

"Yes, he is Reno and he is a good guy. I just cut his hair a few days ago."

"Oh, you did that? Ha-ha, I did that to my cocker spaniel when I was a little kid."

"Yep." I felt the conversation opportunity fade. I needed to initiate charm!

"So, what do you do for a living?" I ask as she looks apprehensive about it and pauses confused. *Oops… did I say something wrong?*

"Well, I am kind of just traveling now." Once again, my head explodes.

"What!? No way! You are traveling?" She looked far too beautiful to be traveling. I think about how many people have told me that same thing. I then glance at the dog and say, "with a dog? Where are you from?"

"Pennsylvania."

"What! Me too! What part?" I ask in astonishment as her body language loosens up to me.

"Harrisburg." *Mind explosion!*

"I cannot believe you are from Harrisburg! I am from Hershey, uh... I mean Lebanon."

"What!?"

"Yes! I am from there and I am on a road trip by myself too! When did you leave?"

"Well… I left and then I was in Georgia first. I left, I think, the 15th."

"Oh my gosh! I left on the 12th!" This is crazy I cannot believe this!"

"Ha-ha yeah! What are the chances? So what are you doing?"

"Oh, I need to change quickly. I am about to ride on an airplane. Can I meet you guys afterward?" She tells me her name is Alice and gives me her number. I change and get over to the plane. Ronnie is waiting for me when I arrive. I say my apologies for being late and he says that he just pulled in not even a minute ago. The gate isn't working properly and he explains that this is possibly the airport 'supposedly' that some of the 9-11 terrorists trained at and the fact that the gate wasn't working was a very big deal. This does not help my fear at all. He calls the hanger to tell them and they said there should be a cop over to patrol the area shortly. We enter and he takes me over to the gates. He opens up his hangar door and proudly says, "There she is."

She was breathtaking. Ronnie tells me that he built her himself and named after the Greek goddess in the picture above the tools. The shop was equipped with all sorts of mechanisms, some I recognized and some that I didn't. Above these tools hung a striking print of a romantic painting of a sculptor and his art. He explained that the picture was by the artist Jean-Leon Gerome in 1890 titled, "Pygmalion and Galatea" about a sculptor who wished for a wife as beautiful as his sculpture, so she-sculpture came to life. That is how Ronnie felt about his plane. She was so beautiful and every time he takes Galatea up into the sky, his sculpture comes to life. She was white with dark green and yellow cleanly painted across her midsection. She was so fresh, nearly spotless and had little cups over the wheels. Her full body wasn't even taller than Ronnie as he stood. I was nervous about getting into her and trusting her with my life, especially when Ronnie pushed her out of the hangar with his own body weight.

I climbed into the back, a shifting body weight balancing act, and he showed me how to work the headset and mic. I put on the goggles and he gave me a few bags in case of emergency stomach ejection. The space was cramped and my legs were bent tightly. My skin boiled in anxiety as he closed the hatch and started the engine. We shakily rolled out on the small tarmac parking lot and I could feel all sorts of bumps and shifts happening under me. I just assumed that hopefully this is standard movement for these types of things. Panic rose inside of me and I momentarily wished that I hadn't manifested this terrifying opportunity. I was horrified. He checked in and asked how I felt and if I was ready. I lied and told him that I was so ready. Deep down, I wanted to be ready. *Deep down, I wanted to be excited and fearless, but the truth was that I was wanting to be, not actually being.* But I decided that conquering fears is what this is all about so bring it on! *The sky's the limit!*

As we quickly rode across the parking lot, rumbling and shaking, I closed my eyes in an attempt to not have a panic attack. I felt a surge of heat rush through my head and as I decided to remember to breathe, I took in a large surge of air and released it just in the moment that I felt weightlessness take hold. Out, came the air from my lungs, dispelling fears and into the air, I flew, increasing my trust in my own abilities to do anything in this world. I felt the release of my own shot blocking characteristics, the forceful needing to be in control of my every aspect of my life. It faded. I was no longer in control here. I was in control of getting here, yes, but I now lived in pure faith that my life brought me here for a reason and I was not in control of the outcome. In this moment of ascension, I surrendered.

I looked around me as the shakiness eased and Ronnie asked me how I was doing. This time I answered him truthfully, saying that this was the most amazing thing that I have ever experienced. I actually had tears in my eyes at how blue the world was below me, the ocean expanding out further than I have ever seen before. The colors in the waters were varied from the depths of the sea to the height of the sand bars. I saw tiny shimmering lines, boats from below, but tiny white vortex trails from up here. The glistening waves were like millions of stars, a whole milky way below us reflecting the sun! I saw our tiny shadow sliding across the earth and he explained islands and things in the water. We spotted sharks and manatees, tiny specks moving around hidden landscapes that are only visible from the heavens. There were islands with mansions and a dock hidden miles from anything. The only way to get to these massive homes was by boat. Ronnie explained that they were owned by millionaires who buy them to just get away. They buy the whole island and then design it how they want it.

What a concept! I have never thought of anything like this. I could see vibrant blue paths down into the land. He explained that these were like roads of water; boat streets with private slips and passageways built into the mainland so when real estate agents sell the homes they can declare water front property. The awakening continued south and I just could not believe my eyes. Flying down the coast over the ocean, seeing the sandy layered land evolve into deep blues, all of it was just so spectacular, an unforgettable feast for my soul. I never felt so alive in my whole entire life and had I not jumped on the opportunity when it presented itself, had I not gone to yoga, had I not gone on that run, had I not started talking to them, had I not asked about his plane and had I not been so confident in myself to stand strong in my question, I would have missed out on this whole opportunity and never even realized it.

Had I given into my fear upon first arrival at the hangar, I never would have experienced the joy I currently possessed. I would have just gone along in life and everything would still be great, but I would not be having this experience. *That is what I mean so strongly when I say to follow the intuitive self. It's not that it will guide me from danger necessarily. The true magic of intuition is that it lines me up exactly with the universe and it's that divine synchronicity that will guide me toward fulfilling my greatest dreams. It's the synchronicity of the universe holding my shoulders and saying, "Way to go, Katie!" It's that feeling of being exactly where you are meant to be right now. It's the feeling of being so present in the moment, so exactly pure and true, right here-right now, that makes life fill with the sweet feelings of being more alive than I ever felt in my entire life.*

That is what I learned on this day. *Everything is possible.* That's when he asked if I wanted to do a barrel roll. I never ride roller coasters because I get belly aches, but the top of the plane was a circular, bubbled, clean glass window. It was a full 360 view. Of course, I accepted the barrel roll! He counts down and I get out my camera and the world becomes a spiral as the horizon line moves from left to above me to my right and then my head was spinning so much I didn't know where I was. I was a blue spiral in that instant, a physical being connected weightlessly in space.

He asked if I wanted to do another. *Challenge accepted.* This is when I began to get a head ache and my stomach began to hurt really badly, like there were bubbles or pouches of angry air rolling in my lower ribs. *Ok. That may be enough.* Fortunately, I didn't only conquer my goal, I went far beyond it. I manifested an unbelievable ride in an airplane with a gentleman pilot that guided me on a sight-seeing tour to lands I never would have been able to dream of.

Live today in limitless possibility- Check.

Chapter Thirty-Six

"In these moments, all I see is beauty."

T he sand is like speckled salt and pepper, a coarse grit of ground shells all sorts of colors and sizes. I walk up to the edge of the ocean to touch the clear gulf waters. I feel the chill of April air contrast the heat of the sun on my skin. The water flows over my feet in gentle laps and I can do nothing other than smile. *Wow...* Here I am, the ocean before me on the coast of Florida, feeling my body surging with zestful spirituality. Surge is the perfect word to describe the flow of energy through my veins. I am alive and more so than I have been in a long time. This world in which I live is incredible.

I told Nina all about the flight back at her place and she couldn't have been happier for me. Honestly, having her treat me like a daughter for this (without being obsessively worried about me), knowing that someone nearby loved me and had my information in case something was to happen, made the flight feel completely comfortable. Had it not been for Nina, I would have been nervous about possibly being kidnapped the whole time, but because we had taken care of the backup safety plan, I was fully able to enjoy and just purely experience. I needed someone to be there for me in a caring way. It had been a month since I felt really cared for and I will always be grateful for her at this time in my life.

That evening was spent with Alice and Reno at the dog beach. We watched the sun drift over the ocean and talked about metaphysical theories as the deep red rainbowing settled beyond the horizon and the stars closed down around us. The evening chill began to take over and we decided to walk back to our cars and head downtown. Alice grabbed a few beers from a gas station and I grabbed a few as well. We park near the most beautiful tree I have seen in my life, a massive banyan tree, so big it could take up an entire block. The initial tree grows up and the branches stretch out these strands of tree-hair that eventually make their way into the ground and become roots to another trunk. So this tree has hundreds of trunks and is absolutely amazing. We sit in it for hours and sip and talk about what we have experienced so far. We park our cars next to each other and say goodnight. I fall asleep instantly with the biggest smile I have ever had in my life.

We stay in Venice for three nights and I spend so much peaceful time on the beach digging for shark teeth and loving the world I have discovered. I meet up with Nina, her husband and Sonny and I meet up with Alice and Reno.

I write- **Day 29-** *Do not be afraid to enjoy. This is an investment. The money spent now will multiply later. This is the greatest investment of my life.*

Lying on the beach, I just needed to take a nap. I pull my shirt over my face and am about to fall asleep when I hear this voice say something odd to me.

"Hello Miss Bathing Beauty." I take the shirt off my head and look over.

"Oh that's not Aunt Debra…" the lady looks surprised, pink sunglasses gleaming above a big welcoming smile. "You are quite the bathing beauty, but just not the bathing beauty I thought you were." So, I go into the water again and two little boys come up to play with me. They see me digging in the sand and ask me what I am up to.

"I'm looking for shark teeth." I tell them as I bend down, this time taking a quick look downward to make sure my swim suit top wasn't dangling anything precious out of it. This adjustment is something that must be done to ensure these wandering knockers don't slip out of the swimsuit constantly. I don't think guys have to worry about this type of thing as much. I rarely think boys wonder if their junk is hanging out and if it is, they don't usually seem to care. I pulled a large foot-long black shell out of the water and was using it to scoop up sand so I could better find fossilized teeth.

The kids and I team up. I find the kids big shells and coral chunks so they can dig in the sand too and we all work as a fossilized shark tooth investigative team.

I leave the shore eventually and stop at huge shower stall to give myself a small bath with a tiny towel and a bit of soap. *I make sure to rinse 'down there' discretely the best way I could.* I get out and sit in the shade and assemble my little shell anklet from random things I collected. I start writing in this enormous cement patio about the previous day's events and, of course, out of the 25 other tables to be sat at, this man with a huge Cuban cigar sits directly in front of me. I try to ignore it, but its scent suffocates me and I can't help but feel the urge to relocate. And it isn't just a simple cigarette contaminating the airflow for two or three minutes. No, this is a tempest of stench wreaking havoc on the eyes and lungs of all the innocent bystanders unlucky enough to be near for almost a half hour. I cough to try to represent the fact that I am very unhappy with his choice of seat, but he is too involved in complaining about his family on his loud phone conversation to even notice me. It was really just a fraudulent display of how unhappy his life really was. He was so caught up in the fact that he had to be here that he couldn't enjoy the simple beauty of the world around him of actually being here. *Fascinating*. I wrote his words as he spoke to ease my mind and remind myself to stay present, stay here, now.

"Walked two miles, yes! I walked two miles and I have to wait a half hour for them. Yep, I have to sit here and wait a half hour. Oh yeah, I'm just sitting here at this pavilion because the beach has all these signs up that says no smoking on the beach. So here I am because the government has to go and ruin everyone's enjoyment. Oh, and then…" I look up and laugh. I move seats. He isn't facing me so I don't care. I notice just in front of him is a pregnant Asian lady sitting at the next table, the only other person in this entire pavilion of 30 tables. He is so caught up in the unhappiness of his life that he doesn't even care who is around to smell the stench of his contaminating identity. There is a lady that approaches me from behind, an older Indian woman asking me if I know anything about the music tonight. She tells me that there is usually free live music here every evening at 6 and it is 5:58 and no one is here yet. We chat a bit and I ask her about her life. She is initially from Portugal and lives half of the year in Maine and the other half in Venice, FL.

She then says my new favorite phrase, "Life is just so beautiful." And it feels so good to hear that from another person. I say it all the time to myself, reminding myself to be thankful for the world around me. It is nice to see so many older people really loving their lives. I was told of a drum circle Wednesday night on the beach in Nokomis. Just being able to reference events like this made me feel as if I am finally alive, living the life I have always dreamed of.

The awakening of possibility started to eclipse the past.

But only for a little…

241

Part Three

The Liberation

Noun

1. *The act of setting someone free from imprisonment, slavery, or oppression; release*

2. *Freedom from limits on thought or behavior.*

Chapter Thirty-Seven

Day 30 - Tuesday

"The untrained mind can be our harshest of enemies, but the subtly trained mind can be our greatest source of personal command."

Alana messaged me about her cousin and her cousin's boyfriend moving in for rent money. This means we are totally done and nothing will ever be the same again. I woke up in my car, stressed beyond the borders of my mind, but it is stunningly beautiful outside so I tried not to let my thoughts get the best of me. I opened the door and kicked off my socks and shoes. 30 seconds later I see Alice's door open and out hops her dog. "Sorry this is taking so long. I am almost done. I'm sorry." She explains as she opens the back of her car.

"No don't be sorry. That's another thing we will work on. Saying sorry. We shouldn't apologize unless we actually do something wrong and feel as if we must apologize. If we say sorry improperly, then that means we are lacking self-confidence so from here on out we will not say sorry unless we mean it." She tells me she'll catch up after I begin doing the bathroom dance. I go for eggs and coffee in the diner. I was told that manatees can be seen next to the power plant off of I-80. I love big animals! Then I realized that I had a golden retriever meeting me for breakfast. *Yes!*

Later this day we leave Venice and drive south, two sexy women, two vehicles and a dog. We end up in Ft. Myers and don't know what to do so we go to a place that I've usually always felt safe, a gay bar. Alice has never been to one before so she is elated. She has decided that she will be gluten free from now on. At the bar they have $5 long Island iced teas with four different types. We both choose the blue Long Island, which proved to be a genius purchase. S*o much alcohol in those drinks!* A guy brought in boxes of pizza. Free pizza caused Alice to reconsider starting her gluten free diet tomorrow.

Alice suggests that we set our sights on Key West since it's the lowest, most tropical point in the continental United States. I say, "Let's do it. Let's allow life to guide us to Key West." Intentions set and we hug, sealing the deal. Like hungry, flamboyant sharks, we are surrounded by new gay friends.

The owner of the gay bar was this massive manatee of a man with equivalently plump Chihuahuas, two little fatties that slugged along the floor panting with their pink collars. Obviously this overweight man fed his dogs the same junk food he was eating, probably a diet of pizza and burgers. We were given permission to sleep in the parking lot in a happily, flashy exclamation. We eventually crawled out into our individual cars again and went to sleep. Before he left he circled the parking lot slowly and looked around every corner for predators, then gave a friendly goodbye wave as he took off into the night, three sweet little circle beings, him and his panting co-pilots, smiling into the salty air around 3 am.

I woke up in the back of the station wagon confused. As I sit up and adjust myself to take in my surroundings, the previous day's events flood my head, putting a smile across my face. *Maybe Alice secretly is gay! Wouldn't that just be the bee's knees! She really wanted to go to that gay club!* But then I realize that if she was at all remotely interested in women, I probably would have at least scored a kiss last night. That thought gets devoured when I realize how badly I have to go to the bathroom. Alice probably won't be awake for a long time and I look around at the warehouses across the road and wonder if there is a place I could go to hide behind a bush, but then I realize that there really is no cover. This is a series of huge corporate buildings and storage facilities all connected by parking lots and roads, a concrete prairie.

But those long islands are begging to release from me and I look around the car searching for a cup, an anything to relieve my urinary tension. Alice surprisingly wakes up, tousles her hair around while she exhaustedly makes her way over with Reno to the side of the building where she and he squat. She returns without a second thought as to who might have seen her. She tells me to just go in a cup under a blanket and that she is going to go back to sleep. *Ugh.* I find a large coffee cup from the day prior and I put the blanket over my head and adjust myself on the edge of the seat at the door and try to get in a relaxed state of mind, but the open air touching my sweetness, balanced to not spill in my car, holds it all back.

I always felt being a man would have been so much easier because when a man has to go, he just doesn't care if someone sees him or not. Women are taught to be more reserved and restrained ever since we are small. Little girls are delicate and treated as dolls while boys are wild and treated like toys. This type of programming, even if struggling for internal sexual justice, can last for the rest of life resulting in a limitation mindset. That is the exact thing I have been working so hard to liberate myself from.

Then again, Alice did just go right now, proving that everything I am thinking is improper since she is a girl. It doesn't matter whether it is a man or woman; it is the mindset that really sets the stage for reality. She had to go. She went. Plain and simple as that. *I have to go and now I am balancing half naked under a blanket unable to go because of all these stupid concerns I am creating within my head about if she'll hear me or if I will overflow the cup or splatter it on the seat and have an even bigger problem. She was smart and did exactly what she needed to do when she needed to do it to achieve peace and now she is sleeping again. I apparently have chosen to struggle.*

I angrily pull up my pants and don't button them because it hurts. I waddle in the morning sun's heat to the electric factory across the street, thinking that the only thing that will bring me to peace at this point today would be a cup of coffee. The grass grows high along the side of the building meeting the burnt looking, rusted, chunky, metal wall bursting with orange foam insulation leaking from within resembling buttered popcorn erupting in the morning heat. *Ugh... Hangover hunger is kicking in...* I go inside to have my presence surprise the three men at a counter. "Hi, if I could please use your bathroom it would be amazing. I slept in that parking lot across the street and I just really have to go. I promise I can pay you in amazing stories!"

The guy looks at me strange and tells me to take my time. *Oh, the relief!* I brushed my teeth and washed my face; was feeling like a serious champion. I found a bathroom and maintained my sophisticated traveler concept, a level up from just plain old homeless traveler peeing in the open at the side of a factory. The guys are no longer at the counter. I am slightly offended that they don't want to hear my stories. Something familiar catches my senses so I look to discover a whole coffee station upon a small counter between the front door and the bathroom. I frantically go up to their main counter and look for someone to beg for coffee. One of the guys finally notices me panting and salivating all over the counter.

"Might I be able to purchase a coffee? I am traveling and have no need for any electrical stuff now so I can't be a customer, but I'll gladly purchase a coffee since I have to wait for my friend to wake up."

"They are complimentary. There is free popcorn too."

247

Chapter Thirty-Eight

"I choose to live life as if everything is a miracle. The only other option isn't nearly as much fun."

Believe and achieve! Even on a small level, such as attracting a cup of coffee, it works. I sip that delicious liquid and 'cheers' myself on having stood firm in my choice not to go to the bathroom outside. Had I gone against my internal judgment, I wouldn't have been granted the opportunity to enjoy a free cup of coffee. *I wonder how often people think I am hyped up on drugs?* There are so many instances in the last few weeks that just continually blow my mind and I can do nothing other than giggle to myself and smile nonstop. Lately, the universe has been brighter and glows with every moment. *It's all about these tiny presents that remind me how amazing this life really is.*

Actually, it's my presence being presented presents for being in the present. I laugh harder, wondering if I am insane...

Back at the car I do the standard protocol for beach life, hanging the towels across the vehicle to dry out, but today it also serves a double purpose. The sun baking down on me is too much to handle, even in the morning so I arrange it to block the sun from hitting me.

Madison texted about the moth tonight; it is one month since I was there. *Wow, a whole month since my first day.* What a month it's been so far...

Eventually Alice and I walk side by side with Reno guiding the way through downtown Fort Myers. It is such a beautiful and clean city, everything being just pretty much perfect. There is a huge banyan tree in front of the courthouse, so massive in size that I stare at it in disbelief that it is even real. The vine stems have morphed into this enormous cylinder coated with tiny lizards and tempting climbing vines. They were so tempting; in fact, that we both climbed it and sat in the tree for a while taking pictures and exploring the insanity of what we were standing on.

There is a very pleasant café downtown that we were both drawn to for some reason. This place just seemed so mesmerizing. I don't know how to describe it other than we just needed to go there. It was like destiny was asking me to arrive in this location at this time.

I wanted the table next to us by the curb because I thought we could have a better view of everything on the street, but two older couples grabbed it instead. So we take the last available outdoor table at the Fresh Connectivity Café and the waitress immediately fetches us some glasses and Reno some water in a bowl.

Alice and I place our orders as I pull out my notebook so we can do written meditations and energy goal writing. These are practices that self-help books often suggest you do to keep you fully engaged with the texts so that the information settles better. I tell her about how I met SkyFly Gypsy, so I put out 'be in airplane energy' into the universe. "In just two days it came to me! I was granted the opportunity to do two flips over the Gulf of Mexico in a plane for free! I decided that it was what I wanted so I fully set my intention to open up the doors for that opportunity. So I know that this Law of Attraction works. Ok, let's focus now. My goal now is boat energy. I will send out energy into the universe to give me boat energy. I want to ride in a boat! No, I will be in a boat on the Gulf of Mexico. I will…" and we continue to make mini declarations, empowerment and desire mantras to attract boat energy into our lives. At this point, I have proven myself worthy of sounding crazy.

As our food comes, I take notice to a beautiful man, tan skin with his dark hair, curly and about three inches long streaked with natural sun highlights. *The first time in my life this has happened…* I can't take my eyes off of him, almost in the same way that I couldn't take my eyes off of Alice at first. He has a huge smile on his face while his two little dogs, one golden Chihuahua puppy and a sweet little black and white puppy hop around so cute, licking everything on the ground they can possibly taste. He laughs as they get tangled and his energy flows massive. He greets Reno as he passes without even really looking at us. Something about my reaction to that man surprised me. *Was I attracted to him? Am I not entirely a lesbian?* I don't know, but as he walked down the sidewalk, something in my chest spiraled or hurt. It's that almost cry feeling that occurs when you watch a movie and something dramatic happens that makes you think it's too late. He continued down the street fading into the crowd and quickly my mind faded him and his puppies from my thoughts. *What on Earth was I just feeling?*

That food was absolutely incredible. I consider myself to be a health-a-tarian more than a vegetarian and I felt I needed some protein so I had a tuna over salad with oil and vinegar and a cup of soup. I leaned back and observed the calmness in the air and the gentle sway of the palm trees in every direction. The beautiful companion before me glistened as we spoke of our dreams and her dog sat patiently at my feet resting in the shade. This was one of those moments when I couldn't stop smiling at what my life has given me.

249

If I were in Erie right now doing what I expected to do, it would be about 5 degrees with an even colder relationship. Instead, I am thousands of miles away in an 80-degree paradise hanging with a beautiful woman and a dog.

Suddenly there is a very brash CA-RAAACK and a woman screams horrifically. Everyone around reacts, looking to see what the sound could be, since no one seemed directly connected to it. The table next to us, the initial table I wanted, had four elderly people sitting at it by the base of a 30 ft. palm tree, one woman had her back to the trunk only about three inches from it. She looks in shock as she stares at the faces of her friends, disturbed by what almost happened. One of the 5 ft. long dead palm husk branches with a base about a foot wide was lying against the back of her chair, having perfectly wedged itself down right behind her in that tiny three inch gap. An older gentleman removes it and lays it along the road and the world continues onward as if nothing happened.

Later when we were about to leave, I picked the fallen branch up and noticed it weighed a surprising 20+ pounds and the base that would have hit her in the top of the skull, had it been just an inch closer, was similar to a blunt hatchet. I held that branch and felt a shiver quake through me. In spite of the beauty around me, the absolute perfection of my current paradise, potential death was always a present force coming from every angle at any given time. Even the thing that I admired most about this place, the trees in the summertime breeze, could produce an instant farewell from this earth and this life. The possibilities surrounding me for what could be possible in any moment seemed to rattle my brain as I did a 360-degree slow spin and looked at the world around me, the blue skies dotted with the occasional cloud and the blissful people smiling in every single direction. I saw it all differently. There was opportunity in all, yes, but there was also a lesson in everything as well. This was, without a doubt, a wake-up call. Not that it happened directly to me, not that anything even really happened, but the fool lives life listening to only the situations that occur to her. I am ready to no longer be a fool in this life. I grabbed the receiver and answered the universe's wake-up call in this moment and I am ready to listen to whatever it has to tell me. Something here wants me to listen. I can feel it.

Alice wants to take Reno to the dog beach and I feel like I don't want to do that, which was strange for me to say even as I said it, but I followed that intuition. So we parted ways after planning to meet up later. I tell her to send out boat vibes. She agrees. I walk all over downtown, checking out the local shops and interesting people. I initially intended to find a place to do magic tricks and make some money, but instead decide to just appreciate the area. Then I head over and walk along the bay that has a lovely park, statues and fountains. There is a dock with many boats and prominent bridges crossing the Caloosahatchee River. I sit and breathe in the surroundings, smiling at where life has brought me so far.

"So what college do you go to?" a voice asks from behind me.

That simple question triggered some irritation in my mind. I don't understand America or people in general, I guess. I just do not get it. It's more expected to have someone my age acting preposterous in a bar than having someone my age simply sitting and observing the world around me. Nearly everyone asks me which college I am in. And when I tell them I am not in school, that I am just enjoying life, they look at me with a tilted head like I am crazy until they ask more questions. Then they look at me with appreciation, but the shock of my just living has begun to wear itself out on me. I am growing tired of explaining the reason, but I guess I am doing my part in sharing a different type of existence with hundreds across these states. It just seems so bizarre to me that a guy screaming at an inanimate object, *(we shall call it a television)* portraying an image of a game is much more acceptable than a young woman sitting alone with a notebook, smiling at the thoughts that come to mind as she observes in the surroundings that she worked so hard to be free in.

All those thoughts stay in my head as I explain to this man the same story I have been repeating to people for weeks now. I am still passionate about it, but talking about me has become repetitive. He talks a little bit more and I answer some more questions about my experiences. He then thanks me for taking the time to talk and hands me five bucks. My jaw drops. He explains that his daughter has been talking about taking a semester off from college to do what I am doing and they have been fighting since she first mentioned it, but after talking to me he feels like he might understand her better. He thanked me again as he wished me well.

Wow. So maybe his destined path today was to randomly take a walk down to the water to cross paths with me to help him understand his daughter and her longing to see more. *You never know how far your ripples will flow when you toss your pebble in the pond of life.*

The water by this dock is deeply dark and has a very strong current, which I find to be quite poetic in my current state of mystery and power strengthening from within. The black metal railing is oddly comforting in my palms, telling me that this is exactly where I need to be right now.

To my left, I see a floating dock about 50 yards long with a pavilion and a bench on the end. Being that no one was out there and it was facing west, I consider this to be a heaven sent spot to watch the sunset and write so I go out

251

to it and sit down on the bench just to discover that the top plank has been snapped off making it pretty awkward to rest against. I sit on an angle against the side pillar and find a tiny bit of relaxation as I breathe deep and stare out across the waters, watching pelicans fly and seagulls hover. I pull out my notebook and start writing, feeling the flow enrich the pages with my mind's creation. *It's magnificent here in this moment.*

Then I hear someone approaching from the path behind me and turn to see a singing man of color with dreads riding a bike equipped with fishing gear. *Great... more distraction by unwanted men while I am trying to write in peace somewhere.*

"Ahh..." he sighs loudly as he parks his bike next to the cement pillar and unloads his bucket. I look up, trying to be a pleasant citizen in the world following that famous Gandhi quote I always try to listen to, *"Be the change you wish to see in the world."*

Chapter Thirty-Nine

"Inspiration is a perpetual energy machine."

I just want the world to be friendly and to slow down a little bit. I'd love the general population to be open minded and accepting to all types of people in all situations. So I smile and shoot a small hello to Fisherman. He mentions how beautiful the night is. I've been on a constant life-high all day, floating around with an endless smile. *The only thing that is rather distressing to me is the inability to document properly.* It seems that I never get caught up in both a day's living and recording. There are many amazing moments where the law of attraction burns through my hours producing so many incredible results. I continually get wrapped up in them and being in the moment of their unraveling, (*which is exactly what I want to do*), but as I continue to experience more events, I just seem to get my life lost in experiencing even more. Every day it has become an addiction to continue attracting amazing circumstances. *I feel I need to share this truth with the world. I want to share this magic with the world.* I need to share this magic with the world, especially now that I have produced airplane results! I am proof that the law of attraction can work. *The power of the mind holds so much more unleashed power than we know!* That is why I feel like I need to continually write every single moment down. That is also why I feel that I need to share every single synchronicity, every divine moment of inspiration I receive that has produced this unending smile. I just need to write it all down because I know it can change lives! *But then I get so caught up in attempting to document that I unintentionally shut off the flow.*

I glance at the scribbled letters on my notebook. *"Live your beliefs and you can turn the world around." Henry David Thoreau.* Now as I write, there is another man of color talking to me. I would like to ignore him and tell him that I need to catch up on my writing, but something in the way he spoke to me as he cut the rotten shrimp and fish parts up, told me that I could learn something from this guy, especially since he was a family man with a wife and kids that went by the name of Rastafarian Ray. He had a genuine smile and energy about him that made me understand the peaceful life of a sunset fisherman. *That's when I felt that inspiration emotion kick in.* I felt it roar through my system as he explained the stinkier the bait, the more fish he will attract. He pulls out a bag of ice dripping from the bottom of that bucket and gently places it on the ground. From within, he pulls out a six pack of the drink that will represent the rest of my Florida life. He holds up a silver torch, shimmering in its entire 8.5 % alcohol splendor. I am hesitant of taking a beer from a random fisherman on a dock in some random city in Florida alone.

I laugh. He asks me why I am laughing. I explain this situation and rapidly feel much better about everything.

"Well, girl, heh. That is awfully funny. Why are you here anyhow?" I crack open the beer myself after robustly wiping the top and take a sip of what felt like one of the most relaxing beers I have ever tasted in my life. I explain to him a general bit of my last few weeks. While we are talking, another interestingly ethnic blended man with a lazy eye walks up. He is super skinny and wearing a white tank top. (I prefer not to call it a wife beater) His tightly woven black hair makes him resemble a close version of Snoop Dogg. We will call him New York. New York greets me, affectionately calling me 'Mami' and starts setting up his fishing gear and jumps right into conversation with us, constantly calling Rasta 'Papi'. Rasta tells him that I am from Pennsylvania.

Rasta reels in a fish. I think it is so awesome that he caught one so quickly. He corrects me. "Ha, honey. This thing ain't a fish! This thing is bait." He cuts it in half with one swift strike, which horrifies me as I watch the bottom end get impaled on a hook and the other end, the head, just looks around stunned. It looks like it is trying to wiggle, attempting to breathe and propel himself back into the water. I look at his little round fishy eyes, doing anything it can to fix the situation and I turn my head. I can't look. There is nothing I can do to save that little guy except just let him die. I almost want to cry, but that is what an inexperienced northerner mostly vegetarian woman would do. I am here for experience and I am here to see how others live, even if it makes me terribly uncomfortable occasionally.

I never was part of fishing before like this and I want these fishermen to respect me, gosh dang it! I never realized how much torture fishing produces. New York says, "Aye yam frahm New Yohk." He tells me. "Aye used to live theh my whole layfe, but I just had to get away from the city. That place is no good. Nope. That place is no good for me. Now look where I am. I wake up in paradise every single day." He looks around and his eyes glimmer. There is something about this man that I feel I can really understand, something about liberation from a personal hell, a life once known, but finally escaped from. He looks smiling in every direction and I can feel his appreciation, the same appreciation I feel for every experience I have had so far. It goes way beyond just happiness. It is a true appreciation coming from deep within, from a place that only real pain can produce. *His is significantly more extreme than mine, but an obvious soul-seeker-for-newness path unites us.* I feel us bond in a deeper spiritual level because we both escaped that other northern world before it killed us. He continues smiling and plops down upon the bench next to me. He reaches into his pocket and asks me if he can borrow my notebook. They begin back and forth fishermen's banter about all the crazy things

254

they've caught off this pier. New York swore the Fort Myers dock right here at the right time was the absolute best place to go fishing.

"Without a boat, ha, there are spots out there that'll blow us land lovers away!" Rasta said to him. They argued about whether that was accurate or not, bringing up this one legendary spot that only a few fishermen know about, a secret fisherman's hot spot about three miles off shore. "I've been there and that spot is great. But in general, this is better."

New York begins trying to roll a blunt. "Papi, I caught a 5 ft. shark here last week." The scent of weed fills the air. I usually decline, but he explains how it is homegrown, not at his place but his buddies place and he gets a bunch for helping him harvest it. I never had homegrown weed before so I figure why not indulge a little bit. Rasta declines explaining that he actually gave up smoking over 15 years ago.

"I am a family man now." My respect for Rasta goes way up.

"Shut up, man! Don't tell me those fisherman lies." New York looks at Rasta as he goes to check the line and we all watch as he reels in another small fish, about 8 inches long. To me, this seems like a large fish. I cannot imagine what types of giant fish they are going to catch with bait that big, but I don't understand the salt life yet. This one gets the fortune of having the rusty hook jammed through the base of its body making a pop sound as it goes through. He tosses it in the water while I cringe and it starts to swim around as if nothing is wrong. Rasta explains how this movement and blood will show the others that it is injured. It will attract something pretty soon.

"Ayam not lying! It was seriously that big! I put a bait fish on and walked down through the dock dragging it through the waters. It was a shark. Papi, when I get some bait, I'll show you." *I cannot believe that he caught a shark*! Big water creatures are not at all blended into my Pennsylvania concept of reality. I can't even imagine a fish that vast, much less a shark this close to land.

"Honey, this water is so dark because this is brackish water. It is where the salt water meets the fresh water and all sorts of fish gather here, both freshwater and saltwater fish. Sharks included. Last month I caught a sea turtle, man he was this big!" New York holds his arms outstretched about 4 feet wide to which Rasta again makes fun of him for lying. This provokes New York to pull out his flip-phone and prove that he actually did catch this mega-turtle.

"And he had three hooks in his mouth. He was a lucky guy because I had wire cutters on me and I cut those things off of him. Usually what happens is when a guy is fishing and they realize that they hooked something that they don't want; they cut the line and leave the hook in the animal. Usually if it is a bad hook, like somewhere vital, it will get infected killing the animal, but then the fisherman doesn't have to bother with it and just sacrifices the hook." *Fishing is brutal!* They hand me the rod and teach me how to properly reel in. I pull up a sail catfish. New York calls him a fatty.

"Whoa, man. Look at this fatty, man!" They teach me the difference between the two types of catfish as he takes Fatty off the hook. He shows me that they have horns. One fin immediately stabs New York's hand and he bleeds down his wrist. He swears and throws the fish back into the water.

"Catfish, you don't want them. They are bottom feeders. Anything on the floor, all that ocean junk, that's what they eat. So, if you eat them, you eat all of that. I used to love me some catfish, but I don't eat that anymore. I eat only the steak of the sea now." New York tells Rasta about his new tattoo which crosses his shoulders. He pulls up his shirt to show him a big tribal design, obviously a cover up, but the thing that catches my eyes are the profuse scars across his spine. He had abundant scarred whip marks, lighter toned, inch-thick at spots, lines all over his back. There had to be over 50 of them ranging in size and color, width and depth. Some were faded and as light as a vein underlying just below the skin. Some were solid and mountainous, forming ranges of what I could only imagine would be previous torture, some type of slave involvement or gang interaction. Possibly they were left over from being whipped as a child, growing longer to cover the entire back as his body grew. *If he received these in adulthood, geez, this guy really must have nearly escaped hell.* Whatever it was, it represented a world that he had known. It represented a world he once knew daily in New York City. He pulls his shirt back on and I try not to let my face show my disturbing observation. This guy escaped something immense and I certainly wasn't about to ask.

"This is what life is all about." New York pulls out his phone and I see something in his character shift. "This is why I moved here. Look at this. Today it's 79 degrees. Tomorrow, 82. This whole week is 80-87 degrees. Now look at New York. 42...45... tomorrow high of 48. Naw man..." he throws arms outwards and gazes at fishing rods and water, "This is life. Every day is paradise for me now."

I knew it was more of a reason to never return than just the temperature difference. Since I took one hit of his prized local weed, my focus was very solid and I really saw his back for what it was. I will never forget the way that looked and I wondered about what the tattoo was that he got covered up on his shoulders. I look at his crooked eye, smiling into the Florida sky and I wonder. He hands me a rod and they explain the tensions of the fishing line and how to read it properly so that I can check the lines myself. I couldn't believe how much the current bent the rod. There were many times that I mistook the current pulling on the line for a fish pulling on it. I'd reel it in really fast and be fooled time and time again. "Mami, you must be patient. Listen to the rod. You will be able to see the difference and feel the difference. The current tugs. Feel the difference." I thought this seemed to be an excellent explanation for a lot in life. *Be patient. Listen to the rod.* Either that or it's a great brand quote for patriarchy uprising.

A father and his three children walked up behind us and started fishing off the left side of the dock. Almost instantly the youngest son catches a fish. Then he does again. Then the third time we all gather around as he pulls up a 6-inch-wide slimy ray. The little rubber disc flutters around and wiggles. Its skin feels rubbery and slick, like a smooth, flat pickle. Jay explains how we have to get him in the water because the out of water shock is going to kill him if we don't. The hook actually was lodged not in its lip, but in its head. And they tried to get it out, but they couldn't get the right angle with it in their hands so they ended up placing it on the ground upside down and having to step on him slightly to get that hook out. The poor little creature gave out a little sigh as it released. The hook's removal gave a firm pop sound, something about that made my jaw clench in disgust. It stopped moving. I thought they had killed it, but they told me it would have died a slow infection death if they didn't get the hook out so at least now it has a chance. He picks it up and throws him in the water where it slaps the surface loudly and just sits there momentarily. I think that the poor thing just died right there in front of us and my stomach turns. Then it starts to flutter awake again and raises the sides of its fins as it descends into the darkness below. *Man… Fish life is a hard life…Yuck.*

We are hanging out as I explain how badly I want to be on a boat. Rasta tells me about his good friend in Key West who would perhaps be more than jubilant to take me on his boat. *What are the chances?* He tells me that he is a crazy old hippie that retired down there and smokes weed all day. He tries to figure out his number, but can't seem to find it. So, he spends the next bit of time calling friends until he finally gets his number. I write Cowboy Bo on my notes next to a number that he swears is the right one. He promises that this guy would just love to take me on his boat, but I have to be careful because his friend is a good guy, but that Key West is very close to Cuba so I have to not just accept any rides from anyone that is offering. I actually hadn't realized how dangerous situations can be next to water until this very moment. *I mean I have been cautious in every moment, but to be kidnapped to another country hadn't crossed my mind before.* Kidnapping on the ocean is a total possibility down here! I appreciate his effort, but I feel as if something about this opportunity is just, well, lacking. Something doesn't feel quite right about this Cowboy offer. That's when I look over to see another guy has come up from behind us. He's holding a red cup in one hand and laughing with his two puppies' leashes in the other. I do a double take and my jaw drops. It is the same guy I was so drawn to earlier that day! *Woah!* I stare at him as he laughs and tries to keep his puppies from licking the disgusting fish scrap off the cement, but they are very determined. I can't stop staring at him while Rasta and Puppy-Man make small talk about the dogs' names. As he is about to leave, I impulsively stand up, "You are the guy from earlier." Those are the words that come out of my mouth. No thought produced that conversation. My reaction startles me.

He looks at me, confused and smiling with a slight giggle. *I am sure this is a dream every guy has, that women just flock to them stumbling over their words to talk.* I disorderly say, "I, uh, I mean, we were eating lunch and you walked by with your puppies earlier." He says his name is Ryan and mentions how he lives close by and loves taking them out. The golden Chihuahua is Diesel and the floppy black and white puppy is Bella. He bought Diesel a month ago and two days later Bella showed up in need of a home so he doesn't know what breed she is, but she is part pit-bull.

We keep talking and he realizes that we were the ones with the beautiful golden retriever. Rasta interrupts and remembers something about what I should say when I call Cowboy on the phone to make him trust me and tells me to get my notebook out quick. I jot down a couple random sentences that make no sense to me, but I assume that it is one of those inside jokes that will prove that I actually do know a friend of his. Rasta says, "I know that he would love to take you out on his boat."

Puppy Man looks over and says, "Wait, you want to go on a boat?" I explain my situation with Alice and why I am where I am. After a few minutes of conversations he offers for us to take a shower at his place if we want. He says we can either sleep in the car or we can sleep there. Doesn't matter, but if we want, he will take us out on his boat tomorrow. "I go out three to four times a week. Usually, it is just me and the puppies so it would be nice to take people out. Hey, we could even take all three dogs out if you want." My eyes light up. He gave me his number and address, but told me to call him before we get there because he has to come let us in. He then mentions how it's no pressure if we don't call, but we can shower if we feel we need to. I cannot even believe this life I am living right now.

The law of attraction, my dream manifested in just one day. I realize that it wasn't even just one day. It was almost instantaneous. The moment I spoke to Alice about what I wanted, the instant I wrote it down on paper at that cafe, Puppyman walked by. He didn't even just walk by; he stopped right in front of us for about 10 seconds. The moment presented itself instantly and I knew it, I felt a drive, a power drawing me to that man. I just didn't act at the moment because I didn't understand what I was feeling. But I was feeling the universal pull of manifestation, the call of the universe. *Manifest Destiny....*

Or, uhh…, something like that…

So here I am again, 8 hours later talking about my great boat desires to a Rasta fisherman on a pier, slightly drunk and high and Ryan shows up again, at the exact moment I'm talking about it!

What are the chances?

I text Alice. 'We have a date with a boat tomorrow!!!!!"

She texts back *(in exact lettering. I thought it was funny and being that this was such a pivotal moment, I took the time to write the texts letter for letter.)* "whatttttttttt?!?! AHHHHHHHHHHH!!!!!!!!!"

The next text says, "Soskldllfnlmgtmngntiklwskkeisopsop20w90e43oiruftt7u7u5492w90090lsxn !!!!!!11!!1! I've never been so excited!" *Neither have I.* This was the first time that I was able to share, step by step, the longing for a situation and the experiencing of it entirely with another person.

That night we hesitantly go to his apartment on the second floor after discussing what to do if he turns out to be a serial killer or something. But as it turns out, he is just a normal bachelor that owns his own business refinishing pavers. He is in love with his two puppies. His apartment is finely furnished and beautifully painted. The floors are spotless tile and everything is very orderly in every room, which struck me as rather impressive considering his current state of solo life. He is a very well kept man.

That shower felt so amazing, so well deserved. After the previous few days' cold, beach, outdoor, bathing stations, I feel as if I have earned this water sanctuary via the law of attraction, my desire and ambitions! I smile and let the heat flow over my face, massaging my eyes and cheeks, relieving stress on my forehead and chest. I envision tension, self-inflicting thoughts, and my weaknesses melting from my body and sliding down my skin, blending with the water to disperse into the drain where it will mix with the energy of the world and be recycled into something not so toxic. I breathe and look around me in absolute happiness. *This life… ahh…* I come out of the shower in my night clothes to see Alice and Ryan having a martini. I still don't fully trust the situation or a random guy making me a drink, so I stick to making a drink myself, claiming that I don't like it dry so as not to offend him. I open his fridge to find a little bit of orange juice, lots of containers of prepared food and a lot of soda, but not just any soda, diet soda. There were about 6 different varieties, but I have this strict intolerance to diet drinks.

"Do you have anything else?" I ask while skimming the refrigerator.

"Nope, trying to lose weight. All I drink is diet." *Shucks. Oh well, It's just one night. I guess a diet ginger ale and captain doesn't sound too bad.* We talk and discuss the boat for the following day. Excitement spreads through my body and Alice and I grabbed each other's hands giggling and smiling. Her gorgeous eyes lit up in disbelief that in just a few hours after we arrived, we had not only found showers, but we also found a place to sleep for all of us! (Including Reno who didn't seem to mind the puppies nipping at him and hopping all over him.) But we also established a boat! *I look at Alice in curiosity as to if she is the one, the soul mate woman of my dreams. She says she is straight, but that lesbian quote states that women are like spaghetti, straight until hot and wet.* Time will tell, I suppose.

While Ryan went to the bathroom, I secretly took pictures of his business card, his name and address on his mail and I sent the information to Madison from Pittsburgh. She understood me. She had contacts to my parents if I didn't message her first thing in the morning and then in the evening after the boat ride. It sounds crazy, but I trusted her more than anyone else in the world right now. She is a stranger that I just met for a few nights a thousand plus miles away, but she's been checking on me daily to make sure I am ok. Plus, she's the only person who really knows all about me and Alana. She wishes me well in the next day's adventures, sounding excited and a little nervous. I feel the same.

These situations result in either the most amazing opportunities ever or the worst. Only time and a little faith in my intuition will tell the tale of Straighty and Katie's open sea voyage. *Ahoy, matey! Batten down the hatches and prepare to set sail! Destiny be a'callin' Arg!*

Chapter Forty

Ft. Myers Florida

"May we dream our greatest happiness into existence."

An overweight woman waddles by, slapping her lumpy, spherical daughter on the booty. From what I saw, I believe the bubbled kid had done something wrong to deserve a booty slap, but the mom seemed too aggressive. Callie and I watch as the mom screams and dangles the kid by the arm as she drags her away yelling profanities. It's a moment like this that makes me wonder where it would be ok to step in, but we just watch that poor child get screamed at as she cries, until the mom puts her in time out on a bench.

"So, what does your mom think about all of this traveling?" Callie asked.

I explain how she hates it and one time convinced my dad that I would be caught by a monster man and killed and eaten. "They screamed into the phone about how Jeffrey Dahmers exist even today. I laughed at them and tried to explain that I was more alright than I had ever been, but they didn't want to hear it. My mom's fear of the unknown followed me like a horrendous shadow for thousands of miles. Honestly, what I was doing prior, drinking and clubbing every weekend while living in my hometown was way more dangerous than nearly anything I was doing on the road."

"Yeah, creepers in the club. That's no joke. I know." Callie shakes her head and a shiver rushes down her body indicating first hand encounters with creeps. "College life is loaded with date rape. Like, the guys were always drugging girls at my school. It was so scary because it was so common. My friends and I just plain old stopped going out because it became too awful. Like, most of my friends at that school were drugged at some point." I confirm that the rape culture is definitely way more acceptable in close encounters like that than anything that I am doing. There are those extremely rare run-ins with crazy people, but that isn't standard life.

"See, Callie. In my opinion, even the creepiest guy that would easily slip a pill in a girl's drink would find some type of respect for me doing what I am doing. Even if he doesn't respect me, he respects what I am doing and a strong woman scares a drug dropper. I mean, I do keep my guard up

261

constantly, but this whole trip has been about maintaining a great state of mind to attract only positive outcomes. I don't have a problem doing that on my own, but when my mom would call and pour her angry fear into my ears, it would absolutely poison my day. I stopped being able to call them at all after some point because it became toxic to my experience. It made me need to distance myself even further from them to the point that I couldn't even bare to call them for weeks. I would see the phone ring in the morning and I would groan that I can't begin my day in the negative. I would see my phone ring at night and I would complain that I couldn't end my day in the negative." Callie stops walking for a second to really look at me. She really wanted to understand what I was saying and it made me wonder if she had some healing to do with her parents too.

"Anyhow, I couldn't allow her fear to leak into my experience. My mom had good intentions somewhere deep down, but I just couldn't handle it. I updated my Facebook daily so they would know I was alive and I would talk to them maybe in the middle of the day when I had enough time to allow their negative opinion of me to fade."

"That's a shame. They just couldn't understand that you were doing what you really wanted for the first time in your life." Callie kicks a rock off the path and puts her hands in her pockets.

"Well, it's funny because the whole time I was gone, they disapproved of everything I was doing. But then when I returned, our friends and family members were so excited to see me and hear about my stories. So many people had followed my online posts about my travels. Then after public acceptance, my parents were proud of me for what I had done. But the whole time I was doing it they did not really support me. In fact, they did the opposite. It's funny to say this now, because I didn't understand why I had so much resentment for them at the time. That resentment lasted years."

We walk by an artist painting on the street. Her work is very airy, fluffy brushstrokes with quotes stamped into it. I am drawn to one that resembles water and it's the same one that Callie is drawn to too. It was a quote from Mahatma Gandhi, 'Before the throne of the Almighty, man will be judged not by his acts, but by his intentions. For God alone reads our hearts.'

Callie reads it out loud twice and we look over to see the irate, fat mother feeding her scolded kid an ice cream cone in the distance. The daughter darts around chasing ducks while giggling, spilling her treat all over her face and increasingly growing belly. She feeds the child sugar, but doesn't want it to act like all it eats is sugar. She shares with her child the kind of love that she was raised to know. Her intention is truly to make her kid happy in the best way she knows how, by satisfying the palate. Callie and I look at each other with deep understanding and compassion for parental intention based upon learned nature.

"Do you want to go to local market and buy an apple?"

I shake my head yes.

....

I wake up on a sofa in a very modern room. *Morning? Where?* I sprung awake with a flicker in my eye as my surroundings separated me from my dream state. I have been waking up in my car the last few nights and am very surprised to see where I am now. *A finely furnished room with an incredibly comfy atmosphere.* I stretch large and look over. Alice is on the other half of the reclining sofa.

Ok. Check one is good. We are both here and we are both ok. I get up and stretch again to look out the window. I see a fresh, early morning view into downtown Fort Myers. *Second floor. Hmm...* Suddenly the previous day's events flow back into my consciousness. *Rasta fishermen, dock, beer, puppies, Ryan and his... his...*

Boat! Yes! His boat! I have acquired a boat into my life! I cannot believe it! I stretch high and smile wide as I once again am floored at the amazing opportunity I have been granted. On the coffee maker, Ryan had a note that stated, 'Please help yourself.' It also included a little smiley face.

The day looked beautiful outside and I could hardly believe that in a few short hours I would be on a boat floating over the salty seas. My notebook seemed to sing me awake as I wrote all my thoughts and experiences from the day prior. Eventually Alice woke up and drank a coffee, appearing very hungover. She said she felt fine although she really did drink a lot last night... Ryan woke up and had some business to tend to calling customers before we embarked on our ocean expedition.

We loaded up the truck with coolers and puppies, swimsuits, towels and whatever else we wanted. We bought beer and snacks at a gas station. I acquired the cheapest stuff I could find on the slightly healthy side including sunflower seeds and protein bars. Alice bought seeds and nuts and Ryan bought a case of beer.

"A case? You think we need a case?" I was unsure why we needed a case of beer for a day trip on a boat with three people and three dogs, but he insisted that we get it. Then Alice bought a six pack of something else. I bought a gallon of water. Ryan was certain that a case would be just the right amount, but insisted also that Alice's 6-pack would definitely be put to a good home too. We loaded the cooler with ice and liquid goodies and loaded the dry cooler with our snacks and bags. The thrill sprinkling through my body was almost too much to bear. It was an emotion of stimulated fear, almost a terror mixed with the most brilliant delight I have ever felt! *I think of the airplane manifestation and remember the emotional rewards.* I realized as that boat was lowered into the water at the dock that I really do not know anything about water life. Water was as foreign to me as the sky! I don't even know the realness of a boat, a craft floating over water with miles of nothing around! The only other boat I had ever actually been on was my uncle's at Raystown Lake in central Pennsylvania. But this was serious water. This was endless ocean water.

Ryan told us stories of his ex-wife and his friends. Alice and I asked how long they were together. He responded, "Fourteen years."

I do the math. "Wait, fourteen years? How old are you?" He replied with the standard question of how old do you think I am? "I thought you were a little older than us like…" *Salt water must be the elixir of youth.* He tells us he is 37. Alice and I can't believe it. *He doesn't look older than 28!* The pelicans watch us at the dock as we take off and the boat roars like a beast. I feel its power pick up strength past the no wake zone buoy and I laugh at the fact that I am here now on a boat! The water is dark, but it eventually looks blue as we keep going out.

The boat roars at full speed, shifting our weight and bouncing us around. Gear keeps flying loose and we catch things before the air takes them into the circulating, churning white water behind us, vibrating to the rhythm below our toes. Our hair is bursting and whipping us in our faces, reminding us to wake up and that, yes, this is real life! The feeling of the warm, yet, chilly wind against my skin, the motor running, our skiing over the water is nothing short of astonishing.

We accelerate, laughing madly across the shimmering surface, flashing the sunlight across my body like a spotlight upon the ultimate point of my life thus far. I can't stop smiling for even a second and my face begins to hurt. Alice grabs my hand and assembles next to me, chuckling as we soar and I wonder if she loves me or just loves this experience. *I hope both.* She said she is straight, but some of her actions don't speak that way. I really began to suspect that she actually did like me. *Well, at least a little bit.*

But I had to keep my head on straight (*or gay*); no way could I possibly get involved with another girl this quick. *I don't even know how she feels, but I do know that her hand feels pretty nice in mine.* Ryan rides us out near a light house and explains that it is Sanibel Island, a very high-class place to live and that the only bridge there has a toll either way. We cruise up the island's coast, checking out all of the waterfront mansions, such ridiculously expensive properties. He points out everything he knows as our personal tour guide, slowing the boat as he speaks, but all of it is so miraculous that it just blends into a collection of awakening experience, the birth of my inner understanding of value and worthiness. *Over my time with Ryan, I would learn more about my limiting beliefs of my monetary worth than ever before. This man was a true mentor for expanding my mind's concept of potential abundance.* We swim when we get hot and we dance on the boat with our drinks, blasting every type of music possible and the puppies are adorable, ears flapping in the wind. The shared experience of my first real ocean boat ride with such incredible people and their puppies is the most amazing feeling I have ever felt in my life. I have never seen a dog so happy; I have never felt myself so happy either. This is what I have been searching for, this emotion of absolute ecstasy, this pure delight in the existence of my being exactly where I feel I need to be. *Yes, this is everything I have been searching for my whole life!* I felt as if my entire focus has been leading me up to be able to appreciate this moment in its finest flavor.

As we pulled up to the dock, Ryan mentioned taking the boat out again in two days to go down the opposite coast. All of us had such an astounding time together that we couldn't help but to accept his offer. He had to do a paver job the next day, but could take the boat out the day after. He lets us hang at the house while he goes to work so he doesn't have to worry about the puppies needing care. This gives me a good time to catch up on my writing. *Good exchange.* Ryan takes us out on the boat again and we stop at Ft. Myers beach. He parks the boat in the choppy, dark water. My legs feel silly as the weight of the boat, non-propelled, shifts against the gentle waves. He shows us the proper way to throw the anchor so that the boat drifts appropriately relative to other boats. Everyone around is giggling and dancing on their luxurious floating crafts. From here, the whole world appears to be cheerful and stress free, such a contrasting universe from that which I escaped. So many people are so happy! I have never been exposed to this amount of pleasure before! We toss the pups into the water and we all hop in after them, helping them to swim to shore. Ft. Myers beach isn't a dog beach, but when you pull up on a boat, you do what you want. All 6 of us run down the beach laughing as the multi-sized pups tackle each other and trip us into the waves. They bounce eagerly as they hop around, saying hi to smiling people sitting in chairs at our prancing puppy surprise. Nearly everyone waves at our size-six paradise parade. I laughed more in this moment out of absolute pure enjoyment, than ever before in my life. Merriment trickled from my spirit so much that I collapsed into the mushy sand by the water's edge as a small wave rolled in. Instantly I was pummeled by puppies vigorously vaulting all over me, continuously kissing and causing even more laugher to erupt. My stomach and face ached again from so much consistent chuckling. My skin baked charmingly in the sun and my heart felt more open as I looked around at this brilliant world I was in.

Oh, how quickly things can change… This was followed up by us returning to the boat, which now had waves beginning to surge. Between all three of us trying to get there and having to keep from allowing the dogs to drown us, we barely made it. I honestly thought one of us was going to die. Reno was panicking and rightfully so. But he was such a big golden retriever and trying to climb on us and we couldn't stand. I was supposed to hold the Chihuahua as I swam, but Diesel wanted to be with Ryan and that little puppy was kicking me, trying to reach Ryan until he unintentionally undid my top. I was holding my waterproof camera and was holding him so I couldn't get my top tied. As the waves splashed up and down, I had to retreat back. I was choking. When I could stand, I called over to a random man and asked him for help as I held the panicked Chihuahua over my exposed boobs. The guy turned red as he tied my suit up the best he could, trying not to look, but laughing at how funny this was. I was worried about Alice and Ryan because from here I could see they were struggling and they had the bigger dogs. I had the smallest. When we got further out, Diesel jumped out of my grip as I was nearly taken under a wave. At this point, I was just struggling to keep myself alive and gulped some water down. I could barely contain myself and just couldn't catch that puppy. Ryan was trying to support Bella back onto the rocking boat, shifting heavily with the increasing waves. He turned around to see Diesel coming toward him and I saw horror in his eyes. He panicked and sank down as he grabbed Diesel and threw him away. He kept having to push him away to ensure that he could stabilize himself as both dogs tried desperately to scramble on him. Alice tried to stay afloat as Reno panicked and tried to climb on her. As I got closer he tried to get on me as well. It was all in all, a horrible scene of near annihilation. Finally, Ryan was able to get up and pull Bella up with him. From there we could get all of us on the saving grace that was our boat. For a moment, we all lay out and snorted nervously. We each admitted that out of the three of us, we all thought at least one of us or the dogs was going to die right then. *Geez, water life... Who knew?*

After we all catch our breath after a day or two, Ryan suggests that we take the boat out and stop at a dog beach called Lover's Key to watch the sunset and let the dogs play at a safe place. *Safe, that sounds great.* We pull up and hop off at this majestic area. It certainly wasn't as clean looking, but it was remote and away from the mass public. There were just a few other people and their dogs strewn here and there. It was located at an inlet surrounded by other island type land masses and sandy shores so the waters were very calm. *Whew. Excellent. Nothing to worry about here.* All the dogs hop around and instantly run over to play with other dogs down the beach. Alice and I observe a gentle water channel and agree to race to the island across from it. It was only about 40 ft. of gentle swimming so it seemed pretty safe.

Ready. Set. Go! We promptly run, giggling as we enter the water, our feet gripping the sand firmly as the water splashes up and across our bodies. We charge through the increasingly high waves until I trip into them, sort of like a dive, and begin swimming as hard as I can. Unfortunately, right as I tripped, I heard her yell, "Oh…" and her voice faded out. "I'm done…" And we were laughing competitively so I kept swimming until I looked back and saw her standing still, slightly hunched over. *What the…*

She was arched over and frozen. I turned back to her instantly because she wasn't responding to me. I put my shoulder under her arm and she couldn't step on her foot. I asked her what happened and she told me that she didn't know, but she stepped on something. Her eyes were closed tightly and she couldn't look at me. She said the pain in her foot was too bad to do anything so I told her to raise her foot above the water so I could inspect what was going on. As her heel rose up, red poured all over the water's surface, spilling all around us in a very disturbing quickness. I told her to not look behind her. I did not want her to see this.

"Use me to walk back to the shore and just look forward toward the beach." She didn't listen; she looked. Instantaneous eruption. She cried and screamed for help as if she was dying. I carried her, limping to the shore, where she collapsed at the water's edge and tried to look at it, but the circle of blood was growing a radius bigger than two ft. within seconds. Only a few people were on this beach at this time of the day and a man was promptly at our side pushing the dogs away. He told her to lie on her stomach and to put her foot into the air. Blood was pouring out of her foot, just streaming down her legs all over the edge of the water. It had begun its trickle into the surf about 4 ft. down where the tide was pulling it into the in swirling decorated patterns, blending her essence into the ocean. I grabbed her head and held it and spoke to her as people began wrapping towels and putting water on it to see what it was.

"Look at me. Don't think about this. Just look at me and think about our amazing boat day. Think about the water." A flashback from Alana's attack in the car when her body froze flashed in my mind as I looked down at the increasing amount of blood surrounding us. "Just look at me." I told her as she cried and held my hand so forcefully that I thought it might break. She screamed as they did anything to it and she grabbed my fist and head so tightly. I knew I had to keep her mind off it. She was losing so much blood and I didn't know how much was a dangerous amount, but I knew that I needed to keep her awake. At this point I didn't know if I was falling in love with her, this beautiful, mystical, traveling goddess, alone with her dog, our destined paths to paradise intertwined... or if this was just an absurdly powerful friendship comrade. But no matter what, this bloody, screaming woman nearly ripping the hair out of my head meant the world to me right now. I held her shrieking body in my arms only a few days after we first met while a bunch of random beach heroes tried to keep the dogs from stepping on her back or dropping tennis balls in our faces. The dogs tried to comfort in the best way they could. If it wasn't such a horrific scene, this part would have been hysterical.

They tell Ryan to take the dogs back, which he is scared to do. Three dogs are a lot of dogs on his own and Reno was already so upset. He didn't want to leave his mom, but Ryan bravely took them into the water and managed to get them into the boat alone as a group helped to carry Alice to the street where an ambulance was waiting. Alice screamed that she was ok and was not paying for their service because she didn't call them. She's traveling and doesn't have any money to pay for an ambulance trip, especially since it was already decided that this couple didn't mind driving us to the Naples hospital. They had two small cocker spaniels and put down the back seat of their car and we climbed inside. They drove us to the Naples emergency room and Ryan called me when he got back and dropped off the dogs and boat at his place. I didn't know what to do since Naples was 45 minutes south of Ryan's place in Ft. Myers, but we didn't have a choice. Alice needed the E.R. fast. And she needed me to help her now. The couple dropped us off and waited with us until we got her into a wheelchair and admitted in. We traded numbers and they asked me to promise that we would tell them how everything went when it was all ok. Alice was drunk this whole time and when the E.R. told her it would be a half hour till they saw her, she begged me to push her wheelchair across the street to this tiny bar so she could buy a beer and chug it quickly. This whole thing was absolutely hilarious at the time, but it was an indicator to what the next few weeks would be like for her.

They removed an inch chunk and several other shards of oyster reef from just under her big toe. There was blood all over the table when I went inside to see her after surgery. Ryan was sitting out in his truck in the parking lot waiting for us to be done. I couldn't believe how much this random man was doing for us. He not only took us out on the adventure of our lives, but he is waiting for us at night in a different city, tailgating in the hospital parking lot. He kept apologizing to me on the phone after I told him her status, saying how sorry he was that this all happened. We finally left the hospital around 10:30 and we were so exhausted. We just couldn't wait to get back to go to sleep. It was such a long day. Ryan helped her get into the truck and he climbed into the driver's side, but his truck wouldn't start. He explained that there is something wrong with the starter occasionally, but it happens so infrequently that he hasn't fixed it. It just needs to sit there for a little bit and then it will start. *Good timing…*

So he pulled out his tablet and started playing a movie for us to watch. We laughed as he hopped in the back of the pickup and opened the cooler that he took off the boat. He pulled out three beers. We sat there in the Naples, Florida hospital parking lot, tailgating and laughing in his massive pickup truck, reminiscing about the crazy day we all shared while watching a movie on Ryan's tablet. *What world am I in?* He told us he never had a day quite like that before. We told him the same thing as we all laughed outrageously. There was a hint of uncertainty as our laughs faded.

We eventually got back, showered and changed. We hung out and helped figure out ways to get Alice to feel comfortable. All comfort suggestions from her included an alcoholic beverage in her hand, which was recommended not to mix with her medicine. She didn't care. After many laughs and jokes, Ryan told us we could stay at his place for as long as it takes for her to heal or to figure out something else. I just couldn't believe this guy's generosity. He was all about sharing his home with us. I was so skeptical when I first met him, but over the course of the next week I would understand how much he really loved having us around. After his divorce, he returned to his friends to discover that they weren't the people he wanted to associate with anymore. He cut them all out of his life for the most part and bought a puppy, invested his time into his business, found another puppy and then spent most of his time alone enjoying his boat and his puppy family. A few weeks later, Alice and I showed up in his life. It was the perfect timing for our overbearing appearance to be appreciated by someone who needed a new kind of friendship and companionship. As we talked about this he laughed in agreement saying, "Ha, yeah. That's true. Wow, what are the chances? Right?"

I helped with the puppies constantly and Alice remained in a drunken stupor on that second story apartment for over a month. My appreciation for Ryan grew by the day and my infatuation with Alice decreased by the day. It's not that she became less beautiful, no. She was still one of the most beautiful women I had ever seen. But I began to see a difference in her mission of travel versus my goal of travel. I really wanted to live life genuinely alive and take on existence and change my core being. At this point in her life, she just wanted to glide by and experience some neat things,

269

mostly in alcoholic inertia. Ryan was patient and willing to share everything that he had during our time there.

We really were the perfect trio for about three weeks. Alice needed rest, Ryan needed companionship and to learn how to trust people again. I needed a rest from the road. I also was necessary at this time, playing the role of a kind of the dog attendant. The day after Alice's injury, the elevator to the apartment broke so she didn't leave the building once until she could walk alright on crutches, which was over two weeks. So during their drunken morning sleep, I took the dogs out on the most incredible walks of my life. During Ryan's work day, I took them out because Alice was stuck. The three of us really were a working unit for the first few weeks, but it is easy to overstay a welcome without ever seeing it transform.

And oh, did it quickly transform.

Chapter Forty-One

*"Begin each day with the enthusiasm that you have another chance
to change everything."*

It became an increasingly difficult task to live, document, share, prepare, and experience all at the same time and it was around this time that my constant documentation of everything began to fade a little more each day. *This could be my excuse for becoming lazy in my travel too*. I also could be giving into female companionship pressure. Whatever the reason, I began to see why it was so important to have a team in life, each with their specific jobs or tasks or titles. *It just is too much to do all by myself*. But I continued with a clear focus in mind of my goals.

Unfortunately, just over the progression of a week, my goals stopped being so clear. Around two weeks stationary, I began to internally slow down. My ambition ceased. My passion hesitated. The world around me began filling with limitations again as my goggles clouded over. The magic of divine opportunity just seemed to disappear from my life by week three.

I had started out so clear, but the constant funnel of alcoholic drinks into my body may have represented not only a momentary slip away from reality, but a monumental slip away from who I essentially am. Yes, the slippery slope from my powerful path had begun and I got caught up in the love of the ocean, but forgot to keep on moving with the flow of the waves. Instead, I dug myself an amusing little hole full of enchantment and good times, but the spirit of my internal self was drowning. And even though I didn't realize it at the time, I actually deep down did become aware of my own disintegration. I just didn't actually know what was wrong, how to stop it or how to fix it.

The absolute hardest thing about traveling is the exact same thing that applies to everything else in life. It is not the circumstances or the reason. It is not the stormy weather or the lack of supplies. It is not the lack of support of family behind you or any reasonable plan of forward action. The hardest thing is challenging the comfort of your own mind, your own general life beliefs and limiting factors. The hardest thing is absolutely mastering your own mind, releasing emotional holds and learning to control your thoughts. Fear stunts the growth of opportunity and it can come in many types of masks.

In the mornings I wrote in my notebooks, drinking coffee until the other two woke up. The pen introduced me to the thoughts that I really am becoming very mentally powerful, while at the same time becoming weak in the category of will power. Almost all of my limiting beliefs are evaporating and being replaced with positive reinforcing thoughts on things that I would like to see in my life currently. The only real problem at this moment in time was that I still had a hold on my heart. I haven't even been able to look at another girl *(besides Alice, kind of)* and I still held a side of sadness with every entrée of amazing life experience. In the back of my mind I knew that no matter what direction things went, no matter where I ended up or what I ended up doing, I still had to return up there to my not real life- to my never was home and attempt to rekindle a love that kicked me out. She tried to call me, many times actually. And I just couldn't muster the strength to talk to her. I wanted to live the world, breathe the universe as fresh and she just represented this misplaced world that I once sought, but was betrayed by. The problem was that no matter where I went, it was still back there waiting for me to clean up those loose ends. I pretended this was the experience of a lifetime and yes, this really was. But the mental anguish and hours spent trying to orchestrate meaning certainly couldn't go to waste. This being lost feeling of living unknown became an escape.

And eventually it became an excuse, even if I didn't realize it at the time.

I graduated from inspirational spiritual living to lost and cowardly drifter during my time in Ft. Myers. I allowed my loyalty to disrupt my goals. I allowed a good situation to devour my ambition. *I did have a really good time doing it.* But my soul yearned for more and even in my moments alone, I felt some type of inner discontentment. I realized quickly that because of this inner dissatisfaction, I became addicted to the concept of bettering my life. *That is why when I first discovered the law of attraction I couldn't get it out of my mind. I craved the change in my life.* I needed it because of the way I was living, the way I was taught to live, was killing me. I needed to learn to think differently so I could learn to live differently. If I failed to learn to see through new eyes, then I was bound for an early grave.

Don't get me wrong. There was good reason to lose myself in Ft. Myers. There were so many amazing moments of absolute bliss with my Ft. Myers family. The constant dog walks resulted in so many joyful memories, one being of little children break dancing while rapping and chanting, "Go Big Dog! Go Big Dog! Go Reno! Go Reno!", while their babysitter allowed them to dance around the fountain that Reno was prancing in after he was finished assaulting a crocodile statue that he thought was real. Often I would grab a husk of a palm branch and run with it, all three pups tripping over each other to catch me. Whenever Reno got a good bite on it, he would run around with it in his mouth and the dogs would chase him, nipping at the leaves. Every single person walking by would stop and laugh because it was an absolutely adorable thing to see. Golden moments sparked from everyday living here and that is how my ambition got stuck.

Everywhere I went people were pleased to introduce me to their type of Florida. The first time I saw a real coconut I thought it was a bomb. This was the day before Alice's accident. A large white van and ethnic men were in a yard walking around with long sticks and I didn't know what they were doing. A foreign, football shaped ball with a string was left by the area that their van was sitting. We stared at it curiously wondering if the brown chunk would blow up so we walked back to the apartment. I then went for a long walk alone where I again encountered the same men. This time I watched them. One held a long pole with a saw on the end. One held a couch cushion and the other stood by the van. Pole Saw would cut coconuts from the 2-3 story trees and as they would drop, Cushion would toss the landing gear below the place the coconut would land. It would bounce and he'd catch it. Then he would toss it to the third man who put it into the van. I asked them what they were doing, but they didn't speak much English. He opened the van to show hundreds of fresh coconuts piled up. *I couldn't believe it!* He pointed at me and said some broken English words indicating if I wanted to try some. Without an answer, he pulled out a foot-long machete. *Ah!* He began hacking off the thick, outer layer of the coconut husk. He sliced it into a makeshift spoon and then bashed a hole in the top after three swift hits. He points and motions for me to drink. *I had no idea that coconuts actually all looked like this. I* am hesitant, being that tiny chunks of husk lined the triangle shaped hole that was just slashed by a tropical sword, but I do it anyhow. It is the sweetest, most delightful thing I have ever tried. When I tilt it back, signifying that I finished the liquid, he asks me to hand it over again. With one swift motion he jams the machete into the hole and it wedges onto the end of the coconut. With a big smile, he looks at me and slams it down and the coconut split in two. He hands the whole thing to me and also places the husk spoon into my hand after demonstrating how to get the sweet meat from the coconut. He hands me his business card, another coconut and smiles huge while simply saying, "Waylcome du Fa-Lar-Ee-Dah." This was the beautiful start of my intense coconut obsession. I don't think this obsession will ever end.

Delicious experiences like that dotted the spell of disintegration, making it very easy to get stuck in Ft. Myers in a drunken vacancy and not even realize it until I'd been there nearly four weeks. I needed to get up north to meet my family to fly out to Los Angeles for our yearly family business/vacation. *Geez, I needed to drive back to Erie first before any of that!* Alana has been threatening that she was going to carry all of my stuff outside with a 'For Free' sign. She was so sick of waiting for my broken promises of another two weeks or another two weeks or another two weeks... I finally told her I'd be back by May first. She told me that I better be back or else. Ryan suggests going to Key West soon and Alice and I look at each other with excited eyes! They tell me that I should fly back down to Florida and go to Key West with them after this is all done. Alice's foot should be entirely better by then. I agree and promise to return after I take care of my PA business. *Ah, Key West opportunity manifested! Yes!* Also, this was something for my dwindling spirit to look forward to after my imminent emotional devastation.

So, I do what I must. I work my way up to Pennsylvania. The first day's drive I decide to take my sister out to Cocoa Beach because she had been in Florida at that 'Disney Insta-life fortress' and hadn't even been able to go to the beach once the whole time she was down there. I couldn't believe it! She hadn't even seen real Florida and all I had been doing was experiencing real Florida! She was just in the tourist frenzy, this 'just add water' concept of life. It was soulfully wrong for me to go about these adventures, having such life altering experiences just two hours from my blood relative's corporate confinement. I had to take her out to the real ocean to touch the real sand and see the real sky. She had to see the actual water, genuine un-chlorinated waves, at least for a day. So we went to Cocoa beach (hardly a purist's location, but definitely the closest fun beach for what she wanted) and we talked and did handstands into the sunset. Even if it was just a few hours that she was able to get away, it was at least enough to allow me to feel justified in my continuation to grow. She had an extra ticket and took me into Epcot for a few hours to check out the diversity of Disney's representation of different cultures from around the world. It really was an enjoyable experience and we were fortunate enough to be there during their annual flower festival. Living statues were constructed two stories high out of flowers, just an unbelievably vibrant portrayal of so many familiar characters from my childhood. We shared, with each other, the entire opposite type of beauty we had been living in for months and something about that bonded us deeper than we had ever connected in our whole lives. Miles apart created thicker glue in our family. Or maybe it was the fact that I had finally begun really living the life I always longed for. Maybe the difference was that this was the first time my sister ever actually saw me. We said goodbye, since corporate wouldn't allow any visitors to stay over behind the gated citadel known as her apartment.

I stop at my friend Krispop's grandparent's house near Leesburg, Florida where I stay the night. The next day we cruise around on a golf cart in the giant retirement home and drink at the country club. We load up the golf cart with a pile of drunken lesbians and drive down to the salt water pool. When we return, her grandma is sitting in the living room watching television with her sunglasses on. We can't stop laughing. We realize that there is a vivid beam of sunlight reflecting off the building across the street straight into her living room. Her grandma mentions that is shines like this every day at this time and it is easier to just put on glasses than to get up and block out all the sunlight from the big window and open it up again in a half hour. That night Krispop drunkenly grabs her grandma's scissors from the kitchen and trims off the inch-long hair side burns I had for some reason allowed myself to grow. I woke up that next morning and looked in the mirror, shocked to see my cheeks! I was so mad, but she told me that she's wanted to hack them off a long time. Haircuts are physical poetry representing deep internal change. I was eventually thankful to see my full face for the first time in my life.

We head into downtown Leesburg, where the 'world's largest' bike fest was happening. It was incredible! There are giant stages and endless vendors selling anything you could imagine! We wandered the streets of this enormous bike show which has all the streets closed down with thousands of motorcycles lining everything as far as I could see. It really is rather absurd and I wanted to stay another day, but I promised Alana I would be back. I leave that day and drive north without a destination. After a few hours, I look at my map to determine possible routes. The name Athens jumps out at me, almost like a flashing light. I decide to go there for some reason. I really don't know why, but my intuition escorts me that way. I hop on the back country highway that direction. It'll be about an hour until arrival. I flicker through the Georgia radio until I hear something funky. After it's over, the radio announcer starts talking about a bike fest. *A bike fest? There's no way they are referencing Leesburg. That's like 5 hours behind me…*they then begin saying that the women's national bike race begins in 20 minutes in downtown Athens.

My ears perk up. *Women's bike race… Hmm…* 15 minutes later I was pulling into downtown Athens, people everywhere and detours all around. After asking someone where the race was, they pointed a few blocks up and told me to park because it's about to start. I hear screams from crowds and a faint announcer when I walk to where many were converged. Bikes race by swiftly in front of the crowds lined up on the sidewalks by giant barriers. After I ask a few questions to people who look like they know what is going on, I find that it is a huge pro-cycling event, an entire city festival called Terrapin Twilight, arguably one of the best bicycle events in the whole country. I had arrived just at the start of the women's pro-am criterion which was a 40k circuit through the downtown. I have never seen bikes compete like this, inches from each other flying around turns in city streets. What an incredible experience to stumble upon! The men's pro am was next and that was an 80k circuit with awards up to $200,000. What are the chances that I would go from one major bike event wandering up the country and be drawn to another major bike event?

I try to make friends my age, but they all seem to be college students that already know each other and aren't really looking to meet new people tonight. I was hoping to find a sofa, but I felt like I was wasting my time not being present in the magic of the moment. I just started to enjoy the scenery without a mission blocking my vision. I met a guitarist and we rapped and played music and were joined by dancing people. It was just what my spirit needed. Then I saw people climbing up a three story balcony and I said why not! I went up and was able to have such a great view of the race, overlooking all the thousands that were watching. I could see down the street quite a distance. I stood there alone and smiled at the greatness that life can be. I noticed some young college kids looking at me, since I didn't really belong there and made direct eye contact with them saying, "Isn't life beautiful?" One of those college kids is a girl named Paris on that balcony. She invites me to stay the night at her apartment after I explained what I was doing. She tells me to meet her there later and gives me her number and address. *So awesome! I knew what I wanted and rather than focusing on it, I put it into my subconscious and simply enjoyed being here and it happened anyhow! Yes!* I considered stopping somewhere for a dessert. I wanted chocolate, but by this time everything in the city was getting wild and everyone was increasingly plastered. I walked into a bar to use the restroom, but could barely squeeze through the crowds. *I was feeling like some joke- A lesbian walks into a bar...* Then I checked out another bar, but I was pretty tired and didn't feel like battling a horde of drunks to make approachable conversation. I gave up on my chocolate dream and went back to the area with the guitarist on the way to get my car. Here, I joined a hacky sack circle and giggled with strangers as we sang and smiled good ambiances in every direction. As the night wore on, people started to filter away; the race was over. The clean-up crews were removing the barriers and opening up the roads again. I said goodbye to my hacky sack alliance, but waited to be the last one to leave for some reason. I felt like I had to wait until the time was right to leave, which didn't actually make sense because as I stood there alone, looking around me at the realm I was in, I just laughed. I laughed a proud laugh with a cheerful smile, so huge that the moon was probably able to see me shimmer back at it. *This world is miraculous and all I had to do was listen to the universe when it called!*

I took a few steps up the street and heard a very strange noise. It was quickness, a metal whip, an air fragmentation and a crunching trombone meets annihilation sound. It was sort of that sound of destruction in movies when things are about to go really bad. There weren't many people in this area, but the few that remained ducked, covering their heads as an enormous adorned metal lamp post came collapsing down, having been caught by a thick steel line that had been holding up a sign hanging in the same place that a delivery truck accidentally caught on the top as it drove through the now open street, pulling the metal rope tight as it drove, therefore ripping the light post nearly in half right in front of me. The metal collapsing sound was horrifying in itself, but was further enhanced by the three ft. glass globe designed to hold the light, shattering on the street. I was the closest person to this being just a few steps away. Crews began yelling, screaming and scrambling around to make sure everyone was ok. Nothing is ever totally secured in this life and had I left a few moments earlier, had I been just a few feet closer, I could have been in the direct path. That was where I was about to cross the street in about 5 steps. Wide eyed, I looked around at the metal and glass chunks before me. Chills spread through me instantly as I waved that I was totally fine. The souvenir of life and death is always present. I clasp my hands to my heart and give a silent thank you to whatever intuition or God or energetic force that was telling me to wait just a few moments longer. Thankfully that ol' joke didn't ring true- *A lesbian walks into a bar...*

I get to Paris's house safely and she has a bed made in the living room and her roommates were in the kitchen having just pulled brownies out of the oven. She already had a plate of them next to my bed expecting me to want some. I smile, "You have no idea how much I wanted these. I just walked around the city looking for chocolate, but gave up!"

She smiles bright and says, "What are the chances?"

The next day I stop in a coffee shop after Paris tours me through her rainy campus. After sipping this steamy, warm coffee, (much appreciated on this Oregon-esque day) I am writing, trying to record the previous day's events. A man asks me what I am doing, then tells me to contact a local writers project because they could possibly help with my book. I thank him, intending to contact them, but felt too overwhelmed with everything I was about to encounter once I got to Pennsylvania. I drive as far as I can until sleep beckons me. I nap in a store's parking lot and woke up the sun shining in front of me. But when I sat up to stretch, I looked to the other side of me to spy a cloud blacker than any sky I have ever seen. My tablet displayed a fat stretch of thunderstorms stretching the entire length of the country and I was sitting directly on the edge of it. The car became dark and I watched the line of sun fade across the parking lot. Time to go.

I made a few miles before the storm caught up to me, but the driving after that point was horrendous. Lightning strikes and high winds made me fear a tornado, especially after the skies grew harsh and deep. I hunched over my steering wheel, a promise to Alana to return invading my desire to just pull over. Eventually, mentally and visually exhausted, I pull over north of Charlotte, NC in a Wal-Mart parking lot. I go inside and buy a 24 oz. beer, a snack, use the bathroom, buy a gallon of water and return to the car where I prop my feet up and watch the rain drizzle down the windows. I think of everything I have gone through and I sip my beer smiling. This is the life I have always wanted. I have never been able to reflect on times with such profound certainty that I have really lived, but now I feel it. *I have really lived my own idea of my current dreams.* I brush my teeth, spit out of the car and fall asleep to the sound of rain.

I wake up to the sun shining and a full bladder. I waddle to the bathroom in the Walmart, barely able to make it. Phone is dead and all I long for is a coffee, but when I return, I notice the car has an almost flat tire. Anger fills me as I wonder what to do. Something tells me to hop in it and start driving, which is strange. I would never do this as a first instinct, had I thought about it, but I felt I needed to and having just woken up, my brain was on slow fire. As I pull out of the parking lot to go right, it finally clicks, *"What the hell am I doing?"*

The very next building was a tire repair center, completely out of view by the hill next to the exit. My jaw drops and I pull in feeling deliriously victorious. They have free coffee. The guy explains that it's a nail in the side and shows me it entirely needs replaced. He tells me they don't have a good used one that same size and that I need to replace both front tires which would cost about $175 for the Volkswagen model recommended. I kind of flip out inside of myself and a surge of pathetic sentences about how "I just slept in the parking lot on my way to maybe lose my home" flutters out and the guy tells me to hold on for like 15 minutes. As I figure out what on Earth I am going to do, he comes back and tells me that my car is ready. I look in disbelief. He hands me a bill for $50 flat and tells me not to worry about the extra. He explains that I only have to pay the price of the employee discounted new tire. The other is a decent used matching tire and is free for me. He wasn't charging me for time either. I ask him why. He explains that he was in a place once where he needed help too. He now has a family and is manager of this service center and is more than happy to help me saying that he believes in me. "Be well. Here is my card if you ever need anything when you are in the area. Take care and always believe in yourself."

I decided I wanted to see some new Appalachian Trail mountains and try to get on the Blue Ridge Parkway at some area. I also still dislike the taste of highways in my eyes. I stopped in small towns everywhere I could. I wandered around Boone, NC after stopping at Blowing Rock, a beautiful tourist attraction called, "The Crown of the Blue Ridge". I stop in Bluefield for the night and unsuccessfully attempted to find some night life. It's located half in Virginia and half in West Virginia. I am not sure which state I slept in my car, but I was chilly until the sun came up. I woke up to one of the most incredible sunrises I have ever seen. I glowed red as stood by Felix, jaw dropped at how I somehow parked at the perfect place to watch the sunrise through these valleys.

Around one mountain curve, I spotted something fluffy along the road and I realized it was a bird, not dead, but just sitting there on the white line like a fuzzy, little muffin. *Ah! It's still alive and so close to danger!* Immediately I hop into the left lane to make a U-turn where the median breaks. Another U-turn puts me in the right lane, flashers on, pulling up a few feet behind the bird. I put on gloves and approach slowly, trying not to scare it. I at least want to scare it off of the road, but it allows me to place my hands around its body so that its petite stick legs step up onto my fingers, gripping them as its small brown feathers semi-flap, a stability action that shows off its fluffy white under arm feathers. Its watchful eyes perceive me curiously as I smile, holding this adorable creature in my palms for many powerful moments, observing everything about this funny situation. I walk gently toward the side of meadow by the highway's edge, but something startles the tiny bird. Its eyes widen as it starts to move quickly, wings flapping frantically and I close my hands around it. *I don't want it to jump the wrong direction into the road!* But I angle my slightly opening hands toward the meadow as it springs from my outreached arms, extended up over my head, my entire body lunging toward the field. It gracefully flies into the air, a weightless elegance flowing between us. *Wow! It's ok*! That bird flew up into the sky and across the field without any hesitation. It must have been in shock and just needed help to awaken. Instantly I hear a strange sound, "WOOOOOOO!" I turn around quickly to see a man cheering, waving his arms as he drives by in his purple, glistening convertible. "YEAHHH!" He yells as he throws me a thumbs up, followed by a powerful upward motion indicating his support. I think about his perspective as he drove by, me standing on the side of the road releasing a bird into a sunny field on the base of a mountain and I burst out laughing, tears forming at how majestic that moment actually was. *Wow. Life is so beautiful.* And to think, all I had to do was to live mindfully and be brave enough to stop and try something different. That whole situation would have never happened if I just kept driving mindlessly or ignored it and never turned around. Who knows how many people he told that story to? Who knows how many individuals can be affected by that simple few minutes, that simple, self-less act? *Maybe no one but you never know how far the life's ripples can go…*

I contact a SofaCruiser named Erin in Charleston, West Virginia. She tells me that if I make it into town by five, I can join her and a group for a Dash Run. I agree, not knowing what it is, but learning that generally saying yes to new experiences works wonders in life. I stop momentarily in Fayetteville and my senses are flooded with acquainted scenes this whole route. What a feeling of familiarity from just one day spent here! I stop at the only place I can remember how to get to, Mike's apartment. I knock hesitantly. Surprisingly, he is home and offers to take me out to the little local vegan restaurant. We catch up and he is so happy to hear about the success of my journey. He again reminds me that whenever I come through, don't be afraid to contact him. I say farewell and tell him to tell all the guys I am sort of on a time crunch, but that I say hi! It's such a fulfilling emotion of meeting up with someone I met from the initial Lost-Katie travel again. I can really see how far my perspective has changed in these miles.

I arrive at Erin's door at 4:58 and she tells me I need sneakers and running clothes now. I quickly change and by 5 we are driving across town to meet a group at a pub. They order beers and chug them and laugh when they realize I don't know what's going on. I just kind of agreed to a fun thing. They explain the rules of the Dash Run- that one person is 'Rabbit' and is out right now creating chalk trails for us to follow. They can go wherever they want to- streets, parking lots, yards, parks, sidewalks- and there are symbols they write on the ground indicating different things for the runners to do or try. The trail can split into two or three trails. This means that someone has to run down each trail until they encounter a chalk mark indicating a false trail or the true trail. Our instant arena circles all over the neighborhoods of the chosen area and participants run and laugh the whole time. We chant and cheer and I feel the intense emotion of 'bro-hood' as we circle around and put our hands in the center while saying a cheer to the day's run. At 5:30 we all yelled, chugged the rest of our drinks and started running like a pack of crazed, colorful animals.

Halfway through the course, we found a symbol indicating beer stop! A guy digs in the bushes and finds a cooler. We all go inside and they have beers lined up in the kitchen. We laugh and they put me in the center of the group and initiate me into their tribe. They sing a drunken Irish style chant and all cheers me as I am told to chug a beer symbolically sealing this initiation. I hold it over the sink as I try my hardest, but the sweat and panting from the running has my stomach constricted and I laugh as it sputters and they all cheer and hug me as they all chug too, putting me up on their shoulders having officially been initiated in the beer run. We finish the race (which someone had clocked at just short of four miles in total) which ended at the bar with the Rabbit sitting there drinking with a huge smile on his face, waiting for us to come back. He said we made it back much faster than he expected. This day was just a perfect conclusion before returning home. *Or before going back to not my home…* I really have no clue what to expect upon return, but I am so scared. I look around me at the positive vibes in the place that I am currently in and consider how I get so lost in the thoughts of the future sometimes that I miss out on the present. It's a big deal, yes; once I get back my whole life will be flipped. But wasting my energy thinking about it now will give me no positive result at all. A guy hands me another beer and we clink bottles as I return my full awareness to this beautiful group.

I realize then that this is the same type of event that the girls in Jacksonville, Florida had invited me to. No wonder they couldn't stop talking about how much fun this was! When they told me about it, I knew I was going to have the opportunity to be part of this again! I just knew that I wanted this experience! What are the chances that it would happen the last day?

Except that it wasn't actually the last day.

Chapter Forty-Two

Pittsburgh, PA- The path back 'home'

"One time I held onto anger, but I quickly realized that all it did was imprison me within my own chamber of non-forgiveness."

I get stuck in traffic the next day on the way to Madison's in Pittsburgh. She was having a small gathering there and invited me to stop for dinner with everyone as I drove through since Erie was still a 2 ½ hour drive from there. I accepted her invite, but was expecting to arrive there about 6 so then I could leave by 7 and be back in Erie that night by 10. But the traffic held me up so that I only arrived in Pittsburgh around 7:45. I needed to eat so I called Alana and asked if it would be ok to stop.

She responded saying, "What does it matter if I get back at midnight or tomorrow." She sounded furious. *But so awesome! An extra night! Reality procrastination initiation!* Madison's house was such a great feeling of familiarity. Her hair had grown slightly. Mine had become slightly shorter. Everything began looking more and more familiar the further north I went. I met everyone on that incredible back porch that overlooked the city. They had the grill on and it smelled divine. It is much more enjoyable here now that it's warmer. Just about everyone was late getting there too and they just finished cooking right as I arrived, which was perfect unplanned timing. We drank so much wine *(which went well with my taste for procrastination)* and laughed as we shared travel stories. I was tired and mostly listened. I had met so many people who just wanted to hear me talk about my solo travels so it was very nice to just sit back and listen to something other than myself speak. I had a big day tomorrow and I had been dreading it since I left. No matter what I experienced, I had the fear that this day was going to come. I tried not to think about it right now and sipped more wine. *Come on, Katie. Control your emotions and stay present. Deal with all of this tomorrow, not now. Be here now.* This night ended with a few bottles of wine and incredible friendship that astonishingly ended in a few healing kisses again. It was the perfect elixir for procrastination of my tomorrow's reality.

The next day I woke up absolutely dreading life, the drive north. *Anxiety. Panic.* This was the day I had avoided for an extensive time. Over and over, I denied my ability to go back. I even squeezed out an extra night last night, but this really was the day of confrontation. I showered away the dirty road and the drunken feels; I loaded up the car and I boldly drove north. I was very excited to see Alana, but I was so petrified. *We hadn't talked for weeks and I have been avoiding all contact with her because… because… well, because I was afraid.* Today was the day of confronting that fear, a fear I didn't even know I had lingering underneath every smile this whole time I had been traveling. It was a fear of confronting broken love and of accepting romantic failure. I really did love Alana this whole time. She was in every sunset and every raindrop, every sunrise and every smile from a stranger. I pulled off the exit for Erie and drove the familiar street that took me past the co-op to Plum Street, the first place I learned of the thing that began this whole journey. The weight of that book, *Contemplate and Welcome Prosperity*, felt exceptionally heavy in my passenger seat as I drove by the parking lot. This is where it all began, 70+ days of changing life. Everything looked so different, so alive compared to the frigid white out world I left here. Erie was blossoming into a beautiful city and I was returning with my wagon full of fear. I didn't know how Alana would greet me. Panic soared through my body as I parked and looked up at our green and white house that once held so much promise.

This is it. This is the moment I have been repeatedly escaping. Fight or flight response shifted from months of flight to fight. I am back to confront that which I had been running from for so long. I ring the doorbell and hold my breath as the door opens. She greets me just as I expect, with an awkward hello and her eyes look at me for a moment before looking at the ground and sliding out of the way for me to enter up the stairs. *It smells just as I remember.* I open the door to 'our' apartment and see our three babies. I greet them and cry; they meow and are afraid of me for a moment. Alana watches as I hug them and say hello to my turtle, Ethel, excitedly kicking against the glass. I put my bag down and I catch Alana looking at me, observing the toned, tan body I have acquired. She looks beautiful, just as beautiful as I remember. She asks me how I am and makes direct eye contact with me, her vibrant blue eyes softening as we hold a moment's gaze. We make lunch and talk about what's been happening in our lives lately. She is very distant to me, almost afraid to talk.

I ask if she wants to join me at the beach for the sunset and she agrees to. We go out to Presque Island and I make a few rock stacks, harnessing the balance of nature and we walk closely, yet distantly down the beach. Up ahead, as the sunset is reaching its max, I see something incredible, like enormous blossoming bubbles. We run up to it and it's a couple that has created these giant bubble makers out of fishing rods and string. They dip the strings into the buckets and hold them out with both hands as the strings create these 20 ft. long caterpillar-shaped bubbles. They float out over the water and dance until they burst into the sunset. I consider how incredible the timing is that we arrived on the day they decided to do this. I smile into that northern sky at the fact that I brought the magic of the synchronicity of divine timing back with me. We return 'home' and I hope for an offer to sleep in the bed, but she is firm in preparing the sofa for me. After she closes the door, I cry myself to sleep under two of our cats.

The next day I cleaned out the car and carried in my things. Feeling defeated, I walk into the bedroom and separate my dirty clothes to do a load of laundry in the basement. She looks at me and I mention about how everything I have needs washed except me and she laughs. She tells me how nice it is to see me again and we hug, our forms fitting together like all of the pieces in a puzzle box morphing into a picture all at once. I feel her familiar nuzzle against my shoulder and it melts my iced heart. I joke about her not wanting to do that unless she wants something else to happen and she tickles me softly. Our hands don't leave each other's embrace and I can feel her nervousness as high as mine. I tickle her gently back and we increase in our tickles until we fall onto the bed, me on top of her back. I freeze, shocked as I feel myself pressed against her butt. She let out a slight gasp, which took us both by surprise. Then I feel her arch her back upward in the way she used to do as we post-sexy-time cuddled. We lay momentarily still, stunned and surprised by the flood of emotions that took over our whole bodies, rising a roaring heat in what I know isn't just me. She rolls over part way and looks into my eyes and I know in this instant that she loves me. She never stopped loving me and I know I loved her all those miles away. I can see it in her and she knows I love her. She reaches her hands up to cup my ears and jaw softly, just like she always did. I lower myself onto her and feel our bodies touch, pressure more intense than we have ever felt before and we kiss. It's the sweetest, gentlest kiss of my entire life that filled us instantly with electricity and our clothing just seemed to melt off of our bodies as we moved together for what felt like the first time. During the end, I told her I loved her and she said it too and we cried, holding each other tightly, kissing with joy and crying at how crazy this all was. It was the last thing either of us expected. We lay there staring at each other in disbelief that I was back and she was in my arms again. I touched her cheek; I kissed her tiny freckles, the cheek I never thought I'd touch again. I slept in the bed that night.

The next day was filled with love. I was doing yoga in the living room and she came in and climbed on top of me. We walked to the co-op to get lunch. I asked the cashier some questions because I had originally applied there to work part time months ago. I figured working here would be a great way to learn more about wellness. The cashier had no answers for me though. After we ate I asked if Alana wanted to go to Presque Isle to watch the sunset again. I had applied here, too, as a park ranger or whatever. *Just being paid to be in nature would have been ideal.* She agreed and we held hands, kissing on the beach until we felt that heat electricity again. We went to the back of the station wagon and parked it in some trees at a secret parking area that the city only uses on big event days. We kissed and she reached for my pants. I was so scared someone would find us, but she told me to be quiet and to trust her. I put my fear to the side and through the view of the back window, staring up at the sky, I saw the stars bursting through the awakening trees.

Then she slid back, pulling me on top of her as she glided my hand down. I was nervous as we kissed and she told me not to worry, but I felt an excessive deal of what seemed like great panic mixed with a great release. She pulled my neck down until our lips met. We kissed and my fear melted away. Eventually I noticed something looked different. I lifted my head and the pale color inside the vehicle altered. *What is that? Lights? Oh no…* I lifted my head and saw a car driving toward us. *Oh my god, someone is here!* I thankfully locate my underwear and pull it on and hook my bra as Alana covers herself in a blanket. *My intuition was right! Or was it that I feared and allowed my mind to wander and since I didn't control my thoughts and emotions, the situation occurred? Was my mind picking up on an external inconsistency, sort of like an antenna receiving distress signals or did I actually energetically create this situation caused by my own internal fear?* I consider this philosophical debate, challenging everything I have been studying this last year as I pull on my clothes. Our intense giggles remind me that my internal philosophy studies don't shine a light quite as bright right now because an actual bright light shines on our vehicle, illuminating our panicking bodies. We are laughing and giggling and Alana can't find any of her clothes. After a firm tap on the window, I tell Alana to stay under the covers and to let me do the talking. I get out of the backseat and stand there in the woods in my underwear in front of a female trooper who looks at me up and down a few times, my tan six-pack shimmering in the pale Erie night.

The trooper's eyebrows rise, followed by a slight smirk as I reach in the car while talking to her. I tell her how thankful I was that her flashlight helped me to find my pants as I slide them up over my Haines boxer briefs while explaining to the officer about how we broke up and I just got back from traveling for two months and we just realized we were still in love after watching the sunset. This short haired female patroller *(of course)* looked me up and down with her fluorescent spotlight many times. She blushed as she shines the light in the back and sees Alana nervously sitting there, eyes like white saucers. She laughs and says about how she didn't expect to see this tonight. She explained that we are on state park lands and that this is extremely illegal. She tells us not to let it happen again because this is family space, again emphasizing the very illegal part. I apologize over and over as I stand there shirtless, but confident. *I look good. I feel great.* I just accomplished the greatest dream in my life and now somehow I have my woman back, naked, here with me right now in public. *Nothing can take me down now!* I joke with her a bit and ask about her job and daily duties because

I had applied to work at Presque Isle as well. I take a confident arms-crossed stance, firming my six-pack and puffing up my boobs with my arm muscles. I am pretty sure that she checks me out nervously the whole time she talks to me, but ultimately lets us go with a jittery warning, shaking her head, laughing as she returns back to her vehicle. What are the chances that a short haired possibly lesbian state trooper would find us out there? We return home laughing so hard and continue to make love for the rest of the night.

I was so conflicted inside. We truly loved each other so very much, but I was expected to go back to my hometown to meet my parents in a week to fly out to California with them, then to then fly down to Florida to meet Ryan and Alice to go to Key West. It was written in my destiny to go to Key West, I knew that. But in the meantime, Alana and I kissed and made love constantly these next few days, completely in love, but the tornado inside of me couldn't figure out a solution. The good news was that my answer happened for me. The bad news was that it completely ripped the fragile skeletal structure of my emotional body apart. We fell into our same arguments those last days and I continued to disappoint her in my over ambitious life discussions and she continued to disappoint me in her limited thinking homebody lifestyle. We broke up for good the second last day I was there. We really did love each other; we just were in such incompatible places in our lives. She asked me if I could take our cats, Lucy and Marshmallow and my turtle Ethel. She wanted to keep our other cat Zola. My mom told me it was fine to bring them to my parents since all their other cats were rescues and were all indoor/outdoor cats. I packed up my car with some things and promised her I would return to clean up the rest of my stuff and figure out what to do. I initially came back to Erie, not to fall in love again, but to pack. We instead spent the entire week in love and now my time was up. I packed up nearly everything except a few things in the living room and put it all in the attic. Then off I went, 6 hours across the state with two screaming cats and a turtle, a car stuffed with all my most important possessions, and tears in my eyes because this time I knew there was really no going back. We really tried, but I just couldn't seem to shake the flight from clouding my inconsistent eyes. (In several months I would again have to return back there to clean out the attic, but Alana was as stiff as stone. I slept at a friend's house for 2 nights as I went through my things, filling the front yard with boxes all of my possessions and a 'Free' sign. I had thrown away our box of shared intimates, sort of a disregarded trophy symbolizing our real end. I was quite pleased to see that all of the piles of objects I had put out there were taken to a new home, but was quite disturbed to find that someone had gone through all of our trash, too, and had taken our strap on, sort of a perversion disgrace of our entire relationship that disturbingly haunted my mind for some time.)

Anyhow, my head was a daze of experience and tragedy on that family trip to L.A. I didn't feel like myself and I couldn't seem to get my energy back. I had returned to Erie with such zest, such exhilaration and I now walked around my family like a zombie with an absolutely broken heart. I over drank at the hotel party celebration and destroyed the next day. I couldn't get my head wrapped around what happened and I couldn't escape the thoughts besides seeing new things to distract from my emotions. I tried to be present on our first family California trip as we drove up the coast. We stopped at the Hearst Castle and saw zebras in a field as we entered the estate. I became inspired by the ambitious life of William Randolph Hearst and his newspaper empire creating the vast wealth that allowed him to travel all over the world, bringing back rare relics and artifacts, creating a castle unlike anything else in America. The view into the valley beyond the vibrant blue Neptune Pool is something I will never forget.

We drove up the coast and I saw cliffs and surging blue ocean waves smashing the rocks hundreds of feet below the simple two lane road. We hiked around Big Sur where we saw a waterfall landing into the sand. As we stood there, I noticed there were people running around on the forbidden beach down below. Signs all around warned of no trespassing. Moments later I would see why. We all watched horrifically as the initial path that the people below had taken to get over there became blocked by the tide coming in. They couldn't get by, being smashed by incoming waves and increasing tide into the cliffs. They helped each other to climb onto a rock as the waves came crashing in. Everyone watched as these kids were bashed and knocked around. Three of them eventually barely made it across the gap and were climbing up the cliffs, thankfully not being swept into the angry ocean. The other two were stuck and we could see the rock disappearing under them, waves rising as they tried desperately to get across, but even from up here we could see the surge getting stronger and stronger. The waves were crashing into them constantly as the kids tried everything they could to get their friends across and out of danger. This disturbing spectacle went on for 20 minutes and everyone on this cliff was gripping the railing, praying, but expecting to watch someone drown. There was nothing to do from up here on these hundred foot cliffs except pray. I thought they would definitely die this day, but hoped somehow they'd make it. And somehow they did.

Our family was returning down the trail to the car as my Dad suggested going down another trail to the other side of the cliffs just see what happened to the Danger Kids. So we wander through the woods and find a campsite at the top of the cliff dwelling loaded with stuff, but no people. I spot a hole in the fence and next to it right by a no trespassing sign about one foot from a 200 ft. drop off into the violent ocean. I look over the fence and lean to get a good look at how insane the water surge really looks from up here; it makes my stomach churn. Then I notice something furry to my left. I freak out for a second, thinking it's a large animal, but then realize that it's actually five large animals. It's the Danger Kids! I see a line of them pasted to the side of the cliff about 8 feet below me, barely maintaining balance on the crumbly cliffs. The front one sees me and I ask if they are ok, but he responds that they can't get a good grip to get up; they have been stuck, unable to reach up safely to get over the last part of this ledge. *So close, yet so far...* I yell to Dad and he comes over and instinctually sits down, holding firmly to the sign post and tells them to grab his foot for support. He looks at me as he exclaims, "I hope they put this sign in properly in cement." I try to figure out a way to help, but there is really nothing I can do. It's too dangerous to get any closer besides standing back, glued to the fence and offering a wobbly hand as they scramble up the edge. Dad pulls them up one at a time as I panic at the thought that just one incorrect move could end their lives. I watch over the edge as I observe the tiny fragments of Earth, the fragmented cliffs that the last two are standing on. Directly beyond that chunk was a several hundred foot drop into cliffs being devoured by the furious ocean, angry that the Danger Kids didn't obey its intensity. It seemed that the water required a sacrifice for the insult of their trespassing and I gulped that thought down, praying it was not true. I was shaking after this was all over because as we spoke to them, it became apparent that they didn't seem to realize how dangerous that whole experience really was. They didn't look or talk like advanced explorers. They just looked like sweet, college kids that really had no idea how close to death they may have been. I once more looked over the crumbly cliff and saw a complete hundred foot drop straight down to the left, the same area they had been balancing on when we found them. A cold chill shudders through me. *Geez.* I have no doubt in my mind that my dad saved their lives this day.

It was great to spend time with the family. We really did share so many wonderful experiences climbing in tidal pools filled with foreign beach creatures and exploring the famous PCH, Pacific Coast Highway- Highway 1 up the cliffs of the Cali coast. But the moment I stopped experiencing, Alana crept into my mind. I needed to keep going. We said our goodbyes in San Francisco and they hopped on their plane to Pennsylvania and I hopped on mine to Florida. In the idle moments, even just idle for a few minutes, I began to feel as if I was waiting on life's doorstep with a killer sneaking up behind me with an ax. I wanted to escape from the prison that became my mind. Everywhere I looked I saw Alana. I tried to distract myself with thoughts of my previous travels or thoughts of my future Key West waters, but Alana's memory leaked into everything. I had to keep moving. I just had to keep going. *She couldn't catch me if I kept going, right?* I watched the world evolve below me as our plane crossed multi-colored states speckled with clouds. *Fight or flight...* I left my distressed emotions in San Francisco and I chose flight. Flight away from the internal was way easier than dealing with my disturbed sensations. At least with Key West goggles on, I knew it could be possible to forget.

At least for a while...

Unfortunately, my thoughts were distressed on that entire flight because as I waited for the plane to board, I decided to listen to my old voicemails from months prior. *I want a fresh start when I land.* Two of the voicemails arrived within a week of each other at the beginning of April. Those two voicemails absolutely shattered all I had left of a heart. I initially told Alana I'd be gone a month. It just so happens that these voicemails revealed that everything I wanted that entire time had actually arrived within that first month. I could have listened. I could have come back, but I never did. I asked and the universe answered everything I had asked for. *Geez, it even left me a fucking voicemail, but I was too scared to answer, too scared to confront the fears I was running from. The call came and I never picked up the phone.* All I had to do was listen and respond and I never did it until it was too late.

One voicemail was my acceptance for the job at the Co-op. The other was my acceptance to the park security job at Presque Isle... Desire and believe; acquire and achieve! *Ask and you shall receive.* Every single thing I had asked for while in Erie arrived in the time I initially told Alana I would be gone, one month... *Everything was in alignment with what I wanted... except me.* I got stuck and didn't have the courage to get out until I was forced to. I bawled in the airport bathroom after hearing those voicemails. It was now too late to answer those calls. The life we planned together vanished. Our love was ruined. She was gone. The opportunity I asked for arrived and I wasted it all, lost in the arms of my stubborn desire to stay on the road even after I felt something shift.

Tears slide down my cheeks. My mind shifts toward thoughts of the seas.

There's absolutely no going back now.

Memories of Florida guide my mind from the clouds and into that blue prevailing ocean.

Desire and believe; acquire and achieve! Ask and you shall receive.

Just be strong enough to answer the universe's call.

Chapter Forty-Three

Getting to Key West

"Live prepared to enjoy all experiences."

Callie lets her blonde curls shake free, ruffling up the back of her hair as she asks me, "So, why do you keep saying that?" I ask her what she means. "Well, about the switching from fight to flight or whatever." I tell her about how I had been seeking truth in its purest form everywhere I had gone and it was a huge turning point to realize that the changes I was seeking were taking place inside of me.

"See, it's like I have been trying to gain some type of stability inside of me. It is something totally non-physical, but it felt like I was a shell of a human, like I had a hard, exquisitely painted exterior shell. But the strength I was seeking through the external was just guiding me to look deeper into myself and when that happened, I realized my inside was empty."

I can see her contemplating all that I said, studying me slightly, and shaking her head up and down. She looks bright as she says, "Cancer, right?"

I shockingly gasp as I reach up to grasp my right shoulder. I think about the strange physical issues I had been having in my chest, digestive tract and stomach these last few years. It is definitely in a state of dis-ease, but I certainly wasn't in a state to declare it to be cancerous. "Geez. What the hell? Why would you ask me that suddenly?" she looks shocked by my response. "Why did you ask me if I had cancer? I wasn't even talking about health."

She bursts in laughter, "No, no! Are you a Cancer? Ya know, a crab. Cancers have a shell of hardness about them, but deep down they are soft and smooshy." *Oh. She was talking about horoscopes. Oh. Ha... Sort of funny.* I shake off my chill. *Ok, cool.*

"Ha! Ok, awesome. No, I'm a Taurus." She tells me she's a Scorpio while raising her eyebrows slightly, mentioning how I don't fit the personality type of a Taurus. We talk more about horoscopes and astrology concepts before moving back to the subject of internal awareness. "So, my goal now is to be that of a massive tree. For instance, have you ever picked up a big branch? It's heavy right? A tree has so much weight and so much mass, but it stands firmly above the earth supporting itself from one central line, the trunk. When there is a storm and the wind blows crazy, a tree doesn't fight it. If it did it would break. It moves with it." I point up at the trees across the park and tell her to pay attention to them because when we get a big gust of wind, they will sway with it. "They usually don't break. They usually move with whatever is happening, maintaining a solidity, a foundation of strength. That's what I have been working on, my foundation and inner stability while remaining flexible."

"Wow. I am so happy we are talking. When you first told me you didn't have a bachelor's degree, I thought you were kind of foolish. But you are just, like, a different type of smart. Like, you speak differently than anyone at college." She jots down some of the things I just said.

"A different kind of smart. I like that. Thanks." I jot that down. Maybe it'll prove to be a confidence booster when I read it again in the future.

....

It was nice to be in Florida without having to worry about my car. Seeing Ryan and Alice again was like seeing family, although over the time that I was gone, they became sort of a couple. Things changed, but it was fine because we were on our way to Key West in the morning!

There is just something about that drive to Key West that just is unlike any other type of thrill I have ever experienced. We were all loaded up into Ryan's truck, Alice and I in the back seat and Mack (Ryan's life-long best friend) and Ryan in the front. All the dogs were dropped off at Ryan's sister's house except for Mack's dog which was given to his friend for the week. The while trip everyone I encountered kept saying 'just wait until you get to Key West.' "Oh, you like this place? Just wait until you get to Key West." It was just like Charleston so I can only imagine how amazing it will be! "Yeah, the whole Gulf coast is nice, but just wait until you see the waters in Key West." And finally, after half a year of traveling, I was actually on my way to the renowned Western Key! I could hardly contain my excitement, even though it was masked by a thick layer of travel jet lag. I could not wait to fill my life with even more experience! Cram my eyes full with the ultimate that America has to experience. *I certainly can't be upset about the break-up then!* We all talked and had a blast the whole way down there. Ryan, of course, had his large Bloody Mary and Mack had his whiskey and weed to keep him company.

Considering my recent digestive problems, I was rather nervous to indulge in too much alcohol, even if I had narrowed it down to soda inflicted sickness rather than a sick alcohol reaction. I knew I would be drinking a lot once there. *Why not just enjoy the travel and sights from a sober perspective?* We were debating on stopping in Miami for a bit, but that plan changed with the introduction of black skies and once we saw the enormous storm about to hit the coast up there, we canceled that plan. Our route was down 75 from Fort Myers to Naples then across Florida on the more scenic route, route 41 which is Tamiami Trail East. We normally would have taken 75 across the state to save time, but that goes directly into the heart of Fort Lauderdale and continues on a web through Miami where, at the time we would be entering, that area would be full of traffic thus allowing us to possibly be stuck in that tropical storm system. We did not want to be driving in heavy traffic with a boat headed for Key West during a large thunderstorm. We wanted to get there and get the boat docked in the water, but the storm may catch us first. The guys tell stories of their previous trips to Key West and strange events that happened. Being that they are guys and have been best friends for years, they compete in travel knowledge, resulting in Ryan drinking and Mack smoking aggressively while nearly yelling at each other. This was generally the thing that happens between them so it struck me as not surprising in the least bit. They tell us about the way boats have to ride the tides in and out of the channels because you can easily get your boat stuck on a sand bar when the tide is low. I have no knowledge of anything with boats so this talk is both very important and very frightening.

"So umm… Ryan, you didn't tell us about getting stuck like this before."

"Well, chances of it happening are usually high, but I've been down here a million times. I know how to travel the channels and have it not happen. See, you need to experience Key West from the water, but you need to be with someone who knows what they are doing."

Mack jumps in. "Yep, everyone, trust Ryan. He's got all the answers."

"Mack, shut up. I only ever got my boat stuck once. And that was with my ex-wife like 12 years ago. We had stopped at this island to explore and when we turned around to go back to the boat, we noticed it was tilted on the one side. I immediately knew it was too late. It was already too shallow and we'd be stuck there a few hours until the tide came back in. So we did what any normal couple would do."

"What's that?" He really has that way of keeping a listener interested.

"We walked around the island naked and had sex all over the place. We were lying naked on the boat when we heard a strange noise and realized it was another boat. They pulled up in the channel and yelled to us from about 25 yards away asking if we were ok. I pulled on my shorts quick and got up to respond, telling them we had water and some snacks and we'd be alright. He asked if we had any alcohol and we told them that we had about three beers left. Ha you won't believe what he did next. Ha-ha, I still can't believe what he did." *He really had this way of making you crave the answer and almost the entire time that he talked, he smiled, making every story so pleasant.* Ryan continues, "He messed around on his boat for a bit. I really couldn't tell what he was doing, but he was definitely doing something. Then he grabbed one of his fishing poles and attached something to it. He cast it out our way and after three attempts, he made it to us. He yelled for us to just cut the line and keep it. So we did and then we realized he had packaged a bud of weed. We yelled thank you and they drove off wishing us well. Man, you don't get that friendly hospitality in Pennsylvania, I bet."

This was so unbelievable to me, the idea that elderly people not only smoked weed, but sent it off to random stranded people. As they told stories that ranged between amazing, drunken and unbelievable, I learned a lot about the culture of the islands, but it is certainly nothing like actually learning from personal experience of the islands. I learned an important lesson from being around Ryan for so long too. He would frequently look at boats, yachts and mansions that I would never ever even dream of possessing. "Whoa, check out that boat. Aw, man. Can you imagine being on that thing?" I'd glance over and see a price tag of $80,000 and wonder how on earth anyone could ever even imagine buying something like that?

But Ryan would. He would consider anything an option. Nothing was a limitation to him, even multi-million dollar houses along the water. He would imagine it as his and I started to understand this newly improved concept of value. Nothing became impossible in his eyes. I constantly would limit my ideas of what I could possess in this life. I would think that I couldn't afford to buy a $400 kayak, much less consider getting a tiny motorized boat. I couldn't even imagine how much gas would cost to power such a craft! And that was the trigger of my limited mindset. I was so financially limited in my mind. But Ryan didn't consider money to be a factor in desire. The object or experience was what he wanted and that was all that mattered. The most important thing I learned from him was to think big and to dream big. That is something that I spoke of, read about, but never really saw before. I was raised in a penny pinching life and everything my whole life seemed too big for me to have and this was the moment in my life when everything about my small mind began to evolve. I was almost able to start seeing big! Well, the first step was to identify it and this was when I started identifying how limited

I was mentally. *Think big.* That is one of the first steps in acquiring anything in life. *Think it. Feel it and it happens.* I had grown very good at acquiring experiences that generally required a lot of money, such as going to Key West with a boat or even being in a plane, but I have such a block in my concept of finance and actual money. The ownership or lack of worthiness block has revealed itself within me.

We make a stop at the Skunk Ape Research Facility (the southern Sasquatch HQ) before making that left hand turn onto Route 1, also known as South Dixie Highway headed for the Florida Keys. I see water and grassy wetlands all over while I read small passing signs for Manatee Bay and Blackwater Sound. It's all an incredibly beach/touristy area which I guess I should have expected along the highway. I keep my eyes on the skies behind us, hoping that they stay away. I do have a massive fear of storms, especially storms on water, such as an ocean which is on both sides of us right now. *Whew, relax.* We turn right and continue toward Key Largo still on Route 1, but at this point it has changed to Overseas Highway. It's a kind of thrilling, yet scary feeling to drive on a road nearly level with the water that filled the boundless distances both left and right. We stop just outside of Key Largo at a small shopping complex to fill our coolers with ice and alcohol. I begin to get very nervous about a possible storm having the ocean surge up and swallow us. *Of course, having a boat in a situation like that could prove to be lifesaving....* It is at this point that I decide it's too late to be a big baby and give into my fear of water. I cannot let it consume me like this. I make a mixed drink with Alice and force myself to not just ignore the fact that there is water in all directions around me, but to plain old face my fear of water. *This is where I am and this is what I am doing. That's it.* If the earth wants to kill me and eat me alive, then so be it! *But I'm done stressing about it.*

And the alcohol goes down easily. I begin to relax and the storm begins to retreat, seemingly sensing my decision to no longer be afraid of it. It's funny how that works sometimes... Was it there just to probe my fear and force me to overcome my fear of stormy weather near water or was it me tapping into a greater blend of energy flowing continuously in the world? Whatever it is, I am thankful for the peace of mind during the sunset which would be taking place about 10 minutes from this point. *I bet Alana would love to see this...* I drink a big gulp and give Alice a huge hug.

We pass upper Matecumbe Key, signifying us getting closer to our goal. Every key we enter is like a key being given to me to a spiritual treasure quest. As I cross the Florida Keys, they are opening treasure chests that hold priceless clues leading to the next treasure chest! Every key unlocks my next clue to life! Craig Key leads to Long Key which leads to Fat Deer Key, which I find extremely funny. *For such a beautiful area of the world, the Florida cartographers couldn't come up with anything more elegant than Fat Deer Key?* The boys explain the reason for it, which is because there really are a bunch of tiny deer that live on the islands out here and they are very special because they exist nowhere else in the world, except at this one location and they are extremely protected. They tell us fun facts and explain that they are not very easy to spot out in the wild. They live, breed and exist only here on the southern Florida Keys. There is a national key deer refuge to the north of the island on Big Pine Key and I imagine a whole frolicking forest of little nymph deer and fairies. I look over to my right and instantly see one standing there at that very second. We pull off the road immediately onto the next right turn and are greeted by several of them crossing the road up ahead. They really are just small, cute, miniature deer.

"Ha! Look at them all! I've never seen this!" shouts Ryan enthusiastically, "What are the chances? Whelp, there you go guys. That completes our portion of the tour on tiny deer." We continue through Marathon, which is an island on the keys home to almost 11,000 residents. The skies in front of us remain clear as the skies behind begin to fade to no longer threatening. The storm we've been racing has stopped following us and instead began to flourish into our visual evolving canvas; a huge feeling of serenity flows over me as we near the 7-mile bridge and the skies prepare for an amazing sunset. My fingers peel the labels on the objects before me as I stand guard with full skyward appreciation on this night. Not a single beam of light, not a single vibrant hue, will go unobserved by me this evening.

Just then I realize that a rainbow is emerging on the right side of us. "Holy kitten whiskers! There is a rainbow!" In front left was a magnificent sunset and in back right was an enormous, expanding rainbow. This would be the first of a series of 14 consecutive rainbows experienced over the course of an 8-day period. As I watched in absolute excitement at the skies evolution into night, I kept a close eye on the rainbow as well, which began sprouting another! "Ahh! It's a double rainbow!" *Whaaa?* After everything with Alana, this felt like such a gift from the Divine saying "Way to go, Katie. Be strong. You are where you need to be." We all began to make quotes from the Double Rainbow guy on YouTube. I don't know if I ever laughed and smiled harder in my life.

The Seven-Mile Bridge is a historical bridge connecting Key West to the rest of Florida. The original bridge is over to the right, crumbling, yet holding tight to its historical relevance. We continued on this two lane road, 30 feet above the waters that spread in all directions with just us and this bridge for seven miles. Panic rises… *There is no landmass under me for 7 miles. I cannot express how significant this moment is. Words will never describe the amount of water-flurried-fear eclipsed by the multitude of sky events taking place at this exact moment.* The shimmer off the water reflected reds and pinks like none I've ever seen before and the double rainbow danced itself into space, slowly fading until its last waves gently kissed my face.

I will never forget the sky on that day or the universal words I heard as it held me in that place. We crossed that bridge and *(although it sounds lame)* that was one of the most real, metaphorical experiences I have ever had. I crossed a bridge into a new life that day. That new life had been waiting for me for years and I finally was arriving.

We finally enter Key West and immediately head to the boat dock at the marina to get the boat in the water. Alice and I watch the guys get it where it needs to be; the boat looks so satisfied being where it is. *So am I.* I check out some signs around the area about fishing trips on these small personal boats. It suddenly dawns on me how lucky I am to have a friend not only guide me to Key West, but also bring his boat and all of his gear for us to use. He is so happy to share this stuff and I just want him to know how much I appreciate it. I hope one day I will be able to really express to him how much he has changed my life. Ryan is an amazing man.

I had thought of myself to be an amazing woman at this point, having recently discovered this new secret to life, the law of attraction, to unveil all of the things I could ever wish to dream for. Ever since I had been studying *Contemplate and Welcome Prosperity* the world has erupted into a vast system of possibilities. I was training my mind to do anything at all that I wanted to do in life, whether it be going somewhere, seeing something, doing anything, even riding in a plane and boat! And I just so happened to meet an amazing guy (who also is a sincerely great man and not a serial killer) who not only brought us to Key West, but also is taking us on the trip of a lifetime. So I was determined to find a place to sleep for the night.

We head downtown, drinking and walking around since they have an open container policy. After being in Savannah, I have a great appreciation for this procedure. We strolled by all of the local tourist bars to get a feel for what Key West is all about and obviously to watch drunk people stumble around. All ages, all types of people intermingling together, flowing out of bars like drift-bound creatures in tide pools and laughing at all sorts of inappropriate things. All the guys are wearing sunglasses, flip-flops and floral shirts and the women are wearing, well, pretty much the same thing. Most importantly is the amount of happiness in every direction. Everyone is happy. It was mostly alcohol induced happiness, but everyone was smiling. This is a theme throughout all of Florida that I have never experienced anywhere else before. It's a collection of people (most are not originally from there) and they have all come to this place to make their lives better.

This is what proves to be a big problem in my homeless-less mission. I cannot find anyone who lives here. To every person I encounter, I use my sleep strategy that I have used this whole year so far. If I like their energy, I tell them that I am traveling and they normally follow up by asking where I am sleeping. The problem with Key West is that only a few of the people here ask where I am sleeping and I am not a fan of being a forceful traveler, but my time is running out to score a place to sleep for the night. Ryan actually canceled his reservation for the night because I accepted my own internal challenge to find a place for us to sleep. I promised my friends I would find one. *Ego driven goal...* I frantically scan the crowds asking hordes of beautiful women what they are doing and asking groups of friends.

Problem #1- No one lives here. Everyone is traveling.

Problem #2- Everyone has loaded rooms in their family/friends' houses.

Problem #3- No one knows anyone that actually lives on the island.

The tourists here either have absolutely no space for anyone or are already the extra guest that shouldn't be there in the first place. Alas, I cannot find anywhere to sleep. I can't even find a single spot for myself, much less a group of four of us. So disappointed, Alice and I return to the truck and hang around it tailgate style and talk about how it's not a big deal. A cat appears from the side of the house and sort of meows at me. *I am so dog esteemed now that I almost forgot what a cat looks like!* I walk over to it and immediately get a horrific scent of cat urine all over the entire area just as another cat emerges from the side of the patio.

"Oh, that is the worst smell ever. I am going to throw up." It looks abandoned, but something about the several food dishes on the porch tells me that someone actually lives in this horrible smelling dwelling. This is not the first time that I have seen someone who takes better care of their pets than themselves. As I watch the cats hop around, I consider that possibly no one actually does live there, but people just feed the cats out of kindness. I return to the truck, stomach in hand, and quickly crack open a carbonated beverage to start making a mixed drink ignoring my digestive issues. A rum and soda on this warm May night, tailgating homeless under palm trees at the southern-most point in the United States sounds just about right to me. *I certainly cannot complain.* These stunning girls walk by while I am expressing my disgust to Alice at my lack of prosperous mind control in succeeding in finding a place to stay for the night. I am not used to having this *'Desire and believe; acquire and achieve!'* concept challenged. I decide to let go and have a little fun with it.

"Can I sleep over with you guys tonight? We have nowhere to go." I yell bluntly at this group of six beautiful gals, all giggly and drunk off of paradise. They stop momentarily to look at me and Alice, average (well, her being gorgeous) looking women hanging out in the back of a pickup truck. Half of them ignore us and continue walking while the other half talk to us surprisingly for a few moments, leading me to believe that they may just take us in! We explain our stories of travel so far and they seem very excited by it. This dazzling blond with enormous knockers almost dangling out of her shirt explains that they are staying at her aunt's house which only has two spare rooms and they already maxed out the amount of friends she was allowed to bring. She genuinely wished she could help us, explaining that there is a spare lot about the size of a picnic table on the side of the house and if we wanted to set up a tent there, we could. I explained how that probably wasn't enough space, but we appreciate the offer regardless. She responded that it's probably for the best because her aunt doesn't clean up after her dogs anyhow.

I arrive at the point of surrender and admit defeat in my quest. I have been unsuccessful in finding a place to sleep for the night. I am so disappointed in myself and I take a shot of whiskey; Alice tells me it's all fine, but to me it's devastating. This mind control, this awareness of longing and correct application of persistence always works out. Everyone I encounter hears me talk about it constantly. Pretty much anyone I spend time with sees the incredible occurrences that happen daily based off of the Law of Attraction's application into my life. *I promised the group to trust me. I promised that I would be successful and that my pure faith in the universe could effortlessly manifest a place for us all to sleep. And here I was, empty handed. I lied to them... They trusted me and this crazy idea of universal gifts and I had nothing to show.* The guys tried to book a hotel last minute at 1 am, but every single thing was completely booked. This moment of defeat was so representative of the destruction of my whole belief system; I was disenchanted. The guys became furious and marched away. I surrendered to the night and just decided to try to enjoy it for what it was. We walked around people watching and soaking up culture. I end up wandering into this strange space alone, standing by a building, thinking about what my life really is. *Am I a fool in pursuit of a fake truth? Is everything I hold to be gold, just an illusion?* This bouncer of a club startles me by expressing how much he likes my spirit. I tilt my head to the side and look at him peculiarly. It's as if he heard my sense of self-doubt and was an angel sent to realign my views before I became stuck in a vortex of negative limiting thoughts. Hearing those words sparked my energy, sort of like a depleted battery being recharged. *Ok... this suddenly feels better* ... I tell him a little bit of background to why I am where I am and he excitedly tells me to talk to a bartender at a gay club up the street. "Tell Lorrie that Big John sent ya. Yeah, she'll take care of you guys." *Big John... ha.*

On this human treasure map, I now continue my life mapping. I am re-determined to find a place to sleep! I am re-determined to be persistent, even in the literal sense of the phrase, being stuck in the Dark Night, which is often referred to in spiritual healing books as the lowest place one comes from in their life, where one must trust that the light will come soon. I go to the club that Big John told me about and I order a drink from the lady. She is a very attractive, older lesbian with a nice energy. I tell her Big John sent me and I explained my story. She tells me to meet her there at 3am when she gets off and we can follow her to her house to sleep for the night. That was it. It was simple and just handed to me in my moment of surrender. My eyes light up. *Yes! I am successful! I am to be justified in my quest!*

So a bit of time passes and we end up somehow missing her. The bar is closed and there is no one around. I call her several times and she doesn't respond and my friends grow frustrated and think I'm a fraud. Ryan makes over $100,000 per year and Mack works his own real estate company so both have never had a reason to be in a predicament of homelessness before tonight. *And voila... I have given them this, um... gift. Or experience. Or perspective...* No, they are very, very angry with me (even though they are trying to control their anger) they are mad that I took charge and told them not to find a hotel for the night. I feel pathetic and worthless and right as we climb into the car to accept defeat and return to the dock to figure out if we are going to sleep on the boat or in the car, the bartender, Lorrie, calls me back and explains that she wished I had texted her so she had my number to contact me. They closed at 2:15 because it was so slow. She then proceeded to give me that gold that I had faith in this whole time- the address to her house.

Despite all of my struggle and determination being shot down, I have accomplished my goal of the evening! It was as if I was just too determined in the outcome, too forceful in my decision on how the world would work tonight. The whole time all I had to do was just relax. Rather than using this opportunity as a shining trophy to show off to others that which I already feel to be true, I just had to enjoy being in the now. I just had to know what it was that I was wanting, while living and remaining in a state of appreciation for where I was at the time. Instead I ignored my now-ness and everything I saw was in the filter of my expectation for the future that evening. *Life can be so simple!* Just know what it is I want while fully enjoying the scenery and being patient while smiling. *That was all I had to do!* I laugh to myself and mark this down as a very important lesson to avoid great frustration in the future. We circle around for a bit in Ryan's huge diesel truck grumbling, noisily at 3 am until finally we find the correct address. I am instantly greeted by the scent of marijuana faintly peeking out what I assumed to be their backyard. *Ah, that familiar scent of freedom.*

We follow voices to the back and open a fat, rusted gate to reveal a very nice patio taking up most of the back yard. The palm trees were overbearing and the growth of tropical foliage was so dense that it seemed like we were in a secret hidden room. Several ladies were sitting on lawn chairs and perched on the stairs. The door to the beautiful shed was open and lit, revealing a fun space. Over time, I realized that it was actually a spare room that they converted into a rental property to a short, spiky blond haired lesbian we shall refer to as Blond Bitty. The whole rest of the night, I would strategically attempt to be nice to Bitty in hopes that maybe we could be friends so I could get in with the local lesbian community here; maybe I could return sooner if I was in, but she would glare at me or not give me any attention when I spoke to her and her friends. She obviously did not approve of me or like me at all and physically let me know it.

All four of us come in and introduce ourselves to the group. It's a whole crew of local 20's to 50's gays that get off bartending work and come over here for an hour or two to hang out after their shifts. They talk and drink and I offer them shots out of my bottle, but they respond by offering me a hit of weed. Mack joins in, proudly displaying his bag and they all instantly exchange weed smells and the ladies say things like, "Baby girl, I gave up the bottle a long time ago." Before cracking open another beer from her personal six pack and shouting, "Damn boy, that's pretty good for Americanized green, but check this stuff out." And Mack would instantly be offended, considering he takes such pride in his constant marijuana intake. But then would be handed a bowl of what could be mistaken as a tiny, hairy octopus that would make him cough his socks off, shouting how amazing that hit was. The alluring verbal exchanges here would provoke me to both drink a little too much and take a hit of weed which always results in a bizarre night for my fumed mind.

Ryan and Alice retire almost instantly to the sofa to fall asleep after thanking Lorrie for all that she did by allowing us to sleep there and Mack and I hung out and met all of Lorrie's late night friends. After some of the people leave and Blond Bitty and her rude friends head out to a local early morning café where you can bring your own bottle, (which by the way, I did attempt to get invited to, but was very offensively forbidden) Mack and I fell asleep on the two reclining patio furniture chairs. I was so thankful that she had two lounge chairs for us to curl up on. I cover myself with the thin sheet Laurie provided us after warning of the terrible mosquitoes that soon will attack at sunrise. I grab my phone to check the time- 4:38 Am. *Geez… it's good I wasn't invited.* I briefly consider staying up to watch the sunrise in Key West and then consider how ruthless the rest of my tomorrow would be if I don't get any sleep now.

The truth is that I really had no idea how ruthless the rest of the day would be no matter what happened. A good night's sleep would never prepare me for the amount of life the next day would bring.

Honestly, nothing could prepare me for what I was about to experience within the next 24 hours.

Chapter Forty-Four

Key West - Day 2

"The magic of perception will awaken even the gentlest, sleeping soul."

I wake up, feeling the heat rising in the early morning and I remove the sheet from my face. With a long stretch, allowing my muscles to deeply lengthen, loosening the tightness of the amount of sitting from the day before, I stare up at the palm trees directly overhead and listen to the morning flurry of birds and insects. Somewhere not too far away, I hear a rooster. There is just something about waking up in a new place that makes me feel so alive and amazing.

I open the door quietly, as to not disturb anyone who is most likely still sleeping in the living room and I am greeted by an elderly man in the kitchen. He does not seem shocked at all to see a strange person in this house, which I find funny. *I think she mentioned something about a dad living there the night before now that I think about it.* He talks to me a lot and sips his coffee slowly, sort of almost reliving the moments that he speaks of. His multi colored socks show bright through his strapped sandals. His name is Ted and for some reason I am very interested in talking to him. His voice purrs depth and soul into everything that he says and there is a gentle grace about the way he speaks that I find myself studying. My approaching post-drinking morning nausea asks him for a generous cup of coffee. He is more than happy to provide me with all that I want as he pulls out a catalogue of creams and sugars. I accept honey and cream.

"I met a girl that used honey all the time. Ahh, yes. But that was years ago." And he sips his coffee and stares up into the corner of the ceiling. *I love watching someone reminisce on a good experience in their life.* He asks me about my life in a very interested, yet distinctly tranquil way. We talk for a half hour as he leans on the corner of the chair. I sipped my hot, delicious coffee. *Very strong.* Almost too strong because I must have made a twitch or a face as I did so.

"Strong enough for ya, eh? Be careful not to grow hair on your chest. We like our coffee like we like our dreams- strong." I had expected him to go with a funnier approach to this sentence, but was remarkably satisfied with the enlightening response he provided. I would have said something along the lines of "I like my coffee like I like my women. Strong and creamy." But his dream line was refreshing.

Everyone slowly begins to wake up and join in the living room. I make my way down the hallway and look at all of these paintings on the walls. There are bizarre paintings of bodies and objects, mixed media including a piece of a violin and other things plastered to a canvas and painted on. Trees, islands, oceans, animals, artists, musicians- there is just so much creativity in this hallway that I cannot help but to walk slowly down the entire thing and stare at every little piece of it.

"These were done by a friend of mine. She's much younger, closer to your age actually." Lorrie appears from a doorway covered by a burgundy sheet. As she walks out, I can see an incredibly peaceful relaxed environment behind her. A peaceful environment doesn't always mean a peaceful mind, but it definitely promotes one. I smile and explain how much I love this one art piece and I am not sure why.

"The colors in that one are remarkable and it's almost as if the detail fell into place as it wanted to be. That is one of Megan's favorites. She always said that it really just painted itself." At this point, I assume that Megan is some young ex-lover of sorts and feel no need to ask questions. "Megan is an artist friend and was kicked out of her home when she came out to her parents. She lived up in Miami, where the gay population is high, but I guess it's always different when it is your kid... She wanted to get an apartment, but her parents gave her until sunrise to get all of her stuff out of their house. We took a couple friends over and all helped her move all of her things. I offered to let her hang her pictures up in here for as long as she wanted. These things take up a lot of space when they aren't on the walls."

I never considered how much space a stack of pictures would take up. There were probably well over 60 paintings in all around here. A few sculptures were placed about on the shelves along with some books too. "Are all of these paintings hers?"

"Yes. They have been here for almost 8 months now too." She takes a long look down the hallway and I see her eyebrows rise a little bit. "hmm... I didn't realize it was that long ago. I don't mind having them up here. This place would be awfully boring without them anyhow."

We make our way back down the hallway and I am met by her father in the middle. She continues into the living room and I say, "I love this artwork. It must be great waking up and walking through so much beauty every single day." He sips his coffee and points to a painting of Joni Joablon and asks me what I think about it. *So much incredible texture and color.* I explain to him that it is one of my favorites in the hallway and he begins to tell a story that would change my life. It is not the story itself that changed my life; it is the sincerity in his voice, the look in his eyes as they began to fill with fond tears of a former world.

"Sharon and I saw her, oh, years back." He began to laugh as I saw him return to the place in the past. "You ever hear of Woodstock? Well, of course you have. We were there. We were in the crowds among the thousands of happy crazy hippies all over. My wife and I lived our lives free. We traveled all over the country, kind of like what you are doing, but we always promised ourselves that we would live our lives free." His eyes began to tear up. He took off his glasses and wiped them a moment while taking in a deep breath. "She passed away on August 18th, three years ago. Breast cancer. But anyhow, we fell in love when we first met and we promised we would always live our lives as full as we could. Nothing would ever hold us back. We would live free and love life as we lived." And he puts his glasses back on and looks at me with such strength that I have never felt before.

"And I will tell you one thing, Katie. What you are doing is what you should be doing. Live. So many people die more every day. They live these jobs they hate. They live this life that is killing them." The certainty in his voice is so compelling that I am certain I am holding my breath. "Live every day like it is your last! It's so generic to say, but I can tell you most of my friends and family are all dead." His blue eyes shine a seeming absolute truth. "They hated me for my free spirit, but when it came down to it, it was my life. And I chose to live a little more every day. Plain and simple. You are doing exactly what you need to be doing in your life right now. Don't ever let anyone make you feel like you are wrong."

He stops talking and the pressurized air surrounding our bodies seems to hold us separate from gravity. It seems to hold a vast interlocking life glow, creating a pause to allow the messages to really sink in. As the silence assists with my mental digestion, he begins again.

"My wife and I stood there, soaked with sweat right in front of Joni Joablon. We were only, I'd say about two people deep in the crowd from the front. We were right there, right there in front of her, swaying with the crowds, all eyes on her and I can still remember her singing..." he begins to gently cry. He stares upwards and I can see in his eyes that he sees her again. He feels the sunlight baking his skin and he feels his arm around his wife again, hands outstretched among thousands, all gathered for love and peace. I see this man see Joni Joablon again, and my jaw tenses and my eyes begin to water too as a section of my chest opens up. It seems to grasp every word he says and pulls it closely into my chest, keeping the memory warm so he can recall even further.

He tenderly sings, "Freedoms, well, it is only another term for…" and his grip tightens around his mug. "Zero left to misplace. And everything…" his eyes light up brighter than they have before, "it ain't nothing, darling, if it ain't lived free." He sees Joni Joablon. He feels his wife's jubilant body in his arms again, their souls combined for one of the most powerfully positive life changing three days in his recent history. He feels the power of his youth again. I see him, right before me on my first full day in Key West, experience Joni Joablon at Woodstock.

Just being part of that moment brought me to a place I've never before experienced. It's similar to the feeling of participating in a drum circle with hundreds of joyful people of all ages at sunset on a beach, but much greater. And it was just me and this man in a hallway. He wipes the tears from his eyes again.

"And that is when we decided to really live our lives and no longer waste anymore of our time. Everything is nothing if it is not free. Enjoy every moment. Every single moment in life is so precious. You are free right now. You are always free right here, right now. Just always remember to be here in the present moment, just be here now and you will really live every moment of your life in freedom." That interwoven moment of blended times will forever take my breath away.

But not as much as what happened later that day.

Chapter Forty-Five

"Nature has a funny way of teaching us the things we seek to learn."

The first full day in Key West has already changed me for the rest of my life. I smile at the world around me and then go to the bathroom. Sure enough, I got my period. *Damn it!* I could not believe that I was finally in the place I desired to go to so badly, this incredible tropical rarity in the United States and I finally wake up here and get this lady limitation curse. *Screw that!* I go to a gas station and buy some tampons and decide that I am not going to let being a woman ruin my trip.

We all get on the boat and Ryan tells us that he wants to take us snorkeling first. Alice and I look at each other with glossy, yearning eyes and the guys prepare the boat. We ask if we can help, but they tell us not to worry about it. We walk down the dock as they prepare it until we board. As the boat revs up, my heart opens with thrill. We speed across these vibrant waters out into endlessness. The waters are more beautiful than anything I have ever seen, shifting from blue to an even more cerulean to an even more dazzling soulful vivacity. My eyes couldn't believe what they were seeing as every 10 seconds unfolded a new shade of blue that I had never before been introduced to.

The boat pulls up and latches onto this small orange buoy in the water. Every 100 ft. there was another little orange buoy snorkeling station for boats to tie to. I hopped off with the flippers and gear and could not believe my eyes. The bluest blue I could ever imagine greeted me right there in my face. I was a part of it, 15 ft. deep of the most loving color I have ever been able to experience in real life. I almost started to cry at the perfection of it. While snorkeling, I was swimming around following all sorts of little fishes through these unhealthy looking reefs that I can only assume were dedicated to teaching tourists how to snorkel. *Like me.* I swam until I had no breath then came back up for air. I repeatedly swam until I had no more energy and rose up until my tired little body was so exhausted that I had nothing left to do except to climb onto the boat and give my gear to the next person. I stood with hands on my hips feeling like I have just taken over the world and realized that this feeling of experience is the greatest emotion I've felt. It's the feeling of just absolute completion, absolute serenity.

After their swim, I grabbed the equipment again. *I couldn't wait to go out and explore some more.* I jumped in and swam around until I looked back at my clan, but spotted some large, awkward fish about 4 ft. in length hanging out under the boat. I realize quickly that it isn't moving. It's alive, but it just seems to be waiting for something.

I yelled to Ryan, "What is that?"

I explained what it looked like and after he said, "uh oh…" he put on some goggles and dipped his head over the edge and looked underneath the boat. *What do you mean uh oh?* I am floating about 10 ft. from the boat, keeping my eyes on the giant fish because this world is totally different to me and I don't know friend from foe. I have never really ever seen a fish the size of my foot much less encountered one the length of most of my body and it actually scares me to know that I am trapped away from my element in its element.

"That's a barracuda. Those things have a nasty bite. Really big teeth and a bad temper. You should be fine though." Ryan gives a thumb up and goes back to what he was doing. But I don't feel comfortable. I look back at that slimy, patient thing and study the way it just kind of floats under the boat. It doesn't look like it is going to attack.

"Are you sure?" I am fighting the feeling of absolute panic taking over my body.

"Yes, lots of fish hang out under boats just to get out of the sunlight for a bit. They use it for shade. They aren't interested in you anyway. You're too big. Just keep away from him and you shouldn't have a problem as long as you aren't fighting him for a dead fish. But if you do that, you aren't getting on this boat, freak." He laughs and starts pulling out some rope. His goofy sense of humor did its job in relaxing me enough to go off exploring some coves and following some Finding Nemo Dori fish. I couldn't believe I was just a few feet behind Doris! They shimmered and swam in their school darting here and there, cautious of my not leaving them alone. I watched fish scurry all over the place, hiding in little underwater canyons and reefs, bubbles dancing all around me while I felt my lungs grow heated from holding my breath so long.

I came up for air and burst through the surface, breathing as deep as I could and returning back down to explore. My right flipper wasn't secured perfectly and made my right calf feel pressure, making me cautious of a cramp, but I felt fine so I gracefully floated through pale pink and purple brain looking coral and wavy, green kelps. Channels were cut or grown in the coral reef like a 10 ft. canyon and I swam through it looking in every direction at the vibrancy of the blue, the sea of heated beauty, this incredible world I have manifested. Several times I went up and down for air and exploration until I paddled my little body to its limit for the time. I wasn't used to swimming so it was important to me to pay attention to not pushing myself too far right away. I take one last breath and go back down once more to watch the little creatures floating in their incredible reef homes.

I was like the reverse little mermaid, a pioneer of a new frontier that I have never known. The world down here swayed and flowed, bubbles sparkled and the sun danced patterns on the already colorfully decorated creations in these waters. I push myself as hard as I can, filling my head with mantras of a better life with every stroke toward greater fulfillment. I think of the first time I heard of *The Secret*. I think of the first time I read Leopold Mountain and I think of the first time that I visualized this exact moment. This is everything I wanted last year. I dreamed this water long before I ever experienced it and I somehow, someway, had it right before me right now. Right here, right now I was living a vision I created months ago. Despite my lack of funds or planning, I was exactly where I wanted to be. As I am about to go up for air, I glance to my left and attempt to get a full 360 view of my true whereabouts right at this moment, the happiest moment of my whole life so far. I am 8 ft. below the water's surface in the most beautiful place I have ever been, chasing schools of vibrant tropical fish. I look to the right and my smile locks in with a strange looking grey fish floating toward me from the distance.

My thoughts go as follows-

Whoa! This is so beautiful! I am so happy, so thankful for the chance to be here! Hmm…That is a strange looking fish over there. I love this! Everything in my body hurts from swimming so hard, but I am so very happy! That fish is really big, huh, it's coming this way still…strange… everything else has been swimming away. I can't believe the type of blue this is! Everything glistens. I'm so happy! I am so truthfully happy, the happiest I have ever been. I really need to go up for air, like now. I am so exhausted.

Wait… That fish… Whoa…That isn't a fish…

And my eyes widen as my brain connects that the grey fish headed toward me is getting bigger and bigger. *I realize my mistake…* As I push my way frantically to the surface, totally unaware that flailing is not what I should be doing, I yell, "Shark! There is a shark!" with barely any breath to yell because I had completely exhausted myself purposefully. I take a tiny breath and lower my head down. I keep my eyes on it as it glides so gently and determined, getting closer and closer just 5 ft. below me. Like a giant meaty torpedo, it glides so fast, yet, so slow right for me, every second seemingly taking a lifetime of flashing panics of my outrageous swimming toward the boat which was 15 ft. away. Every ounce of strength in my entire being is exerted with virtually no oxygen. I look up and yell to them, "It's coming. It's definitely a shark and it's almost under me." But I honestly don't know how much of that I actually yelled since I was so exhausted, trying to swim while maintaining a firm stare at this predator. They don't know what to do. Ryan was anxiously getting on swim gear, but it takes so long to do that and I feel like I am nearly drowning from fear and actual oxygen deprivation. I pull my legs up high and kick little kicks while in constant preparation to propel a foot downward as fast as possible. 12 years of soccer playing defense taught me something. And still, it approaches and I transform my right paddling arm into a fist as my left arm keeps paddling. The horrifying feeling of absolute dread washes over me as I realize that I just got my period this morning... *oh no... fresh blood...*

It glides even closer, a water monster about six ft. long, slightly longer than my body. As it is a few feet from beneath me I realize that there is absolutely no way for me to make it another 10 ft. to the boat and pure fear floods my whole entire self, all of my energy in this moment transformed from the happiest I have ever been to the most horrified and realizing there is nowhere to hide. In just 30 seconds a complete shift of emotional contrast happens inside of me. I honestly might die right now- happiest in life to life gone instantly. I crunch my legs up as tight as possible, as if doing this would levitate me out of that fish tank feeding session. But it's my instinct to scrunch up and tighten every muscle. And it feels like everything in my whole body pauses, like a burst of an old time camera just captured this two seconds in slow motion and held it in my life, forever a still frame image in perfect clarity. The shark now slid directly underneath me, pausing just four feet below me where I could see it slowly turning an angle to its left, directly under my coiled body as everything in my internal clock stopped. *Was it going to rotate sideways and attack like in those shark movies, clenching my screaming body as we both fly viciously above the surface for my friends to witness, me dangling from its clenched jaw in bloody terror?* Was it going to rip me limb from limb, dragging me across the sea floor where I would ultimately fill the bellies of bottom feeders, literally fulfilling my spiritual quest of becoming one with the entire ocean?

This is the point that something happened. Something enormous happened inside of me. Up until this prevailing second of a fat shark sitting underneath me, seeking a scent I was giving off and me realizing that there is nothing in this world that can save me except myself right now, there really was no retreating, this was it. Something about staring potential death in the eye triggered something powerful inside of me. I transformed, a bleeding lesbian in fetal position, floating above a monster in the most beautiful place I have ever been, I transformed. Fight or flight response changed. There was no flight. I tried to get out, but there was no flight. I instantly converted into fight and the fear within me shifted as my fist pulled up and back, shoulder blades angled to punch the hardest I have ever punched in my whole life. *The only thing I knew about sharks- they don't like being punched in the nose.* And every single particle of my body shifted to prepare for the most incredible punch of my whole life. My head stayed submerged with my body in full battle mode, oxygen didn't matter anymore.

The whole world goes silent and for a second it is just me floating in absolute stillness, fetal position and something about the poetry of this moment having been the most fulfilling of my life creates a sense of internal wealth, almost a state of understanding. For a second I consider this to be the most beautiful moment that I could die and as crazy as it sounds, I find peace in the idea that this could be it. Nothing seemed to be more fitting than the most beautiful, blue water moment that I had been dreaming of my whole life being the precursor of death. I wasn't going out without a fight.

All that mattered was that in my head I went from, *"Oh my god! Oh my god! I'm trapped! I am going to die!"* to, *"Bring it on."* In that two second camera flash instance of my life, the only thing running through my mind was *"I will punch the shit out of a mother fucking shark today if I must."* Directly underneath me it shifted and pivoted, angling its passively aggressive body completely below my pulsing body, heart beating in time with the countdown to attack.

I am about to beat the shit out of a shark.

I stare strongly, the most real moment in my life, ready to respond to any type of engaging movement, ready to kick-scream-punch Tekken style like where I hit all the buttons of my life controller at once. And just like that, its emotionless face begins to rotate. It makes a 45 degree turn and slowly swims away just as gently threatening as it had come in.

I stare in disbelief. I don't have enough oxygen pumping in my brain to believe it. It swims away, swaying back and forth very slowly and my last itty bit of priceless breath is literally taken away as I raise my head up and scream/pant/cry/breathe. I don't know if it might come back. I don't know shark feeding patterns. Maybe they do a psyche you out thing like that and come back when your guard is down! I begin swimming harder than I ever have in my whole life, crying, "It's leaving! Get me out of here." Full panic again, swimming to a boat with a 4 ft. barracuda under it doesn't even matter

310

anymore. I just want on that fucking boat. I don't even have enough breath to scream, but that doesn't stop me. "Get me out of this water! That was a fucking shark! That was a 6 ft. shark! It was longer than my body. Get me out."

That was the longest 10 feet of my life, those panicked strokes separating me from the boat after the shark decided I was unworthy. *Or too intimidating...* Honestly, sharks don't care for the taste of human blood so it probably realized that it didn't actually want what I had to offer. *But, uh...I like to think that I intimidated him with my muscles and mind.* I was already entirely exhausted, fully exerted before it even appeared. And as I reached the ladder and climbed aboard, I took everything off of me, explained my story and passed out. *That took all of my energy away. That was the scariest thing I have ever experienced.*

Unfortunately, this day was nowhere near done with its terrifying surprises. This would be a day of conquering my greatest fears unlike anything else I have ever experienced in my life.

Chapter Forty-Six

"Fear isn't actually real. It's pretend, imaginary possibilities that are usually worse than most outcomes. Danger does exist, but fear does not."

I wake up with a towel covering my head as the boat shifted me into the wall. I pretend to keep sleeping on the floor as Ryan drives, the humming of the vessel silencing my shaky fears. I wonder momentarily where I am and realize what just happened. I gasp and sit up, looking around as the boat speeds across the crystal waters; sun greets my eyes and blinds me. He slows down and yells to us that we are going to a party island. *Ok, cool that sounds safe and fun.* I could totally use a party island after what just happened. I was shaking inside, a nervousness rising that I tried to blame on the boat's continuous moving, but I knew better. I was really scared deep down and my spirit was trembling.

On the island, they asked me questions and I tried to remain calm as I explained what happened again. Ryan told me that he never saw a shark there before and asked me if I was sure of what I saw. *What! Am I sure of what I saw?* I flipped out because I will never forget what that shark looked like sliding below me. I will never forget that creature's approaching face. I know what a giant 6-7 ft. grey mass shaped like a shark looks like. I told him he never saw one before because he never worried about getting his period before.

"Oh… yes. That is a good point… I haven't hit puberty so I didn't get mine yet." He laughed as he handed me another beer and told me to relax because it's all over. Alice put her arms around me, hugged me and told me to breathe deep, but it was as if I was preventing a panic attack. I had all this surging energy pulsing though me. I hopped into the water and swam around alone and then decided to go for a solo walk down the beach and contemplate life. That occurrence really put me in a strange state of mind. I looked around at all the people dancing on their boats or sitting out on their chairs as I passed by. Almost all had a drink in their hand and no matter what age they were- teens to 70's they all had fit, sexy, tan bodies. I think about the happiness they all had here, free to express themselves as they desired. No one was out here judging. *Not even time was judging bodies.* I observed the people I walked by and thought about the average people I know back in Pennsylvania. A man offered me a beer and his wife asked if I was ok after I tripped over their anchor line. I laughed because it didn't hurt. I learned how to collapse my body so that I would avoid skateboarding injuries when I was younger and it has proven itself a valuable resource after I hit 21. I brushed the sand off of me and looked at them and said, "I am so alright." I raise my hands above me toward the skies yelling, "I just tripped over an anchor on an island; what world is this? I just had a 6ft. shark under me! You have no idea how alright I am! This is the most beautiful place I have ever been in and I am alive and here to experience it! I am so alright I could cry." Crazy eruption took over. I didn't care who heard me. This was the beginning of my randomly asking people I encounter if they would like to hear an incredible story because I just couldn't contain it inside of me any longer. And they cheered me and laughed, saying how happy they were for me. I declined their beer, feeling it would just suppress the incredible emotions of my naturally flourishing existence.

I finished the walk up the left coast, hopping over tiny creatures, shells and hermit crabs. They were scattered all over the place, just living their little hermit lives as pebbles beside my wandering feet. I held their delicate bodies on my fingertips watching them slowly trust that my predator hands wouldn't harm them. Some were barely the size of my thumbnail. They had shells so rough and chunky that I hadn't even noticed the tiny transparent stems popping out of the bottom until I took a moment to pause and really observe my surroundings when I encountered mangroves ending the path. There was tiny life existing around me the whole time. All I had to do was slow down enough to notice.

When I returned to the boat, everyone was ridiculously drunk and two other boats pulled up next to ours. *They were playful and splashing around in the water.* The new thing was that the girls had their tops off and the guys had their bottoms off. It wasn't quite what I expected to come back to, but Mack was kind of reserved in the clothes category so I joined him on the boat. We drank shots from the bottle as everyone encouraged me belligerently, begging me to join them naked in the water. I am not free flowing in physical body confidence yet and haven't really ever been naked in front of anyone besides a lover. *Or a few weeks back when I wore the puppy as a top.* But shots happen. Persuasion happens and I look around at the life surrounding me. *Whoa, I'm on an island and I can hang with beautiful topless women in between boats and I could sink down below the surface so no one could really see my goods.* The sand was stirred up, making the water milky as the boats swayed. There were a few male body parts to avoid with my eyes, but it wasn't hard to avoid them being that they were under the water too. My top comes undone and I hold my breasts with my hands, completely covering them and their renewed bounce as I hop off the side of the boat. Once in the water, I felt comfortable since they were covered by the bra of natural stirred up water. I relax, breathe out and let them go. Alice shouts and comes over laughing about how free we are. My short hair was slicked back out of my eyes. Her dark, curly hair is

313

long enough to hang in front of her shoulders and cover her nipples like a sexy sports model smiling right in front of me. I was speaking her favorite language- drunk, naked and free.

But I didn't rise out of the water beyond my shoulders until I covered up, so I wasn't fully exposed at all. I felt like I was properly pushing my boundaries to my personal comfort until I put my top back on.

Alice and Ryan eventually climbed on the giant 6-person raft and undid the rope tied to it. Ryan gave a huge grin and thumbs up. *Ok. We get it.* They floated out to sea pretty fast. It didn't look like the current out there was that strong, but within a few minutes, I was afraid they wouldn't be able to get back. Mack tells me not to worry and that we will give them some alone time until we pick them up with the boat. Mack and I talk for about 10 minutes about some very personal topics. *As I write this, I cannot recall, but I remember the emotion of feeling so lucky to be here to share this moment of his opening up finally.* For weeks he kept himself boarded up, a secret closed personality, as to not release his true emotional side. It took being stoned and drunk on a boat on a naked island for him to really relax and open up. It really was such a beautiful moment to see unfold giving me some insight into all of humanity having an access code to emotional sensitivity under the right circumstances.

A loud sound startles us from discussion. A boat a few down from us speeds away toward our friends on their naked party raft. *Ah! We don't want others to find them doing whatever they are doing!* By now, they were about three miles off shore, appearing as just a tiny multi-colored dot in the distance. Mack had assured me that they were fine, but now a boat was going to beat us to them! We speed off and as we do, we see someone's personal plane fly over us and turn to go out toward them. *Ha!* We laugh so very hard as it flies over and inspects them, then circles around to fly over again. *They are being spotted by another boat and by a plane! Ha-ha! As above, so below!* It circles around once more before flying away. The hilarity in this moment as we are racing into the ocean to save our naked friends from humiliation on the water, to be overthrown by humiliation of the skies, was almost too much for me to handle. We laughed freely as if the previous events of the day had no hold on my heart anymore.

We arrive as the other boat is talking to them. The boat captain waves at us explaining that they just wanted to make sure they were ok because they were pretty far out to sea. Mack yells that he wanted to give them the alone time they wanted and they laugh and tell us to be careful. Boat life is like a giant adult playground of danger and excitement, but it's like everyone is drunk so it's really funny. *And really dangerous.* But people are meaty action figures in real life and can definitely die easily in water. Alice is embarrassed and holding onto the side of the raft, having climbed off so no one would see her exposure since she didn't have a suit on the raft. Ryan tells us to tie the rope to the raft and gently pull them back to shore. After their rope is secured, Mack starts the boat and I look toward the island; it's so far in the distance. I consider for a second how scary it is to be miles out in the water like this. *Geez, if something were to happen I don't think I could swim that far. Fear rising.* I think about the creatures that the guys fished out of the water right along Ft. Myers city. I think about the shark earlier that day and wonder what is below me right now out here. *Fear rises.* A shiver runs down my spine like an anxiety tornado, but I breathe deep and close my eyes as the boat starts to gently roar.

I tell myself, *"We will be back to land soon, ya Katie land-lubber."* As I gulp away my stress, I hear Ryan and Alice scream for Mack to stop. I open my eyes in panic as I prepare to see the worst. The raft had caught water on the front and was going under the surface rather than over it because of Ryan and Alice sitting forward, thus causing the front to go under water as we picked up speed. They screamed and laughed as they flipped off. Even though everything was fine, my nervousness didn't relax any; in fact, it was even worse. I just wanted to get back to shore; the feeling in my gut was making me nauseous and the alcohol with the sun was making me feel like I had a fever. *Fear rising.* Mack walks back, amused, as he asks if they need help getting back on the raft and tells me to hold the wheel facing toward the island so the rope for the raft doesn't get tangled in the motor. Ryan yells to go slower next time and helps Alice onto the raft again. My smile fades as my eyes go from an uneasy amusement watching them climb aboard the raft to shifting upward and beyond them, focusing very muddled at the sky, which was beginning to do something dreadfully strange. I blink as I try to make sense out of the vortexes I see.

No way… is that a… No…

I see the ocean on the horizon begin to rise up in a type of faint arch, the shape of a grey teepee forming a cone from below. *That doesn't make sense.* Then I look above it as the clouds begin to do the same, forming a thin V from the sky. For the second time today, everything about my existence stops; my body freezes completely. The others' laughter fades into a slow motion rhythm, a warped resonance while my eyes lock in on the funnel coming down out of the clouds, pulling the faded gray water up progressively to meet it in the middle of the sky. The spiraling vortex of darkness reveals itself as it fills in that gray gap. I am speechless as I try to make sense out of what I am seeing. *This cannot be real.* I watch in absolute horror as the sky becomes the ground and the ground becomes the sky. *As above, so below…* I have always

315

been terrified of storms. Panic rises in me every time there is a thunderstorm. I have always been unpracticed and honestly, very scared of water life. Now, I am confronted with both at the same time and we are three miles off shore.

I scream, "Oh my God! What is that?" They ignore me slightly, having already had a crazy unproven Katie outburst today. So I point into the distance behind them yelling, "That's a tornado! That is an ocean tornado!" This finally gets their attention. They look behind them and undeniably I am freaking out, watching the tornado grow stronger and angle around. The upper portion of it thickens as the middle of it remains a long curling cylinder, a thin funnel resembling a fluctuating pipe.

As above, so below. As within, so without... So many mixed emotions exist on that boat. Ryan screams in excitement that this is only the second one he has ever seen in his life and the last one wasn't a complete funnel. "Ah! This is amazing! It's a total water spout! This is so rare!" The three of them are all smiles, staring at it like a prized trophy. Mack says that he never saw one before, but heard a lot about them. Ryan yells, "Let's go toward it!" And they laugh and stare in amazement at the nightmare I have had for years, manifesting itself before me in this moment. They couldn't be happier to see that colossal funnel and I couldn't have been more of an exact opposite reflection of that terrible ocean chimney.

I flip the fuck out. I scream the loudest I have ever screamed. I shake in distress and horror at the thought of the boat flipping like all those stories I have heard since in Florida. I think of the shark earlier and I think about how I haven't changed my tampon and I would create another delicious trail for even bigger sharks to follow as I desperately attempt to swim to shore after our boat flips and the raft pops and my head goes all over the place. I pull out my camera and take pictures as we fight about what to do. The vortex grows and seems to be getting closer. Ryan tries to tell me that it is totally harmless and we will be fine and that we should go closer.

I yell and protest, finally deciding within myself that yes, I will kill them all if they don't go now. I honestly threaten to cut the cord to the raft and push Mack overboard. *Yes, I am going to touch ground and I don't care if I have to kill them to do it.* "I will kill you all to steal this boat to survive today! I don't care. I am going back now. I am taking this boat and I am getting out of the ocean right now. That ocean tornado can take you fools, but it's not taking me!" I look at the controls of the boat and realize that I really don't know how to drive it properly, but I don't care. I am determined to survive today and nothing is getting in my way. Not even drunken naked chumps.

They really try to calm me down and get me to go toward it, but they can't even get me to relax. I was practically crying as I was screaming. Maybe if the shark event hadn't just happened two hours prior, I could have handled contemplating this rationally, but no. There was no rational thriving drive to go toward that thing I have feared my whole life. *Fight or flight? Fuck fighting the weather. Get this girl to shore.* I have never threatened to kill anyone before. I certainly never ever meant it, but I was honestly in such a state of horror that I was actually considering having to kill them. But that is what they say- desperate times call for desperate measures and I was desperately holding on to any fabric of sanity at this moment. There was no logic in this world right now to me and I was purely living in a state of survival. There is no reasoning or longing for excitement in a state of utter survival. The fact that they all laughed the whole time that I was having a nervous breakdown just made me more upset. I have never in my whole life been so hysterical, so petrified, and so distraught.

Eventually they give in and treat me like a person standing on the edge of a building about to commit suicide, gently telling me to step back, put my verbal gun down and slowly ride back to shore. When we got back I was in such a state of panic that I couldn't even see. I couldn't breathe. I couldn't relax. I couldn't sit or sleep. I was horrified and the feelings of unrest inside of me just made me fill with panic. To top it all off they were all furious at the fact that I was making them come back to shore. I overheard them telling the other boat about how I had ruined the opportunity to see a waterspout, but they wouldn't have ever even seen it behind them if I hadn't seen it in the first place!

Honestly, we probably would have been fine if we stayed out. Water miles are so deceiving and it was most likely a mile away from us out there. But I was so panicked and ungrounded that I had to stand on solid ground. On shore I was shaking uncontrollably and told them that I needed to do something to get this energy out. I needed to get grounded.

So I took off my flip flops and began running up the coast the opposite direction. I ran as hard as I could and I dug my toes deep into the sand, feeling the mush surround my feet as my soles slapped hard. I felt the raspy pepper-sand feel begin to hurt my skin while my muscles extorted fully releasing tension from my influences, my joints and my spirit. I was shaken and I felt the only way to relax it was to shake up my whole body. I hit the end of the beach and was panting and sweating more than I had in years perhaps, but I wasn't tired. It was as if I was on a drug, a steroid of death's confrontation pumping energy through me. I did push-ups and jumped into the water, flicking my hair back while doing yoga. I cried into the sky as I told myself I would be alright. The sun beat down on me, massaging my back as I pushed into more push-ups and downward facing dogs. I collapsed into the sand and stared across the horizon feeling the earth beneath me, the sand cradling my quaking body, the planet holding me in the time I needed it most. And I panted and breathed in the salty air, noticing that I was the only one anywhere within eyesight.

Thank God because I look totally crazy now. I was on the furthest side of the island where boats don't go. No one was out at sea in front of me. No one was in a plane above me. My phone was back in the truck so no one knew where I was. It was just me out here alone at this moment. Not a single human being knew where I was right now because I initially set off the other direction on the island, but turned around because I felt compelled to go this way so even the crew didn't know where I was. This was my life. This was my existence and the only proof here was my own consciousness in this moment. And I felt the tension melt out of me and suddenly I didn't feel alone. I felt so peaceful and alive. The hard, wet, warm sand smeared against my cheek, gritty and pressing into my skin, was the most real thing I have ever felt. I pressed my face harder into it, allowing it to compress and remind me that I am really here. *Sand! I really am here!* I rolled my hands through it and gently slid the sand granules between my fingers and felt their crunchy composition grind against itself. I felt the sun and the wind dry the sand stuck to my face. I felt the hair dripping with exuberance down my neck and into my ear. The waves gently pressed compassion against the shoreline and sang to me songs of peaceful realization of being really in the present moment. My mind wasn't straying elsewhere. It wasn't caught up in panic or thinking about what was happening later or what previously happened. My mind was fully in the now. All of my senses were present, feeling and smelling the earth, seeing and tasting the salty ocean waves and hearing the island sounds that were naturally occurring around me. Nothing mattered except for my happiness in this moment and I have to say, considering how irrational I felt moments prior, I was feeling pretty darn relaxed just catching my breath and breathing in the sun.

Eventually I ran back much more gentle than the run there. They became entirely wasted with the two boats next to us doing exactly what they were doing when I left, only like a level up in absurdity. I looked around and noticed that for some reason a lot of boats had gone and it seemed that we had practically the whole island to ourselves, which was kind of neat to think about. *Our own personal island.* I felt very calm and relaxed, which seemed odd to me, and I chose water over a beer so I could maintain my nature infused high. I smile and confirm that I am peaceful for the first time this day. The sun felt great. The water felt amazing and I had survived some of my biggest fears. Peace was everywhere. *"As above, so below. As within, so without."*

Ryan climbs on the boat and looks off toward the North West with his hand covering his eyebrows, "Uh oh…" he says. My ears perk up instantly, very displeased with that sound. "It looks like there is a storm coming. I guess that explains why everyone else was leaving"

An instant shift to horror happens inside of me. "Well, let's go! We need to get out of here!" I say very fast as Mack slaps his head saying something about here she goes again. Alice is incessantly drunk and just laughs.

"Well, it's kind of too late. We should have left when all those other boats were leaving. See that boat out there? That's a shrimp boat. When they leave you know it's too late." I could cry or throw up. I ask what 'too late' means. "We can't leave because we don't want to be stuck on the water when the storm hits. That would be really bad and dangerous." He nonchalantly takes a sip of beer while I ask if we could just try to race it back, "Yeah, we really just have to wait it out here on the island. I highly doubt we would beat it back and a storm on a boat is a terrible time. We don't want it to flip. So Katie, just crack a beer and hang tight." I didn't like that answer. He then mentions that it looked like it would be a bad one, but most storms come and go quickly in Florida every day, as I had already experienced. *It does rain often, but not often when I am stuck on an island!* He hoped it would be over before it was too late to get through the sand bars as the tides shifted, closing the passages through the sand dunes at low tide. I hoped so too.

Within a very quick 5 minutes, the storm was fully on us. The next half hour was spent crouched down in the water on the side of the neighboring boat because it was larger than ours. The waves slapped up rapidly as the boats crudely swayed. High winds held my fears of more water spouts and hurricanes. The horizontal rain felt like ice bullets when we weren't covered by the boat. I was shaking in fear as that storm approached. I didn't know if lighting would strike the water and electrocute us. *Was this a quick hurricane force?* I didn't know anything and after the day's previous events, I couldn't figure out if I was going to cry or laugh. So I laughed at the longing to cry! I laughed at all the chaos in this day! As I became covered in painfully giant, hard rain drops, we all decided to really crouch down together at this boat shelter and I cried at the insanity of this day. The laughing and crying blended as these wild emotions burst from inside of me! The chilly water I previously avoided became a warm shelter from the frigid sky elements. I kneeled down as all of us remaining on the island took refuge and my body became one with the waves. My skin prickled with cold, fast air and the occasional insane rapid fire of freezing bullet drops. I felt the panic inside of me instantly ease away; as the storm roared over us, I laughed wildly and I just let go. Everything around me was absurd! I laughed like a mad wo-man. I had no control here and I just gave up! I let go. I just fully, energetically let go.

319

I looked around me and could barely see from the downpour. Everyone else continues to drink and laugh despite what was going on. I watched the boats aggressively trying to maintain composure, anchors holding fast to the agitating seafloor. I watched the black churning sky stare at me with wicked, driving eyes. The warmth of the water melted the anxiety I held onto so strongly. It strained the fear right out of my entire being. I observed the chaos my life had become from an outside perspective and it's as if once again, everything became slow motion. I filled with such an overwhelmingly intense joy, smiling and laughing. *I can only say it was that I just gave up. I let go of everything.* I let go of the circumstance- being stranded on an island during an ugly storm. This is just what it was. There was nothing I could do. There was no fight. There was no flight. I just had to sit back and let go. And when I did this, the world around me changed instantly, like a frustrated filter lens was removed from my vision. The icy rain became a cleansing tool and it stripped pain from my body. I stood and raised my arms up feeling the heated water slap my thighs. I stepped out into the ferocious storm and let go of every single thing I held onto my whole entire life and watched the world erupt. I walked back alone onto the shore. Here, I allowed the storm to hit me with its full power. My mantras began flowing as free as the angry gravitational rain. *I am alive! I am free! I am well! I am strong! I am so powerful!*

I screamed a mighty roar into the storm mirroring its raging fury. I yelled in crazed exhilaration, "Woooooooooooo! Yeahhhhhh!" jumping up and the ice bullets beat me hard so I yelled again and again. The wind whipped my body, but I cheered into the sky and I didn't care how crazy I looked because this day was the craziest day I have ever encountered. *Crazy doesn't exist out here*! This storm doesn't matter. We are all perfectly coexisting right here, right now! "I am here and I am alive!" I yell into the air. Everyone is watching and cheering too, but Alice is really watching me.

"Thank you, Universe! You are right! I guess this is what I wanted! I guess I wanted to face my fears and grow. Ok, Fine! Universe, I give up! I give up everything!" I yell into the storm, fairly confident that no one can actually hear me from the sound of nature pounding everything. I laugh outrageously as I am blended into the sounds of this divine seafaring reality. I didn't care if the others heard me or not. The world was a brilliant silvery existence of vibrational, water droplets chiming vibrations in every direction, ocean air harboring pressurized surprises and no matter what my ego decided, this realm is full of surprises! *I cannot control every single thing with my mind*! I spent so much time studying and applying the law of attraction to my life that I proved to myself that I can do amazing things, but I can't control every single thing. *That's an ego override.* I can't control all energetic existence! There is such incredible truth in the manifestation of one's dreams, but there is also a divine prevailing truth in the simplicity of intuition and

320

letting go of expectation. There is such godlike truth in allowing the world to just simply be. That is where inner happiness resides. And that is what happened to me here on this day. I let go. I allowed myself to just be and I surrendered, a forced surrender that I was running from this whole time. *Yes, I fought so very hard to hold on, to control the situation, but what it came down to was the fact that it was required for me to just let go of this current situational instant, but more so to let go of the internal ridged structure that my life had grown so fond of forcefully living in.* And standing like a crazed islander, bawling, laughing absurdly and dancing in the midst of a giant storm at the southernmost point of the United States, screaming at the sky, confronting possible death several times, feeling more flamboyantly alive than I have ever felt in my whole life, feeling more awakened, more spiritually liberated, freer than ever, I, for the first time in my life, met my true self.

The storm eased. The beating missiles on my body stopped firing and the wind thanked me for honoring it as it moved on. It was never going to be there forever, but for the time that it was, it wanted my respect. And I finally gave Mother Nature the respect she always deserved. The sky smiled eventually as the sun greeted me. I began to shake at how cold I had grown standing out there. I didn't even know it then, but I was shaking from bigger things than just chill. After the wind settled, everyone said goodbye and cheered the fact that we all survived. *Getting stuck on an island in Key West isn't such an absurdly uncommon event to those who are familiar with that type of life, but to me it was absolutely life changing.* We boarded our boats to return to the mainland, my mind fuzzy in a dream-like state. We hit gently onto one low sand bar on the way back and saw two boats stuck on sand bars in the distance. Ryan tells us that there is nothing we can do to help the stranded passengers now because they were just plain old in the wrong channels for low tide.

He again reminded us how lucky we were to have such an intelligent captain. I was very grateful to have someone to guide me. He indicated that we needed to get back to shore now just in case the storm hits again.

I'm not sure what it was that I was feeling at this point. Everything was cold and fuzzy as I ducked down behind the captain's window, huddled with our crew to block the wind and chilled air whipping by us, but I was a world away from them in my mind. They laughed about the day's events and to me it seemed as if I were listening to them through a window. I was in a world of my own, a perspective of undigested reflection of what this day was composed of, of what this soul had been exposed to. There was so much speeding through me as we sped to safety across the sleek, patient waters. This exploratory feeling was so very foreign, but it was oddly familiar too. It may have been the feeling of revival or reawakening. It may have been the feeling of clarity for the first time or the ecstasy of just letting go of everything. It could have been the shock of forcefully discovering absolute inner peace in the most intense moment of chaos or the feeling of having faced my most prevalent fear- the fear of death.

One thing was certain.

I was so alive.

....

I snap back into reality as Callie gasps.

Woah…

I realize that an instant captivated audience surrounds us and I remember what is actually happening right now.

Chapter Forty-Seven

"Every day I am standing at the beginning of the rest of my life."

Callie squirms as I tell these last few stories. She covers her face as she listens, an outburst which draws attention from the other tables at the cute café that we had stopped at for some kombucha, a tart fermented tea. A table next to us asks me if they can listen in on the rest of the story, claiming that they weren't intending to eavesdrop, but couldn't help it. *Yes! Delightful!* More people chimed in until there was a whole story telling group eating their kale chips, organic sandwiches, sipping smoothies and juices while listening to my tales of the almighty sea. *Ahoy Mateys, arrrrgh!*

They exclaim together in loud "ohhh's" and "ahhh's", cheering and asking questions while synchronizing their emotional responses to heighten my story telling ability. They, too, share their stories of ocean adventure, but eventually return to my story. *Hmm… some of their stories seemed way more extreme than mine…* My eyes tear up as I speak and some of theirs tear up too. I see them embark on a mental recreation of the details I provide. My Italian heritage shows itself as my arms move about.

They want to have a question and answer session of sorts and I fondly introduce 'The great day of the real Shark-nado'. It would fundamentally mark the most essential moments in my life, a theatrical replay for years to come, a resounding internal drama that would perform occasionally for me in my quiet moments, my solemn moments of self-ceremony such as a night drive alone when my eyes would again fill with the purest blue waters and the fish would swim with me as I paddled toward them with that mesmerized smile upon my face until the appearance of that all too familiar mysterious blur, that shape-shifting fish as it came closer, where my chest would tighten as my vision focused, where my energy shifted from life's greatest bliss to horrifyingly disturbed and overtaken by dread, where I felt death accept me, where I transformed from flight to fight. I re-experience the entire event over and over, but I tell Callie and the group that the vision wasn't all of it.

The emotional rollercoaster greeted me in those most delicate moments, taking my hand and pulling me through a hallway of introspection unlike anything I had ever felt before. It was a reoccurring vision flashing on repeat of my giving up my forced power in this life to the Universe, to God, to Allah, to Buddha, to Vishnu, to spirit, to whatever loving energy was out there teaching me all these thousands of miles. Every time it flashed through me, my perspective would change and my appreciation for life would increase.

323

My head would be filled again with the exact moments of personalized horror, of exposing another personal growth perspective. "Every day I learn from that day and every day I see my current life in a more beautiful way." I explain that this is the end of this story, BUT that isn't the end of my traveling. "That was just a couple of trips. I mean, we haven't even touched Tennessee or Oregon stories yet."

An older woman in a multi-colored shirt asks me, "So honey, if that isn't all of it, then what the best day of your life so far?" Callie bursts out loud as she realizes that the whole reason I was telling these stories was because she asked me that same exact question. She whispers, "What are the chances?"

My laughter elaborates, "See, the best day of my life is also the worst day of my life." I smile, looking in each of their eyes, observing their forward leaning body postures. *Entranced.... Enchanted....* "It is that day that I was forced to face my greatest fears. It marks the moment that I truly became alive and empowered inside myself, a personal renaissance. It is the day I learned to let go and the day that I learned to breathe."

They look around and respond, "That's so crazy! The best day of your life is also the worst day of your life? Wow! What are the chances?"

Callie smiles and touches my shoulder. "And to think, I almost didn't get out of bed this morning. I just wanted to binge watch shows all day, but something told me to get up. What are the chances that I would have run into you by that bench? Wait, this reminds me... You never told me what happened before we met." I gently touch my sore elbows and reflect.

"Yeah, I did have quite an interesting morning before we even met." I giggle. My elbow and shoulder irritation snaps my mind right back into that old growth Oak tree at the top of the hill.

Everyone anxiously leans in again.

Chapter Forty-Eight

Lancaster, PA

"I delight in the opportunity to live life with a jubilant, excited state of positive influence."

*W*here should I go? I walked around the hills of the park. *What am I doing?* I had woken up feeling overwhelmed and stuck so I just began wandering. I usually end up at Buchanan Park when I feel like this and I usually choose a spot either by the huge 300+ year trees, sprawled out under the dogwoods and magnolias or hanging on a blanket by the rose garden. Today, however, I wandered through the field and was drawn toward the dog park, but not quite to the dog park. I was drawn to the top of the hill across from it where I sat at a table under a fat, beautiful tree whose belly was so full that I could probably hug my body around it 5 times easily.

What a massive structure above me… that closest branch is bigger than an elephant's leg and it's just hanging right above me on a 90 degree angle. So beautiful! I pulled out my notebook to do some writing, but my words were met with hesitation as I continuously became more in love with this tree. *I bet if I stood up on top of this table, I could probably jump and pull my body up there! I do yoga. My core muscles can probably do this if I jump and kick off the right way.* I threw my blanket up high onto a branch and pulled my book bag tight.

I was right. I practically levitated into that thing and I was so proud of myself for maintaining such a strong body despite my lack of working out lately. I climbed around on the thick branches and found a comfortable spot to lay my blanket and lean back like a lounge chair. My bag hung off a branch next to me and I was able to easily access everything. I intended to pull out a notebook to write, but spotted a tiny religious book I was given last week. The gal I had been dating invited me to spend time with her and her family two weeks prior. Her mom had given me a tiny booklet, a biblical guide book that I had tossed into my bag. The spiritual revolution inside of me since I first began traveling has been remarkable. For about two weeks now, that gal decided not to be as interested in me anymore, but something about this little book seemed very compelling.

I cracked it open and read a few pages, feeling the relatability concept of comfort and compassion flow through me. I felt that surge of connectivity to the world open up and I smiled as the squirrels ran through the branches. It felt as if something amazing was happening during this moment, but I wasn't sure exactly what it was. The sunlight was sparkling like my own spiritual disco ball through the gentle sway of the leaves. The flight of birds singing around me met the patter of the squirrels, mixing with the delicate sound of the subtle sprinkle that had just begun dabbling tiny dots of popping sounds all around me, blocking out the echoes of the distant traffic entirely in some type of synchronized isochronic frequencies. Something about this moment made everything inside of me feel illuminated. After several minutes of feeling this tender display of nature, I opened my eyes and everything seemed a bit more vivid. I grabbed that religious booklet (something I have never actually done before) and opened it to a random page as I spoke out loud in an almost mocking sense, "Ok, Universe. What do I need to know?" I began reading about Jesus living like a homeless traveler for the purpose of continuously being humbled. It mentioned that he never had more than he could carry and most of the time never knew where his next meal was coming from or where he was sleeping. He wasn't born poor, but he lived each moment and each day with the trust that the world would provide him with what he needed when he needed it. He lived on the streets with the homeless, like the homeless and was never ever above them and because of that, he always held compassion. He was humbled daily.

This sparked something dazzling inside of me as I thought back to those times from Georgia and the later times in Tennessee, California and Oregon. I thought of how I longed to understand the world through the eyes of the homeless. I realized that the thing I was seeking this whole time was to simply be humbled, to live a humble life of compassion and understanding for my fellow man. I had been seeking an emotion to really encompass the entirety of this humble concept. I had to be stripped down to my basic essentials (giving everything away in Erie) and trust that the universe would present me with what I needed as I needed it (living out of my car on the open road for months).

I closed that little booklet slowly, as if closing an ancient text of wisdom with delicate pages, as my gaze moved beyond the interior of this tree to the world waking up in the distance. I laughed in the way that I do when life's poetry seems almost too beautiful for me to handle, but this was it! This was life and it is amazing. Three children walk below the tree carrying a basketball, just a few feet underneath me and I laugh at how funny this whole thing is. *Ego Rises*...Up in this tree, I am becoming enlightened and feel more alive than I possibly ever have and humans are walking underneath me, completely unaware of the revelation happening just above them. I wondered if this was like a metaphor for awareness, but chuckled to myself at how far I have come since I first began traveling. *But have I?*

I was sitting here in a tree feeling 'enlightened' when my ego chimed in like it likes to do. *Gee, when I climb out of this tree people will think I am so cool, like 'that girl just got so humble from sitting in a tree.'*

This was the ego, the self-righteous subconscious coming through *(the thought process that generally gets me into trouble in life),* but I masked it to myself with the ideology that I was becoming like Christ, Christ-consciousness, or the Buddha under the Bodhi tree whom sat in silence claiming that he was not moving until he attained total understanding. *I am like the truthful Buddha, or loving Lord Krishna, or the virtuous Muhammad or the humble, homeless Jesus, or the compassionate Vishnu, or ethical Gandhi or Mother Tree-sa, only I am the seeker-Katie-of-the-Oak-tree. Maybe I am the bridge, our current day prophet and I will be as celebrated as these spiritual leaders in the world! Maybe this is my calling, my purpose being revealed to me in this moment in this tree! Maybe generations of people will be guided by my life's understanding and mission! Ego rises…*

I packed up my belongings and said 'thank you' to the tree for the 'wisdom' it whispered to me. I listened. I really did listen, but the only problem was that it wasn't just my spirit listening; it was my ego too and it wasn't actually listening, but hearing what the ego wanted to hear…

I turned to lower myself out of the tree between the two massive branches I originally climbed up. *I can't wait for people to see an incredibly enlightened girl climb out of this tree…* And as I lowered myself down, my arms kind of locked and got stuck. So I decided that it would be a good idea to pop my body up a bit and rotate, but the fact that my bookbag was attached to my back made this incorrect. I rotated to the right as my body shifted hard on an angle to the left causing my arm to not reach its destination. From that motion of attempted grip, my body was propelled backwards and my elbows shredded down the sides of that un-grabbably massive branch.

I turtled 5 ft. out of this tree, completely backwards, backpack down. I collapsed on my spine, my back landing conveniently upon the top of the picnic table like a platform, a platter of supreme understanding, arms spread wide as a display of Katie-shame for the entire world to behold. *The wide-spread of the offended ego.*

I was in shock. My eyes teared up instantly. I hurt everywhere and laughed as tears formed because I realized how stupid this actually must have looked to any potential onlookers. Then after checking to make sure I was alright, I instantly realized the power of this experience. I needed to be humbled internally and spiritually as well. Life threw me out of a tree, sort of like screaming "WAKE UP." In the act of becoming conscious of my thousands of miles and four years of dedication to my longing of being humbled, and becoming aware of my humbling intentions, my ego produced a non-humble intention that needed to be made known.

Therefore, I fell out of the humbling tree upon a platform on the top of a hill, sprawled out flat like a pancake platter of perspective topped with sympathetic syrup and whipped compassion for self. I grabbed all the parts of my body that ached. *I'm ok.* So I just laughed, walking away filled with shame and understanding. Crazy comes in many forms and sometimes crazy is the most beautiful, most powerful thing I experience. This hill overlooks a lot of residential property on a college campus. *Someone somewhere must have seen this absurd revelation…*

……………………………………………………………………………………………

About a football field's length away, Harold mows his lawn like he does nearly every other morning. He finished his early, annoying neighborhood ritual and stands proudly before his fine cut lines, placing his hands on his hips as he analyzes what can be gently tweaked next. He gazes across his yard looking out at the view he inspects every morning. A young woman is running with bright sneakers down the sidewalk. A man is walking his large, black dog. A bird wails as it flies from tree to tree. Harold then sees a body fall from a large tree up on the hill. Wait…What?

"Charlotte! Uh… Something weird just happened!" He yells to his wife, but she doesn't hear him and squawks back. He watches as the person lies flat momentarily on the table and he becomes concerned that something is really wrong. But the figure gets up and inspects itself and looks around. "Charlotte! I think a homeless girl just fell out of that huge tree on the hill up there! Call the cops!"

Charlotte comes outside to inspect, but only sees the person sitting at the table on the hill as if nothing is going on. "Harold, why are you talking so crazy? It's 8:30am and that doesn't even make sense. Here, I just made pancakes. Have some coffee and sit down for a rest or I'…"

Harold adjusts his glasses as he watches the figure slowly wander off down the tree line toward the day's next strange adventure.

……………………………………………………………………………………………

328

Callie's eyes widen. "And that's when you met me!"

"Yep, well, like a half hour after that. I didn't know what I was doing or where I was going after I fell from that tree, but I felt compelled to go somewhere. Like Leopold says, 'When intuition compels, have your preparation be brave enough to meet it!'"

An older man wearing a fine fedora speaks up suddenly from the back table, gargling slightly in his first few words, "Well, that's all good and fun, Sweetie, but you know your idol, Mr. Mountain, was a fraud, right?" I spill my attention from the joyous conversation and turn as he speaks. "Leopold Mountain. I've been sort of tuning into your story. You seem like a nice girl so you should know the actual truth. Some consider him to be the biggest scoundrel ever." *My stomach churns...* He turns his head up from his paper as he continues," Don't get me wrong, a great deal of what he speaks of and writes of does have truth. His philosophies are sound, but he isn't. Sorry, honey, I have been listening and biting my tongue this whole time, waiting for the right moment to break it to you, but Leopold was a terrible man. He swindled countless dollars from countless people."

I am speechless. I have no idea how to respond because I have never heard any accusation such as this before, especially not in front of my insta-audience and insta-crush. Everyone who had been paying attention to the stories has hushed and all sights are on my response. Dread, horror, fear, sadness, anger, fury, disappointment- it all floods my eyes and I am truly at a loss for words other than, "Wha-wha...what do you mean?"

"Well, Sweetie. You've got passion. Anyone can see that and spiritual predators will latch on to that in a heartbeat if you let them." He adjusts his hat. "Like I was saying, Leopold swindled thousands of dollars from thousands of people and lied about nearly every encounter in that book."

I think of the stories I nearly worshipped, the stories I carried on my back, the stories that started a multi-billion dollar industry, a revolution of self-help and business development; I can't imagine... "No, I have never heard this. You are probably lying and trying to make me look bad. There is no way that I studied this philosophy for years and never have heard of this!" I stammer my words and a lady jumps in to defend me, asking the man about what he's trying to do by distorting a young girl's passion. He smiles gently from his eyes.

"Listen. During his lifetime Leopold started several fake schools, started several fake businesses, was known to run when he was caught and lied about just about every encounter with anyone he mentions in his books. There is no proof that he ever interviewed or met with any of those millionaires and he claimed that all of his files burned up with a mysterious Boston fire while he was travelling the country researching and interviewing the world's most successful people, *aka starting these fake businesses*. The timelines that he speaks of do not line up if he dedicated 20 plus years of his life to research and interviews while having a track record all over this country of fraudulence over and over again. That alone is proof that he never did any of what he wrote about."

I ask him to elaborate and he responds, "Fake insurance education classes. He published many editions of the Mount Truth's Prosperity Magazine and advertised his fake business in it, such as his railroad ownership courses. None of it was accredited so after getting his apprentices' tuitions, he would shut it down and take off with the money of hundreds of hopeful students each time." He studies my face as it sinks in. "You want more?" *I'm not sure if I do, but it's like an accident that I can't take my eyes off of...*

"He sold countless fake educational courses under others' names. He sold false lumber businesses and loaned close to a million on credit under others' names to start fake projects as the steel industry was expanding. That was begun as a way to buy in bulk and distribute for more. It would have been fine, except he never distributed any of the supplies and guess what? He again took off with the funds. You would think that this was all fine and dandy, a father returning home with success to his family, but he hardly ever saw them. And when he did, he was so absent minded and non-attentive that his children hardly knew him." I think back to one story Leopold emphasized so strongly about how he helped his son to achieve eyesight even though he was born blind. *I always thought that the story seemed out of place, but maybe there is more to its reason for existing than just being there to inspire...* "He established a scam formula and reinvented it over and over. *"*

"It's amazing what he has been able to do, though. He created a legacy of falsehood that actually does somehow inspire people... It's fascinating really." He looks off into the distance, pausing quite a while as if he was studying someone out there somewhere. After sipping his tea he says, "This lying, false man spent his whole life believing that he was something bigger than he was and now he has a legacy as a brilliant creator and a passionate philanthropist. He thought himself into power, yes, but his real life was nothing like what he speaks. He was a corrupt man, BUT he truly believed that the secrets to success shouldn't remain hidden." *I feel sick to my stomach, a roaring churn pitted in my soul, my chest throbbing and heating up something fragile and hurt in my gut...*

Fedora seems to sense my uneasiness. "Sweetie, I am not saying that the philosophies are bogus. Heh, The Law of Attraction is very real; as is everything else he speaks of. He did learn it and he did spend his life studying it. BUT he is a fake, a false prophet of sorts." My eyes clear slightly.

"Heck, if you think about it, he really did believe himself into royalty. He was an honest to goodness scoundrel of a human and to overcome his reality to portray this sense of purity, to actually achieve it to some degree, does make him rather truthful. Heh, heh, if truthful is a flexible description. I have a love/hate relationship with the man. I wish he was a better person than he was, but I learned and applied so much of his teachings to my life that I can't say he is wrong. He is a corrupt man, but I owe a lot of my life's success to his writings and research."

"Well, I get that. That's how I feel too. I just can't imagine it to be a phony thing." I feel uneasy, but slightly better, like I was hit by a car, but wearing bubble wrap around my body when it happened. I'm just in shock.

"The mind is a powerful thing with such limitless potential; it's impossible to say what it can and cannot do. If you believe it, then you can achieve it. He is right."

I look at my hands, feeling foolish for practically worshipping his text. "But if what you are saying is true, then how right is he really? I mean, think of all of the people who were hurt by his abuse."

He sips his tea. "It depends on what you consider truth to be. For instance, let's say a friend is wearing something you can't stand, but it is their favorite thing and it brings them so much joy. Does it do good to tell them about it? Will they be offended and embarrassed? Well, what if they have something in their teeth after eating? Will they still be embarrassed if you tell them about that? What if you are in a formal place and you didn't notice it for a very long time? What is the difference? Will you be causing damage or affecting positive change?"

"I'm not sure. It's hard to say."

"Yes! It is indeed. And it's just the same thing with Leopold, isn't it? Does the action of his lifestyle overpower the positivity of mind power's education in our society? His intentions were to share secrets, to expose hidden truths! It is arguable that he's generated our mass consumerism *must-have-must-have-now mindset*, but none-the-less, he has assisted in writing an educational series of books with the goal of getting rich and famous, but also the goal of educating the masses of their own individual ability to take control of their lives through the power of the mind, to release the secrets of the ancient societies that he was initiated into from his youth. So here we come back to the scale of 'Which truth weighs more?' Does the damage outweigh the good or vice versa? He was gifted the removal of the veil of hidden mind powers and misused them, but also set them free to the public. So I ask you, what is the truth?"

"Wow, I don't know." Callie holds up her phone with a collection of Leopold Mountain websites claiming that what Fedora speaks of is quite possibly true. I am heartbroken and yet, somehow optimistic.

"His books make him out to be God-like. He certainly isn't. So the truth of his actual existence being so nauseating made me question, heh, back in the day. That was the day before these science boxes." He holds up his phone and points a finger at it. "See, when I learned about his spiritual hiccups, I actually did travel all over the country and interview people, sort of in the fashion he claimed to have done, to find out the truth about him. He became my piece-by-piece treasure map." *I gasp as I remember this feeling of being on a treasure hunt of secret information! I too followed the trail he laid out toward truth!* "It's funny how much my life became exactly what he described his life to be, yet never was. Now you can just look down at your phone and type a few words and the world opens up to you with answers. I had to work damn hard to find out the truth about him, but through all of that, I understand that he was really onto something." I allow Fedora's words to sink in. *Wow... I could really relate to his experience of feeling enchanted by this information.*

He sips his tea again as he folds his paper up. "Yessir, did our boy want a quick buck. But, Sweetheart, keep in mind that the truth of the words may actually balance the actions. After all, they say that everything in life is intention. If his intention was to share hidden secrets and if he lived his life trying to share them as true as he could, then he lived his intention true, despite his actions. There is a famous saying, 'Some do and those who can't, teach.'" *I have heard that before, but never thought about it too much.*

"Well, it's the same with him! He taught. He couldn't live it. He didn't embody it, but he taught it. He spent a lifetime dedicated to the subject of self-empowerment, even if he did stray away from his integrity for most of it." Fedora stands up slowly and shakes my hand. "Young lady, it's been a pleasure to meet you. Don't let this shake your stones of solidity. Don't become disenchanted. Use THE words and do good, just like you are doing. And after that, use YOUR words to do good too. You woke me up this morning and it's been a long time since anyone sparked this ol' scallywag's soul-passion. Thank you for the gift." He reaches out his hand. *Whoa, I never thought of it as a gift...* "The name's Robert. And there are many others to

332

wake up in this lifetime. Be well. Stay enchanted. And just know that truth comes in many forms." Our hands met firmly and his eyes smiled vividly. He turned to leave, giving me a nod as he shuffled out of the courtyard.

Callie says, "Wow, can I read you some of these website titles?" I nod, gulping as I prepare for the words. "Leopold Mountain: the supreme self-help scammer of our era. How Leopold Mountain actually got wealthy. The Liar in Print: Leopold Mountain… Katie, the list goes on…" My audience retreated to their phones, researching as well. Nearly everyone else has taken off on their own individual unraveling of the truth at this point. My version of the story has lost its authenticity in the moment. *Sigh…*

But isn't that the truest truth; shine a light on the unknown, on potentials previously dim and step back to allow others to determine what they see, to learn what their own truths are?

The teacher presents the unknown and students discover it for themselves to make their truths known…

Maybe that is the same thing as Leopold… misguided, yet, a beacon.

I look at the phone, already knowing what I am going to see. Callie asks me what I am going to do now. *I'm not sure.* I just spent the whole day preaching to her, telling her the depths of my soul's ambition to do more in life and have now discovered that everything I hold sacred has been ripped out from beneath me, my grounding fully collapsed in this moment… *heck, I just spent the last five years of my life practicing this and essentially idolizing this man and his philosophy…*

I look at her while remaining silent for a moment, just like I did when I stared out the window this morning, seeing my reflection in respect to my old photograph from my first day of travels. Only this time, I stare longingly at the ice melting in her glass behind my warped, blurred reflection, the drips slowly trickling to blend a distorted world of liquid refraction within a cup cuddled in her hand. It moves so slowly, so gently and I think of how rushed my life has become. Water chooses the path of least resistance and all I have been doing lately is going against the current. I sigh, "I don't know what to do, Callie. I'm stuck. I mean, what are the chances that this would be the case?"

"I don't know, Katie. I think I know where I am going, but just like a college degree, life isn't guaranteed. Like you said before, so many people ended up with jobs in another field than their degree. It is just a stepping stone or a door to the next place."

My mind becomes misted again, a fog of uncertainty, a subtle apprehension to my even existing. She seems to notice, grabbing my hand and says, "Well, you have really caught my attention today. Like, I feel as if I have been on vacation from my life and it's all because of our conversation. It's been an absolutely magical day! I mean, how crazy is all of this? Like, I can't believe I was with you when you found this all out! It's wild, but I love that this astonishes your gypsy soul." My eyes brighten instantly as she continues. "You seriously should totally write a book. Like Fedora Robbie said- Stay Enchanted" She holds my hand and smiles so sweet into my eyes, blending my fears into a swirl, sending them off as we float somewhere together for a moment, transforming my misted mind into some grand voyage into the mystic waters of fortune.

I laugh, "You're right. I should write… yeah. Everything Leopold fundamentally spoke of was true in essence so it's not like I wasted time. I just need to think of it differently."

She brushes her short, blond hair back to reveal those lovely, sexy, brown eyes, almost as if she's metaphorically seeing clearer as well. "Yeah, switch your perspective and just stay enchanted. Also, if it wasn't for all of this, would we have ever met? Think about that!" Her eyes lit with a sizzling brilliance. *Wow, she is absolutely beautiful.* "How many little things could have changed the course of our lives to have never run into each other?" She now places her hand on my thigh, this time holding eye contact with me as she speaks, "Like I said before, what are the chances that we ever would have crossed paths?" *The heat in my chest begins to spiral in anticipation.*

I grab her soft hand, so thankful for her existence in my life today. I feel the gentle tug, a longing, as my breath is taken away for a second, some mystical delight in the back of my mind that disallows me to speak for a moment; we hold eye contact and the instant seems to thicken into something profoundly beautiful. *What is this emotion that has swarmed over me? Well, golly, this feels good… I wonder if this is the moment of our first kiss…*

I smile as she laughs and slowly repeats, "What are the chances?" *She returns an insightful, genuine smile.*

I nervously, yet confidently reply, "Hey, the chances are pretty good when you allow them to be."

Book Follow Up

- *Alana and I never did get back together, although this book is in honor of her too. The unfulfilling cycle that I was stuck in would probably have continued without her. She really was an angel to me when I needed her most.*

- *The Everything Show never really took off. I lost most footage over the years and most was never recorded properly anyhow. I began posting some videos as KT Travels, but certainly not all of them survived, nor is any of it of great quality.*

- *I returned home and people all over explained that they had been following my posts online the whole time and sharing them with their friends and family. This would inspire me to continue inspiring others in the art of daily living.*

- *Compiling all the scraps of papers, photos, and journals to write this book is single-handedly the hardest thing I have ever done in my life. But with dedication and persistence, I finished it.*

- *I continued traveling for years after this book was complete, but that's another story.*

Remember,

This is the <u>Unconventional First Edition</u> and was created as such intentionally.

Refer to the Editor's Note at the beginning for any questions about the validity of this book and its perfection in its raw form for this first publication.

Thank you for reading and look forward to my next books and quite possibly a movie about this book one day.

After all, everything begins with a thought. What Are the Chances?

Also, please check out some of my murals and large scale public art pieces.

Instagram- Katietrainer.Art
Facebook- Katie Trainer Artist/Author/Magic

*Check out some of my **What Are the Chances?** Merchandise!*
www.Katietrainer.com

Editors of Content

- *Alex Stanilla*
- *Daniel Meyer (Deuscain)*
- *Candy Sparks*
- *Erika Firestone*
- *SCORE Mentor – Lawrence Keating*
- *Rose Luciano – Fruition Collective*
- *Abby Drye*
- *Henry Quiles*
- *Deb Bybee*
- *Candice Elise*
- *Taylor Sharp*
- *Alexandria Maier*
- *Lindsey Snyder*
- *Rachel Hostetter*
- *Emily Truman*
- *Molly Swisher*
- *Lindsey Haldeman*
- *Jennifer Tobin*
- *Amanda W.*
- *Laura Putt*
- *Nikki Weems*
- *Cathie Ambron*
- *Alicia Zelazny*
- *Jamie Mack*
- *Camellia Natalini*
- *Ashley Wampler*
- *Kody Brown*
- *Ashley Orndorff*
- *Larry Merris*
- *Amber Ackerley*
- *Zanabella Skincare and Valoree Skiles*
- *Ashley Cooper*
- *Several others that wished to remain anonymous*

A Special Thanks To

HACC Harrisburg Area Community College-
Lebanon/Lancaster You've helped me more than you know. The final stages of this book would not be possible without you and the helpful library staff.

Assets of Lancaster

SCORE Mentorship Program

About the Author

K. A. Trainer was born as Katrina Ann Trainer in Lebanon, Pennsylvania on May 16th, 1989. (Photo taken one of the first days of traveling in 2013. Look at those hopeful eyes!)

'What Are the Chances?' is her first printed publication. Katie developed a Science Meets Art series and became a professional muralist in the first year of being back while finishing the final edits of 'What Are the Chances?' She graduated with an Art and Communications degree from Harrisburg Area Community College in 2012, while being a magician, a landscaper, and a full-time co-manager at her family's third-generation restaurant, Trainer's Midway Diner, Exit 16 off of Interstate 78 in Pennsylvania.

From an early age, she always loved the arts and filled all of her school years with as many creative writing and art classes as she could. She received her Reiki 1&2 certification in Oregon in 2015 and received her Yoga Certification in Pennsylvania in 2016 and hopes to live her life full of creative harmony and inspiration.

SCIENCE MEETS ART.

KATIE TRAINER
Energetic Vibrational Artist

At the time of publication, Katie became an award winning muralist with science, technology, engineering, art, & math, infused into a community revitalization and sustainability focus, completing over 35 murals across PA in her first two years while finishing this book.

Some photos from the travel gallery. Others are available online at www.Katietrainer.com

Live Life Limitless

"If life were to be a lake and you, a stone, you never really know how far the ripples can go from every single action."

"It is true that if you never try, you never fail. But it is also true that you will never know what you have missed out on in life."

"Life Is Art"

My First
Murals

Follow my adventures on Instagram- KatieTrainer.Art
www.KatieTrainer.com

Made in the USA
Middletown, DE
07 September 2019